OECD Research and Development Expenditure in Industry 2020

ANBERD

2011-2018

OECD

BETTER POLICIES FOR BETTER LIVES

This document, as well as any data and map included herein, are without prejudice to the status of or sovereignty over any territory, to the delimitation of international frontiers and boundaries and to the name of any territory, city or area.

The statistical data for Israel are supplied by and under the responsibility of the relevant Israeli authorities. The use of such data by the OECD is without prejudice to the status of the Golan Heights, East Jerusalem and Israeli settlements in the West Bank under the terms of international law.

Note by Turkey
The information in this document with reference to "Cyprus" relates to the southern part of the Island. There is no single authority representing both Turkish and Greek Cypriot people on the Island. Turkey recognises the Turkish Republic of Northern Cyprus (TRNC). Until a lasting and equitable solution is found within the context of the United Nations, Turkey shall preserve its position concerning the "Cyprus issue".

Note by all the European Union Member States of the OECD and the European Union
The Republic of Cyprus is recognised by all members of the United Nations with the exception of Turkey. The information in this document relates to the area under the effective control of the Government of the Republic of Cyprus.

Please cite this publication as:
OECD (2020), *OECD Research and Development Expenditure in Industry 2020: ANBERD*, OECD Publishing, Paris, *https://doi.org/10.1787/c86631b8-en*.

ISBN 978-92-64-79973-8 (print)
ISBN 978-92-64-90419-4 (pdf)

OECD Research and Development Expenditure in Industry
ISSN 2223-7917 (print)
ISSN 2223-7925 (online)

Table of contents

Readers' guide

Main features

This publication includes business R&D data in ISIC Rev. 4 for 31 OECD member economies and four non-member economies. The reported data follow the International Standard Industrial Classification, Revision 4 (ISIC Rev. 4).

The data according to different versions of ISIC classification are published in the following database: STAN R&D: Research and development expenditure in industry - ISIC Rev. 4, STAN: OECD Structural Analysis Statistics (database), *https://doi.org/10.1787/data-00689-en*.

Signs and abbreviations

..	Not available
.	Decimal point
n.e.c.	Not elsewhere classified

Sources and methods

Documentation (PDF): *www.oecd.org/sti/inno/ANBERD_full_documentation.pdf*.

Industry coverage (XLS): *www.oecd.org/sti/inno/ANBERDcoverage.xls*.

Contact details

For any enquiries, please contact *oecdilibrary@oecd.org* or *RDSurvey@oecd.org*.

Classification

The International Standard Industrial Classification (ISIC) Rev. 4 is available online at *http://unstats.un.org/unsd/publication/SeriesM/seriesm_4rev4e.pdf*.

ISIC Rev. 4 classification

Section	Division	Description
A	10-99	**TOTAL BUSINESS ENTERPRISE**
A	01-03	**AGRICULTURE, HUNTING, FORESTRY AND FISHING**
B	05-09	**MINING AND QUARRYING**
C	10-33	**MANUFACTURING**
	10-12	**Food products, beverages and tobacco**
	13-15	**Textiles, wearing apparel, leather and related products**
	13	Textiles
	14	Wearing apparel
	15	Leather and related products
	16-18	**Wood and paper products; printing**
	16	Wood, wood and cork products
	17	Paper and paper products
	18	Printing and reproduction of recorded media
	19-23	**Chemicals and non-metallic products**
	19	Coke and refined petroleum products
	20-21	Chemicals and pharmaceutical products
	20	Chemicals and chemical products
	21	Pharmaceutical products
	22	Rubber and plastics products
	23	Other non-metallic mineral products
	24-25	**Basic metals and fabricated metal products**
	24	Basic metals
	25	Fabricated metal products
	26-30	**Machinery and transport equipment**
	26	Computer, electronic and optical products
	27	Electrical equipment
	28	Machinery and equipment n.e.c.
	29	Motor vehicles, trailers and semi-trailers
	30	Other transport equipment
	31-33	**Other manufacturing; repair, installation of mach. and equip.**
	31	Furniture,
	32	Other manufacturing
	33	Repair and installation of machinery and equipment
D+E	35-39	**ELECTRICITY, GAS, WATER AND WASTE MANAGEMENT**
D	35-36	Electricity, gas and water
E	37-39	Sewerage, waste and remediation activities
F	41-43	**CONSTRUCTION**
G-U	45-99	**TOTAL SERVICES**
G-N	45-82	**BUSINESS SECTOR SERVICES**
G	45-47	**Wholesale and retail trade; repair of motor vehicles**
H	49-53	**Transportation and storage**
I	55-56	**Accommodation and food service activities**
J	58-63	**Information and communication**
	58-60	Publishing, audio visual and broadcasting activities
	58	Publishing activities
	59	Video, television programme, sound recording and music publishing
	60	Programming and broadcasting activities
	61	Telecommunications
	62-63	IT and other information services
	62	Computer programming, consultancy and related activities
	63	Information service activities
K	64-66	**Financial and insurance activities**
L-N	68-82	**Real estate; professional, scientific and technical; administrative and support service activities**
L	68	**Real estate activities**
Mx72	69-75x72	**Professional, scientific and technical activities, except scientific R&D**
	72	Scientific research and development
N	77-82	**Administrative and support service activities**
O-U	84-99	**COMMUNITY, SOCIAL AND PERSONAL SERVICES**
O-P	84-85	**Public administration, defence; compulsory social security, education**
Q	86-88	Human health and social work activities
R-U	90-99	**Arts, entertainment, recreation and other personal services**
R	90-93	Arts, entertainment and recreation
S-U	94-99	Other services; households as employers; goods- and services-producing activities of households for own use; extraterritorial bodies, activities of extraterritorial organizations and bodies

R&D expenditure in industry

AUSTRALIA

R&D expenditure in industry by main activity of the enterprise, current prices
ISIC Rev. 4

Million USD PPP

		2011	2012	2013	2014	2015	2016	2017	2018
	TOTAL BUSINESS ENTERPRISE	12 124.9	11 970.0 e	13 025.4	12 202.7 e	11 301.5	11 868.8	11 896.1	..
01-03	**AGRICULTURE, FORESTRY AND FISHING**	125.5	138.6 e	167.7	168.7 e	168.3	194.5 e	213.9	..
05-09	**MINING AND QUARRYING**	2 716.1	2 315.2 e	1 955.8	1 556.3 e	1 272.7	1 050.6 e	716.2	..
10-33	**MANUFACTURING**	2 978.7	2 966.0 e	3 373.3	3 052.5 e	2 676.3	2 904.3 e	3 168.4	..
10-12	Food products, beverages and tobacco	362.9	379.0 e	476.1	..	..	..	..	..
13-15	Textiles, wearing apparel, leather and related products	34.9	33.6 e	31.8	..	..	..	..	..
13	Textiles	16.8	..	..	..	..	..	..	..
14	Wearing apparel	4.6	..	..	..	..	..	..	..
15	Leather and related products, footwear	13.6	..	..	..	..	..	..	..
16-18	Wood and paper products and printing	68.7	47.3 e	68.6	..	..	..	..	..
16	Wood and wood products, except furniture	25.3	..	..	..	..	..	..	..
17	Paper and paper products	32.0	..	..	..	..	..	..	..
18	Printing and reproduction of recorded media	11.4	..	..	..	..	..	..	..
19-23	Chemical, rubber, plastic, non-metallic mineral products	712.9	755.5 e	856.9	..	..	..	..	..
19	Coke and refined petroleum products	59.9	77.1 e	115.0	..	..	..	..	..
20-21	Chemical and pharmaceutical products	517.9	532.7 e	570.9	..	..	..	..	..
20	Chemicals and chemical products	250.6	229.7 e	204.6	..	..	..	..	..
21	Pharmaceuticals, medicinal, chemical and botanical products	267.2	303.0 e	366.2	..	..	..	..	..
22	Rubber and plastic products	67.6	68.3 e	75.0	..	..	..	..	..
23	Other non-metallic mineral products	67.6	77.4 e	96.1	..	..	..	..	..
24-25	Basic metals, metal products, except machinery and equipment	482.6	417.4 e	402.0 e	..	..	..	..	..
24	Basic metals	334.5	280.3 e	229.0	..	..	..	..	..
25	Fabricated metal products, except machinery and equipment	148.1	137.2 e	173.0 e	..	..	..	..	..
26-30	Computer, electronic, optical products; electrical machinery, transport equipment	1 110.8	1 113.3 e	1 297.5 e	..	..	..	..	..
26	Computer, electronic and optical products	237.9	..	..	..	..	..	..	..
27	Electrical equipment	86.8	..	..	..	..	..	..	..
28	Machinery and equipment n.e.c.	239.2	..	..	..	..	..	..	..
29	Motor vehicles, trailers and semi-trailers	440.7	..	..	..	..	..	..	..
30	Other transport equipment	106.2	..	..	..	..	..	..	..
31-33	Furniture; repair, installation of machinery and equipment	205.9	219.9 e	240.3	..	..	..	..	..
31	Furniture	12.2	13.1 e	11.5	..	..	..	..	..
32	Other manufacturing	175.8	184.9 e	203.0	..	..	..	..	..
33	Repair and installation of machinery and equipment	17.9	21.9 e	25.8	..	..	..	..	..
35-39	**ELECTRICITY, GAS, WATER AND WASTE MANAGEMENT**	250.2	219.5 e	217.9	187.4 e	170.6	203.0 e	240.8	..
35-36	Electricity, gas and water	173.7	148.1 e	129.2	99.0 e	86.9 e	99.8 e	119.6	..
37-39	Sewerage, waste management and remediation activities	76.6	71.5 e	88.7	88.3 e	83.7 e	103.1 e	121.2	..
41-43	**CONSTRUCTION**	542.3	515.6 e	597.1	495.3 e	343.3	277.9 e	238.2	..
45-99	**TOTAL SERVICES**	5 512.0	5 815.0 e	6 713.6	6 742.6 e	6 670.3	7 238.6 e	7 318.4	..
45-82	**Business sector services**	5 362.8	5 649.8 e	6 506.4	6 484.0 e	6 365.6	6 901.6 e	7 000.7	..
45-47	**Wholesale and retail trade; motor vehicle and motorcycle repairs**	573.1	676.2 e	846.9	818.0 e	742.4	780.9 e	800.0	..
49-53	**Transportation and storage**	193.8	215.6 e	250.8	200.5 e	129.6	98.3 e	82.1	..
55-56	**Accommodation and food service activities**	14.2	15.4 e	16.8	19.0 e	22.0	25.4 e	25.8	..
58-63	**Information and communication**	1 215.2	1 365.6 e	1 655.8	1 637.9 e	1 610.0	1 880.9 e	2 113.6	..
58-60	Publishing, audiovisual and broadcasting activities	119.4	138.9 e	189.5	..	..	..	..	..
58	Publishing activities	84.6	99.1 e	132.4	..	..	..	..	..
59-60	Motion picture, video and TV programme production; broadcasting activities	34.7	39.8 e	57.1	..	..	..	..	..
59	Motion picture, video and TV programme production; sound and music	13.4	..	..	..	..	..	..	..
60	Programming and broadcasting activities	21.4	..	..	..	..	..	..	..
61	Telecommunications	319.0	277.9 e	164.7	..	..	..	..	..
62-63	IT and other information services	776.7	948.8 e	1 301.5	..	..	..	..	..
62	Computer programming, consultancy and related activities	751.1	915.9 e	1 258.6	..	..	..	..	..
63	Information service activities	25.6	32.9 e	42.9	..	..	..	..	..
64-66	**Financial and insurance activities**	1 975.6	1 960.7 e	2 137.2	2 179.8 e	2 181.0	2 196.5 e	1 942.3	..
68-82	**Real estate; professional, scientific and technical; administrative and support**	1 391.0	1 416.3 e	1 598.8	1 628.9 e	1 680.7	1 919.6 e	2 036.8	..
68	Real estate activities	15.2	22.0 e	32.8	41.1 e	48.0	56.6 e	59.4	..
69-75x72	Professional, scientific and technical activities, except scientific R&D	668.0	..	..	..	..	..	..	..
72	Scientific research and development	454.9	..	..	..	..	..	..	..
77-82	Administrative and support service activities	252.9	245.7 e	264.2 e	267.0 e	259.5	241.7 e	186.7	..
84-99	Community, social and personal services	149.2	165.2 e	207.2	258.6 e	304.7	337.0 e	317.8	..
84-85	Public administration and defence; compulsory social security and education	17.5	18.6 e	23.1	30.6 e	40.3 e	48.3 e	49.5	..
86-88	Human health and social work activities	62.5	54.6 e	50.9	56.4 e	74.7 e	89.5 e	96.1	..
90-93	Arts, entertainment and recreation	47.9	60.8 e	77.9	92.8 e	98.3 e	99.4 e	83.8	..
94-99	Other services; household-employers; extraterritorial bodies	21.2	31.2 e	55.3	78.8 e	91.3 e	99.7 e	88.6	..

.. Not available; e Estimated value

Note: Detailed metadata at: *http://metalinks.oecd.org/anberd/20200813/2abe.*

R&D expenditure in industry by main activity of the enterprise, constant prices
ISIC Rev. 4

2010 USD PPP

		2011	2012	2013	2014	2015	2016	2017	2018
	TOTAL BUSINESS ENTERPRISE	**12 438.6**	**12 535.3 e**	**12 634.4**	**11 964.3 e**	**11 301.5**	**11 255.3**	**11 201.0**	..
01-03	**AGRICULTURE, FORESTRY AND FISHING**	**128.8**	**145.1 e**	**162.7**	**165.4 e**	**168.3**	**184.5 e**	**201.4**	..
05-09	**MINING AND QUARRYING**	**2 786.3**	**2 424.5 e**	**1 897.1**	**1 525.9 e**	**1 272.7**	**996.3 e**	**674.3**	..
10-33	**MANUFACTURING**	**3 055.7**	**3 106.1 e**	**3 272.1**	**2 992.8 e**	**2 676.3**	**2 754.2 e**	**2 983.3**	..
10-12	Food products, beverages and tobacco	372.2	396.9 e	461.8	..	..	..	..	..
13-15	Textiles, wearing apparel, leather and related products	35.8	35.2 e	30.8	..	..	..	..	..
13	Textiles	17.2	..	..	..	..	..	..	..
14	Wearing apparel	4.7	..	..	..	..	..	..	..
15	Leather and related products, footwear	13.9	..	..	..	..	..	..	..
16-18	Wood and paper products and printing	70.5	49.5 e	66.6	..	..	..	..	..
16	Wood and wood products, except furniture	25.9	..	..	..	..	..	..	..
17	Paper and paper products	32.8	..	..	..	..	..	..	..
18	Printing and reproduction of recorded media	11.7	..	..	..	..	..	..	..
19-23	Chemical, rubber, plastic, non-metallic mineral products	731.4	791.2 e	831.2	..	..	..	..	..
19	Coke and refined petroleum products	61.4	80.7 e	111.5	..	..	..	..	..
20-21	Chemical and pharmaceutical products	531.3	557.8 e	553.7	..	..	..	..	..
20	Chemicals and chemical products	257.1	240.5 e	198.5	..	..	..	..	..
21	Pharmaceuticals, medicinal, chemical and botanical products	274.1	317.3 e	355.3	..	..	..	..	..
22	Rubber and plastic products	69.4	71.5 e	72.7	..	..	..	..	..
23	Other non-metallic mineral products	69.3	81.1 e	93.2	..	..	..	..	..
24-25	Basic metals, metal products, except machinery and equipment	495.1	437.1 e	389.9 e	..	..	..	..	..
24	Basic metals	343.1	293.5 e	222.1	..	..	..	..	..
25	Fabricated metal products, except machinery and equipment	151.9	143.6 e	167.8 e	..	..	..	..	..
26-30	Computer, electronic, optical products; electrical machinery, transport equipment	1 139.6	1 165.8 e	1 258.6 e	..	..	..	..	..
26	Computer, electronic and optical products	244.1	..	..	..	..	..	..	..
27	Electrical equipment	89.0	..	..	..	..	..	..	..
28	Machinery and equipment n.e.c.	245.4	..	..	..	..	..	..	..
29	Motor vehicles, trailers and semi-trailers	452.1	..	..	..	..	..	..	..
30	Other transport equipment	109.0	..	..	..	..	..	..	..
31-33	Furniture; repair, installation of machinery and equipment	211.2	230.2 e	233.1	..	..	..	..	..
31	Furniture	12.5	13.7 e	11.2	..	..	..	..	..
32	Other manufacturing	180.4	193.6 e	196.9	..	..	..	..	..
33	Repair and installation of machinery and equipment	18.3	23.0 e	25.0	..	..	..	..	..
35-39	**ELECTRICITY, GAS, WATER AND WASTE MANAGEMENT**	**256.7**	**229.9 e**	**211.4**	**183.7 e**	**170.6**	**192.5 e**	**226.7**	..
35-36	Electricity, gas and water	178.1	155.1 e	125.3	97.1 e	86.9 e	94.7 e	112.6	..
37-39	Sewerage, waste management and remediation activities	78.6	74.8 e	86.1	86.6 e	83.7 e	97.8 e	114.1	..
41-43	**CONSTRUCTION**	**556.4**	**539.9 e**	**579.2**	**485.6 e**	**343.3**	**263.5 e**	**224.3**	..
45-99	**TOTAL SERVICES**	**5 654.6**	**6 089.6 e**	**6 512.1**	**6 610.9 e**	**6 670.3**	**6 864.5 e**	**6 890.8**	..
45-82	**Business sector services**	**5 501.6**	**5 916.6 e**	**6 311.1**	**6 357.3 e**	**6 365.6**	**6 544.9 e**	**6 591.6**	..
45-47	**Wholesale and retail trade; motor vehicle and motorcycle repairs**	**587.9**	**708.2 e**	**821.5**	**802.0 e**	**742.4**	**740.5 e**	**753.3**	..
49-53	**Transportation and storage**	**198.8**	**225.8 e**	**243.3**	**196.6 e**	**129.6**	**93.2 e**	**77.3**	..
55-56	**Accommodation and food service activities**	**14.6**	**16.1 e**	**16.3**	**18.6 e**	**22.0**	**24.1 e**	**24.3**	..
58-63	**Information and communication**	**1 246.6**	**1 430.1 e**	**1 606.1**	**1 605.8 e**	**1 610.0**	**1 783.7 e**	**1 990.1**	..
58-60	Publishing, audiovisual and broadcasting activities	122.5	145.5 e	183.8	..	..	..	..	..
58	Publishing activities	86.8	103.8 e	128.4	..	..	..	..	..
59-60	Motion picture, video and TV programme production; broadcasting activities	35.6	41.7 e	55.4	..	..	..	..	..
59	Motion picture, video and TV programme production; sound and music	13.7	..	..	..	..	..	..	..
60	Programming and broadcasting activities	21.9	..	..	..	..	..	..	..
61	Telecommunications	327.2	291.0 e	159.8	..	..	..	..	..
62-63	IT and other information services	796.8	993.6 e	1 262.5	..	..	..	..	..
62	Computer programming, consultancy and related activities	770.6	959.1 e	1 220.9	..	..	..	..	..
63	Information service activities	26.3	34.4 e	41.6	..	..	..	..	..
64-66	**Financial and insurance activities**	**2 026.7**	**2 053.3 e**	**2 073.1**	**2 137.2 e**	**2 181.0**	**2 083.0 e**	**1 828.8**	..
68-82	**Real estate; professional, scientific and technical; administrative and support**	**1 426.9**	**1 483.2 e**	**1 550.8**	**1 597.1 e**	**1 680.7**	**1 820.4 e**	**1 917.8**	..
68	Real estate activities	15.5	23.0 e	31.8	40.3 e	48.0	53.7 e	55.9	..
69-75x72	Professional, scientific and technical activities, except scientific R&D	685.3	..	..	..	..	..	..	..
72	Scientific research and development	466.7	..	..	..	..	..	..	..
77-82	Administrative and support service activities	259.4	257.3 e	256.2 e	261.8 e	259.5	229.2 e	175.7	..
84-99	Community, social and personal services	153.0	173.0 e	201.0	253.5 e	304.7	319.6 e	299.3	..
84-85	Public administration and defence; compulsory social security and education	18.0	19.5 e	22.4	30.0 e	40.3 e	45.8 e	46.6	..
86-88	Human health and social work activities	64.1	57.2 e	49.4	55.3 e	74.7 e	84.9 e	90.4	..
90-93	Arts, entertainment and recreation	49.2	63.6 e	75.5	90.9 e	98.3 e	94.3 e	78.9	..
94-99	Other services; household-employers; extraterritorial bodies	21.8	32.6 e	53.6	77.3 e	91.3 e	94.6 e	83.4	..

.. Not available; e Estimated value

Note: Detailed metadata at: *http://metalinks.oecd.org/anberd/20200813/2abe.*

AUSTRIA

R&D expenditure in industry by main activity of the enterprise, current prices
ISIC Rev. 4

Million USD PPP

		2011	2012	2013	2014	2015	2016	2017	2018
	TOTAL BUSINESS ENTERPRISE	**6 847.5**	**8 038.4**	**8 504.0**	**9 118.3**	**9 389.6**	**10 061.5**	**10 239.8**	..
01-03	**AGRICULTURE, FORESTRY AND FISHING**	**2.4**	**4.0 e**	**4.3**	**2.8 e**	**2.8**	**8.4 e**	**17.3**	..
05-09	**MINING AND QUARRYING**	**7.2**	**5.0 e**	**3.7**	**8.4 e**	**13.7**	**15.0 e**	**12.3**	..
10-33	**MANUFACTURING**	**4 361.2**	**5 039.7 e**	**5 276.3**	**5 600.3 e**	**5 781.4**	**6 351.4 e**	**6 702.3**	..
10-12	Food products, beverages and tobacco	34.5	45.7 e	54.3	56.6 e	54.8	59.9 e	65.4	..
13-15	Textiles, wearing apparel, leather and related products	23.3 e	26.3 e	26.3 e	25.1 e	23.4 e	25.6 e	28.6 e	..
13	Textiles	12.8	15.7 e	16.8	16.7 e	15.6	16.0 e	16.2	..
14	Wearing apparel	7.3 e	7.1 e	5.9 e	4.6 e	3.8 e	4.5 e	6.0 e	..
15	Leather and related products, footwear	3.2	3.5 e	3.6	3.7 e	4.0	5.1 e	6.4	..
16-18	Wood and paper products and printing	65.3	71.4 e	72.8	76.3 e	76.6	78.8 e	76.2	..
16	Wood and wood products, except furniture	18.4	21.2 e	25.2	30.5 e	33.1	33.6 e	30.1	..
17	Paper and paper products	28.4	30.5 e	28.2	29.5 e	31.9	35.9 e	38.1	..
18	Printing and reproduction of recorded media	18.6	19.7 e	19.4	16.2 e	11.6	9.3 e	8.0	..
19-23	Chemical, rubber, plastic, non-metallic mineral products	745.5 e	896.6 e	950.8 e	985.7 e	975.1 e	1 027.1 e	1 043.9 e	..
19	Coke and refined petroleum products	12.9 e	12.6 e	10.4 e	8.1 e	6.7 e	8.0 e	10.5 e	..
20-21	Chemical and pharmaceutical products	462.9	560.0 e	593.9	604.7 e	592.8	642.3 e	685.0	..
20	Chemicals and chemical products	258.0	267.1 e	236.8	225.1 e	224.7	253.7 e	281.8	..
21	Pharmaceuticals, medicinal, chemical and botanical products	204.8	292.9 e	357.1	379.6 e	368.1	388.6 e	403.2	..
22	Rubber and plastic products	157.6	201.5 e	227.7	246.2 e	242.2	236.1 e	210.8	..
23	Other non-metallic mineral products	112.1	122.5 e	118.7	126.7 e	133.4	140.8 e	137.5	..
24-25	Basic metals, metal products, except machinery and equipment	325.8	438.3 e	503.5	505.3 e	471.8	506.4 e	550.9	..
24	Basic metals	145.6	229.8 e	288.1	278.0 e	238.7	254.6 e	291.0	..
25	Fabricated metal products, except machinery and equipment	180.2	208.4 e	215.3	227.3 e	233.1	251.8 e	259.9	..
26-30	Computer, electronic, optical products; electrical machinery, transport equipment	2 962.4	3 337.5 e	3 456.1	3 736.1 e	3 958.9	4 409.7 e	4 678.0	..
26	Computer, electronic and optical products	630.1	713.9 e	772.3	854.1 e	909.9	1 012.9 e	1 072.0	..
27	Electrical equipment	885.0	909.1 e	863.1	891.6 e	929.7	1 028.1 e	1 085.7	..
28	Machinery and equipment n.e.c.	817.6	1 016.1 e	1 116.4	1 215.3 e	1 258.5	1 357.8 e	1 393.5	..
29	Motor vehicles, trailers and semi-trailers	489.4	562.7 e	581.0	626.8 e	675.0	782.6 e	870.9	..
30	Other transport equipment	140.3	135.6 e	123.3	148.3 e	185.9	228.3 e	255.8	..
31-33	Furniture; repair, installation of machinery and equipment	204.3	223.9 e	212.5	215.2 e	220.8	243.9 e	259.5	..
31	Furniture	24.1	23.1 e	16.4	12.9 e	11.6	12.3 e	12.9	..
32	Other manufacturing	111.1	115.4 e	108.0	105.7 e	107.4	125.3 e	144.5	..
33	Repair and installation of machinery and equipment	69.1	85.4 e	88.1	96.6 e	101.8	106.3 e	102.1	..
35-39	**ELECTRICITY, GAS, WATER AND WASTE MANAGEMENT**	**24.4**	**25.0 e**	**22.9**	**27.2 e**	**33.8**	**41.7 e**	**47.2**	..
35-36	Electricity, gas and water	19.2	20.5 e	18.5	18.6 e	21.6	30.2 e	40.3	..
37-39	Sewerage, waste management and remediation activities	5.2	4.5 e	4.4	8.6 e	12.3	11.5 e	6.9	..
41-43	**CONSTRUCTION**	**57.1**	**54.1 e**	**50.3**	**70.6 e**	**93.3**	**104.6 e**	**99.6**	..
45-99	**TOTAL SERVICES**	**2 395.3**	**2 910.6 e**	**3 146.5**	**3 409.1 e**	**3 464.5**	**3 540.3 e**	**3 361.1**	..
45-82	**Business sector services**	**2 389.7**	**2 904.8 e**	**3 141.3**	**3 403.3 e**	**3 456.5**	**3 527.3 e**	**3 342.3**	..
45-47	**Wholesale and retail trade; motor vehicle and motorcycle repairs**	**361.3**	**418.1 e**	**426.6**	**434.3 e**	**430.9**	**463.2 e**	**484.3**	..
49-53	**Transportation and storage**	**6.6**	**9.1 e**	**12.7**	**17.5 e**	**19.0**	**15.4 e**	**7.2**	..
55-56	**Accommodation and food service activities**	**0.0**	**0.0 e**	**0.0**	**0.0 e**	**0.0**	**0.0 e**	**0.0**	..
58-63	**Information and communication**	**415.9**	**512.5 e**	**535.1**	**575.4 e**	**600.7**	**649.9 e**	**665.2**	..
58-60	Publishing, audiovisual and broadcasting activities	26.4	39.0 e	44.8	51.5 e	55.0	57.7 e	55.3	..
58	Publishing activities	24.7	36.9 e	42.5	48.3 e	50.4	51.0 e	46.7	..
59-60	Motion picture, video and TV programme production; broadcasting activities	1.7	2.1 e	2.3	3.2 e	4.6	6.7 e	8.6	..
59	Motion picture, video and TV programme production; sound and music	..	..	..	..	..	..	..	..
60	Programming and broadcasting activities	..	..	..	..	..	..	..	..
61	Telecommunications	60.3	58.2 e	48.3	45.5 e	44.8	46.0 e	44.4	..
62-63	IT and other information services	329.2	415.2 e	442.0	478.4 e	500.9	546.3 e	565.5	..
62	Computer programming, consultancy and related activities	223.1	295.8 e	341.9	382.5 e	406.2	454.9 e	487.4	..
63	Information service activities	106.1	119.4 e	100.1	95.9 e	94.7	91.3 e	78.2	..
64-66	**Financial and insurance activities**	**36.0**	**21.9 e**	**14.5**	**18.2 e**	**22.9**	**21.3 e**	**13.3**	..
68-82	**Real estate; professional, scientific and technical; administrative and support**	**1 569.7**	**1 943.2 e**	**2 152.5**	**2 358.0 e**	**2 383.0**	**2 377.6 e**	**2 172.3**	..
68	Real estate activities	0.7	1.8 e	2.8	3.1 e	3.0	2.9 e	2.6	..
69-75x72	Professional, scientific and technical activities, except scientific R&D	625.3	739.3 e	796.5	899.7 e	940.0	928.7 e	811.0	..
72	Scientific research and development	931.0	1 191.4 e	1 345.9	1 446.4 e	1 427.9	1 431.0 e	1 342.6	..
77-82	Administrative and support service activities	12.8	10.6 e	7.3	8.8 e	12.1	14.9 e	16.1	..
84-99	Community, social and personal services	5.6	5.7 e	5.1	5.8 e	8.0	13.0 e	18.8	..
84-85	Public administration and defence; compulsory social security and education	3.1	3.1 e	2.3	1.6 e	1.2	1.3 e	1.7	..
86-88	Human health and social work activities	0.8	1.3 e	1.9	2.5 e	2.8	2.8 e	2.5	..
90-93	Arts, entertainment and recreation	0.6	0.4 e	0.3	0.8 e	2.1	4.5 e	7.3	..
94-99	Other services; household-employers; extraterritorial bodies	1.2	1.0 e	0.6	0.8 e	2.0	4.4 e	7.3	..

.. Not available; e Estimated value

Note: Detailed metadata at: *http://metalinks.oecd.org/anberd/20200813/2abe*.

AUSTRIA

R&D expenditure in industry by main activity of the enterprise, constant prices
ISIC Rev. 4

2010 USD PPP

		2011	2012	2013	2014	2015	2016	2017	2018
	TOTAL BUSINESS ENTERPRISE	**7 727.8**	**8 699.7**	**8 872.1**	**9 330.5**	**9 389.6**	**9 628.9**	**9 607.0**	..
01-03	**AGRICULTURE, FORESTRY AND FISHING**	**2.7**	**4.3 e**	**4.5**	**2.9 e**	**2.8**	**8.1 e**	**16.2**	..
05-09	**MINING AND QUARRYING**	**8.1**	**5.4 e**	**3.8**	**8.6 e**	**13.7**	**14.4 e**	**11.5**	..
10-33	**MANUFACTURING**	**4 921.9**	**5 454.3 e**	**5 504.7**	**5 730.6 e**	**5 781.4**	**6 078.3 e**	**6 288.1**	..
10-12	Food products, beverages and tobacco	38.9	49.5 e	56.7	58.0 e	54.8	57.3 e	61.3	..
13-15	Textiles, wearing apparel, leather and related products	26.3 e	28.5 e	27.5 e	25.6 e	23.4 e	24.5 e	26.8 e	..
13	Textiles	14.5	17.0 e	17.5	17.1 e	15.6	15.4 e	15.2	..
14	Wearing apparel	8.3 e	7.7 e	6.2 e	4.7 e	3.8 e	4.3 e	5.6 e	..
15	Leather and related products, footwear	3.6	3.8 e	3.7	3.8 e	4.0	4.9 e	6.0	..
16-18	Wood and paper products and printing	73.7	77.3 e	75.9	78.1 e	76.6	75.4 e	71.5	..
16	Wood and wood products, except furniture	20.7	22.9 e	26.2	31.2 e	33.1	32.1 e	28.2	..
17	Paper and paper products	32.0	33.1 e	29.4	30.2 e	31.9	34.3 e	35.7	..
18	Printing and reproduction of recorded media	21.0	21.3 e	20.2	16.6 e	11.6	8.9 e	7.5	..
19-23	Chemical, rubber, plastic, non-metallic mineral products	841.3 e	970.4 e	991.9 e	1 008.6 e	975.1 e	983.0 e	979.3 e	..
19	Coke and refined petroleum products	14.6 e	13.6 e	10.9 e	8.3 e	6.7 e	7.7 e	9.9 e	..
20-21	Chemical and pharmaceutical products	522.4	606.0 e	619.6	618.7 e	592.8	614.7 e	642.7	..
20	Chemicals and chemical products	291.2	289.1 e	247.1	230.3 e	224.7	242.8 e	264.4	..
21	Pharmaceuticals, medicinal, chemical and botanical products	231.2	317.0 e	372.6	388.4 e	368.1	371.9 e	378.3	..
22	Rubber and plastic products	177.8	218.1 e	237.6	251.9 e	242.2	225.9 e	197.7	..
23	Other non-metallic mineral products	126.5	132.6 e	123.8	129.6 e	133.4	134.7 e	129.0	..
24-25	Basic metals, metal products, except machinery and equipment	367.7	474.3 e	525.3	517.0 e	471.8	484.6 e	516.9	..
24	Basic metals	164.4	248.7 e	300.6	284.5 e	238.7	243.7 e	273.0	..
25	Fabricated metal products, except machinery and equipment	203.4	225.6 e	224.7	232.6 e	233.1	241.0 e	243.8	..
26-30	Computer, electronic, optical products; electrical machinery, transport equipment	3 343.3	3 612.1 e	3 605.7	3 823.1 e	3 958.9	4 220.1 e	4 388.9	..
26	Computer, electronic and optical products	711.1	772.7 e	805.7	874.0 e	909.9	969.4 e	1 005.7	..
27	Electrical equipment	998.8	983.9 e	900.5	912.4 e	929.7	983.9 e	1 018.6	..
28	Machinery and equipment n.e.c.	922.7	1 099.7 e	1 164.7	1 243.6 e	1 258.5	1 299.4 e	1 307.4	..
29	Motor vehicles, trailers and semi-trailers	552.3	609.0 e	606.1	641.4 e	675.0	749.0 e	817.1	..
30	Other transport equipment	158.3	146.8 e	128.6	151.7 e	185.9	218.5 e	240.0	..
31-33	Furniture; repair, installation of machinery and equipment	230.6	242.3 e	221.7	220.2 e	220.8	233.4 e	243.4	..
31	Furniture	27.2	24.9 e	17.1	13.2 e	11.6	11.7 e	12.1	..
32	Other manufacturing	125.4	124.9 e	112.7	108.2 e	107.4	119.9 e	135.5	..
33	Repair and installation of machinery and equipment	78.0	92.4 e	91.9	98.8 e	101.8	101.7 e	95.8	..
35-39	**ELECTRICITY, GAS, WATER AND WASTE MANAGEMENT**	**27.5**	**27.1 e**	**23.9**	**27.8 e**	**33.8**	**39.9 e**	**44.3**	..
35-36	Electricity, gas and water	21.7	22.2 e	19.3	19.0 e	21.6	28.9 e	37.8	..
37-39	Sewerage, waste management and remediation activities	5.8	4.9 e	4.6	8.8 e	12.3	11.1 e	6.5	..
41-43	**CONSTRUCTION**	**64.4**	**58.6 e**	**52.5**	**72.3 e**	**93.3**	**100.1 e**	**93.5**	..
45-99	**TOTAL SERVICES**	**2 703.2**	**3 150.0 e**	**3 282.7**	**3 488.4 e**	**3 464.5**	**3 388.1 e**	**3 153.4**	..
45-82	**Business sector services**	**2 696.9**	**3 143.8 e**	**3 277.3**	**3 482.5 e**	**3 456.5**	**3 375.7 e**	**3 135.8**	..
45-47	**Wholesale and retail trade; motor vehicle and motorcycle repairs**	**407.8**	**452.5 e**	**445.0**	**444.4 e**	**430.9**	**443.3 e**	**454.4**	..
49-53	**Transportation and storage**	**7.5**	**9.9 e**	**13.3**	**17.9 e**	**19.0**	**14.7 e**	**6.8**	..
55-56	**Accommodation and food service activities**	**0.0**	**0.0 e**	**0.0**	**0.0 e**	**0.0**	**0.0 e**	**0.0**	..
58-63	**Information and communication**	**469.4**	**554.7 e**	**558.2**	**588.7 e**	**600.7**	**621.9 e**	**624.1**	..
58-60	Publishing, audiovisual and broadcasting activities	29.8	42.3 e	46.7	52.7 e	55.0	55.2 e	51.9	..
58	Publishing activities	27.9	39.9 e	44.3	49.4 e	50.4	48.8 e	43.8	..
59-60	Motion picture, video and TV programme production; broadcasting activities	2.0	2.3 e	2.4	3.3 e	4.6	6.4 e	8.1	..
59	Motion picture, video and TV programme production; sound and music	..	..	..	..	..	..	..	..
60	Programming and broadcasting activities	..	..	..	..	..	..	..	..
61	Telecommunications	68.1	63.0 e	50.4	46.5 e	44.8	44.0 e	41.7	..
62-63	IT and other information services	371.5	449.4 e	461.2	489.6 e	500.9	522.8 e	530.6	..
62	Computer programming, consultancy and related activities	251.8	320.1 e	356.7	391.4 e	406.2	435.4 e	457.2	..
63	Information service activities	119.7	129.3 e	104.4	98.1 e	94.7	87.4 e	73.3	..
64-66	**Financial and insurance activities**	**40.7**	**23.7 e**	**15.1**	**18.6 e**	**22.9**	**20.3 e**	**12.4**	..
68-82	**Real estate; professional, scientific and technical; administrative and support**	**1 771.5**	**2 103.0 e**	**2 245.7**	**2 412.8 e**	**2 383.0**	**2 275.3 e**	**2 038.1**	..
68	Real estate activities	0.7	2.0 e	2.9	3.2 e	3.0	2.8 e	2.5	..
69-75x72	Professional, scientific and technical activities, except scientific R&D	705.7	800.2 e	831.0	920.6 e	940.0	888.8 e	760.8	..
72	Scientific research and development	1 050.7	1 289.4 e	1 404.1	1 480.0 e	1 427.9	1 369.5 e	1 259.6	..
77-82	Administrative and support service activities	14.4	11.5 e	7.6	9.0 e	12.1	14.3 e	15.1	..
84-99	Community, social and personal services	6.3	6.2 e	5.4	5.9 e	8.0	12.4 e	17.6	..
84-85	Public administration and defence; compulsory social security and education	3.5	3.3 e	2.4	1.6 e	1.2	1.2 e	1.6	..
86-88	Human health and social work activities	0.9	1.5 e	2.0	2.6 e	2.8	2.7 e	2.3	..
90-93	Arts, entertainment and recreation	0.6	0.4 e	0.3	0.8 e	2.1	4.3 e	6.8	..
94-99	Other services; household-employers; extraterritorial bodies	1.3	1.1 e	0.7	0.9 e	2.0	4.2 e	6.9	..

.. Not available; e Estimated value

Note: Detailed metadata at: *http://metalinks.oecd.org/anberd/20200813/2abe.*

BELGIUM

R&D expenditure in industry by main activity of the enterprise, current prices
ISIC Rev. 4

Million USD PPP

		2011	2012	2013	2014	2015	2016	2017	2018
	TOTAL BUSINESS ENTERPRISE	**6 747.6**	**7 479.2**	**7 885.3**	**8 342.7**	**8 847.8**	**9 531.2**	**10 782.6**	..
01-03	**AGRICULTURE, FORESTRY AND FISHING**	31.1	18.6	20.4	7.7	13.6	7.9	9.8	..
05-09	**MINING AND QUARRYING**	7.7	1.5	2.3	6.0	7.8	1.6	2.0	..
10-33	**MANUFACTURING**	**4 246.0**	**4 468.8**	**4 663.3**	**4 605.5**	**4 833.1**	**5 440.9**	**6 029.7**	..
10-12	Food products, beverages and tobacco	146.3	132.7	138.3	168.8 e	184.9 e	240.8	260.9	..
13-15	Textiles, wearing apparel, leather and related products	68.0	59.7	67.7	82.6 e	90.6 e	66.2	81.0	..
13	Textiles	52.4	40.6	46.2	..	..	..	..	..
14	Wearing apparel	6.4	7.4	8.7	..	..	..	..	..
15	Leather and related products, footwear	9.2	11.6	12.8	..	..	..	..	..
16-18	Wood and paper products and printing	23.4	32.3	36.4	30.9	30.4	28.7	33.6	..
16	Wood and wood products, except furniture	6.8	14.9	17.0	5.9	6.0	7.4	8.1	..
17	Paper and paper products	12.5	13.2	14.6	22.0	20.9	16.2	17.9	..
18	Printing and reproduction of recorded media	4.1	4.3	4.8	3.0	3.5	5.1	7.6	..
19-23	Chemical, rubber, plastic, non-metallic mineral products	2 331.7	2 505.7	2 583.4	2 612.8 e	2 687.7 e	3 227.9 e	3 586.2 e	..
19	Coke and refined petroleum products	7.9	11.5	12.1	14.8 e	16.2 e	19.0 e	12.4 e	..
20-21	Chemical and pharmaceutical products	2 137.4	2 314.4	2 390.1	2 391.6	2 448.2	3 014.8	3 337.0	..
20	Chemicals and chemical products	421.0	458.4	460.7	443.1	458.4	397.6	455.5	..
21	Pharmaceuticals, medicinal, chemical and botanical products	1 716.4	1 856.0	1 929.4	1 948.5	1 989.8	2 617.2	2 881.5	..
22	Rubber and plastic products	109.6	111.9	112.9	129.3	141.8	126.0	161.7	..
23	Other non-metallic mineral products	76.9	68.0	68.3	77.1	81.5	68.2	75.1	..
24-25	Basic metals, metal products, except machinery and equipment	276.0	299.5	287.8	301.1 e	312.5 e	293.5	342.1	..
24	Basic metals	169.0	171.7	155.1	174.5 e	180.5 e	178.0	208.9	..
25	Fabricated metal products, except machinery and equipment	107.0	127.9	132.7	126.6	132.1	115.5	133.2	..
26-30	Computer, electronic, optical products; electrical machinery, transport equipment	1 359.4	1 378.5	1 481.1	1 358.8	1 466.6	1 509.4	1 639.7	..
26	Computer, electronic and optical products	511.4	555.7	593.4	550.1	578.7	624.9	684.8	..
27	Electrical equipment	266.7	169.4	170.4	184.3	183.6	142.4	149.2	..
28	Machinery and equipment n.e.c.	289.0	359.7	376.0	324.7	356.7	404.9	450.7	..
29	Motor vehicles, trailers and semi-trailers	136.2	153.6	183.6	143.9	162.8	173.9	200.6	..
30	Other transport equipment	156.2	140.1	157.7	155.9	184.8	163.3	154.4	..
31-33	Furniture; repair, installation of machinery and equipment	41.1	60.4	68.5	50.4	60.4	74.4	86.3	..
31	Furniture	10.4	12.5	12.6	9.6	10.4	17.4	21.4	..
32	Other manufacturing	16.2	21.1	25.0	21.3	25.6	20.9	29.0	..
33	Repair and installation of machinery and equipment	14.5	26.8	30.9	19.5	24.4	36.1	35.9	..
35-39	**ELECTRICITY, GAS, WATER AND WASTE MANAGEMENT**	**68.8**	**107.3**	**127.4**	**101.4**	**108.5**	**100.9**	**82.6**	..
35-36	Electricity, gas and water	51.7	91.3	104.9	76.7	83.7	81.4	59.4	..
37-39	Sewerage, waste management and remediation activities	17.2	15.9	22.5	24.7	24.8	19.5	23.2	..
41-43	**CONSTRUCTION**	**67.6**	**44.0**	**48.6**	**49.8**	**65.3**	**83.5**	**96.3**	..
45-99	**TOTAL SERVICES**	**2 326.4**	**2 839.0**	**3 023.3**	**3 572.5**	**3 819.5**	**3 896.4**	**4 562.2**	..
45-82	**Business sector services**	**2 311.9**	**2 833.5**	**3 017.7**	**3 552.3**	**3 790.8**	**3 866.1**	**4 527.0**	..
45-47	**Wholesale and retail trade; motor vehicle and motorcycle repairs**	**162.1**	**339.3**	**353.4**	**405.1**	**425.0**	**477.0**	**510.9**	..
49-53	**Transportation and storage**	**18.1**	**17.0**	**21.5**	**31.8**	**35.6**	**29.8**	**30.1**	..
55-56	**Accommodation and food service activities**	**0.0**	**0.1**	**0.0**	**0.0 e**	**0.0 e**	**0.3 e**	**0.2 e**	..
58-63	**Information and communication**	**670.6**	**659.9**	**673.2**	**769.1**	**812.6**	**972.2**	**1 157.2**	..
58-60	Publishing, audiovisual and broadcasting activities	31.9	51.1	55.8	79.2	91.1	83.6	84.5	..
58	Publishing activities	22.1	44.8	47.8	58.7	69.6	74.5	75.2	..
59-60	Motion picture, video and TV programme production; broadcasting activities	9.8	6.2	8.0	20.5	21.4	9.1	9.3	..
59	Motion picture, video and TV programme production; sound and music	7.5	3.6	4.5	..	..	..	..	..
60	Programming and broadcasting activities	2.3	2.6	3.5	..	..	..	..	..
61	Telecommunications	249.7	112.4	94.5	85.4	90.5	163.7	185.8	..
62-63	IT and other information services	389.0	496.5	522.9	604.5	631.0	724.9	886.9	..
62	Computer programming, consultancy and related activities	353.3	460.9	485.5	555.7	583.0	675.4	832.0	..
63	Information service activities	35.7	35.6	37.3	48.8	48.0	49.5	54.9	..
64-66	**Financial and insurance activities**	**125.9**	**214.1**	**218.3**	**306.1**	**316.2**	**328.2**	**437.0**	..
68-82	**Real estate; professional, scientific and technical; administrative and support**	**1 335.2**	**1 603.2**	**1 751.3**	**2 040.2 e**	**2 201.4 e**	**2 058.6**	**2 391.7**	..
68	Real estate activities	0.9	1.4	1.5	0.9 e	0.9 e	1.3	1.3	..
69-75x72	Professional, scientific and technical activities, except scientific R&D	682.0	743.2	830.9	892.0	980.2	1 090.8	1 212.7	..
72	Scientific research and development	618.6	809.8	869.8	1 017.7	1 086.9	922.0	1 125.1	..
77-82	Administrative and support service activities	33.7	48.8	49.1	129.6	133.3	44.5	52.7	..
84-99	Community, social and personal services	14.5	5.5	5.6	20.1	28.7	30.3	35.1	..
84-85	Public administration and defence; compulsory social security and education	1.0	0.7 e	0.6 e	0.3	0.8	0.4	0.5	..
86-88	Human health and social work activities	12.0	4.1	4.0	17.3	25.2	28.5	33.0	..
90-93	Arts, entertainment and recreation	0.0	0.2 e	0.4 e	0.6	0.8	0.7	0.9	..
94-99	Other services; household-employers; extraterritorial bodies	1.5	0.6	0.7	1.9	2.0	0.6	0.7	..

.. Not available; e Estimated value

Note: Detailed metadata at: *http://metalinks.oecd.org/anberd/20200813/2abe.*

BELGIUM

R&D expenditure in industry by main activity of the enterprise, constant prices
ISIC Rev. 4

2010 USD PPP

		2011	2012	2013	2014	2015	2016	2017	2018
	TOTAL BUSINESS ENTERPRISE	**7 416.5**	**7 967.8**	**8 133.8**	**8 459.0**	**8 847.8**	**9 148.9**	**10 068.3**	..
01-03	**AGRICULTURE, FORESTRY AND FISHING**	34.1	19.8	21.1	7.8	13.6	7.6	9.2	..
05-09	**MINING AND QUARRYING**	8.5	1.6	2.3	6.1	7.8	1.6	1.9	..
10-33	**MANUFACTURING**	**4 666.9**	**4 760.7**	**4 810.3**	**4 669.6**	**4 833.1**	**5 222.7**	**5 630.3**	..
10-12	Food products, beverages and tobacco	160.8	141.3	142.7	171.1 e	184.9 e	231.2	243.6	..
13-15	Textiles, wearing apparel, leather and related products	74.8	63.6	69.9	83.8 e	90.6 e	63.5	75.7	..
13	Textiles	57.6	43.3	47.7	..	..	..	..	..
14	Wearing apparel	7.0	7.9	9.0	..	..	..	..	..
15	Leather and related products, footwear	10.2	12.4	13.2	..	..	..	..	..
16-18	Wood and paper products and printing	25.7	34.4	37.6	31.4	30.4	27.5	31.4	..
16	Wood and wood products, except furniture	7.5	15.9	17.6	6.0	6.0	7.1	7.6	..
17	Paper and paper products	13.8	14.0	15.0	22.3	20.9	15.5	16.7	..
18	Printing and reproduction of recorded media	4.5	4.6	5.0	3.1	3.5	4.9	7.1	..
19-23	Chemical, rubber, plastic, non-metallic mineral products	2 562.9	2 669.4	2 664.8	2 649.3 e	2 687.7 e	3 098.5 e	3 348.6 e	..
19	Coke and refined petroleum products	8.7	12.2	12.5	15.0 e	16.2 e	18.2 e	11.5 e	..
20-21	Chemical and pharmaceutical products	2 349.3	2 465.5	2 465.4	2 425.0	2 448.2	2 893.8	3 116.0	..
20	Chemicals and chemical products	462.7	488.3	475.2	449.3	458.4	381.7	425.3	..
21	Pharmaceuticals, medicinal, chemical and botanical products	1 886.6	1 977.2	1 990.2	1 975.7	1 989.8	2 512.2	2 690.6	..
22	Rubber and plastic products	120.4	119.2	116.5	131.1	141.8	120.9	151.0	..
23	Other non-metallic mineral products	84.5	72.4	70.4	78.2	81.5	65.5	70.1	..
24-25	Basic metals, metal products, except machinery and equipment	303.3	319.1	296.9	305.3 e	312.5 e	281.7	319.4	..
24	Basic metals	185.8	182.9	160.0	176.9 e	180.5 e	170.9	195.0	..
25	Fabricated metal products, except machinery and equipment	117.6	136.2	136.9	128.3	132.1	110.9	124.4	..
26-30	Computer, electronic, optical products; electrical machinery, transport equipment	1 494.2	1 468.5	1 527.8	1 377.7	1 466.6	1 448.9	1 531.1	..
26	Computer, electronic and optical products	562.1	592.0	612.1	557.8	578.7	599.9	639.4	..
27	Electrical equipment	293.1	180.4	175.8	186.9	183.6	136.7	139.4	..
28	Machinery and equipment n.e.c.	317.6	383.2	387.8	329.2	356.7	388.6	420.8	..
29	Motor vehicles, trailers and semi-trailers	149.7	163.7	189.4	145.9	162.8	166.9	187.3	..
30	Other transport equipment	171.6	149.2	162.7	158.0	184.8	156.8	144.2	..
31-33	Furniture; repair, installation of machinery and equipment	45.1	64.3	70.6	51.1	60.4	71.4	80.5	..
31	Furniture	11.4	13.3	13.0	9.7	10.4	16.7	19.9	..
32	Other manufacturing	17.8	22.5	25.8	21.5	25.6	20.0	27.1	..
33	Repair and installation of machinery and equipment	15.9	28.5	31.8	19.8	24.4	34.7	33.5	..
35-39	**ELECTRICITY, GAS, WATER AND WASTE MANAGEMENT**	75.6	114.3	131.4	102.8	108.5	96.9	77.1	..
35-36	Electricity, gas and water	56.8	97.3	108.2	77.7	83.7	78.2	55.5	..
37-39	Sewerage, waste management and remediation activities	18.9	17.0	23.2	25.0	24.8	18.7	21.6	..
41-43	**CONSTRUCTION**	74.3	46.9	50.2	50.5	65.3	80.1	89.9	..
45-99	**TOTAL SERVICES**	**2 557.0**	**3 024.5**	**3 118.5**	**3 622.2**	**3 819.5**	**3 740.1**	**4 260.0**	..
45-82	**Business sector services**	2 541.1	3 018.6	3 112.8	3 601.8	3 790.8	3 711.0	4 227.2	..
45-47	**Wholesale and retail trade; motor vehicle and motorcycle repairs**	178.1	361.4	364.5	410.8	425.0	457.9	477.1	..
49-53	**Transportation and storage**	19.9	18.1	22.1	32.2	35.6	28.6	28.1	..
55-56	**Accommodation and food service activities**	0.0	0.1	0.0	0.0 e	0.0 e	0.3 e	0.2 e	..
58-63	**Information and communication**	737.1	703.0	694.4	779.9	812.6	933.2	1 080.5	..
58-60	Publishing, audiovisual and broadcasting activities	35.1	54.4	57.6	80.3	91.1	80.2	78.9	..
58	Publishing activities	24.3	47.7	49.3	59.5	69.6	71.5	70.2	..
59-60	Motion picture, video and TV programme production; broadcasting activities	10.8	6.7	8.2	20.8	21.4	8.7	8.7	..
59	Motion picture, video and TV programme production; sound and music	8.2	3.9	4.6	..	..	..	..	..
60	Programming and broadcasting activities	2.5	2.8	3.7	..	..	..	..	..
61	Telecommunications	274.4	119.7	97.5	86.6	90.5	157.1	173.5	..
62-63	IT and other information services	427.6	528.9	539.3	613.0	631.0	695.8	828.1	..
62	Computer programming, consultancy and related activities	388.3	491.0	500.9	563.4	583.0	648.3	776.8	..
63	Information service activities	39.3	37.9	38.5	49.5	48.0	47.5	51.3	..
64-66	**Financial and insurance activities**	138.3	228.0	225.2	310.4	316.2	315.0	408.0	..
68-82	**Real estate; professional, scientific and technical; administrative and support**	1 467.5	1 707.9	1 806.5	2 068.6 e	2 201.4 e	1 976.0	2 233.3	..
68	Real estate activities	1.0	1.5	1.5	0.9 e	0.9 e	1.2	1.2	..
69-75x72	Professional, scientific and technical activities, except scientific R&D	749.6	791.8	857.1	904.5	980.2	1 047.0	1 132.4	..
72	Scientific research and development	679.9	862.6	897.2	1 031.9	1 086.9	885.0	1 050.5	..
77-82	Administrative and support service activities	37.1	52.0	50.6	131.4	133.3	42.7	49.2	..
84-99	Community, social and personal services	15.9	5.9	5.8	20.4	28.7	29.1	32.8	..
84-85	Public administration and defence; compulsory social security and education	1.1	0.7 e	0.6 e	0.3	0.8	0.4	0.5	..
86-88	Human health and social work activities	13.2	4.3	4.1	17.5	25.2	27.4	30.8	..
90-93	Arts, entertainment and recreation	0.0	0.2 e	0.4 e	0.6	0.8	0.7	0.8	..
94-99	Other services; household-employers; extraterritorial bodies	1.6	0.7	0.7	1.9	2.0	0.6	0.7	..

.. Not available; e Estimated value

Note: Detailed metadata at: *http://metalinks.oecd.org/anberd/20200813/2abe.*

BELGIUM

R&D expenditure in industry by industry orientation, current prices
ISIC Rev. 4

Million USD PPP

		2011	2012	2013	2014	2015	2016	2017	2018
	TOTAL BUSINESS ENTERPRISE	**6 747.6**	**7 479.2**	**7 885.3**	**8 342.7**	**8 847.8**	**9 531.2**	**10 782.6**	..
01-03	**AGRICULTURE, FORESTRY AND FISHING**	104.3	79.0	89.8	69.6	82.0	95.6	102.4	..
05-09	**MINING AND QUARRYING**	7.8	6.8	6.0	6.2	8.3	1.9	2.3	..
10-33	**MANUFACTURING**	**5 071.8**	**5 724.4**	**5 993.2**	**6 065.9**	**6 363.9**	**6 778.7**	**7 551.6**	..
10-12	Food products, beverages and tobacco	180.8	200.7	202.0	297.5 e	318.9 e	313.6	334.9	..
13-15	Textiles, wearing apparel, leather and related products	71.0	74.6	84.2	124.1 e	133.0 e	82.9	97.8	..
13	Textiles	52.0	50.3	56.9	..	..	..	..	..
14	Wearing apparel	6.5	12.6	14.5	..	..	..	..	..
15	Leather and related products, footwear	12.4	11.6	12.8	..	..	..	..	..
16-18	Wood and paper products and printing	21.9	32.8	37.6	30.9	30.6	35.0	41.2	..
16	Wood and wood products, except furniture	6.3	14.6	17.2	6.2	6.8	8.0	8.7	..
17	Paper and paper products	12.5	14.0	15.6	21.6	20.3	21.9	24.9	..
18	Printing and reproduction of recorded media	3.1	4.2	4.8	3.0	3.5	5.1	7.6	..
19-23	Chemical, rubber, plastic, non-metallic mineral products	3 016.1	3 269.2 e	3 376.9 e	3 571.4 e	3 681.6 e	4 131.8 e	4 636.5 e	..
19	Coke and refined petroleum products	8.0	12.0 e	12.4 e	18.3 e	19.6 e	81.4 e	75.5 e	..
20-21	Chemical and pharmaceutical products	2 756.5	3 035.3	3 140.5	3 297.5	3 386.3	3 817.2	4 287.8	..
20	Chemicals and chemical products	688.2	774.8	778.4	795.6	802.7	781.3	832.8	..
21	Pharmaceuticals, medicinal, chemical and botanical products	2 068.3	2 260.5	2 362.2	2 501.8	2 583.6	3 035.9	3 455.0	..
22	Rubber and plastic products	160.0	129.7	129.9	150.6	165.3	143.1	170.5	..
23	Other non-metallic mineral products	91.5	92.2	94.0	105.0	110.4	90.1	102.7	..
24-25	Basic metals, metal products, except machinery and equipment	345.9	342.8	333.1	358.3	372.2	347.6	394.7	..
24	Basic metals	199.3	210.1	193.7	217.9	225.3	215.7	246.5	..
25	Fabricated metal products, except machinery and equipment	146.5	132.7	139.4	140.4	146.9	131.9	148.2	..
26-30	Computer, electronic, optical products; electrical machinery, transport equipment	1 401.2	1 747.1	1 892.8	1 594.2	1 713.9	1 746.7	1 895.5	..
26	Computer, electronic and optical products	541.4	643.7	685.0	650.3	678.6	703.4	759.4	..
27	Electrical equipment	201.6	172.5	173.7	186.7	186.2	160.4	170.2	..
28	Machinery and equipment n.e.c.	295.4	371.9	389.4	327.8	363.2	432.8	484.4	..
29	Motor vehicles, trailers and semi-trailers	201.8	400.1	460.6	266.2	291.7	269.4	309.7	..
30	Other transport equipment	161.0	158.9	184.1	163.1	194.4	180.7	171.9	..
31-33	Furniture; repair, installation of machinery and equipment	35.0	57.1 e	66.6 e	89.7	113.6	121.1	151.0	..
31	Furniture	9.2	13.8 e	14.2 e	12.2	13.0	20.1	24.3	..
32	Other manufacturing	23.3	39.6	48.5	62.0	81.8	66.6	89.0	..
33	Repair and installation of machinery and equipment	2.5	3.7 e	3.9 e	15.4	18.8	34.3	37.7	..
35-39	**ELECTRICITY, GAS, WATER AND WASTE MANAGEMENT**	70.0	132.2	154.9	145.4	174.9	146.9	131.9	..
35-36	Electricity, gas and water	52.1	113.7	129.6	114.6	140.9	126.2	107.4	..
37-39	Sewerage, waste management and remediation activities	17.9	18.5	25.4	30.8	33.9	20.8	24.5	..
41-43	**CONSTRUCTION**	73.7	79.2	84.8	79.1	98.6	110.3	124.3	..
45-99	**TOTAL SERVICES**	**1 420.0**	**1 457.6**	**1 556.6**	**1 976.6**	**2 120.2**	**2 397.7**	**2 870.1**	..
45-82	**Business sector services**	**1 399.8**	**1 407.4**	**1 497.6**	**1 937.2**	**2 072.8**	**2 330.4**	**2 788.8**	..
45-47	**Wholesale and retail trade; motor vehicle and motorcycle repairs**	75.7	63.8	75.6	220.1	232.0	130.6	157.4	..
49-53	**Transportation and storage**	18.4	16.3	20.0	35.0	39.6	39.6	41.4	..
55-56	**Accommodation and food service activities**	0.0	0.1 e	0.2 e	0.2	0.3	0.3 e	0.2 e	..
58-63	**Information and communication**	775.2	748.6	772.6	840.4	891.1	1 036.8	1 252.2	..
58-60	Publishing, audiovisual and broadcasting activities	31.7	29.8	31.1	78.4	89.0	87.7	86.8	..
58	Publishing activities	21.9	22.7	22.1	58.0	67.6	75.1	74.8	..
59-60	Motion picture, video and TV programme production; broadcasting activities	9.8	7.1	9.0	20.4	21.4	12.6	12.0	..
59	Motion picture, video and TV programme production; sound and music	..	..	..	..	..	..	..	..
60	Programming and broadcasting activities	..	..	..	..	..	..	..	..
61	Telecommunications	350.2	161.4	145.5	157.6	161.9	180.1	203.4	..
62-63	IT and other information services	393.2	557.5	596.0	604.4	640.2	769.0	962.0	..
62	Computer programming, consultancy and related activities	356.8	512.0	548.5	535.7	563.2	712.7	898.3	..
63	Information service activities	36.5	45.6	47.6	68.7	77.0	56.4	63.7	..
64-66	**Financial and insurance activities**	119.5	111.5	106.5	235.0	246.5	292.5	385.6	..
68-82	**Real estate; professional, scientific and technical; administrative and support**	411.0	467.0 e	522.8 e	606.5	663.3	830.6	952.0	..
68	Real estate activities	0.9	2.9 e	3.0 e	0.5	0.6	1.4	1.4	..
69-75x72	Professional, scientific and technical activities, except scientific R&D	370.1	446.2	500.0	536.6	594.8	775.7	881.1	..
72	Scientific research and development	6.2	7.4	7.6	42.4	39.7	17.9	23.6	..
77-82	Administrative and support service activities	33.8	10.5	12.2	26.9	28.3	35.7	45.9	..
84-99	Community, social and personal services	20.2	50.2	58.9	39.4	47.4	67.3	81.3	..
84-85	Public administration and defence; compulsory social security and education	1.1	3.0 e	1.9 e	0.4	0.8	0.7	0.7	..
86-88	Human health and social work activities	18.7	44.3	52.7	36.2	43.5	64.5	77.8	..
90-93	Arts, entertainment and recreation	0.0	0.6 e	1.1 e	0.8	0.9	1.6	2.2	..
94-99	Other services; household-employers; extraterritorial bodies	0.4	2.3 e	3.3 e	2.1	2.2	0.6	0.7	..

.. Not available; e Estimated value

Note: Detailed metadata at: *http://metalinks.oecd.org/anberd/20200813/2abe.*

BELGIUM

R&D expenditure in industry by industry orientation, constant prices
ISIC Rev. 4

2010 USD PPP

		2011	2012	2013	2014	2015	2016	2017	2018
	TOTAL BUSINESS ENTERPRISE	**7 416.5**	**7 967.8**	**8 133.8**	**8 459.0**	**8 847.8**	**9 148.9**	**10 068.3**	..
01-03	**AGRICULTURE, FORESTRY AND FISHING**	114.7	84.1	92.7	70.6	82.0	91.8	95.6	..
05-09	**MINING AND QUARRYING**	8.5	7.3	6.2	6.2	8.3	1.8	2.2	..
10-33	**MANUFACTURING**	**5 574.6**	**6 098.3**	**6 182.0**	**6 150.5**	**6 363.9**	**6 506.8**	**7 051.4**	..
10-12	Food products, beverages and tobacco	198.8	213.8	208.3	301.7 e	318.9 e	301.1	312.8	..
13-15	Textiles, wearing apparel, leather and related products	78.0	79.4	86.9	125.8 e	133.0 e	79.6	91.4	..
13	Textiles	57.2	53.6	58.7	..	..	..	..	..
14	Wearing apparel	7.2	13.5	15.0	..	..	..	..	..
15	Leather and related products, footwear	13.6	12.4	13.2	..	..	..	..	..
16-18	Wood and paper products and printing	24.1	34.9	38.8	31.3	30.6	33.6	38.5	..
16	Wood and wood products, except furniture	6.9	15.6	17.8	6.3	6.8	7.7	8.1	..
17	Paper and paper products	13.8	14.9	16.1	21.9	20.3	21.0	23.3	..
18	Printing and reproduction of recorded media	3.4	4.5	5.0	3.1	3.5	4.9	7.1	..
19-23	Chemical, rubber, plastic, non-metallic mineral products	3 315.0	3 482.8 e	3 483.3 e	3 621.1 e	3 681.6 e	3 966.1 e	4 329.4 e	..
19	Coke and refined petroleum products	8.8	12.8 e	12.8 e	18.6 e	19.6 e	78.1 e	70.5 e	..
20-21	Chemical and pharmaceutical products	3 029.7	3 233.6	3 239.5	3 343.4	3 386.3	3 664.1	4 003.8	..
20	Chemicals and chemical products	756.4	825.4	802.9	806.7	802.7	750.0	777.6	..
21	Pharmaceuticals, medicinal, chemical and botanical products	2 273.3	2 408.2	2 436.6	2 536.7	2 583.6	2 914.1	3 226.2	..
22	Rubber and plastic products	175.9	138.2	134.0	152.7	165.3	137.3	159.2	..
23	Other non-metallic mineral products	100.6	98.2	97.0	106.5	110.4	86.5	95.9	..
24-25	Basic metals, metal products, except machinery and equipment	380.2	365.2	343.6	363.3	372.2	333.6	368.5	..
24	Basic metals	219.1	223.8	199.8	220.9	225.3	207.0	230.1	..
25	Fabricated metal products, except machinery and equipment	161.1	141.4	143.8	142.3	146.9	126.6	138.4	..
26-30	Computer, electronic, optical products; electrical machinery, transport equipment	1 540.1	1 861.3	1 952.5	1 616.4	1 713.9	1 676.7	1 769.9	..
26	Computer, electronic and optical products	595.1	685.8	706.6	659.4	678.6	675.2	709.1	..
27	Electrical equipment	221.6	183.8	179.2	189.3	186.2	154.0	158.9	..
28	Machinery and equipment n.e.c.	324.7	396.1	401.7	332.4	363.2	415.4	452.3	..
29	Motor vehicles, trailers and semi-trailers	221.8	426.2	475.1	269.9	291.7	258.6	289.2	..
30	Other transport equipment	177.0	169.3	189.9	165.4	194.4	173.5	160.5	..
31-33	Furniture; repair, installation of machinery and equipment	38.4	60.9 e	68.7 e	90.9	113.6	116.2	141.0	..
31	Furniture	10.1	14.7 e	14.7 e	12.4	13.0	19.3	22.7	..
32	Other manufacturing	25.6	42.2	50.0	62.9	81.8	63.9	83.1	..
33	Repair and installation of machinery and equipment	2.7	4.0 e	4.0 e	15.6	18.8	33.0	35.2	..
35-39	**ELECTRICITY, GAS, WATER AND WASTE MANAGEMENT**	76.9	140.9	159.8	147.4	174.9	141.0	123.1	..
35-36	Electricity, gas and water	57.2	121.1	133.7	116.2	140.9	121.1	100.3	..
37-39	Sewerage, waste management and remediation activities	19.7	19.7	26.2	31.2	33.9	19.9	22.8	..
41-43	**CONSTRUCTION**	**81.0**	**84.4**	**87.5**	**80.2**	**98.6**	**105.9**	**116.1**	..
45-99	**TOTAL SERVICES**	**1 560.8**	**1 552.8**	**1 605.6**	**2 004.1**	**2 120.2**	**2 301.6**	**2 680.0**	..
45-82	**Business sector services**	**1 538.6**	**1 499.3**	**1 544.8**	**1 964.2**	**2 072.8**	**2 237.0**	**2 604.0**	..
45-47	**Wholesale and retail trade; motor vehicle and motorcycle repairs**	**83.2**	**68.0**	**78.0**	**223.1**	**232.0**	**125.3**	**147.0**	..
49-53	**Transportation and storage**	**20.3**	**17.4**	**20.6**	**35.5**	**39.6**	**38.0**	**38.7**	..
55-56	**Accommodation and food service activities**	**0.0**	**0.1 e**	**0.2 e**	**0.3**	**0.3**	**0.3 e**	**0.2 e**	..
58-63	**Information and communication**	**852.1**	**797.6**	**797.0**	**852.1**	**891.1**	**995.2**	**1 169.2**	..
58-60	Publishing, audiovisual and broadcasting activities	34.9	31.7	32.0	79.5	89.0	84.2	81.1	..
58	Publishing activities	24.1	24.1	22.8	58.8	67.6	72.1	69.8	..
59-60	Motion picture, video and TV programme production; broadcasting activities	10.8	7.6	9.3	20.7	21.4	12.1	11.3	..
59	Motion picture, video and TV programme production; sound and music	..	..	..	..	..	..	..	..
60	Programming and broadcasting activities	..	..	..	..	..	..	..	..
61	Telecommunications	384.9	171.9	150.1	159.8	161.9	172.8	189.9	..
62-63	IT and other information services	432.2	594.0	614.8	612.8	640.2	738.2	898.3	..
62	Computer programming, consultancy and related activities	392.1	545.4	565.7	543.2	563.2	684.1	838.8	..
63	Information service activities	40.1	48.5	49.1	69.6	77.0	54.1	59.5	..
64-66	**Financial and insurance activities**	**131.3**	**118.7**	**109.8**	**238.3**	**246.5**	**280.8**	**360.1**	..
68-82	**Real estate; professional, scientific and technical; administrative and support**	**451.7**	**497.5 e**	**539.3 e**	**614.9**	**663.3**	**797.3**	**888.9**	..
68	Real estate activities	1.0	3.1 e	3.1 e	0.5	0.6	1.3	1.3	..
69-75x72	Professional, scientific and technical activities, except scientific R&D	406.8	475.3	515.8	544.1	594.8	744.5	822.8	..
72	Scientific research and development	6.8	7.9	7.9	43.0	39.7	17.2	22.1	..
77-82	Administrative and support service activities	37.2	11.2	12.5	27.3	28.3	34.3	42.8	..
84-99	Community, social and personal services	22.2	53.5	60.8	39.9	47.4	64.6	75.9	..
84-85	Public administration and defence; compulsory social security and education	1.2	3.2 e	1.9 e	0.4	0.8	0.6	0.7	..
86-88	Human health and social work activities	20.5	47.2	54.4	36.7	43.5	61.9	72.6	..
90-93	Arts, entertainment and recreation	0.0	0.7 e	1.1 e	0.8	0.9	1.5	2.0	..
94-99	Other services; household-employers; extraterritorial bodies	0.4	2.5 e	3.4 e	2.1	2.2	0.6	0.7	..

.. Not available; e Estimated value

Note: Detailed metadata at: *http://metalinks.oecd.org/anberd/20200813/2abe.*

R&D expenditure in industry by main activity of the enterprise, current prices
ISIC Rev. 4

Million USD PPP

		2011	2012	2013	2014	2015	2016	2017	2018
	TOTAL BUSINESS ENTERPRISE	**13 625.3**	**13 417.9**	**13 560.5**	**14 798.1**	**14 386.2**	**15 514.1**	**15 514.6**	..
01-03	**AGRICULTURE, FORESTRY AND FISHING**	**116.9 e**	**77.9**	**72.7**	**67.5**	**81.0 e**	**130.3 e**	**137.7 e**	..
05-09	**MINING AND QUARRYING**	**1 118.6**	**1 292.0**	**1 344.0**	**1 177.7**	**704.8 e**	**697.8 e**	**621.6 e**	..
10-33	**MANUFACTURING**	**5 973.0**	**5 782.5**	**5 718.1**	**4 938.7 e**	**5 301.2 e**	**5 560.0**	**5 415.3**	..
10-12	Food products, beverages and tobacco	136.3	126.9	128.3 e	126.8	120.2	163.2	156.9	..
13-15	Textiles, wearing apparel, leather and related products	66.9	48.1 e	33.5	36.8 e	33.7 e	28.2	29.1	..
13	Textiles	35.0 e	25.7	22.1	25.2	24.0	..	..	..
14	Wearing apparel	28.7 e	19.1 e	9.0	8.9	7.2	..	..	..
15	Leather and related products, footwear	3.2	3.2 e	2.5	2.7 e	2.5 e	..	..	..
16-18	Wood and paper products and printing	234.7	214.5 e	213.6 e	242.2	311.7	288.4	249.0	..
16	Wood and wood products, except furniture	71.0	70.7 e	61.3 e	50.4	70.5	82.0	60.6	..
17	Paper and paper products	121.8	105.3	113.6	154.4	196.3	159.1	136.1	..
18	Printing and reproduction of recorded media	41.9	38.6	38.8 e	38.2	44.9	47.2	52.3	..
19-23	Chemical, rubber, plastic, non-metallic mineral products	953.3	791.6	780.6	727.4	898.5 e	909.0	960.4	..
19	Coke and refined petroleum products	74.2 e	49.8 e	53.9 e	3.3	26.7 e	27.3	24.9	..
20-21	Chemical and pharmaceutical products	675.9	543.9	543.3	551.9	718.7	693.6	739.6	..
20	Chemicals and chemical products	258.1	180.0	202.6	176.4	318.1	282.6	283.9	..
21	Pharmaceuticals, medicinal, chemical and botanical products	417.8	364.0	340.7	375.5	400.6	411.0	455.7	..
22	Rubber and plastic products	137.9 e	144.8 e	127.9 e	127.6	114.6	145.0	157.7	..
23	Other non-metallic mineral products	65.3	53.0	55.6	44.7	38.5 e	43.1	38.2	..
24-25	Basic metals, metal products, except machinery and equipment	409.7	384.9 e	414.2 e	496.3 e	487.8 e	503.0	370.2	..
24	Basic metals	172.6	167.1 e	194.4 e	279.6 e	276.0 e	285.9	161.0	..
25	Fabricated metal products, except machinery and equipment	237.1	217.7	219.8	216.7 e	211.8 e	217.1	209.2	..
26-30	Computer, electronic, optical products; electrical machinery, transport equipment	3 989.8	4 035.8	3 982.8	3 166.8	3 264.1	3 449.5	3 424.0	..
26	Computer, electronic and optical products	1 980.8	2 012.7	1 820.3	838.8	877.4	952.1	981.1	..
27	Electrical equipment	118.6	117.3	138.9	147.9 e	155.4	186.4	207.5	..
28	Machinery and equipment n.e.c.	516.2	472.4	473.0	571.6 e	564.9	672.0	632.5	..
29	Motor vehicles, trailers and semi-trailers	162.1 e	149.4 e	143.0	112.2	148.2 e	192.2	226.6	..
30	Other transport equipment	1 212.2 e	1 283.9 e	1 407.7	1 496.3	1 518.2 e	1 446.8	1 377.1	..
31-33	Furniture; repair, installation of machinery and equipment	182.3	180.8	165.0	142.2	185.2	122.6	135.3	..
31	Furniture	29.0	23.3	18.0	19.5	31.5 e	25.7	28.2	..
32	Other manufacturing	125.8	131.8	121.7	72.3	100.9 e	72.1	91.3	..
33	Repair and installation of machinery and equipment	27.4	25.7	25.3	50.4	52.7 e	24.9	15.8	..
35-39	**ELECTRICITY, GAS, WATER AND WASTE MANAGEMENT**	**160.5 e**	**171.1**	**189.5**	**406.1 e**	**366.1 e**	**343.0**	**304.6**	..
35-36	Electricity, gas and water	..	..	..	..	..	..	..	..
37-39	Sewerage, waste management and remediation activities	..	..	..	..	..	..	..	..
41-43	**CONSTRUCTION**	**127.4**	**88.4**	**68.6**	**73.1**	**63.3 e**	**80.7 e**	**78.3 e**	..
45-99	**TOTAL SERVICES**	**6 128.7**	**6 005.9**	**6 167.5**	**8 135.0**	**7 869.8 e**	**8 702.3 e**	**8 957.1 e**	..
45-82	**Business sector services**	**6 019.8**	**5 904.7**	**6 059.6**	**8 014.7**	**7 741.2**	**8 562.9**	**8 811.1**	..
45-47	**Wholesale and retail trade; motor vehicle and motorcycle repairs**	**1 198.5**	**1 255.8**	**1 170.8**	**1 296.4**	**1 404.6**	**1 433.5**	**1 447.6**	..
49-53	**Transportation and storage**	**49.2**	**50.6**	**68.1 e**	**70.7**	**97.0**	**83.7**	**88.0**	..
55-56	**Accommodation and food service activities**	**2.4 e**	**2.4**	**1.6**	**1.7 e**	**1.8 e**	**3.3**	**2.5**	..
58-63	**Information and communication**	**2 171.9**	**2 076.2**	**2 238.6**	**3 551.0**	**3 405.4**	**4 606.3**	**4 641.7**	..
58-60	Publishing, audiovisual and broadcasting activities	494.4	593.8	568.6	1 408.5	1 213.1 e	..	..	..
58	Publishing activities	470.2	563.2	535.1	1 367.1	1 170.7	..	..	..
59-60	Motion picture, video and TV programme production; broadcasting activities	24.2	30.5	33.5	41.5	42.4 e	..	..	..
59	Motion picture, video and TV programme production; sound and music	23.4	28.9 e	31.0	38.4 e	39.3 e	..	..	..
60	Programming and broadcasting activities	0.8	1.6 e	2.5	3.0 e	3.1 e	..	..	..
61	Telecommunications	347.6	322.2	356.2	311.3	318.5 e	..	..	..
62-63	IT and other information services	1 329.9	1 161.0	1 313.7	1 831.2	1 873.8 e	..	..	..
62	Computer programming, consultancy and related activities	1 254.9	1 079.9	1 212.4	1 700.3	1 739.9 e	..	..	..
63	Information service activities	75.0	81.2	101.3	130.9	133.9 e	..	..	..
64-66	**Financial and insurance activities**	**260.5**	**278.0**	**379.9**	**377.1**	**359.8**	**203.8**	**353.6**	..
68-82	**Real estate; professional, scientific and technical; administrative and support**	**2 337.3 e**	**2 241.7**	**2 200.6 e**	**2 717.9 e**	**2 472.6 e**	**2 233.1**	**2 277.7**	..
68	Real estate activities	6.5 e	6.4	8.7 e	8.9 e	9.4 e	7.5	8.3	..
69-75x72	Professional, scientific and technical activities, except scientific R&D	575.0	555.2	539.6	700.6	629.8	567.1 e	585.3	..
72	Scientific research and development	1 641.3	1 564.3	1 533.5	1 888.1	1 737.2	1 564.1 e	1 614.4 e	..
77-82	Administrative and support service activities	114.5	115.7	118.9 e	119.5	96.2	94.5 e	69.7	..
84-99	Community, social and personal services	108.9	101.2	108.7	120.3	128.7 e	139.4 e	146.0 e	..
84-85	Public administration and defence; compulsory social security and education	10.4 e	11.2	11.4	13.8	14.8	..	..	..
86-88	Human health and social work activities	79.0	72.3	78.4	86.2	92.1	99.8 e	104.6	..
90-93	Arts, entertainment and recreation	4.0 e	4.0	4.1	4.9	5.2	..	..	..
94-99	Other services; household-employers; extraterritorial bodies	15.4 e	13.7	14.7	15.4	16.5	..	..	..

.. Not available; e Estimated value

Note: Detailed metadata at: *http://metalinks.oecd.org/anberd/20200813/2abe.*

R&D expenditure in industry by main activity of the enterprise, constant prices
ISIC Rev. 4

2010 USD PPP

		2011	2012	2013	2014	2015	2016	2017	2018
	TOTAL BUSINESS ENTERPRISE	**14 085.6**	**13 756.9**	**13 439.4**	**14 461.0**	**14 386.2**	**14 890.1**	**14 508.1**	..
01-03	**AGRICULTURE, FORESTRY AND FISHING**	**120.9 e**	**79.9**	**72.1**	**65.9**	**81.0 e**	**125.1 e**	**128.7 e**	..
05-09	**MINING AND QUARRYING**	**1 156.4**	**1 324.6**	**1 332.0**	**1 150.9**	**704.8 e**	**669.7 e**	**581.3 e**	..
10-33	**MANUFACTURING**	**6 174.8**	**5 928.7**	**5 667.1**	**4 826.1 e**	**5 301.2 e**	**5 336.3**	**5 064.0**	..
10-12	Food products, beverages and tobacco	140.9	130.2	127.1 e	123.9	120.2	156.7	146.7	..
13-15	Textiles, wearing apparel, leather and related products	69.2	49.3 e	33.2	36.0 e	33.7 e	27.0	27.2	..
13	Textiles	36.1 e	26.4	21.9	24.6	24.0	..	..	..
14	Wearing apparel	29.7 e	19.6 e	8.9	8.7	7.2	..	..	..
15	Leather and related products, footwear	3.3	3.3 e	2.4	2.6 e	2.5 e	..	..	..
16-18	Wood and paper products and printing	242.6	219.9 e	211.7 e	236.7	311.7	276.8	232.9	..
16	Wood and wood products, except furniture	73.4	72.5 e	60.7 e	49.2	70.5	78.7	56.7	..
17	Paper and paper products	125.9	107.9	112.5	150.9	196.3	152.7	127.3	..
18	Printing and reproduction of recorded media	43.4	39.5	38.5 e	37.3	44.9	45.3	48.9	..
19-23	Chemical, rubber, plastic, non-metallic mineral products	985.5	811.6	773.7	710.9	898.5 e	872.4	898.1	..
19	Coke and refined petroleum products	76.7 e	51.1 e	53.4 e	3.2	26.7 e	26.2	23.3	..
20-21	Chemical and pharmaceutical products	698.7	557.7	538.5	539.3	718.7	665.7	691.6	..
20	Chemicals and chemical products	266.8	184.5	200.8	172.4	318.1	271.2	265.5	..
21	Pharmaceuticals, medicinal, chemical and botanical products	431.9	373.2	337.6	366.9	400.6	394.5	426.1	..
22	Rubber and plastic products	142.6 e	148.4 e	126.7 e	124.7	114.6	139.2	147.5	..
23	Other non-metallic mineral products	67.5	54.4	55.1	43.7	38.5 e	41.4	35.7	..
24-25	Basic metals, metal products, except machinery and equipment	423.6	394.6 e	410.5 e	485.0 e	487.8 e	482.7	346.2	..
24	Basic metals	178.4	171.3 e	192.7 e	273.2 e	276.0 e	274.4	150.6	..
25	Fabricated metal products, except machinery and equipment	245.1	223.2	217.8	211.8 e	211.8 e	208.4	195.6	..
26-30	Computer, electronic, optical products; electrical machinery, transport equipment	4 124.6	4 137.8	3 947.3	3 094.7	3 264.1	3 310.8	3 201.9	..
26	Computer, electronic and optical products	2 047.7	2 063.5	1 804.0	819.7	877.4	913.8	917.5	..
27	Electrical equipment	122.6	120.3	137.6	144.6 e	155.4	178.9	194.1	..
28	Machinery and equipment n.e.c.	533.6	484.4	468.8	558.6 e	564.9	645.0	591.5	..
29	Motor vehicles, trailers and semi-trailers	167.6 e	153.2 e	141.7	109.6	148.2 e	184.5	211.9	..
30	Other transport equipment	1 253.1 e	1 316.4 e	1 395.1	1 462.2	1 518.2 e	1 388.6	1 287.7	..
31-33	Furniture; repair, installation of machinery and equipment	188.4	185.3	163.6	139.0	185.2	117.7	126.5	..
31	Furniture	30.0	23.9	17.8	19.1	31.5 e	24.7	26.4	..
32	Other manufacturing	130.1	135.1	120.6	70.7	100.9 e	69.2	85.4	..
33	Repair and installation of machinery and equipment	28.3	26.4	25.1	49.2	52.7 e	23.9	14.7	..
35-39	**ELECTRICITY, GAS, WATER AND WASTE MANAGEMENT**	**165.9 e**	**175.5**	**187.9**	**396.9 e**	**366.1 e**	**329.2**	**284.9**	..
35-36	Electricity, gas and water	..	..	..	..	..	..	..	..
37-39	Sewerage, waste management and remediation activities	..	..	..	..	..	..	..	..
41-43	**CONSTRUCTION**	**131.7**	**90.6**	**68.0**	**71.5**	**63.3 e**	**77.5 e**	**73.2 e**	..
45-99	**TOTAL SERVICES**	**6 335.7**	**6 157.7**	**6 112.4**	**7 949.7**	**7 869.8 e**	**8 352.2 e**	**8 376.0 e**	..
45-82	**Business sector services**	**6 223.2**	**6 053.9**	**6 005.5**	**7 832.1**	**7 741.2**	**8 218.4**	**8 239.5**	..
45-47	**Wholesale and retail trade; motor vehicle and motorcycle repairs**	**1 239.0**	**1 287.6**	**1 160.3**	**1 266.8**	**1 404.6**	**1 375.8**	**1 353.7**	..
49-53	**Transportation and storage**	**50.9**	**51.9**	**67.5 e**	**69.1**	**97.0**	**80.3**	**82.3**	..
55-56	**Accommodation and food service activities**	**2.5 e**	**2.5**	**1.6**	**1.6 e**	**1.8 e**	**3.2**	**2.3**	..
58-63	**Information and communication**	**2 245.3**	**2 128.6**	**2 218.6**	**3 470.1**	**3 405.4**	**4 421.0**	**4 340.6**	..
58-60	Publishing, audiovisual and broadcasting activities	511.1	608.8	563.6	1 376.4	1 213.1 e	..	..	..
58	Publishing activities	486.1	577.5	530.4	1 335.9	1 170.7	..	..	..
59-60	Motion picture, video and TV programme production; broadcasting activities	25.0	31.3	33.2	40.5	42.4 e	..	..	..
59	Motion picture, video and TV programme production; sound and music	24.2	29.6 e	30.8	37.5 e	39.3 e	..	..	..
60	Programming and broadcasting activities	0.8	1.7 e	2.4	3.0 e	3.1 e	..	..	..
61	Telecommunications	359.4	330.3	353.0	304.2	318.5 e	..	..	..
62-63	IT and other information services	1 374.9	1 190.3	1 302.0	1 789.5	1 873.8 e	..	..	..
62	Computer programming, consultancy and related activities	1 297.3	1 107.1	1 201.6	1 661.6	1 739.9 e	..	..	..
63	Information service activities	77.5	83.2	100.4	127.9	133.9 e	..	..	..
64-66	**Financial and insurance activities**	**269.3**	**285.0**	**376.5**	**368.5**	**359.8**	**195.6**	**330.7**	..
68-82	**Real estate; professional, scientific and technical; administrative and support**	**2 416.2 e**	**2 298.3**	**2 181.0 e**	**2 655.9 e**	**2 472.6 e**	**2 143.3**	**2 129.9**	..
68	Real estate activities	6.7 e	6.6	8.6 e	8.7 e	9.4 e	7.2	7.8	..
69-75x72	Professional, scientific and technical activities, except scientific R&D	594.5	569.2	534.8	684.6	629.8	544.3 e	547.3	..
72	Scientific research and development	1 696.7	1 603.9	1 519.8	1 845.1	1 737.2	1 501.2 e	1 509.6 e	..
77-82	Administrative and support service activities	118.4	118.6	117.8 e	116.8	96.2	90.7 e	65.2	..
84-99	Community, social and personal services	112.6	103.8	107.7	117.5	128.7 e	133.8 e	136.6 e	..
84-85	Public administration and defence; compulsory social security and education	10.7 e	11.5	11.3	13.5	14.8	..	..	..
86-88	Human health and social work activities	81.7	74.1	77.7	84.2	92.1	95.8 e	97.8	..
90-93	Arts, entertainment and recreation	4.2 e	4.1	4.0	4.8	5.2	..	..	..
94-99	Other services; household-employers; extraterritorial bodies	16.0 e	14.0	14.6	15.1	16.5	..	..	..

.. Not available; e Estimated value

Note: Detailed metadata at: *http://metalinks.oecd.org/anberd/20200813/2abe.*

CHILE

R&D expenditure in industry by main activity of the enterprise, current prices
ISIC Rev. 4

Million USD PPP

		2011	2012	2013	2014	2015	2016	2017	2018
	TOTAL BUSINESS ENTERPRISE	419.5	466.7	536.4	506.5	532.4	575.6	532.8	..
01-03	**AGRICULTURE, FORESTRY AND FISHING**	50.8 e	48.0	87.9	69.5	69.6	70.4	63.3	..
05-09	**MINING AND QUARRYING**	41.6 e	66.6	93.7	52.7	105.6	89.3	66.3	..
10-33	**MANUFACTURING**	93.6 e	117.0	120.9	153.2	147.6	171.1	159.1	..
10-12	Food products, beverages and tobacco	..	25.1	26.1	58.8	63.6	..	..	..
13-15	Textiles, wearing apparel, leather and related products	..	1.5	0.6	1.3	0.4	..	..	..
13	Textiles	..	0.6	0.4	1.0	0.1	..	..	..
14	Wearing apparel	..	0.0	0.0	0.0	0.0	..	..	..
15	Leather and related products, footwear	..	0.9	0.3	0.3	0.2	..	..	..
16-18	Wood and paper products and printing	..	7.2	6.2	5.0	5.7	..	..	..
16	Wood and wood products, except furniture	..	0.5	1.7	1.2	1.7	..	..	..
17	Paper and paper products	..	6.7	4.5	3.8	4.0	..	..	..
18	Printing and reproduction of recorded media	..	0.0	0.0	0.0	0.1	..	..	..
19-23	Chemical, rubber, plastic, non-metallic mineral products	..	60.0	66.7	67.6	60.9	..	..	..
19	Coke and refined petroleum products	..	0.5	1.2	0.4	0.2	..	..	..
20-21	Chemical and pharmaceutical products	..	55.8	56.8	60.7	53.2	..	..	..
20	Chemicals and chemical products	..	37.4	23.2	32.6	24.4	..	..	..
21	Pharmaceuticals, medicinal, chemical and botanical products	..	18.5	33.7	28.0	28.8	..	..	..
22	Rubber and plastic products	..	1.1	5.8	4.7	5.1	..	..	..
23	Other non-metallic mineral products	..	2.5	2.9	1.8	2.4	..	..	..
24-25	Basic metals, metal products, except machinery and equipment	..	11.2	11.5	10.7	8.9	..	..	..
24	Basic metals	..	6.2	6.6	6.4	4.6	..	..	..
25	Fabricated metal products, except machinery and equipment	..	5.1	4.9	4.2	4.3	..	..	..
26-30	Computer, electronic, optical products; electrical machinery, transport equipment	..	8.4	6.8	6.9	6.9	..	..	..
26	Computer, electronic and optical products	..	0.5	1.2	1.7	1.0	..	..	..
27	Electrical equipment	..	1.3	1.2	1.5	2.1	..	..	..
28	Machinery and equipment n.e.c.	..	3.8	3.8	2.7	2.9	..	..	..
29	Motor vehicles, trailers and semi-trailers	..	1.3	0.0	0.7	0.8	..	..	..
30	Other transport equipment	..	1.4	0.5	0.4	0.2	..	..	..
31-33	Furniture; repair, installation of machinery and equipment	..	3.6	3.1	2.8	1.2	..	..	..
31	Furniture	..	0.5	1.7	0.8	0.5	..	..	..
32	Other manufacturing	..	0.0	0.9	1.1	0.1	..	..	..
33	Repair and installation of machinery and equipment	..	3.1	0.5	1.0	0.5	..	..	..
35-39	**ELECTRICITY, GAS, WATER AND WASTE MANAGEMENT**	7.8 e	10.9	12.5	7.1	4.1	3.8	2.9	..
35-36	Electricity, gas and water	..	10.9	9.0	4.3	3.2	2.5	2.0	..
37-39	Sewerage, waste management and remediation activities	..	0.0	3.5	2.8	0.9	1.3	0.9	..
41-43	**CONSTRUCTION**	3.8 e	3.7	3.3	3.2	3.1	3.2	3.4	..
45-99	**TOTAL SERVICES**	221.9 e	219.1	218.1	220.9	202.4	237.9	237.9	..
45-82	**Business sector services**	220.5 e	216.1	207.9	215.5	193.6	228.7	224.5	..
45-47	**Wholesale and retail trade; motor vehicle and motorcycle repairs**	..	63.6	42.5	59.3	50.4	52.2	60.8	..
49-53	**Transportation and storage**	..	3.1	1.7	8.4	4.6	3.6	1.3	..
55-56	**Accommodation and food service activities**	..	0.0	0.6	0.5	0.0	0.2	0.0	..
58-63	**Information and communication**	..	32.0	47.6	28.2	35.2	31.2	31.0	..
58-60	Publishing, audiovisual and broadcasting activities	..	1.7	8.4	1.8	0.0	..	..	..
58	Publishing activities	..	0.1	6.3	1.8	0.0	..	..	..
59-60	Motion picture, video and TV programme production; broadcasting activities	..	1.6	2.1	0.0	0.0	..	..	..
59	Motion picture, video and TV programme production; sound and music	..	1.6	2.0	0.0	0.0	..	..	..
60	Programming and broadcasting activities	..	0.0	0.1	0.0	0.0	..	..	..
61	Telecommunications	..	1.5	1.9	0.4	2.5	..	..	..
62-63	IT and other information services	..	28.8	37.3	26.1	32.7	..	..	..
62	Computer programming, consultancy and related activities	..	23.3	35.5	25.0	31.9	..	..	..
63	Information service activities	..	5.6	1.8	1.0	0.8	..	..	..
64-66	**Financial and insurance activities**	..	35.0	24.8	28.4	11.2	24.0	3.2	..
68-82	**Real estate; professional, scientific and technical; administrative and support**	..	82.4	90.8	90.6	92.2	117.6	128.2	..
68	Real estate activities	..	0.6	0.0	0.0	0.0	0.4	0.1	..
69-75x72	Professional, scientific and technical activities, except scientific R&D	..	59.2	50.1	49.2	33.9	39.3	47.1	..
72	Scientific research and development	..	20.8	37.8	39.8	55.9	72.0	78.6	..
77-82	Administrative and support service activities	..	1.7	2.9	1.7	2.3	5.8	2.4	..
84-99	Community, social and personal services	1.4 e	3.0	10.2	5.4	8.9	9.2	13.4	..
84-85	Public administration and defence; compulsory social security and education	..	0.0	2.3	1.9	0.9	2.0	0.1	..
86-88	Human health and social work activities	..	2.9	5.1	2.2	6.6	6.4	12.6	..
90-93	Arts, entertainment and recreation	..	0.1	2.0	0.0	0.3	0.0	0.0	..
94-99	Other services; household-employers; extraterritorial bodies	..	0.0	0.8	1.2	1.0	0.8	0.7	..

.. Not available; e Estimated value

Note: Detailed metadata at: *http://metalinks.oecd.org/anberd/20200813/2abe*.

CHILE

R&D expenditure in industry by main activity of the enterprise, constant prices
ISIC Rev. 4

2010 USD PPP

		2011	2012	2013	2014	2015	2016	2017	2018
	TOTAL BUSINESS ENTERPRISE	427.6	469.3	532.7	498.8	532.4	577.2	510.5	..
01-03	**AGRICULTURE, FORESTRY AND FISHING**	51.8 e	48.2	87.3	68.4	69.6	70.5	60.7	..
05-09	**MINING AND QUARRYING**	42.4 e	66.9	93.1	51.9	105.6	89.5	63.5	..
10-33	**MANUFACTURING**	95.4 e	117.7	120.1	150.8	147.6	171.6	152.4	..
10-12	Food products, beverages and tobacco	..	25.2	25.9	57.9	63.6	..	..	..
13-15	Textiles, wearing apparel, leather and related products	..	1.6	0.6	1.2	0.4	..	..	..
13	Textiles	..	0.6	0.4	1.0	0.1	..	..	..
14	Wearing apparel	..	0.0	0.0	0.0	0.0	..	..	..
15	Leather and related products, footwear	..	0.9	0.3	0.3	0.2	..	..	..
16-18	Wood and paper products and printing	..	7.3	6.2	4.9	5.7	..	..	..
16	Wood and wood products, except furniture	..	0.5	1.7	1.2	1.7	..	..	..
17	Paper and paper products	..	6.7	4.4	3.7	4.0	..	..	..
18	Printing and reproduction of recorded media	..	0.0	0.0	0.0	0.1	..	..	..
19-23	Chemical, rubber, plastic, non-metallic mineral products	..	60.3	66.3	66.6	60.9	..	..	..
19	Coke and refined petroleum products	..	0.5	1.2	0.4	0.2	..	..	..
20-21	Chemical and pharmaceutical products	..	56.2	56.5	59.7	53.2	..	..	..
20	Chemicals and chemical products	..	37.6	23.0	32.1	24.4	..	..	..
21	Pharmaceuticals, medicinal, chemical and botanical products	..	18.6	33.4	27.6	28.8	..	..	..
22	Rubber and plastic products	..	1.1	5.8	4.7	5.1	..	..	..
23	Other non-metallic mineral products	..	2.5	2.9	1.8	2.4	..	..	..
24-25	Basic metals, metal products, except machinery and equipment	..	11.3	11.4	10.5	8.9	..	..	..
24	Basic metals	..	6.2	6.5	6.3	4.6	..	..	..
25	Fabricated metal products, except machinery and equipment	..	5.1	4.8	4.1	4.3	..	..	..
26-30	Computer, electronic, optical products; electrical machinery, transport equipment	..	8.4	6.7	6.8	6.9	..	..	..
26	Computer, electronic and optical products	..	0.5	1.2	1.7	1.0	..	..	..
27	Electrical equipment	..	1.3	1.2	1.5	2.1	..	..	..
28	Machinery and equipment n.e.c.	..	3.9	3.8	2.6	2.9	..	..	..
29	Motor vehicles, trailers and semi-trailers	..	1.3	0.0	0.7	0.8	..	..	..
30	Other transport equipment	..	1.4	0.5	0.4	0.2	..	..	..
31-33	Furniture; repair, installation of machinery and equipment	..	3.6	3.0	2.8	1.2	..	..	..
31	Furniture	..	0.5	1.7	0.8	0.5	..	..	..
32	Other manufacturing	..	0.0	0.9	1.1	0.1	..	..	..
33	Repair and installation of machinery and equipment	..	3.1	0.5	1.0	0.5	..	..	..
35-39	**ELECTRICITY, GAS, WATER AND WASTE MANAGEMENT**	7.9 e	11.0	12.4	7.0	4.1	3.8	2.7	..
35-36	Electricity, gas and water	..	10.9	8.9	4.2	3.2	2.5	1.9	..
37-39	Sewerage, waste management and remediation activities	..	0.0	3.5	2.8	0.9	1.3	0.9	..
41-43	**CONSTRUCTION**	3.8 e	3.7	3.3	3.2	3.1	3.2	3.2	..
45-99	**TOTAL SERVICES**	226.2 e	220.4	216.6	217.5	202.4	238.5	227.9	..
45-82	**Business sector services**	224.8 e	217.3	206.5	212.2	193.6	229.3	215.1	..
45-47	**Wholesale and retail trade; motor vehicle and motorcycle repairs**	..	63.9	42.2	58.4	50.4	52.4	58.3	..
49-53	**Transportation and storage**	..	3.1	1.7	8.3	4.6	3.6	1.2	..
55-56	**Accommodation and food service activities**	..	0.0	0.6	0.5	0.0	0.2	0.0	..
58-63	**Information and communication**	..	32.2	47.3	27.8	35.2	31.2	29.7	..
58-60	Publishing, audiovisual and broadcasting activities	..	1.7	8.3	1.8	0.0	..	..	..
58	Publishing activities	..	0.1	6.2	1.8	0.0	..	..	..
59-60	Motion picture, video and TV programme production; broadcasting activities	..	1.6	2.1	0.0	0.0	..	..	..
59	Motion picture, video and TV programme production; sound and music	..	1.6	2.0	0.0	0.0	..	..	..
60	Programming and broadcasting activities	..	0.0	0.1	0.0	0.0	..	..	..
61	Telecommunications	..	1.5	1.9	0.4	2.5	..	..	..
62-63	IT and other information services	..	29.0	37.1	25.7	32.7	..	..	..
62	Computer programming, consultancy and related activities	..	23.4	35.3	24.6	31.9	..	..	..
63	Information service activities	..	5.6	1.8	1.0	0.8	..	..	..
64-66	**Financial and insurance activities**	..	35.2	24.6	28.0	11.2	24.1	3.0	..
68-82	**Real estate; professional, scientific and technical; administrative and support**	..	82.8	90.1	89.2	92.2	117.9	122.9	..
68	Real estate activities	..	0.6	0.0	0.0	0.0	0.4	0.1	..
69-75x72	Professional, scientific and technical activities, except scientific R&D	..	59.6	49.7	48.4	33.9	39.4	45.1	..
72	Scientific research and development	..	21.0	37.5	39.2	55.9	72.2	75.3	..
77-82	Administrative and support service activities	..	1.7	2.9	1.6	2.3	5.8	2.3	..
84-99	Community, social and personal services	1.4 e	3.1	10.1	5.3	8.9	9.2	12.9	..
84-85	Public administration and defence; compulsory social security and education	..	0.0	2.3	1.9	0.9	2.0	0.1	..
86-88	Human health and social work activities	..	2.9	5.1	2.1	6.6	6.4	12.1	..
90-93	Arts, entertainment and recreation	..	0.1	1.9	0.0	0.3	0.0	0.0	..
94-99	Other services; household-employers; extraterritorial bodies	..	0.0	0.8	1.2	1.0	0.8	0.6	..

.. Not available; e Estimated value

Note: Detailed metadata at: http://metalinks.oecd.org/anberd/20200813/2abe.

CZECH REPUBLIC

R&D expenditure in industry by main activity of the enterprise, current prices
ISIC Rev. 4

Million USD PPP

		2011	2012	2013	2014	2015	2016	2017	2018
	TOTAL BUSINESS ENTERPRISE	2 558.8	2 874.8	3 246.9	3 698.3	3 722.4	3 894.2	4 589.8	5 133.6
01-03	**AGRICULTURE, FORESTRY AND FISHING**	8.5	10.0	11.4	11.7	13.8	15.3	15.2	14.5
05-09	**MINING AND QUARRYING**	1.4	1.5	1.1	2.4	2.7	4.1	4.1	3.3
10-33	**MANUFACTURING**	1 341.7	1 468.4	1 725.9	1 910.1	1 954.2	2 083.3	2 465.7	2 802.6
10-12	Food products, beverages and tobacco	24.6	22.8	25.0	18.0	19.5	19.1	24.3	19.8
13-15	Textiles, wearing apparel, leather and related products	32.9	15.7	24.7	27.0	26.1	25.3	24.5	26.3
13	Textiles	16.8	12.9	21.9	24.7	23.8	23.0	21.6	23.2
14	Wearing apparel	14.8	1.7	1.3	0.8	1.0	1.1	1.5	1.7
15	Leather and related products, footwear	1.4	1.1	1.5	1.5	1.3	1.2	1.4	1.4
16-18	Wood and paper products and printing	6.1	3.2	2.7	4.0	9.6	6.9	10.3	7.5
16	Wood and wood products, except furniture	3.1	0.4	0.8	1.6	4.5	3.7	3.9	2.9
17	Paper and paper products	2.4	2.1	1.0	1.1	4.3	2.1	4.2	2.6
18	Printing and reproduction of recorded media	0.5	0.7	0.9	1.3	0.9	1.1	2.2	2.0
19-23	Chemical, rubber, plastic, non-metallic mineral products	239.5	243.0	281.0	304.1	317.2	290.3	304.4	334.6
19	Coke and refined petroleum products	0.8	0.5	0.5	0.6	0.9	0.7	0.7	0.9
20-21	Chemical and pharmaceutical products	156.4	155.9	165.1	177.7	177.1	162.5	178.9	203.5
20	Chemicals and chemical products	75.7	72.0	88.2	93.1	90.2	72.0	89.0	92.4
21	Pharmaceuticals, medicinal, chemical and botanical products	80.7	83.9	76.9	84.6	86.9	90.5	89.9	111.1
22	Rubber and plastic products	52.0	51.4	66.5	83.5	93.1	83.6	77.3	77.5
23	Other non-metallic mineral products	30.2	35.2	48.9	42.3	46.2	43.5	47.5	52.7
24-25	Basic metals, metal products, except machinery and equipment	79.8	92.4	86.5	113.3	118.2	96.3	123.9	139.7
24	Basic metals	22.0	23.6	17.8	23.5	24.9	12.7	16.3	15.2
25	Fabricated metal products, except machinery and equipment	57.8	68.8	68.7	89.9	93.3	83.6	107.6	124.5
26-30	Computer, electronic, optical products; electrical machinery, transport equipment	874.8	1 004.9	1 244.2	1 373.7	1 374.1	1 559.7	1 882.5	2 162.7
26	Computer, electronic and optical products	86.1	92.7	119.1	147.5	152.7	185.6	207.5	235.9
27	Electrical equipment	121.3	154.1	147.2	239.0	259.1	302.0	335.0	357.8
28	Machinery and equipment n.e.c.	219.7	289.1	335.3	330.1	301.0	314.5	342.9	374.0
29	Motor vehicles, trailers and semi-trailers	298.3	345.4	508.4	511.6	548.9	621.5	838.1	1 019.2
30	Other transport equipment	149.3	123.6	134.2	145.5	112.4	136.0	159.1	175.8
31-33	Furniture; repair, installation of machinery and equipment	84.0	86.4	61.7	70.0	89.5	85.7	95.7	112.0
31	Furniture	5.4	4.0	3.7	3.1	3.3	2.4	3.8	5.0
32	Other manufacturing	26.8	34.0	27.0	28.1	31.1	44.3	45.8	42.0
33	Repair and installation of machinery and equipment	51.7	48.4	31.0	38.9	55.1	39.1	46.1	65.0
35-39	**ELECTRICITY, GAS, WATER AND WASTE MANAGEMENT**	10.6	10.5	14.8	13.0	18.2	11.1	12.6	13.1
35-36	Electricity, gas and water	3.1	3.7	7.6	5.1	4.4	4.2	4.5	4.2
37-39	Sewerage, waste management and remediation activities	7.4	6.7	7.2	7.9	13.8	6.9	8.2	8.9
41-43	**CONSTRUCTION**	27.2	31.7	41.3	53.0	47.8	42.0	48.1	54.2
45-99	**TOTAL SERVICES**	1 169.5	1 352.7	1 452.4	1 708.1	1 685.7	1 738.4	2 044.1	2 245.9
45-82	**Business sector services**	1 161.3	1 341.7	1 422.5	1 686.0	1 658.1	1 712.3	2 025.8	2 224.0
45-47	**Wholesale and retail trade; motor vehicle and motorcycle repairs**	69.8	69.1	75.0	70.8	84.3	76.2	85.5	103.6
49-53	**Transportation and storage**	0.4	1.5	1.7	1.8	1.5	1.4	1.4	1.3
55-56	**Accommodation and food service activities**	0.1	0.1	0.1	0.1	0.1	0.1	0.2	0.3
58-63	**Information and communication**	371.5	421.2	458.3	607.6	613.1	686.1	854.8	1 033.0
58-60	Publishing, audiovisual and broadcasting activities	16.0	18.3	18.1	21.5	21.5	22.4	25.0	63.5
58	Publishing activities	16.0	18.0	17.6	21.0	21.0	21.9	24.5	63.0
59-60	Motion picture, video and TV programme production; broadcasting activities	0.1	0.3	0.5	0.5	0.4	0.5	0.5	0.5
59	Motion picture, video and TV programme production; sound and music	0.1	0.3	0.4	0.5	0.4	0.4	0.4	0.4
60	Programming and broadcasting activities	0.0	0.0	0.1	0.0	0.0	0.1	0.0	0.0
61	Telecommunications	41.1	45.7	46.3	47.5	48.9	54.5	58.7	64.6
62-63	IT and other information services	314.4	357.2	393.9	538.7	542.7	609.1	771.1	904.9
62	Computer programming, consultancy and related activities	229.7	267.5	287.9	414.3	459.2	534.5	670.0	816.1
63	Information service activities	84.7	89.6	106.0	124.4	83.5	74.6	101.1	88.8
64-66	**Financial and insurance activities**	35.2	45.8	60.2	58.2	50.5	71.2	87.7	89.5
68-82	**Real estate; professional, scientific and technical; administrative and support**	684.4	804.0	827.3	947.5	908.6	877.3	996.2	996.3
68	Real estate activities	9.4	23.4	37.5	15.5	2.9	2.7	1.8	3.5
69-75x72	Professional, scientific and technical activities, except scientific R&D	176.3	174.5	152.9	170.9	202.6	214.9	254.6	290.6
72	Scientific research and development	497.2	601.1	629.1	753.4	697.3	656.2	724.5	679.2
77-82	Administrative and support service activities	1.4	4.9	7.8	7.7	5.9	3.5	15.2	23.0
84-99	Community, social and personal services	8.1	11.0	29.9	22.1	27.6	26.1	18.3	21.8
84-85	Public administration and defence; compulsory social security and education	1.0	2.0	12.1	9.8	10.4	4.2	8.6	12.2
86-88	Human health and social work activities	3.2	5.2	10.9	6.0	5.0	5.2	4.9	3.2
90-93	Arts, entertainment and recreation	0.9	0.7	0.9	0.7	0.7	0.9	1.2	0.5
94-99	Other services; household-employers; extraterritorial bodies	3.1	3.2	5.8	5.6	11.4	15.8	3.6	5.9

Note: Detailed metadata at: *http://metalinks.oecd.org/anberd/20200813/2abe.*

R&D expenditure in industry by main activity of the enterprise, constant prices
ISIC Rev. 4

2010 USD PPP

		2011	2012	2013	2014	2015	2016	2017	2018
	TOTAL BUSINESS ENTERPRISE	**2 816.8**	**3 108.0**	**3 327.4**	**3 674.5**	**3 722.4**	**3 739.5**	**4 275.6**	**4 671.3**
01-03	**AGRICULTURE, FORESTRY AND FISHING**	9.4	10.8	11.7	11.7	13.8	14.7	14.1	13.2
05-09	**MINING AND QUARRYING**	1.6	1.7	1.2	2.4	2.7	3.9	3.9	3.0
10-33	**MANUFACTURING**	1 476.9	1 587.5	1 768.6	1 897.8	1 954.2	2 000.5	2 296.9	2 550.2
10-12	Food products, beverages and tobacco	27.1	24.6	25.6	17.9	19.5	18.3	22.6	18.0
13-15	Textiles, wearing apparel, leather and related products	36.2	17.0	25.3	26.8	26.1	24.3	22.8	23.9
13	Textiles	18.5	14.0	22.5	24.5	23.8	22.1	20.1	21.1
14	Wearing apparel	16.2	1.8	1.3	0.8	1.0	1.1	1.4	1.5
15	Leather and related products, footwear	1.5	1.2	1.5	1.5	1.3	1.2	1.3	1.3
16-18	Wood and paper products and printing	6.7	3.4	2.8	4.0	9.6	6.6	9.6	6.8
16	Wood and wood products, except furniture	3.4	0.4	0.9	1.6	4.5	3.6	3.6	2.7
17	Paper and paper products	2.6	2.2	1.0	1.1	4.3	2.0	3.9	2.3
18	Printing and reproduction of recorded media	0.6	0.8	0.9	1.3	0.9	1.0	2.0	1.8
19-23	Chemical, rubber, plastic, non-metallic mineral products	263.6	262.7	288.0	302.2	317.2	278.7	283.6	304.5
19	Coke and refined petroleum products	0.9	0.5	0.5	0.6	0.9	0.7	0.7	0.8
20-21	Chemical and pharmaceutical products	172.2	168.6	169.2	176.6	177.1	156.0	166.6	185.2
20	Chemicals and chemical products	83.4	77.8	90.4	92.5	90.2	69.1	82.9	84.1
21	Pharmaceuticals, medicinal, chemical and botanical products	88.8	90.7	78.8	84.0	86.9	86.9	83.8	101.1
22	Rubber and plastic products	57.3	55.6	68.2	83.0	93.1	80.3	72.0	70.5
23	Other non-metallic mineral products	33.3	38.0	50.1	42.0	46.2	41.8	44.2	48.0
24-25	Basic metals, metal products, except machinery and equipment	87.9	99.9	88.7	112.6	118.2	92.5	115.4	127.1
24	Basic metals	24.3	25.6	18.2	23.3	24.9	12.2	15.2	13.8
25	Fabricated metal products, except machinery and equipment	63.6	74.4	70.5	89.3	93.3	80.3	100.2	113.3
26-30	Computer, electronic, optical products; electrical machinery, transport equipment	963.0	1 086.4	1 275.0	1 364.8	1 374.1	1 497.7	1 753.7	1 968.0
26	Computer, electronic and optical products	94.8	100.2	122.0	146.5	152.7	178.2	193.3	214.7
27	Electrical equipment	133.6	166.6	150.9	237.5	259.1	290.0	312.1	325.6
28	Machinery and equipment n.e.c.	241.9	312.6	343.6	328.0	301.0	302.0	319.4	340.3
29	Motor vehicles, trailers and semi-trailers	328.4	373.4	521.0	508.3	548.9	596.8	780.7	927.4
30	Other transport equipment	164.3	133.6	137.5	144.5	112.4	130.6	148.2	159.9
31-33	Furniture; repair, installation of machinery and equipment	92.4	93.4	63.2	69.5	89.5	82.3	89.1	101.9
31	Furniture	6.0	4.3	3.8	3.0	3.3	2.3	3.5	4.6
32	Other manufacturing	29.5	36.7	27.7	27.9	31.1	42.5	42.7	38.2
33	Repair and installation of machinery and equipment	56.9	52.4	31.8	38.6	55.1	37.5	42.9	59.1
35-39	**ELECTRICITY, GAS, WATER AND WASTE MANAGEMENT**	11.6	11.3	15.2	12.9	18.2	10.7	11.8	11.9
35-36	Electricity, gas and water	3.4	4.0	7.8	5.1	4.4	4.1	4.2	3.8
37-39	Sewerage, waste management and remediation activities	8.2	7.3	7.4	7.9	13.8	6.6	7.6	8.1
41-43	**CONSTRUCTION**	29.9	34.2	42.3	52.7	47.8	40.3	44.8	49.3
45-99	**TOTAL SERVICES**	1 287.4	1 462.5	1 488.4	1 697.1	1 685.7	1 669.3	1 904.1	2 043.6
45-82	**Business sector services**	1 278.4	1 450.5	1 457.8	1 675.1	1 658.1	1 644.3	1 887.1	2 023.7
45-47	**Wholesale and retail trade; motor vehicle and motorcycle repairs**	76.8	74.7	76.8	70.3	84.3	73.1	79.7	94.3
49-53	**Transportation and storage**	0.5	1.6	1.8	1.8	1.5	1.4	1.3	1.2
55-56	**Accommodation and food service activities**	0.1	0.1	0.1	0.1	0.1	0.1	0.2	0.3
58-63	**Information and communication**	409.0	455.3	469.6	603.7	613.1	658.8	796.3	940.0
58-60	Publishing, audiovisual and broadcasting activities	17.6	19.8	18.5	21.4	21.5	21.5	23.2	57.8
58	Publishing activities	17.6	19.5	18.1	20.9	21.0	21.0	22.8	57.3
59-60	Motion picture, video and TV programme production; broadcasting activities	0.1	0.4	0.5	0.5	0.4	0.5	0.5	0.4
59	Motion picture, video and TV programme production; sound and music	0.1	0.4	0.4	0.5	0.4	0.4	0.4	0.4
60	Programming and broadcasting activities	0.0	0.0	0.1	0.0	0.0	0.1	0.0	0.0
61	Telecommunications	45.3	49.4	47.5	47.2	48.9	52.3	54.7	58.8
62-63	IT and other information services	346.1	386.1	403.7	535.2	542.7	584.9	718.3	823.4
62	Computer programming, consultancy and related activities	252.8	289.3	295.1	411.6	459.2	513.3	624.1	742.6
63	Information service activities	93.3	96.9	108.6	123.6	83.5	71.6	94.2	80.8
64-66	**Financial and insurance activities**	38.8	49.5	61.7	57.8	50.5	68.4	81.7	81.5
68-82	**Real estate; professional, scientific and technical; administrative and support**	753.4	869.3	847.8	941.4	908.6	842.5	928.0	906.6
68	Real estate activities	10.3	25.3	38.4	15.4	2.9	2.6	1.7	3.1
69-75x72	Professional, scientific and technical activities, except scientific R&D	194.1	188.7	156.7	169.8	202.6	206.3	237.2	264.4
72	Scientific research and development	547.4	649.9	644.7	748.6	697.3	630.1	674.9	618.1
77-82	Administrative and support service activities	1.6	5.3	8.0	7.6	5.9	3.4	14.2	20.9
84-99	Community, social and personal services	9.0	11.9	30.6	22.0	27.6	25.1	17.0	19.9
84-85	Public administration and defence; compulsory social security and education	1.1	2.1	12.4	9.7	10.4	4.0	8.0	11.1
86-88	Human health and social work activities	3.5	5.6	11.2	6.0	5.0	5.0	4.6	2.9
90-93	Arts, entertainment and recreation	1.0	0.8	1.0	0.7	0.7	0.9	1.1	0.5
94-99	Other services; household-employers; extraterritorial bodies	3.4	3.5	6.0	5.5	11.4	15.2	3.3	5.4

Note: Detailed metadata at: *http://metalinks.oecd.org/anberd/20200813/2abe.*

CZECH REPUBLIC

R&D expenditure in industry by industry orientation, current prices
ISIC Rev. 4

Million USD PPP

		2011	2012	2013	2014	2015	2016	2017	2018
	TOTAL BUSINESS ENTERPRISE	**2 558.8**	**2 874.8**	**3 246.9**	**3 698.3**	**3 722.4**	**3 894.2**	**4 589.8**	**5 133.6**
01-03	**AGRICULTURE, FORESTRY AND FISHING**	**15.6 e**	**15.7 e**	**20.1**	**22.9**	**23.8**	**25.4**	**33.1**	**37.5**
05-09	**MINING AND QUARRYING**	**4.6 e**	**1.8 e**	**2.1**	**3.2**	**3.0**	**5.3**	**3.8**	**3.9**
10-33	**MANUFACTURING**	**1 616.0 e**	**1 711.7 e**	**2 033.3**	**2 352.1**	**2 393.2**	**2 503.4**	**2 915.0**	**3 247.2**
10-12	Food products, beverages and tobacco	21.0 e	27.0 e	23.3	19.4	21.7	18.5	27.8	23.3
13-15	Textiles, wearing apparel, leather and related products	26.7 e	17.7 e	28.2	36.0	30.1	26.6	28.5	27.7
13	Textiles	23.5 e	15.2 e	25.1	30.8	27.2	24.1	26.1	25.5
14	Wearing apparel	2.3 e	1.5 e	2.5	2.3	1.9	1.8	1.3	1.2
15	Leather and related products, footwear	0.9 e	1.0 e	0.6	2.9	1.1	0.7	1.1	1.0
16-18	Wood and paper products and printing	7.6 e	5.2 e	3.5	4.0	5.7	2.7	5.3	9.2
16	Wood and wood products, except furniture	4.5 e	2.6 e	1.4	2.2	2.8	1.1	1.9	4.3
17	Paper and paper products	2.3 e	2.4 e	1.1	1.1	1.8	1.1	2.3	4.0
18	Printing and reproduction of recorded media	0.8 e	0.2 e	1.0	0.7	1.1	0.5	1.1	0.9
19-23	Chemical, rubber, plastic, non-metallic mineral products	268.7 e	239.5 e	271.6	296.4	328.1	310.3	322.7	342.1
19	Coke and refined petroleum products	1.2 e	1.7 e	1.8	4.4	3.9	1.6	1.5	2.0
20-21	Chemical and pharmaceutical products	189.1 e	144.1 e	160.1	176.7	204.1	193.7	201.4	220.8
20	Chemicals and chemical products	59.3 e	52.0 e	55.8	53.6	59.3	58.6	64.7	50.4
21	Pharmaceuticals, medicinal, chemical and botanical products	129.8 e	92.1 e	104.3	123.0	144.8	135.1	136.7	170.4
22	Rubber and plastic products	48.1 e	55.6 e	63.9	74.4	81.2	76.7	80.4	80.1
23	Other non-metallic mineral products	30.3 e	38.1 e	45.7	40.8	38.9	38.2	39.4	39.3
24-25	Basic metals, metal products, except machinery and equipment	108.5 e	124.0 e	123.8	148.7	166.2	126.5	153.5	174.3
24	Basic metals	15.6 e	14.8 e	12.8	12.7	11.2	9.6	17.5	11.8
25	Fabricated metal products, except machinery and equipment	92.9 e	109.3 e	111.0	136.0	155.0	116.9	136.0	162.5
26-30	Computer, electronic, optical products; electrical machinery, transport equipment	1 080.6 e	1 236.4 e	1 494.1	1 745.9	1 753.4	1 935.1	2 267.3	2 585.9
26	Computer, electronic and optical products	183.9 e	235.0 e	264.3	309.1	301.1	363.8	344.7	436.2
27	Electrical equipment	126.5 e	206.2 e	124.6	155.6	155.8	156.0	184.6	197.0
28	Machinery and equipment n.e.c.	293.8 e	250.5 e	357.8	390.5	379.8	378.9	387.8	393.2
29	Motor vehicles, trailers and semi-trailers	266.2 e	361.5 e	556.3	671.9	728.6	826.6	1 081.8	1 274.4
30	Other transport equipment	210.2 e	183.2 e	190.9	218.7	188.0	209.8	268.3	285.1
31-33	Furniture; repair, installation of machinery and equipment	102.9 e	61.8 e	88.9	101.6	87.9	83.7	109.9	84.7
31	Furniture	1.7 e	4.4 e	5.0	10.5	3.4	2.4	2.6	5.5
32	Other manufacturing	35.4 e	29.1 e	39.9	36.8	32.7	39.9	46.0	45.2
33	Repair and installation of machinery and equipment	65.8 e	28.3 e	44.0	54.4	51.8	41.4	61.3	34.0
35-39	**ELECTRICITY, GAS, WATER AND WASTE MANAGEMENT**	**21.3 e**	**22.9 e**	**29.8**	**28.2**	**30.3**	**23.8**	**22.9**	**31.4**
35-36	Electricity, gas and water	10.7 e	9.8 e	10.5	10.6	10.7	13.6	9.1	9.0
37-39	Sewerage, waste management and remediation activities	10.7 e	13.1 e	19.3	17.6	19.6	10.2	13.7	22.4
41-43	**CONSTRUCTION**	**25.9 e**	**28.0 e**	**35.1**	**40.4**	**39.5**	**33.9**	**39.9**	**44.7**
45-99	**TOTAL SERVICES**	**875.3 e**	**1 094.6 e**	**1 126.6**	**1 251.6**	**1 232.7**	**1 302.5**	**1 575.1**	**1 768.8**
45-82	**Business sector services**	**839.3 e**	**1 061.3 e**	**1 087.7**	**1 219.6**	**1 193.4**	**1 283.2**	**1 553.4**	**1 746.2**
45-47	**Wholesale and retail trade; motor vehicle and motorcycle repairs**	**21.3 e**	**1.9 e**	**0.0**	**0.2**	**3.5**	**3.9**	**6.0**	**0.6**
49-53	**Transportation and storage**	**2.1 e**	**2.7 e**	**4.6**	**4.4**	**4.2**	**3.1**	**4.8**	**2.6**
55-56	**Accommodation and food service activities**	**0.1 e**	**1.2 e**	**0.0**	**0.0**	**0.1**	**0.2**	**0.2**	**0.0**
58-63	**Information and communication**	**385.0 e**	**442.2 e**	**478.9**	**642.4**	**651.0**	**722.3**	**903.0**	**1 084.7**
58-60	Publishing, audiovisual and broadcasting activities	2.0 e	16.9 e	0.0	2.4	0.6	0.5	1.0	2.3
58	Publishing activities	..	..	..	..	0.1	..	0.5	0.1
59-60	Motion picture, video and TV programme production; broadcasting activities	..	..	..	..	0.5	..	0.4	2.2
59	Motion picture, video and TV programme production; sound and music	..	..	..	..	..	..	0.4	2.0
60	Programming and broadcasting activities	..	..	..	..	..	..	0.1	0.2
61	Telecommunications	47.3 e	51.8 e	60.4	70.4	65.3	73.5	72.6	72.0
62-63	IT and other information services	335.6 e	373.5 e	418.5	569.6	585.1	648.3	829.5	1 010.3
62	Computer programming, consultancy and related activities	248.6 e	264.9 e	285.6	427.3	498.6	584.8	730.4	914.7
63	Information service activities	87.1 e	108.6 e	132.9	142.3	86.5	63.5	99.1	95.6
64-66	**Financial and insurance activities**	**34.1 e**	**36.9 e**	**48.3**	**46.7**	**24.5**	**52.2**	**59.3**	**57.2**
68-82	**Real estate; professional, scientific and technical; administrative and support**	**396.7 e**	**576.4 e**	**555.8**	**526.0**	**510.1**	**501.4**	**580.0**	**601.1**
68	Real estate activities	4.4 e	0.2 e	0.0	0.0	0.0	0.0	0.0	0.0
69-75x72	Professional, scientific and technical activities, except scientific R&D	105.0 e	28.2 e	32.1	36.2	49.3	36.8	41.3	47.0
72	Scientific research and development	286.6 e	547.7 e	523.0	489.3	460.8	464.6	538.4	553.7
77-82	Administrative and support service activities	0.7 e	0.4 e	0.6	0.5	0.0	0.1	0.3	0.4
84-99	Community, social and personal services	36.0 e	33.3 e	39.0	32.0	39.3	19.3	21.7	22.6
84-85	Public administration and defence; compulsory social security and education	10.4 e	11.0 e	15.5	10.2	12.3	6.9	9.3	9.1
86-88	Human health and social work activities	20.2 e	20.1 e	18.2	17.9	21.7	5.9	7.3	6.2
90-93	Arts, entertainment and recreation	3.8 e	0.2 e	0.1	0.1	0.0	0.0	0.0	1.1
94-99	Other services; household-employers; extraterritorial bodies	1.6 e	1.9 e	5.2	3.8	5.3	6.5	5.0	6.3

.. Not available; e Estimated value

Note: Detailed metadata at: *http://metalinks.oecd.org/anberd/20200813/2abe.*

CZECH REPUBLIC

R&D expenditure in industry by industry orientation, constant prices
ISIC Rev. 4

2010 USD PPP

		2011	2012	2013	2014	2015	2016	2017	2018
	TOTAL BUSINESS ENTERPRISE	**2 816.8**	**3 108.0**	**3 327.4**	**3 674.5**	**3 722.4**	**3 739.5**	**4 275.6**	**4 671.3**
01-03	**AGRICULTURE, FORESTRY AND FISHING**	17.2 e	17.0 e	20.6	22.7	23.8	24.4	30.9	34.1
05-09	**MINING AND QUARRYING**	5.1 e	2.0 e	2.2	3.2	3.0	5.1	3.5	3.6
10-33	**MANUFACTURING**	1 778.9 e	1 850.5 e	2 083.7	2 336.9	2 393.2	2 403.9	2 715.5	2 954.8
10-12	Food products, beverages and tobacco	23.1 e	29.2 e	23.9	19.3	21.7	17.7	25.9	21.2
13-15	Textiles, wearing apparel, leather and related products	29.4 e	19.2 e	28.9	35.8	30.1	25.5	26.6	25.2
13	Textiles	25.8 e	16.5 e	25.7	30.6	27.2	23.2	24.3	23.2
14	Wearing apparel	2.6 e	1.6 e	2.6	2.2	1.9	1.7	1.2	1.1
15	Leather and related products, footwear	1.0 e	1.1 e	0.6	2.9	1.1	0.7	1.0	0.9
16-18	Wood and paper products and printing	8.4 e	5.6 e	3.6	4.0	5.7	2.6	4.9	8.4
16	Wood and wood products, except furniture	5.0 e	2.8 e	1.4	2.2	2.8	1.1	1.8	3.9
17	Paper and paper products	2.5 e	2.6 e	1.2	1.1	1.8	1.0	2.1	3.6
18	Printing and reproduction of recorded media	0.9 e	0.2 e	1.0	0.7	1.1	0.5	1.0	0.8
19-23	Chemical, rubber, plastic, non-metallic mineral products	295.8 e	259.0 e	278.3	294.5	328.1	298.0	300.6	311.3
19	Coke and refined petroleum products	1.3 e	1.9 e	1.9	4.4	3.9	1.5	1.4	1.8
20-21	Chemical and pharmaceutical products	208.2 e	155.8 e	164.1	175.5	204.1	186.0	187.6	200.9
20	Chemicals and chemical products	65.3 e	56.2 e	57.1	53.3	59.3	56.3	60.2	45.8
21	Pharmaceuticals, medicinal, chemical and botanical products	142.9 e	99.6 e	106.9	122.3	144.8	129.7	127.4	155.0
22	Rubber and plastic products	53.0 e	60.1 e	65.5	73.9	81.2	73.7	74.9	72.9
23	Other non-metallic mineral products	33.3 e	41.2 e	46.9	40.6	38.9	36.7	36.7	35.7
24-25	Basic metals, metal products, except machinery and equipment	119.4 e	134.1 e	126.8	147.8	166.2	121.5	143.0	158.6
24	Basic metals	17.1 e	16.0 e	13.1	12.6	11.2	9.2	16.3	10.7
25	Fabricated metal products, except machinery and equipment	102.3 e	118.1 e	113.7	135.2	155.0	112.2	126.7	147.9
26-30	Computer, electronic, optical products; electrical machinery, transport equipment	1 189.5 e	1 336.6 e	1 531.1	1 734.7	1 753.4	1 858.2	2 112.1	2 353.1
26	Computer, electronic and optical products	202.5 e	254.1 e	270.9	307.1	301.1	349.3	321.1	396.9
27	Electrical equipment	139.3 e	222.9 e	127.7	154.6	155.8	149.8	172.0	179.3
28	Machinery and equipment n.e.c.	323.4 e	270.8 e	366.7	388.0	379.8	363.9	361.3	357.8
29	Motor vehicles, trailers and semi-trailers	293.0 e	390.8 e	570.1	667.6	728.6	793.7	1 007.8	1 159.6
30	Other transport equipment	231.4 e	198.0 e	195.7	217.3	188.0	201.5	250.0	259.5
31-33	Furniture; repair, installation of machinery and equipment	113.3 e	66.8 e	91.1	101.0	87.9	80.4	102.4	77.1
31	Furniture	1.9 e	4.7 e	5.1	10.4	3.4	2.3	2.4	5.0
32	Other manufacturing	39.0 e	31.5 e	40.9	36.5	32.7	38.3	42.8	41.1
33	Repair and installation of machinery and equipment	72.4 e	30.6 e	45.1	54.0	51.8	39.8	57.1	31.0
35-39	**ELECTRICITY, GAS, WATER AND WASTE MANAGEMENT**	23.5 e	24.8 e	30.5	28.0	30.3	22.9	21.3	28.6
35-36	Electricity, gas and water	11.7 e	10.6 e	10.7	10.5	10.7	13.1	8.5	8.2
37-39	Sewerage, waste management and remediation activities	11.7 e	14.2 e	19.8	17.5	19.6	9.8	12.8	20.4
41-43	**CONSTRUCTION**	28.6 e	30.3 e	35.9	40.1	39.5	32.5	37.1	40.7
45-99	**TOTAL SERVICES**	963.6 e	1 183.4 e	1 154.5	1 243.6	1 232.7	1 250.7	1 467.3	1 609.5
45-82	**Business sector services**	923.9 e	1 147.4 e	1 114.6	1 211.8	1 193.4	1 232.2	1 447.1	1 589.0
45-47	**Wholesale and retail trade; motor vehicle and motorcycle repairs**	23.5 e	2.0 e	0.0	0.2	3.5	3.8	5.6	0.6
49-53	**Transportation and storage**	2.3 e	2.9 e	4.7	4.4	4.2	3.0	4.5	2.4
55-56	**Accommodation and food service activities**	0.1 e	1.3 e	0.0	0.0	0.1	0.2	0.2	0.0
58-63	**Information and communication**	423.8 e	478.1 e	490.8	638.2	651.0	693.6	841.2	987.0
58-60	Publishing, audiovisual and broadcasting activities	2.2 e	18.3 e	0.0	2.3	0.6	0.5	0.9	2.1
58	Publishing activities	..	..	..	..	0.1	..	0.5	0.1
59-60	Motion picture, video and TV programme production; broadcasting activities	..	..	..	..	0.5	..	0.4	2.0
59	Motion picture, video and TV programme production; sound and music	..	..	..	..	..	..	0.3	1.8
60	Programming and broadcasting activities	..	..	..	..	..	..	0.1	0.2
61	Telecommunications	52.1 e	56.0 e	61.9	69.9	65.3	70.6	67.6	65.5
62-63	IT and other information services	369.5 e	403.8 e	428.9	565.9	585.1	622.5	772.7	919.4
62	Computer programming, consultancy and related activities	273.6 e	286.4 e	292.7	424.6	498.6	561.6	680.4	832.3
63	Information service activities	95.8 e	117.4 e	136.2	141.3	86.5	61.0	92.3	87.0
64-66	**Financial and insurance activities**	37.6 e	39.9 e	49.5	46.4	24.5	50.1	55.2	52.1
68-82	**Real estate; professional, scientific and technical; administrative and support**	436.7 e	623.2 e	569.6	522.6	510.1	481.5	540.3	547.0
68	Real estate activities	4.8 e	0.2 e	0.0	0.0	0.0	0.0	0.0	0.0
69-75x72	Professional, scientific and technical activities, except scientific R&D	115.6 e	30.5 e	32.9	36.0	49.3	35.3	38.5	42.8
72	Scientific research and development	315.5 e	592.1 e	536.0	486.1	460.8	446.1	501.6	503.8
77-82	Administrative and support service activities	0.8 e	0.4 e	0.7	0.5	0.0	0.1	0.3	0.3
84-99	Community, social and personal services	39.7 e	36.0 e	39.9	31.8	39.3	18.5	20.2	20.6
84-85	Public administration and defence; compulsory social security and education	11.4 e	11.9 e	15.9	10.2	12.3	6.6	8.7	8.3
86-88	Human health and social work activities	22.3 e	21.8 e	18.6	17.8	21.7	5.7	6.8	5.6
90-93	Arts, entertainment and recreation	4.2 e	0.2 e	0.1	0.1	0.0	0.0	0.0	1.0
94-99	Other services; household-employers; extraterritorial bodies	1.7 e	2.1 e	5.3	3.7	5.3	6.2	4.7	5.7

.. Not available; e Estimated value

Note: Detailed metadata at: *http://metalinks.oecd.org/anberd/20200813/2abe.*

DENMARK

R&D expenditure in industry by main activity of the enterprise, current prices
ISIC Rev. 4

Million USD PPP

		2011	2012	2013	2014	2015	2016	2017	2018
	TOTAL BUSINESS ENTERPRISE	4 859.9	4 897.4	4 936.6	5 023.4	5 406.7	5 990.8	6 260.1	..
01-03	**AGRICULTURE, FORESTRY AND FISHING**	7.0	5.8	7.1	6.5	6.7	4.2	56.3	..
05-09	**MINING AND QUARRYING**	5.6	1.9	6.4	11.1	11.2	10.4	10.9	..
10-33	**MANUFACTURING**	2 524.4	2 754.5	2 870.2	2 913.6	3 048.2	3 162.8	3 496.9	..
10-12	Food products, beverages and tobacco	69.0	81.9	64.8	54.0	64.4	72.1	79.9	..
13-15	Textiles, wearing apparel, leather and related products	2.4	2.7	2.7	2.7	3.1	4.3	7.6	..
13	Textiles	1.5	1.7	2.3	2.3	2.7	4.1	7.0	..
14	Wearing apparel	..	1.0	0.5	0.4	0.5	0.3	0.5	..
15	Leather and related products, footwear	..	0.0	0.0	0.0	0.0	0.0	0.0	..
16-18	Wood and paper products and printing	5.9	4.6	46.7	7.9	3.1	2.5	5.9	..
16	Wood and wood products, except furniture	1.4	1.5	43.4	2.3	1.9	1.4	1.8	..
17	Paper and paper products	4.2	3.1	3.3	5.6	1.2	1.1	1.4	..
18	Printing and reproduction of recorded media	0.3	0.0	0.0	0.0	0.0	0.0	2.7	..
19-23	Chemical, rubber, plastic, non-metallic mineral products	1 185.8	1 418.6	1 476.6	1 541.9	1 678.3	1 870.3	1 776.6	..
19	Coke and refined petroleum products	..	..	..	..	..	..	..	..
20-21	Chemical and pharmaceutical products	..	..	..	..	..	..	..	..
20	Chemicals and chemical products	..	..	..	..	..	..	..	..
21	Pharmaceuticals, medicinal, chemical and botanical products	892.2	1 065.8	1 127.2	1 162.6	1 239.0	1 484.7	1 414.4	..
22	Rubber and plastic products	50.3	53.8	55.0	55.8	62.4	16.5	19.7	..
23	Other non-metallic mineral products	4.7	22.4	23.4	24.7	26.2	6.3	24.8	..
24-25	Basic metals, metal products, except machinery and equipment	19.5	19.8	19.8	17.5	24.1	28.0	26.3	..
24	Basic metals	3.1	3.2	2.9	2.9	3.3	4.5	5.9	..
25	Fabricated metal products, except machinery and equipment	16.4	16.6	16.8	14.6	20.8	23.5	20.4	..
26-30	Computer, electronic, optical products; electrical machinery, transport equipment	1 112.5	1 079.5	1 078.1	1 081.8	1 014.6	983.6	1 398.4	..
26	Computer, electronic and optical products	325.7	373.3	406.2	412.4	438.4	492.0	518.8	..
27	Electrical equipment	78.6	73.1	69.0	67.7	57.4	74.2	72.4	..
28	Machinery and equipment n.e.c.	687.7	612.4	581.1	583.3	498.4	396.0	784.4	..
29	Motor vehicles, trailers and semi-trailers	14.9	15.3	15.6	11.6	10.8	14.3	12.4	..
30	Other transport equipment	5.5	5.4	6.1	6.8	9.7	7.2	10.4	..
31-33	Furniture; repair, installation of machinery and equipment	129.3	147.3	181.5	208.0	261.0	201.9	202.1	..
31	Furniture	6.1	4.5	4.0	5.6	6.8	7.6	8.8	..
32	Other manufacturing	123.2	141.3	177.5	202.4	253.7	194.2	193.3	..
33	Repair and installation of machinery and equipment	0.0	1.5	0.0	0.0	0.4	0.1	0.0	..
35-39	**ELECTRICITY, GAS, WATER AND WASTE MANAGEMENT**	37.3	13.2	12.4	13.5	27.9	19.8	23.4	..
35-36	Electricity, gas and water	34.2	9.2	10.9	8.9	13.0	14.5	18.7	..
37-39	Sewerage, waste management and remediation activities	3.1	4.0	1.5	4.6	14.9	5.3	4.6	..
41-43	**CONSTRUCTION**	5.3	5.9	7.2	5.0	5.1	6.4	5.3	..
45-99	**TOTAL SERVICES**	2 280.4	2 116.1	2 033.2	2 073.6	2 307.6	2 787.1	2 667.0	..
45-82	**Business sector services**	2 250.4	2 072.9	1 996.2	2 043.6	2 294.4	2 773.1	2 608.3	..
45-47	**Wholesale and retail trade; motor vehicle and motorcycle repairs**	255.7	236.8	160.8	224.2	240.3	252.3	364.9	..
49-53	**Transportation and storage**	7.5	15.6	8.9	7.8	9.3	8.9	7.9	..
55-56	**Accommodation and food service activities**	0.3	0.1	1.9	1.2	3.0	1.7	2.4	..
58-63	**Information and communication**	749.3	594.8	492.3	480.6	552.9	703.4	469.0	..
58-60	Publishing, audiovisual and broadcasting activities	89.3	74.3	71.4	86.0	133.6	78.1	43.4	..
58	Publishing activities	86.9	73.0	67.3	80.9	123.0	75.9	40.1	..
59-60	Motion picture, video and TV programme production; broadcasting activities	2.5	1.3	4.1	5.0	10.7	2.2	3.3	..
59	Motion picture, video and TV programme production; sound and music	2.5	1.3	4.1	3.5	9.3	2.2	1.1	..
60	Programming and broadcasting activities	0.0	0.0	0.0	1.5	1.4	0.0	2.2	..
61	Telecommunications	52.0	64.0	52.8	30.6	37.5	27.8	14.0	..
62-63	IT and other information services	607.9	456.5	368.1	364.0	381.7	597.4	411.6	..
62	Computer programming, consultancy and related activities	595.7	444.5	353.7	350.5	360.2	560.7	392.9	..
63	Information service activities	12.2	12.0	14.3	13.5	21.5	36.8	18.7	..
64-66	**Financial and insurance activities**	531.7	541.5	541.4	547.7	632.4	697.1	764.0	..
68-82	**Real estate; professional, scientific and technical; administrative and support**	705.8	684.1	790.9	782.3	856.6	1 109.6	1 000.1	..
68	Real estate activities	1.3	3.1	6.8	2.0	2.3	2.1	8.3	..
69-75x72	Professional, scientific and technical activities, except scientific R&D	164.9	161.7	174.9	159.1	248.8	230.5	245.0	..
72	Scientific research and development	530.1	512.2	604.6	611.2	601.9	864.8	675.2	..
77-82	Administrative and support service activities	9.5	7.0	4.6	10.0	3.6	12.2	71.6	..
84-99	Community, social and personal services	30.0	43.2	37.1	30.0	13.1	14.1	58.7	..
84-85	Public administration and defence; compulsory social security and education	..	..	..	..	..	..	..	..
86-88	Human health and social work activities	..	..	..	..	..	..	..	..
90-93	Arts, entertainment and recreation	0.1	6.1	5.2	5.0	4.4	6.8	16.4	..
94-99	Other services; household-employers; extraterritorial bodies	29.9	29.6	31.5	24.7	8.9	7.2	42.2	..

.. Not available

Note: Detailed metadata at: http://metalinks.oecd.org/anberd/20200813/2abe.

DENMARK

R&D expenditure in industry by main activity of the enterprise, constant prices
ISIC Rev. 4

2010 USD PPP

		2011	2012	2013	2014	2015	2016	2017	2018
	TOTAL BUSINESS ENTERPRISE	**5 207.0**	**5 192.5**	**5 044.4**	**5 062.6**	**5 406.7**	**5 793.2**	**5 792.4**	..
01-03	**AGRICULTURE, FORESTRY AND FISHING**	7.5	6.2	7.3	6.6	6.7	4.0	52.1	..
05-09	**MINING AND QUARRYING**	6.0	2.0	6.6	11.1	11.2	10.1	10.1	..
10-33	**MANUFACTURING**	**2 704.7**	**2 920.4**	**2 932.9**	**2 936.4**	**3 048.2**	**3 058.5**	**3 235.7**	..
10-12	Food products, beverages and tobacco	73.9	86.9	66.2	54.5	64.4	69.7	73.9	..
13-15	Textiles, wearing apparel, leather and related products	2.6	2.9	2.8	2.8	3.1	4.2	7.0	..
13	Textiles	1.6	1.8	2.3	2.3	2.7	3.9	6.5	..
14	Wearing apparel	..	1.0	0.5	0.4	0.5	0.3	0.5	..
15	Leather and related products, footwear	..	0.0	0.0	0.0	0.0	0.0	0.0	..
16-18	Wood and paper products and printing	6.3	4.9	47.7	8.0	3.1	2.4	5.4	..
16	Wood and wood products, except furniture	1.5	1.6	44.3	2.3	1.9	1.3	1.6	..
17	Paper and paper products	4.5	3.2	3.4	5.6	1.2	1.1	1.3	..
18	Printing and reproduction of recorded media	0.3	0.0	0.0	0.0	0.0	0.0	2.5	..
19-23	Chemical, rubber, plastic, non-metallic mineral products	1 270.5	1 504.1	1 508.8	1 553.9	1 678.3	1 808.6	1 643.9	..
19	Coke and refined petroleum products	..	..	..	..	..	..	..	..
20-21	Chemical and pharmaceutical products	..	..	..	..	..	..	..	..
20	Chemicals and chemical products	..	..	..	..	..	..	..	..
21	Pharmaceuticals, medicinal, chemical and botanical products	955.9	1 130.1	1 151.8	1 171.6	1 239.0	1 435.7	1 308.8	..
22	Rubber and plastic products	53.9	57.0	56.2	56.2	62.4	16.0	18.2	..
23	Other non-metallic mineral products	5.0	23.8	24.0	24.9	26.2	6.1	23.0	..
24-25	Basic metals, metal products, except machinery and equipment	20.9	21.0	20.2	17.6	24.1	27.1	24.4	..
24	Basic metals	3.4	3.4	3.0	2.9	3.3	4.3	5.5	..
25	Fabricated metal products, except machinery and equipment	17.6	17.6	17.2	14.7	20.8	22.8	18.9	..
26-30	Computer, electronic, optical products; electrical machinery, transport equipment	1 191.9	1 144.5	1 101.6	1 090.2	1 014.6	951.2	1 294.0	..
26	Computer, electronic and optical products	348.9	395.8	415.1	415.6	438.4	475.8	480.1	..
27	Electrical equipment	84.3	77.5	70.6	68.2	57.4	71.7	67.0	..
28	Machinery and equipment n.e.c.	736.8	649.3	593.8	587.9	498.4	383.0	725.8	..
29	Motor vehicles, trailers and semi-trailers	16.0	16.2	16.0	11.7	10.8	13.8	11.5	..
30	Other transport equipment	5.9	5.7	6.2	6.9	9.7	7.0	9.7	..
31-33	Furniture; repair, installation of machinery and equipment	138.6	156.1	185.5	209.6	261.0	195.3	187.0	..
31	Furniture	6.5	4.7	4.1	5.6	6.8	7.3	8.2	..
32	Other manufacturing	132.0	149.8	181.4	203.9	253.7	187.8	178.8	..
33	Repair and installation of machinery and equipment	0.0	1.6	0.0	0.0	0.4	0.1	0.0	..
35-39	**ELECTRICITY, GAS, WATER AND WASTE MANAGEMENT**	**40.0**	**14.0**	**12.7**	**13.6**	**27.9**	**19.2**	**21.6**	..
35-36	Electricity, gas and water	36.6	9.8	11.2	8.9	13.0	14.1	17.3	..
37-39	Sewerage, waste management and remediation activities	3.3	4.2	1.5	4.7	14.9	5.1	4.3	..
41-43	**CONSTRUCTION**	**5.7**	**6.3**	**7.3**	**5.1**	**5.1**	**6.2**	**4.9**	..
45-99	**TOTAL SERVICES**	**2 443.3**	**2 243.6**	**2 077.7**	**2 089.8**	**2 307.6**	**2 695.2**	**2 467.8**	..
45-82	**Business sector services**	**2 411.1**	**2 197.8**	**2 039.8**	**2 059.6**	**2 294.4**	**2 681.6**	**2 413.5**	..
45-47	**Wholesale and retail trade; motor vehicle and motorcycle repairs**	**274.0**	**251.1**	**164.3**	**225.9**	**240.3**	**244.0**	**337.7**	..
49-53	**Transportation and storage**	**8.1**	**16.6**	**9.1**	**7.8**	**9.3**	**8.6**	**7.3**	..
55-56	**Accommodation and food service activities**	**0.4**	**0.1**	**1.9**	**1.2**	**3.0**	**1.7**	**2.2**	..
58-63	**Information and communication**	**802.8**	**630.6**	**503.0**	**484.3**	**552.9**	**680.2**	**433.9**	..
58-60	Publishing, audiovisual and broadcasting activities	95.7	78.8	73.0	86.6	133.6	75.6	40.1	..
58	Publishing activities	93.1	77.4	68.7	81.5	123.0	73.4	37.1	..
59-60	Motion picture, video and TV programme production; broadcasting activities	2.7	1.4	4.2	5.1	10.7	2.2	3.0	..
59	Motion picture, video and TV programme production; sound and music	2.7	1.4	4.2	3.6	9.3	2.2	1.0	..
60	Programming and broadcasting activities	0.0	0.0	0.0	1.5	1.4	0.0	2.0	..
61	Telecommunications	55.7	67.9	54.0	30.8	37.5	26.9	12.9	..
62-63	IT and other information services	651.3	484.0	376.1	366.9	381.7	577.7	380.9	..
62	Computer programming, consultancy and related activities	638.3	471.3	361.5	353.3	360.2	542.2	363.6	..
63	Information service activities	13.1	12.7	14.6	13.6	21.5	35.6	17.3	..
64-66	**Financial and insurance activities**	**569.7**	**574.1**	**553.3**	**552.0**	**632.4**	**674.1**	**706.9**	..
68-82	**Real estate; professional, scientific and technical; administrative and support**	**756.2**	**725.3**	**808.2**	**788.4**	**856.6**	**1 073.0**	**925.4**	..
68	Real estate activities	1.4	3.3	6.9	2.1	2.3	2.0	7.7	..
69-75x72	Professional, scientific and technical activities, except scientific R&D	176.7	171.5	178.7	160.3	248.8	222.9	226.7	..
72	Scientific research and development	568.0	543.0	617.8	615.9	601.9	836.3	624.7	..
77-82	Administrative and support service activities	10.2	7.5	4.7	10.0	3.6	11.8	66.3	..
84-99	Community, social and personal services	32.1	45.8	37.9	30.3	13.1	13.6	54.3	..
84-85	Public administration and defence; compulsory social security and education	..	..	..	..	..	..	..	..
86-88	Human health and social work activities	..	..	..	..	..	..	..	..
90-93	Arts, entertainment and recreation	0.1	6.5	5.3	5.1	4.4	6.5	15.2	..
94-99	Other services; household-employers; extraterritorial bodies	32.1	31.4	32.2	24.9	8.9	7.0	39.1	..

.. Not available

Note: Detailed metadata at: *http://metalinks.oecd.org/anberd/20200813/2abe.*

ESTONIA

R&D expenditure in industry by main activity of the enterprise, current prices
ISIC Rev. 4

Million USD PPP

		2011	2012	2013	2014	2015	2016	2017	2018
	TOTAL BUSINESS ENTERPRISE	474.7	420.3	297.8	236.9	259.5	263.7	269.1	..
01-03	**AGRICULTURE, FORESTRY AND FISHING**	0.1	..	..	..	0.0	0.0	0.0	..
05-09	**MINING AND QUARRYING**	..	..	..	..	..	..	..	..
10-33	**MANUFACTURING**	302.8	182.3	102.9	51.0	70.0	65.0	79.6	..
10-12	Food products, beverages and tobacco	2.7	2.6	9.0	6.0	6.3	10.2	3.4	..
13-15	Textiles, wearing apparel, leather and related products	1.0	0.9	1.0	1.2	1.2	1.0	1.0	..
13	Textiles	..	..	..	..	..	..	..	..
14	Wearing apparel	..	..	..	..	..	..	..	..
15	Leather and related products, footwear	..	..	..	..	..	..	..	..
16-18	Wood and paper products and printing	1.1	0.2	0.6	0.1	1.1	0.6	0.2	..
16	Wood and wood products, except furniture	..	..	0.6	0.1	0.0	0.3	0.2	..
17	Paper and paper products	0.0	0.0	0.0	0.0	0.0	0.0	0.0	..
18	Printing and reproduction of recorded media	..	..	0.0	0.0	1.0	0.3	0.0	..
19-23	Chemical, rubber, plastic, non-metallic mineral products	..	..	..	..	..	..	..	..
19	Coke and refined petroleum products	263.9	146.3	64.5	9.1	22.2	1.5	8.6	..
20-21	Chemical and pharmaceutical products	9.2	8.5	6.7	5.9	6.3	5.1	5.4	..
20	Chemicals and chemical products	3.0	6.8	4.8	3.7	4.6	4.3	4.0	..
21	Pharmaceuticals, medicinal, chemical and botanical products	6.2	1.7	1.9	2.1	1.6	0.8	1.4	..
22	Rubber and plastic products	1.7	1.6	0.8	7.6	0.4	0.7	1.0	..
23	Other non-metallic mineral products	..	..	..	..	..	..	..	..
24-25	Basic metals, metal products, except machinery and equipment	0.7	0.4	..	..	..	..	..	..
24	Basic metals	0.0	0.0	..	..	..	..	..	..
25	Fabricated metal products, except machinery and equipment	0.7	0.4	1.6	1.4	0.9	1.0	1.0	..
26-30	Computer, electronic, optical products; electrical machinery, transport equipment	19.2	18.7	16.0	16.7	29.4	42.2	56.3	..
26	Computer, electronic and optical products	5.7	4.5	5.0	8.0	12.4	17.0	26.2	..
27	Electrical equipment	7.9	8.4	3.4	4.7	9.1	10.3	19.0	..
28	Machinery and equipment n.e.c.	1.6	1.4	5.2	1.2	1.6	3.0	6.4	..
29	Motor vehicles, trailers and semi-trailers	3.7	4.4	2.3	2.8	3.3	8.6	4.7	..
30	Other transport equipment	..	..	..	..	..	..	..	..
31-33	Furniture; repair, installation of machinery and equipment	3.0	..	2.2	..	..	..	..	..
31	Furniture	0.4	0.6	0.4	..	..	..	..	..
32	Other manufacturing	2.4	1.6	1.5	1.5	0.6	1.3	1.5	..
33	Repair and installation of machinery and equipment	0.1	..	0.4	0.2	0.2	0.4	0.0	..
35-39	**ELECTRICITY, GAS, WATER AND WASTE MANAGEMENT**	23.7	33.0	9.6	25.2	15.4	16.4	16.2	..
35-36	Electricity, gas and water	..	..	..	..	..	..	..	..
37-39	Sewerage, waste management and remediation activities	..	..	..	..	..	..	..	..
41-43	**CONSTRUCTION**	0.7	5.9	..	..	..	1.1	2.2	..
45-99	**TOTAL SERVICES**	147.0	198.7	181.1	155.0	173.3	175.4	170.5	..
45-82	**Business sector services**	144.5	196.2	178.9	151.1	170.9	175.0	170.3	..
45-47	**Wholesale and retail trade; motor vehicle and motorcycle repairs**	2.9	3.3	2.7	2.7	0.2	2.4	4.2	..
49-53	**Transportation and storage**	..	..	..	..	..	..	..	..
55-56	**Accommodation and food service activities**	0.0	0.0	0.0	0.0	0.0	0.0	0.0	..
58-63	**Information and communication**	68.9	101.0	85.2	71.6	93.9	105.1	93.2	..
58-60	Publishing, audiovisual and broadcasting activities	..	..	..	..	..	..	..	..
58	Publishing activities	..	..	..	..	..	..	..	..
59-60	Motion picture, video and TV programme production; broadcasting activities	0.0	0.0	0.0	0.0	0.0	0.0	0.0	..
59	Motion picture, video and TV programme production; sound and music	0.0	0.0	0.0	0.0	0.0	0.0	0.0	..
60	Programming and broadcasting activities	0.0	0.0	0.0	0.0	0.0	0.0	0.0	..
61	Telecommunications	11.5	25.0	11.9	10.8	10.1	13.8	16.6	..
62-63	IT and other information services	57.3	75.9	..	..	..	..	..	..
62	Computer programming, consultancy and related activities	54.6	73.2	69.6	59.4	78.1	85.1	70.6	..
63	Information service activities	2.7	2.7	..	..	..	..	..	..
64-66	**Financial and insurance activities**	22.5	22.5	25.4	25.1	24.5	23.2	30.0	..
68-82	**Real estate; professional, scientific and technical; administrative and support**	49.4	69.4	65.4	50.0	49.9	39.8	38.5	..
68	Real estate activities	0.0	0.0	0.0	0.0	0.0	0.0	0.0	..
69-75x72	Professional, scientific and technical activities, except scientific R&D	7.9	11.2	10.8	9.6	11.2	9.2	2.6	..
72	Scientific research and development	40.5	57.5	54.1	40.2	33.3	30.5	34.4	..
77-82	Administrative and support service activities	..	..	..	..	..	..	..	..
84-99	Community, social and personal services	2.6	2.5	2.2	3.9	2.5	0.4	0.2	..
84-85	Public administration and defence; compulsory social security and education	0.0	0.0	0.0	0.0	0.0	0.1	0.0	..
86-88	Human health and social work activities	2.6	2.5	2.2	3.9	2.5	0.3	0.2	..
90-93	Arts, entertainment and recreation	0.0	0.0	0.0	0.0	0.0	0.0	0.0	..
94-99	Other services; household-employers; extraterritorial bodies	0.0	0.0	0.0	0.0	0.0	0.0	0.0	..

.. Not available

Note: Detailed metadata at: *http://metalinks.oecd.org/anberd/20200813/2abe*.

ESTONIA

R&D expenditure in industry by main activity of the enterprise, constant prices
ISIC Rev. 4

2010 USD PPP

		2011	2012	2013	2014	2015	2016	2017	2018
	TOTAL BUSINESS ENTERPRISE	**509.1**	**441.3**	**301.4**	**234.9**	**259.5**	**254.7**	**253.5**	..
01-03	**AGRICULTURE, FORESTRY AND FISHING**	**0.1**	..	..	..	**0.0**	**0.0**	**0.0**	..
05-09	**MINING AND QUARRYING**	..	..	..	..	..	..	..	..
10-33	**MANUFACTURING**	**324.7**	**191.4**	**104.1**	**50.6**	**70.0**	**62.8**	**75.0**	..
10-12	Food products, beverages and tobacco	2.9	2.7	9.1	5.9	6.3	9.9	3.2	..
13-15	Textiles, wearing apparel, leather and related products	1.1	0.9	1.0	1.2	1.2	1.0	1.0	..
13	Textiles	..	..	..	..	..	..	..	..
14	Wearing apparel	..	..	..	..	..	..	..	..
15	Leather and related products, footwear	..	..	..	..	..	..	..	..
16-18	Wood and paper products and printing	1.2	0.2	0.6	0.1	1.1	0.6	0.2	..
16	Wood and wood products, except furniture	..	..	0.6	0.1	0.0	0.2	0.2	..
17	Paper and paper products	0.0	0.0	0.0	0.0	0.0	0.0	0.0	..
18	Printing and reproduction of recorded media	..	..	0.0	0.0	1.0	0.3	0.0	..
19-23	Chemical, rubber, plastic, non-metallic mineral products	..	..	..	..	..	..	..	..
19	Coke and refined petroleum products	283.0	153.6	65.3	9.0	22.2	1.5	8.1	..
20-21	Chemical and pharmaceutical products	9.9	9.0	6.8	5.8	6.3	4.9	5.1	..
20	Chemicals and chemical products	3.2	7.1	4.8	3.7	4.6	4.1	3.8	..
21	Pharmaceuticals, medicinal, chemical and botanical products	6.7	1.8	1.9	2.1	1.6	0.8	1.3	..
22	Rubber and plastic products	1.9	1.7	0.8	7.5	0.4	0.7	0.9	..
23	Other non-metallic mineral products	..	..	..	..	..	..	..	..
24-25	Basic metals, metal products, except machinery and equipment	0.8	0.5	..	..	..	..	..	..
24	Basic metals	0.0	0.0	..	..	..	..	..	..
25	Fabricated metal products, except machinery and equipment	0.8	0.5	1.7	1.4	0.9	0.9	1.0	..
26-30	Computer, electronic, optical products; electrical machinery, transport equipment	20.6	19.7	16.2	16.5	29.4	40.8	53.1	..
26	Computer, electronic and optical products	6.1	4.7	5.1	7.9	12.4	16.4	24.7	..
27	Electrical equipment	8.5	8.8	3.5	4.7	9.1	9.9	17.9	..
28	Machinery and equipment n.e.c.	1.7	1.5	5.3	1.2	1.6	2.9	6.0	..
29	Motor vehicles, trailers and semi-trailers	4.0	4.6	2.3	2.7	3.3	8.3	4.4	..
30	Other transport equipment	..	..	..	..	..	..	..	..
31-33	Furniture; repair, installation of machinery and equipment	3.2	..	2.2	..	..	..	..	..
31	Furniture	0.5	0.6	0.4	..	..	..	..	..
32	Other manufacturing	2.6	1.6	1.5	1.5	0.6	1.3	1.4	..
33	Repair and installation of machinery and equipment	0.1	..	0.4	0.2	0.2	0.4	0.0	..
35-39	**ELECTRICITY, GAS, WATER AND WASTE MANAGEMENT**	**25.5**	**34.6**	**9.7**	**25.0**	**15.4**	**15.9**	**15.2**	..
35-36	Electricity, gas and water	..	..	..	..	..	..	..	..
37-39	Sewerage, waste management and remediation activities	..	..	..	..	..	..	..	..
41-43	**CONSTRUCTION**	**0.7**	**6.2**	..	..	..	**1.0**	**2.1**	..
45-99	**TOTAL SERVICES**	**157.7**	**208.6**	**183.2**	**153.7**	**173.3**	**169.4**	**160.6**	..
45-82	**Business sector services**	**155.0**	**206.0**	**181.0**	**149.8**	**170.9**	**169.0**	**160.4**	..
45-47	**Wholesale and retail trade; motor vehicle and motorcycle repairs**	**3.1**	**3.4**	**2.8**	**2.7**	**0.2**	**2.3**	**3.9**	..
49-53	**Transportation and storage**	..	..	..	..	..	..	..	..
55-56	**Accommodation and food service activities**	**0.0**	**0.0**	**0.0**	**0.0**	**0.0**	**0.0**	**0.0**	..
58-63	**Information and communication**	**73.9**	**106.1**	**86.2**	**70.9**	**93.9**	**101.5**	**87.8**	..
58-60	Publishing, audiovisual and broadcasting activities	..	..	..	..	..	..	..	..
58	Publishing activities	..	..	..	..	..	..	..	..
59-60	Motion picture, video and TV programme production; broadcasting activities	0.0	0.0	0.0	0.0	0.0	0.0	0.0	..
59	Motion picture, video and TV programme production; sound and music	0.0	0.0	0.0	0.0	0.0	0.0	0.0	..
60	Programming and broadcasting activities	0.0	0.0	0.0	0.0	0.0	0.0	0.0	..
61	Telecommunications	12.4	26.3	12.0	10.7	10.1	13.3	15.6	..
62-63	IT and other information services	61.4	79.7	..	..	..	..	..	..
62	Computer programming, consultancy and related activities	58.5	76.9	70.5	58.8	78.1	82.2	66.5	..
63	Information service activities	2.9	2.9	..	..	..	..	..	..
64-66	**Financial and insurance activities**	**24.1**	**23.6**	**25.7**	**24.9**	**24.5**	**22.4**	**28.2**	..
68-82	**Real estate; professional, scientific and technical; administrative and support**	**52.9**	**72.9**	**66.1**	**49.6**	**49.9**	**38.4**	**36.3**	..
68	Real estate activities	0.0	0.0	0.0	0.0	0.0	0.0	0.0	..
69-75x72	Professional, scientific and technical activities, except scientific R&D	8.5	11.8	10.9	9.5	11.2	8.9	2.5	..
72	Scientific research and development	43.4	60.4	54.7	39.8	33.3	29.4	32.4	..
77-82	Administrative and support service activities	..	..	..	..	..	..	..	..
84-99	Community, social and personal services	2.8	2.6	2.2	3.9	2.5	0.4	0.2	..
84-85	Public administration and defence; compulsory social security and education	0.0	0.0	0.0	0.0	0.0	0.1	0.0	..
86-88	Human health and social work activities	2.8	2.6	2.2	3.9	2.5	0.3	0.2	..
90-93	Arts, entertainment and recreation	0.0	0.0	0.0	0.0	0.0	0.0	0.0	..
94-99	Other services; household-employers; extraterritorial bodies	0.0	0.0	0.0	0.0	0.0	0.0	0.0	..

.. Not available

Note: Detailed metadata at: *http://metalinks.oecd.org/anberd/20200813/2abe.*

FINLAND

R&D expenditure in industry by main activity of the enterprise, current prices
ISIC Rev. 4

Million USD PPP

		2011	2012	2013	2014	2015	2016	2017	2018
	TOTAL BUSINESS ENTERPRISE	**5 620.3**	**5 167.9**	**5 083.5**	**4 860.5**	**4 459.8**	**4 428.8**	**4 665.1**	..
01-03	**AGRICULTURE, FORESTRY AND FISHING**	5.5	2.0	3.2	1.7	1.8	1.9	5.0	..
05-09	**MINING AND QUARRYING**	9.3	10.9	9.4	6.9	7.5	10.6	19.3	..
10-33	**MANUFACTURING**	**4 318.3**	**3 728.4**	**3 626.2**	**3 446.2**	**2 992.9**	**2 845.7**	**2 918.4**	..
10-12	Food products, beverages and tobacco	71.5	65.6	75.7	78.2	66.7	55.1	66.7	..
13-15	Textiles, wearing apparel, leather and related products	7.6	5.4	7.0	9.7	12.2	8.6	7.1	..
13	Textiles	1.0 e	0.8 e	1.7 e	0.7 e	4.4	5.4	4.1	..
14	Wearing apparel	6.5 e	4.5 e	5.1 e	9.0 e	7.6	3.1 e	3.0 e	..
15	Leather and related products, footwear	0.1 e	0.1 e	0.1 e	0.0 e	0.1	0.0 e	0.0 e	..
16-18	Wood and paper products and printing	101.1	109.1	105.0	99.8	114.4	114.4	118.2	..
16	Wood and wood products, except furniture	10.7	8.5	8.4	8.8	5.6	9.5	9.8	..
17	Paper and paper products	84.5	94.3	90.0	85.0	99.5	96.9	99.9	..
18	Printing and reproduction of recorded media	5.8	6.4	6.6	6.0	9.3	8.1	8.5	..
19-23	Chemical, rubber, plastic, non-metallic mineral products	390.1 e	385.0 e	385.5 e	363.5 e	387.6 e	427.2 e	449.4 e	..
19	Coke and refined petroleum products	45.6 e	41.9 e	41.4 e	28.7 e	38.6 e	42.6 e	44.8 e	..
20-21	Chemical and pharmaceutical products	273.6	267.2	273.8	264.3	276.9	307.4	309.2	..
20	Chemicals and chemical products	143.5	117.1	141.4	115.8	133.7	144.5	138.3	..
21	Pharmaceuticals, medicinal, chemical and botanical products	130.1	150.1	132.4	148.5	143.3	162.9	170.9	..
22	Rubber and plastic products	37.2	38.6	40.0	38.0	41.1	43.8	63.8	..
23	Other non-metallic mineral products	33.7	37.3	30.3	32.4	31.0	33.4	31.6	..
24-25	Basic metals, metal products, except machinery and equipment	108.3	98.9	93.6	82.1	81.3	81.5	94.0	..
24	Basic metals	56.4	51.9	44.7	35.6	41.2	41.5	36.6	..
25	Fabricated metal products, except machinery and equipment	51.9	47.0	48.8	46.5	40.1	40.0	57.4	..
26-30	Computer, electronic, optical products; electrical machinery, transport equipment	3 604.0	3 023.4	2 926.6	2 783.4	2 301.1	2 123.3	2 148.7	..
26	Computer, electronic and optical products	2 794.6	2 097.5	1 966.8	1 916.4	1 507.0	1 318.0	1 292.5	..
27	Electrical equipment	289.4	318.4	331.7	334.4	258.7	253.5	257.8	..
28	Machinery and equipment n.e.c.	444.2	518.7	557.1	487.8	471.2	471.0	507.4	..
29	Motor vehicles, trailers and semi-trailers	22.9	23.2	27.8	28.3	44.0	46.0	49.9	..
30	Other transport equipment	52.9	65.5	43.1	16.4	20.3	35.0	41.0	..
31-33	Furniture; repair, installation of machinery and equipment	35.8 e	40.9 e	32.9 e	29.6 e	29.6 e	35.6 e	34.2 e	..
31	Furniture	8.5	9.7	7.5	6.8	5.3	4.2	8.1	..
32	Other manufacturing	15.4	20.3	14.7	15.3	14.3	20.3	14.5	..
33	Repair and installation of machinery and equipment	11.8 e	10.9 e	10.7 e	7.5 e	10.0 e	11.1 e	11.6 e	..
35-39	**ELECTRICITY, GAS, WATER AND WASTE MANAGEMENT**	57.4	62.4	53.5	40.6	44.4	73.7	71.7	..
35-36	Electricity, gas and water	26.0	33.7	27.7	21.1	23.7	51.4	67.4	..
37-39	Sewerage, waste management and remediation activities	31.4	28.7	25.7	19.6	20.7	22.2	4.3	..
41-43	**CONSTRUCTION**	55.3	56.5	50.4	87.9	111.1	115.6	136.2	..
45-99	**TOTAL SERVICES**	**1 174.5**	**1 307.7**	**1 340.9**	**1 277.3**	**1 302.1**	**1 381.5**	**1 514.5**	..
45-82	**Business sector services**	**1 153.6**	**1 278.5**	**1 315.6**	**1 248.3**	**1 271.4**	**1 345.2**	**1 484.2**	..
45-47	**Wholesale and retail trade; motor vehicle and motorcycle repairs**	101.7	129.0	93.4	79.4	96.1	101.5	86.4	..
49-53	**Transportation and storage**	17.3	19.6	17.2	16.1	18.6	17.3	13.9	..
55-56	**Accommodation and food service activities**	0.7	1.1	0.5 e	0.1 e	0.1 e	0.1 e	0.3 e	..
58-63	**Information and communication**	500.5	514.4	602.6	563.4	604.4	657.0	795.8	..
58-60	Publishing, audiovisual and broadcasting activities	64.4	64.0	75.2	90.2	94.1	68.4	128.2	..
58	Publishing activities	61.3	62.2	74.1	86.6	91.0	65.8	125.4	..
59-60	Motion picture, video and TV programme production; broadcasting activities	3.1	1.8	1.1	3.5	3.2	2.5	2.8	..
59	Motion picture, video and TV programme production; sound and music	..	..	..	..	..	..	..	..
60	Programming and broadcasting activities	..	..	..	..	..	..	..	..
61	Telecommunications	42.3	27.4	38.8	40.0	34.9	35.0	30.9	..
62-63	IT and other information services	393.8	423.0	488.6	433.3	475.3	553.6	636.7	..
62	Computer programming, consultancy and related activities	383.3	416.9	473.4	409.9	455.4	530.7	555.8	..
63	Information service activities	10.5	6.1	15.2	23.4	19.8	22.9	80.9	..
64-66	**Financial and insurance activities**	**79.3**	**94.8**	**75.6**	**103.7**	**139.5**	**109.1**	**135.1**	..
68-82	**Real estate; professional, scientific and technical; administrative and support**	454.1	519.6	526.3 e	485.7 e	412.7 e	460.3 e	452.6 e	..
68	Real estate activities	3.1	3.2	1.4 e	0.2 e	0.3 e	0.2 e	0.9 e	..
69-75x72	Professional, scientific and technical activities, except scientific R&D	170.0	192.3	154.1	140.4	190.1	188.1	178.0	..
72	Scientific research and development	276.4	318.8	367.1	338.1	216.6	260.5	268.7	..
77-82	Administrative and support service activities	4.5	5.3	3.5	6.8	5.7	11.6	5.1	..
84-99	Community, social and personal services	21.0	29.2	25.3	29.0	30.7	36.4	30.3	..
84-85	Public administration and defence; compulsory social security and education	1.4 e	3.3	1.4	1.9 e	0.0	0.1	0.1 e	..
86-88	Human health and social work activities	3.0	4.0	5.3	2.2	2.9	3.2	4.2	..
90-93	Arts, entertainment and recreation	13.2 e	16.8	16.7	22.5	26.2	31.7	24.5 e	..
94-99	Other services; household-employers; extraterritorial bodies	3.4 e	5.1	1.9	2.4 e	1.5	1.5	1.6	..

.. Not available; e Estimated value

Note: Detailed metadata at: *http://metalinks.oecd.org/anberd/20200813/2abe.*

FINLAND

R&D expenditure in industry by main activity of the enterprise, constant prices
ISIC Rev. 4

2010 USD PPP

		2011	2012	2013	2014	2015	2016	2017	2018
	TOTAL BUSINESS ENTERPRISE	**6 068.9**	**5 482.1**	**5 239.9**	**4 939.7**	**4 459.8**	**4 291.3**	**4 397.9**	..
01-03	**AGRICULTURE, FORESTRY AND FISHING**	**5.9**	**2.1**	**3.3**	**1.7**	**1.8**	**1.9**	**4.7**	..
05-09	**MINING AND QUARRYING**	**10.0**	**11.5**	**9.7**	**7.1**	**7.5**	**10.2**	**18.2**	..
10-33	**MANUFACTURING**	**4 662.9**	**3 955.1**	**3 737.8**	**3 502.3**	**2 992.9**	**2 757.3**	**2 751.2**	..
10-12	Food products, beverages and tobacco	77.2	69.6	78.0	79.4	66.7	53.3	62.9	..
13-15	Textiles, wearing apparel, leather and related products	8.2	5.8	7.2	9.9	12.2	8.4	6.7	..
13	Textiles	1.1 e	0.8 e	1.8 e	0.7 e	4.4	5.3	3.8	..
14	Wearing apparel	7.0 e	4.8 e	5.3 e	9.1 e	7.6	3.0 e	2.8 e	..
15	Leather and related products, footwear	0.1 e	0.1 e	0.1 e	0.0 e	0.1	0.0 e	0.0 e	..
16-18	Wood and paper products and printing	109.1	115.8	108.3	101.4	114.4	110.9	111.5	..
16	Wood and wood products, except furniture	11.5	9.0	8.7	9.0	5.6	9.2	9.3	..
17	Paper and paper products	91.3	100.0	92.8	86.4	99.5	93.9	94.2	..
18	Printing and reproduction of recorded media	6.3	6.8	6.8	6.0	9.3	7.8	8.0	..
19-23	Chemical, rubber, plastic, non-metallic mineral products	421.2 e	408.4 e	397.3 e	369.4 e	387.6 e	413.9 e	423.7 e	..
19	Coke and refined petroleum products	49.2 e	44.5 e	42.7 e	29.2 e	38.6 e	41.3 e	42.2 e	..
20-21	Chemical and pharmaceutical products	295.4	283.5	282.2	268.6	276.9	297.8	291.5	..
20	Chemicals and chemical products	154.9	124.2	145.7	117.7	133.7	140.0	130.4	..
21	Pharmaceuticals, medicinal, chemical and botanical products	140.5	159.3	136.5	150.9	143.3	157.8	161.1	..
22	Rubber and plastic products	40.2	40.9	41.2	38.6	41.1	42.5	60.2	..
23	Other non-metallic mineral products	36.4	39.5	31.2	32.9	31.0	32.3	29.8	..
24-25	Basic metals, metal products, except machinery and equipment	116.9	104.9	96.4	83.5	81.3	79.0	88.6	..
24	Basic metals	60.9	55.1	46.1	36.2	41.2	40.3	34.5	..
25	Fabricated metal products, except machinery and equipment	56.0	49.9	50.3	47.3	40.1	38.7	54.2	..
26-30	Computer, electronic, optical products; electrical machinery, transport equipment	3 891.7	3 207.2	3 016.6	2 828.7	2 301.1	2 057.4	2 025.6	..
26	Computer, electronic and optical products	3 017.6	2 225.0	2 027.4	1 947.7	1 507.0	1 277.0	1 218.5	..
27	Electrical equipment	312.5	337.8	341.9	339.9	258.7	245.6	243.0	..
28	Machinery and equipment n.e.c.	479.6	550.3	574.3	495.7	471.2	456.3	478.3	..
29	Motor vehicles, trailers and semi-trailers	24.7	24.7	28.7	28.8	44.0	44.5	47.1	..
30	Other transport equipment	57.2	69.5	44.4	16.7	20.3	33.9	38.6	..
31-33	Furniture; repair, installation of machinery and equipment	38.6 e	43.4 e	34.0 e	30.1 e	29.6 e	34.5 e	32.2 e	..
31	Furniture	9.2	10.3	7.7	6.9	5.3	4.1	7.6	..
32	Other manufacturing	16.6	21.6	15.1	15.6	14.3	19.7	13.6	..
33	Repair and installation of machinery and equipment	12.8 e	11.5 e	11.1 e	7.6 e	10.0 e	10.7 e	11.0 e	..
35-39	**ELECTRICITY, GAS, WATER AND WASTE MANAGEMENT**	**62.0**	**66.2**	**55.1**	**41.2**	**44.4**	**71.4**	**67.6**	..
35-36	Electricity, gas and water	28.1	35.8	28.6	21.4	23.7	49.8	63.5	..
37-39	Sewerage, waste management and remediation activities	33.9	30.4	26.5	19.9	20.7	21.6	4.0	..
41-43	**CONSTRUCTION**	**59.7**	**59.9**	**51.9**	**89.3**	**111.1**	**112.0**	**128.4**	..
45-99	**TOTAL SERVICES**	**1 268.3**	**1 387.2**	**1 382.2**	**1 298.1**	**1 302.1**	**1 338.6**	**1 427.8**	..
45-82	**Business sector services**	**1 245.6**	**1 356.3**	**1 356.1**	**1 268.7**	**1 271.4**	**1 303.4**	**1 399.2**	..
45-47	**Wholesale and retail trade; motor vehicle and motorcycle repairs**	**109.8**	**136.9**	**96.3**	**80.7**	**96.1**	**98.3**	**81.4**	..
49-53	**Transportation and storage**	**18.7**	**20.8**	**17.8**	**16.4**	**18.6**	**16.7**	**13.1**	..
55-56	**Accommodation and food service activities**	**0.7**	**1.2**	**0.5 e**	**0.1 e**	**0.1 e**	**0.1 e**	**0.3 e**	..
58-63	**Information and communication**	**540.4**	**545.7**	**621.2**	**572.6**	**604.4**	**636.6**	**750.2**	..
58-60	Publishing, audiovisual and broadcasting activities	69.5	67.9	77.5	91.6	94.1	66.3	120.9	..
58	Publishing activities	66.2	66.0	76.4	88.1	91.0	63.8	118.2	..
59-60	Motion picture, video and TV programme production; broadcasting activities	3.4	1.9	1.1	3.6	3.2	2.4	2.6	..
59	Motion picture, video and TV programme production; sound and music	..	..	..	..	..	..	..	..
60	Programming and broadcasting activities	..	..	..	..	..	..	..	..
61	Telecommunications	45.6	29.1	40.0	40.7	34.9	33.9	29.1	..
62-63	IT and other information services	425.2	448.7	503.7	440.4	475.3	536.4	600.2	..
62	Computer programming, consultancy and related activities	413.9	442.2	488.0	416.6	455.4	514.2	523.9	..
63	Information service activities	11.3	6.5	15.7	23.7	19.8	22.2	76.3	..
64-66	**Financial and insurance activities**	**85.7**	**100.6**	**77.9**	**105.4**	**139.5**	**105.7**	**127.4**	..
68-82	**Real estate; professional, scientific and technical; administrative and support**	**490.3**	**551.2**	**542.5 e**	**493.6 e**	**412.7 e**	**446.0 e**	**426.7 e**	..
68	Real estate activities	3.3	3.4	1.4 e	0.3 e	0.3 e	0.2 e	0.8 e	..
69-75x72	Professional, scientific and technical activities, except scientific R&D	183.6	204.0	158.8	142.7	190.1	182.2	167.8	..
72	Scientific research and development	298.5	338.1	378.4	343.6	216.6	252.4	253.3	..
77-82	Administrative and support service activities	4.9	5.7	3.6	6.9	5.7	11.2	4.8	..
84-99	Community, social and personal services	22.7	30.9	26.1	29.5	30.7	35.3	28.6	..
84-85	Public administration and defence; compulsory social security and education	1.5 e	3.5	1.5	1.9 e	0.0	0.1	0.1 e	..
86-88	Human health and social work activities	3.3	4.2	5.5	2.2	2.9	3.1	3.9	..
90-93	Arts, entertainment and recreation	14.2 e	17.8	17.2	22.9	26.2	30.7	23.1 e	..
94-99	Other services; household-employers; extraterritorial bodies	3.6 e	5.4	1.9	2.5 e	1.5	1.4	1.5	..

.. Not available; e Estimated value

Note: Detailed metadata at: *http://metalinks.oecd.org/anberd/20200813/2abe.*

FINLAND

R&D expenditure in industry by industry orientation, current prices
ISIC Rev. 4

Million USD PPP

		2011	2012	2013	2014	2015	2016	2017	2018
	TOTAL BUSINESS ENTERPRISE	**5 620.3**	**5 167.9**	**5 083.5**	**4 860.5**	**4 459.8**	**4 428.8**	**4 665.1**	..
01-03	**AGRICULTURE, FORESTRY AND FISHING**	22.3	21.0	13.8	12.2	18.0	21.0	27.2	..
05-09	**MINING AND QUARRYING**	40.8	18.4	15.5	15.7	20.1	22.4	24.0	..
10-33	**MANUFACTURING**	**4 500.8**	**3 916.0**	**3 800.2**	**3 664.6**	**3 310.4**	**3 137.1**	**3 207.9**	..
10-12	Food products, beverages and tobacco	71.0	81.2	82.1	86.7	75.5	60.3	76.0	..
13-15	Textiles, wearing apparel, leather and related products	14.1	9.4	10.2	11.2	16.9	8.9	10.0	..
13	Textiles	8.7	5.8	7.8	5.1	14.5	5.3	5.2	..
14	Wearing apparel	4.8	2.8	2.0	5.9	2.1	3.4	4.5 e	..
15	Leather and related products, footwear	0.6	0.8	0.4	0.2	0.3	0.2	0.2 e	..
16-18	Wood and paper products and printing	95.4	109.5	108.1	99.6	117.3	118.9	123.2	..
16	Wood and wood products, except furniture	7.8	7.2	8.6	8.0	3.7	5.5	7.9	..
17	Paper and paper products	82.0	95.3	92.0	85.0	103.7	100.5	96.6	..
18	Printing and reproduction of recorded media	5.6	6.0	7.5	6.6	9.9	12.9	18.8	..
19-23	Chemical, rubber, plastic, non-metallic mineral products	432.9	406.1	402.6	368.2	405.5	444.9	485.7 e	..
19	Coke and refined petroleum products	47.9	49.1	51.0	33.7	42.2	49.8	44.3 e	..
20-21	Chemical and pharmaceutical products	326.0	297.1	292.6	279.5	301.3	325.7	344.6	..
20	Chemicals and chemical products	134.6	100.8	125.7	94.5	115.2	114.1	119.7	..
21	Pharmaceuticals, medicinal, chemical and botanical products	191.4	196.3	166.9	185.0	186.1	211.5	224.9	..
22	Rubber and plastic products	41.6	43.0	48.3	40.7	46.3	45.6	70.8	..
23	Other non-metallic mineral products	17.5	16.9	10.7	14.2	15.7	23.8	26.1	..
24-25	Basic metals, metal products, except machinery and equipment	150.9	94.4	145.2	157.9	170.4	185.4	183.3	..
24	Basic metals	37.4	35.1	31.0	42.3	33.6	26.3	28.7	..
25	Fabricated metal products, except machinery and equipment	113.5	59.3	114.2	115.6	136.8	159.1	154.6	..
26-30	Computer, electronic, optical products; electrical machinery, transport equipment	3 658.3	3 133.7	2 968.6	2 854.2	2 430.8	2 179.1	2 209.0	..
26	Computer, electronic and optical products	2 937.1	2 256.8	2 117.0	2 056.9	1 620.0	1 391.7	1 343.5	..
27	Electrical equipment	278.5	314.7	320.2	330.5	265.8	253.4	261.6	..
28	Machinery and equipment n.e.c.	348.6	457.9	452.3	415.4	460.1	443.4	524.5	..
29	Motor vehicles, trailers and semi-trailers	18.7	5.9	11.7	8.5	40.4	30.6	24.7	..
30	Other transport equipment	75.4	98.5	67.4	42.9	44.4	60.3	54.8	..
31-33	Furniture; repair, installation of machinery and equipment	78.2	81.8	83.4	86.8	94.0	139.6	120.6 e	..
31	Furniture	6.3	7.6	6.1	7.0	5.8	5.7	7.3	..
32	Other manufacturing	60.5	61.9	66.8	73.2	78.2	104.7	87.3	..
33	Repair and installation of machinery and equipment	11.4	12.3	10.5	6.6	10.0	29.3	26.0 e	..
35-39	**ELECTRICITY, GAS, WATER AND WASTE MANAGEMENT**	41.7	32.6	27.9	22.0	19.3	19.0	34.5	..
35-36	Electricity, gas and water	30.1	27.7	20.9	17.2	12.3	16.5	29.3	..
37-39	Sewerage, waste management and remediation activities	11.6	4.9	7.1	4.9	7.0	2.6	5.2	..
41-43	**CONSTRUCTION**	**74.0**	**72.4**	**62.3**	**26.2**	**34.0**	**42.8**	**39.5**	..
45-99	**TOTAL SERVICES**	**940.7**	**1 107.5**	**1 164.0**	**1 119.9**	**1 058.1**	**1 186.3**	**1 331.9**	..
45-82	**Business sector services**	**900.8**	**1 034.6**	**1 097.9**	**1 044.6**	**1 020.2**	**1 138.4**	**1 265.0**	..
45-47	**Wholesale and retail trade; motor vehicle and motorcycle repairs**	15.7	3.4	7.8	6.9	12.2	6.0	6.9	..
49-53	**Transportation and storage**	17.4	18.3	14.8	17.1	17.9	18.2	13.4 e	..
55-56	**Accommodation and food service activities**	8.2	1.1	0.4	0.2	0.5	0.0	0.0 e	..
58-63	**Information and communication**	644.7	760.1	805.4	723.9	698.6	811.2	833.5	..
58-60	Publishing, audiovisual and broadcasting activities	11.6	15.3	19.9	15.1	18.2	19.8	43.9	..
58	Publishing activities	9.1	13.1	17.8	12.7	16.0	18.7	41.5 e	..
59-60	Motion picture, video and TV programme production; broadcasting activities	2.5	2.3	2.1	2.4	2.3	1.1	2.4 e	..
59	Motion picture, video and TV programme production; sound and music	1.0	1.1	0.2	0.9	0.6	0.3 e	0.6 e	..
60	Programming and broadcasting activities	1.5	1.2	1.9	1.5	1.7	0.8 e	1.8 e	..
61	Telecommunications	227.9	290.3	272.9	218.0	95.3	130.5	85.1	..
62-63	IT and other information services	405.1	454.4	512.6	490.8	585.1	660.9	704.3	..
62	Computer programming, consultancy and related activities	279.4	327.9	366.3	360.4	493.5	541.7	581.1	..
63	Information service activities	125.8	126.6	146.4	130.4	91.6	119.2	123.2	..
64-66	**Financial and insurance activities**	**75.2**	**92.6**	**71.8**	**102.2**	**131.6**	**111.1**	**138.5**	..
68-82	**Real estate; professional, scientific and technical; administrative and support**	139.6	159.0	197.6	194.3	159.5	191.9	272.6	..
68	Real estate activities	2.7	5.7	4.5	3.6	2.1	1.8	5.6	..
69-75x72	Professional, scientific and technical activities, except scientific R&D	21.8	22.9	22.8	31.5	39.1	53.9	41.8	..
72	Scientific research and development	107.1	126.9	164.6	154.6	107.2	131.7	219.7	..
77-82	Administrative and support service activities	8.0	3.6	5.7	4.6	11.2	4.5	5.4	..
84-99	Community, social and personal services	39.9	72.9	66.1	75.3	37.8	48.0	66.9	..
84-85	Public administration and defence; compulsory social security and education	1.8	4.4	1.7	3.4	1.5	2.0	2.8 e	..
86-88	Human health and social work activities	4.2	7.4	11.3	8.2	8.0	6.0	9.3	..
90-93	Arts, entertainment and recreation	10.1	10.2	11.8	11.7	15.1	17.9	25.6 e	..
94-99	Other services; household-employers; extraterritorial bodies	23.8	51.0	41.3	52.1	13.2	22.1	29.2	..

.. Not available; e Estimated value

Note: Detailed metadata at: *http://metalinks.oecd.org/anberd/20200813/2abe.*

FINLAND

R&D expenditure in industry by industry orientation, constant prices
ISIC Rev. 4

2010 USD PPP

		2011	2012	2013	2014	2015	2016	2017	2018
	TOTAL BUSINESS ENTERPRISE	**6 068.9**	**5 482.1**	**5 239.9**	**4 939.7**	**4 459.8**	**4 291.3**	**4 397.9**	..
01-03	**AGRICULTURE, FORESTRY AND FISHING**	**24.1**	**22.3**	**14.2**	**12.4**	**18.0**	**20.3**	**25.7**	..
05-09	**MINING AND QUARRYING**	**44.1**	**19.5**	**15.9**	**15.9**	**20.1**	**21.7**	**22.6**	..
10-33	**MANUFACTURING**	**4 860.1**	**4 154.1**	**3 917.1**	**3 724.3**	**3 310.4**	**3 039.7**	**3 024.1**	..
10-12	Food products, beverages and tobacco	76.7	86.1	84.6	88.2	75.5	58.4	71.6	..
13-15	Textiles, wearing apparel, leather and related products	15.2	10.0	10.5	11.4	16.9	8.6	9.4	..
13	Textiles	9.4	6.2	8.1	5.2	14.5	5.1	4.9	..
14	Wearing apparel	5.2	3.0	2.0	6.0	2.1	3.3	4.3 e	..
15	Leather and related products, footwear	0.6	0.8	0.5	0.2	0.3	0.2	0.2 e	..
16-18	Wood and paper products and printing	103.0	116.1	111.5	101.3	117.3	115.2	116.2	..
16	Wood and wood products, except furniture	8.5	7.6	8.9	8.2	3.7	5.3	7.4	..
17	Paper and paper products	88.5	101.1	94.8	86.4	103.7	97.4	91.1	..
18	Printing and reproduction of recorded media	6.0	6.3	7.7	6.7	9.9	12.5	17.7	..
19-23	Chemical, rubber, plastic, non-metallic mineral products	467.5	430.8	415.0	374.2	405.5	431.1	457.9 e	..
19	Coke and refined petroleum products	51.7	52.1	52.6	34.2	42.2	48.3	41.7 e	..
20-21	Chemical and pharmaceutical products	352.0	315.1	301.6	284.1	301.3	315.5	324.9	..
20	Chemicals and chemical products	145.3	106.9	129.6	96.1	115.2	110.6	112.9	..
21	Pharmaceuticals, medicinal, chemical and botanical products	206.6	208.2	172.0	188.0	186.1	205.0	212.0	..
22	Rubber and plastic products	44.9	45.7	49.8	41.4	46.3	44.2	66.7	..
23	Other non-metallic mineral products	18.9	17.9	11.0	14.5	15.7	23.1	24.6	..
24-25	Basic metals, metal products, except machinery and equipment	163.0	100.1	149.7	160.5	170.4	179.6	172.8	..
24	Basic metals	40.4	37.2	32.0	43.0	33.6	25.5	27.1	..
25	Fabricated metal products, except machinery and equipment	122.6	62.9	117.7	117.4	136.8	154.2	145.7	..
26-30	Computer, electronic, optical products; electrical machinery, transport equipment	3 950.2	3 324.2	3 059.9	2 900.7	2 430.8	2 111.4	2 082.5	..
26	Computer, electronic and optical products	3 171.6	2 394.0	2 182.1	2 090.4	1 620.0	1 348.5	1 266.5	..
27	Electrical equipment	300.7	333.8	330.1	335.9	265.8	245.5	246.6	..
28	Machinery and equipment n.e.c.	376.4	485.7	466.2	422.1	460.1	429.6	494.4	..
29	Motor vehicles, trailers and semi-trailers	20.2	6.3	12.1	8.6	40.4	29.7	23.3	..
30	Other transport equipment	81.4	104.4	69.4	43.6	44.4	58.4	51.6	..
31-33	Furniture; repair, installation of machinery and equipment	84.5	86.7	86.0	88.2	94.0	135.3	113.7 e	..
31	Furniture	6.9	8.0	6.3	7.1	5.8	5.5	6.9	..
32	Other manufacturing	65.3	65.7	68.9	74.4	78.2	101.4	82.3	..
33	Repair and installation of machinery and equipment	12.3	13.0	10.8	6.7	10.0	28.4	24.5 e	..
35-39	**ELECTRICITY, GAS, WATER AND WASTE MANAGEMENT**	**45.0**	**34.6**	**28.8**	**22.4**	**19.3**	**18.4**	**32.5**	..
35-36	Electricity, gas and water	32.5	29.3	21.5	17.5	12.3	15.9	27.6	..
37-39	Sewerage, waste management and remediation activities	12.5	5.2	7.3	4.9	7.0	2.5	4.9	..
41-43	**CONSTRUCTION**	**79.9**	**76.8**	**64.2**	**26.7**	**34.0**	**41.5**	**37.2**	..
45-99	**TOTAL SERVICES**	**1 015.8**	**1 174.8**	**1 199.8**	**1 138.2**	**1 058.1**	**1 149.5**	**1 255.6**	..
45-82	**Business sector services**	**972.7**	**1 097.5**	**1 131.7**	**1 061.7**	**1 020.2**	**1 103.0**	**1 192.5**	..
45-47	**Wholesale and retail trade; motor vehicle and motorcycle repairs**	**16.9**	**3.6**	**8.1**	**7.1**	**12.2**	**5.8**	**6.6**	..
49-53	**Transportation and storage**	**18.8**	**19.5**	**15.3**	**17.4**	**17.9**	**17.7**	**12.7 e**	..
55-56	**Accommodation and food service activities**	**8.8**	**1.1**	**0.5**	**0.2**	**0.5**	**0.0**	**0.0 e**	..
58-63	**Information and communication**	**696.2**	**806.3**	**830.2**	**735.7**	**698.6**	**786.0**	**785.7**	..
58-60	Publishing, audiovisual and broadcasting activities	12.6	16.3	20.5	15.3	18.2	19.2	41.4	..
58	Publishing activities	9.8	13.9	18.3	12.9	16.0	18.1	39.1 e	..
59-60	Motion picture, video and TV programme production; broadcasting activities	2.7	2.4	2.2	2.5	2.3	1.0	2.3 e	..
59	Motion picture, video and TV programme production; sound and music	1.1	1.2	0.2	0.9	0.6	0.3 e	0.6 e	..
60	Programming and broadcasting activities	1.6	1.2	1.9	1.6	1.7	0.8 e	1.7 e	..
61	Telecommunications	246.1	308.0	281.3	221.5	95.3	126.5	80.2	..
62-63	IT and other information services	437.5	482.1	528.4	498.8	585.1	640.4	664.0	..
62	Computer programming, consultancy and related activities	301.7	347.8	377.5	366.3	493.5	524.9	547.8	..
63	Information service activities	135.8	134.3	150.9	132.5	91.6	115.5	116.2	..
64-66	**Financial and insurance activities**	**81.2**	**98.2**	**74.0**	**103.9**	**131.6**	**107.6**	**130.6**	..
68-82	**Real estate; professional, scientific and technical; administrative and support**	**150.8**	**168.7**	**203.7**	**197.4**	**159.5**	**185.9**	**257.0**	..
68	Real estate activities	2.9	6.0	4.7	3.6	2.1	1.7	5.2	..
69-75x72	Professional, scientific and technical activities, except scientific R&D	23.6	24.3	23.5	32.0	39.1	52.2	39.4	..
72	Scientific research and development	115.7	134.6	169.6	157.1	107.2	127.6	207.1	..
77-82	Administrative and support service activities	8.6	3.8	5.9	4.7	11.2	4.3	5.1	..
84-99	Community, social and personal services	43.1	77.3	68.1	76.5	37.8	46.5	63.1	..
84-85	Public administration and defence; compulsory social security and education	2.0	4.6	1.7	3.5	1.5	1.9	2.7 e	..
86-88	Human health and social work activities	4.6	7.8	11.6	8.3	8.0	5.8	8.7	..
90-93	Arts, entertainment and recreation	10.9	10.8	12.2	11.8	15.1	17.4	24.2 e	..
94-99	Other services; household-employers; extraterritorial bodies	25.7	54.1	42.6	53.0	13.2	21.4	27.5	..

.. Not available; e Estimated value

Note: Detailed metadata at: http://metalinks.oecd.org/anberd/20200813/2abe.

R&D expenditure in industry by main activity of the enterprise, current prices
ISIC Rev. 4

Million USD PPP

		2011	2012	2013	2014	2015	2016	2017	2018
	TOTAL BUSINESS ENTERPRISE	**34 290.4**	**35 581.4**	**37 688.6 e**	**38 551.3**	**39 279.2 e**	**41 436.6**	**43 100.6**	..
01-03	**AGRICULTURE, FORESTRY AND FISHING**	**179.9**	**185.4**	**218.3 e**	**224.3 e**	**228.4 e**	**262.9**	**273.3**	..
05-09	**MINING AND QUARRYING**	**14.1**	**17.5**	**18.4 e**	**18.2 e**	**17.8 e**	**18.1**	**22.1**	..
10-33	**MANUFACTURING**	**17 057.9**	**17 866.7**	**19 134.7 e**	**19 608.0 e**	**19 894.9 e**	**20 777.6**	**20 968.6**	..
10-12	Food products, beverages and tobacco	396.1	414.1	443.4 e	470.7 e	485.1 e	483.6	499.1	..
13-15	Textiles, wearing apparel, leather and related products	134.5	134.9	153.9 e	139.7 e	140.6 e	194.1	215.7	..
13	Textiles	89.8	88.1	97.8 e	97.6 e	103.0 e	129.8	153.1	..
14	Wearing apparel	37.4	39.9	49.8 e	37.2 e	32.1 e	55.4	52.2	..
15	Leather and related products, footwear	7.2	7.0	6.3 e	4.9 e	5.5 e	9.0	10.4	..
16-18	Wood and paper products and printing	78.0	87.8	92.2 e	93.0 e	86.8 e	78.0	95.1	..
16	Wood and wood products, except furniture	17.1	22.6	22.7 e	24.0 e	24.4 e	21.0	19.7	..
17	Paper and paper products	48.5	47.3	52.2 e	47.4 e	40.0 e	42.9	53.4	..
18	Printing and reproduction of recorded media	12.5	17.9	17.3 e	21.7 e	22.4 e	14.2	22.1	..
19-23	Chemical, rubber, plastic, non-metallic mineral products	3 166.3	3 285.7	3 436.8 e	3 478.9 e	3 543.4 e	3 693.1	3 617.8	..
19	Coke and refined petroleum products	127.8	91.8	123.5 e	110.2 e	75.2 e	70.4	60.2	..
20-21	Chemical and pharmaceutical products	1 988.2	2 031.0	2 147.1 e	2 211.7 e	2 266.8 e	2 352.1	2 405.5	..
20	Chemicals and chemical products	990.5	1 074.4	1 159.1 e	1 153.0 e	1 166.6 e	1 264.4	1 321.6	..
21	Pharmaceuticals, medicinal, chemical and botanical products	997.7	956.6	988.0 e	1 058.7 e	1 100.2 e	1 087.6	1 083.9	..
22	Rubber and plastic products	832.8	943.3	931.8 e	930.5 e	964.1 e	991.1	954.0	..
23	Other non-metallic mineral products	217.5	219.6	234.4 e	226.6 e	237.3 e	279.5	198.1	..
24-25	Basic metals, metal products, except machinery and equipment	1 074.2	1 105.3	1 161.4 e	1 157.4 e	1 123.8 e	1 122.3	1 070.1	..
24	Basic metals	289.7	290.5	304.4 e	305.1 e	259.7 e	189.2	183.1	..
25	Fabricated metal products, except machinery and equipment	784.5	814.8	857.0 e	852.2 e	864.0 e	933.2	887.0	..
26-30	Computer, electronic, optical products; electrical machinery, transport equipment	11 540.5	12 107.4	13 084.9 e	13 406.2 e	13 611.7 e	14 355.5	14 427.8	..
26	Computer, electronic and optical products	3 795.6	4 007.9	4 502.6 e	4 648.8 e	4 676.9 e	4 928.8	4 909.0	..
27	Electrical equipment	771.2	790.5	810.3 e	822.0 e	835.7 e	902.0	1 091.8	..
28	Machinery and equipment n.e.c.	1 219.0	1 293.3	1 270.4 e	1 249.8 e	1 286.6 e	1 390.2	1 490.2	..
29	Motor vehicles, trailers and semi-trailers	2 280.0	2 251.7	2 341.1 e	2 382.6 e	2 608.5 e	3 123.0	3 139.0	..
30	Other transport equipment	3 474.7	3 763.9	4 160.5 e	4 303.0 e	4 204.0 e	4 011.6	3 797.8	..
31-33	Furniture; repair, installation of machinery and equipment	668.3	731.5	762.2 e	862.1 e	903.6 e	850.9	1 043.0	..
31	Furniture	20.8	20.7	22.6 e	19.6 e	15.8 e	15.3	12.7	..
32	Other manufacturing	328.3	345.5	376.2 e	404.9 e	403.8 e	388.0	455.2	..
33	Repair and installation of machinery and equipment	319.2	365.3	363.4 e	437.6 e	484.0 e	447.6	575.1	..
35-39	**ELECTRICITY, GAS, WATER AND WASTE MANAGEMENT**	**643.7**	**647.8**	**705.5 e**	**771.2 e**	**860.0 e**	**940.8**	**741.1**	..
35-36	Electricity, gas and water	611.8	621.1	666.8 e	727.7 e	817.7 e	898.7	697.2	..
37-39	Sewerage, waste management and remediation activities	31.9	26.8	38.7 e	43.5 e	42.3 e	42.2	43.8	..
41-43	**CONSTRUCTION**	**153.5**	**173.2**	**180.0 e**	**144.0 e**	**124.6 e**	**159.7**	**172.5**	..
45-99	**TOTAL SERVICES**	**16 241.2**	**16 690.9**	**17 431.6 e**	**17 785.5 e**	**18 153.5 e**	**19 277.4**	**20 923.0**	..
45-82	**Business sector services**	**16 177.5**	**16 625.1**	**17 352.1 e**	**17 709.0 e**	**18 061.8 e**	**19 128.9**	**20 760.3**	..
45-47	**Wholesale and retail trade; motor vehicle and motorcycle repairs**	**1 757.4**	**1 819.0**	**2 014.8 e**	**2 016.3 e**	**2 132.7 e**	**2 625.1**	**2 746.7**	..
49-53	**Transportation and storage**	**57.6**	**55.5**	**56.5 e**	**148.5 e**	**224.4 e**	**203.1**	**226.6**	..
55-56	**Accommodation and food service activities**	**0.4**	**4.1**	**5.2 e**	**3.9 e**	**2.5 e**	**2.4**	**1.6**	..
58-63	**Information and communication**	**3 581.2**	**3 935.3**	**4 461.5 e**	**4 634.5 e**	**4 664.1 e**	**5 013.7**	**5 909.2**	..
58-60	Publishing, audiovisual and broadcasting activities	939.2	1 067.4	1 214.6 e	1 259.1 e	1 316.2 e	1 485.8	1 587.0	..
58	Publishing activities	870.4	983.2	1 146.8 e	1 202.7 e	1 259.8 e	1 432.3	1 529.1	..
59-60	Motion picture, video and TV programme production; broadcasting activities	68.8	84.2	67.7 e	56.4 e	56.4 e	53.5	57.9	..
59	Motion picture, video and TV programme production; sound and music	58.9	74.9	60.8 e	52.9 e	55.4 e	53.0	54.6	..
60	Programming and broadcasting activities	10.0	9.4	7.0 e	3.5 e	1.0 e	0.5	3.2	..
61	Telecommunications	708.4	853.8	1 030.7 e	1 025.5 e	953.9 e	1 009.1	1 273.2	..
62-63	IT and other information services	1 933.6	2 014.1	2 216.2 e	2 350.0 e	2 394.1 e	2 518.8	3 049.0	..
62	Computer programming, consultancy and related activities	1 797.5	1 892.7	2 079.2 e	2 200.1 e	2 230.1 e	2 327.8	2 842.5	..
63	Information service activities	136.1	121.4	137.0 e	149.9 e	164.0 e	191.1	206.5	..
64-66	**Financial and insurance activities**	**311.0**	**302.9**	**311.0 e**	**297.0 e**	**302.9 e**	**376.0**	**462.7**	..
68-82	**Real estate; professional, scientific and technical; administrative and support**	**10 469.8**	**10 508.2**	**10 503.2 e**	**10 608.8 e**	**10 735.1 e**	**10 908.8**	**11 413.4**	..
68	Real estate activities	4.3	2.1	2.7 e	0.8 e	1.3 e	7.5	7.4	..
69-75x72	Professional, scientific and technical activities, except scientific R&D	5 970.7	5 926.6	5 840.0 e	5 907.3 e	5 946.6 e	5 881.1	6 078.6	..
72	Scientific research and development	4 332.2	4 388.8	4 416.1 e	4 478.7 e	4 608.2 e	4 812.8	5 061.7	..
77-82	Administrative and support service activities	162.6	190.7	244.4 e	222.0 e	179.0 e	207.4	265.7	..
84-99	Community, social and personal services	63.7	65.7	79.5 e	76.6 e	91.7 e	148.5	162.7	..
84-85	Public administration and defence; compulsory social security and education	4.6	4.5	5.8 e	6.2 e	8.3 e	16.3	32.7	..
86-88	Human health and social work activities	16.9	18.0	24.7 e	26.1 e	30.0 e	44.4	53.6	..
90-93	Arts, entertainment and recreation	4.1	6.9	8.1 e	2.6 e	5.5 e	22.1	12.9	..
94-99	Other services; household-employers; extraterritorial bodies	38.2	36.4	41.0 e	41.6 e	47.9 e	65.7	63.5	..

.. Not available; e Estimated value
Note: Detailed metadata at: *http://metalinks.oecd.org/anberd/20200813/2abe.*

FRANCE

R&D expenditure in industry by main activity of the enterprise, constant prices
ISIC Rev. 4

2010 USD PPP

		2011	2012	2013	2014	2015	2016	2017	2018
	TOTAL BUSINESS ENTERPRISE	**37 007.0**	**38 091.9**	**38 487.6 e**	**38 946.1**	**39 279.2 e**	**39 775.5**	**40 462.1**	..
01-03	**AGRICULTURE, FORESTRY AND FISHING**	194.2	198.4	223.0 e	226.6 e	228.4 e	252.3	256.6	..
05-09	**MINING AND QUARRYING**	15.3	18.8	18.8 e	18.4 e	17.8 e	17.4	20.8	..
10-33	**MANUFACTURING**	**18 409.3**	**19 127.3**	**19 540.4 e**	**19 808.9 e**	**19 894.9 e**	**19 944.7**	**19 684.9**	..
10-12	Food products, beverages and tobacco	427.5	443.3	452.8 e	475.5 e	485.1 e	464.3	468.5	..
13-15	Textiles, wearing apparel, leather and related products	145.2	144.4	157.2 e	141.2 e	140.6 e	186.4	202.5	..
13	Textiles	97.0	94.3	99.9 e	98.6 e	103.0 e	124.6	143.8	..
14	Wearing apparel	40.4	42.7	50.9 e	37.6 e	32.1 e	53.2	49.0	..
15	Leather and related products, footwear	7.8	7.5	6.4 e	4.9 e	5.5 e	8.6	9.8	..
16-18	Wood and paper products and printing	84.2	94.0	94.1 e	94.0 e	86.8 e	74.9	89.3	..
16	Wood and wood products, except furniture	18.4	24.2	23.2 e	24.2 e	24.4 e	20.2	18.5	..
17	Paper and paper products	52.3	50.6	53.3 e	47.9 e	40.0 e	41.1	50.1	..
18	Printing and reproduction of recorded media	13.5	19.1	17.7 e	21.9 e	22.4 e	13.6	20.7	..
19-23	Chemical, rubber, plastic, non-metallic mineral products	3 417.2	3 517.5	3 509.6 e	3 514.6 e	3 543.4 e	3 545.0	3 396.3	..
19	Coke and refined petroleum products	138.0	98.3	126.1 e	111.4 e	75.2 e	67.5	56.5	..
20-21	Chemical and pharmaceutical products	2 145.7	2 174.3	2 192.6 e	2 234.3 e	2 266.8 e	2 257.8	2 258.2	..
20	Chemicals and chemical products	1 069.0	1 150.2	1 183.7 e	1 164.8 e	1 166.6 e	1 213.7	1 240.7	..
21	Pharmaceuticals, medicinal, chemical and botanical products	1 076.7	1 024.1	1 008.9 e	1 069.5 e	1 100.2 e	1 044.0	1 017.5	..
22	Rubber and plastic products	898.8	1 009.8	951.5 e	940.0 e	964.1 e	951.4	895.6	..
23	Other non-metallic mineral products	234.7	235.1	239.4 e	228.9 e	237.3 e	268.3	186.0	..
24-25	Basic metals, metal products, except machinery and equipment	1 159.3	1 183.3	1 186.0 e	1 169.2 e	1 123.8 e	1 077.3	1 004.6	..
24	Basic metals	312.6	311.0	310.8 e	308.3 e	259.7 e	181.6	171.9	..
25	Fabricated metal products, except machinery and equipment	846.7	872.2	875.2 e	861.0 e	864.0 e	895.8	832.7	..
26-30	Computer, electronic, optical products; electrical machinery, transport equipment	12 454.8	12 961.7	13 362.3 e	13 543.5 e	13 611.7 e	13 780.1	13 544.6	..
26	Computer, electronic and optical products	4 096.3	4 290.7	4 598.0 e	4 696.4 e	4 676.9 e	4 731.2	4 608.5	..
27	Electrical equipment	832.3	846.2	827.5 e	830.4 e	835.7 e	865.8	1 024.9	..
28	Machinery and equipment n.e.c.	1 315.6	1 384.5	1 297.3 e	1 262.6 e	1 286.6 e	1 334.5	1 399.0	..
29	Motor vehicles, trailers and semi-trailers	2 460.7	2 410.6	2 390.8 e	2 407.0 e	2 608.5 e	2 997.8	2 946.8	..
30	Other transport equipment	3 750.0	4 029.5	4 248.7 e	4 347.1 e	4 204.0 e	3 850.8	3 565.3	..
31-33	Furniture; repair, installation of machinery and equipment	721.2	783.1	778.3 e	871.0 e	903.6 e	816.8	979.1	..
31	Furniture	22.4	22.2	23.1 e	19.8 e	15.8 e	14.7	11.9	..
32	Other manufacturing	354.4	369.9	384.2 e	409.0 e	403.8 e	372.5	427.3	..
33	Repair and installation of machinery and equipment	344.4	391.0	371.1 e	442.1 e	484.0 e	429.6	539.9	..
35-39	**ELECTRICITY, GAS, WATER AND WASTE MANAGEMENT**	**694.7**	**693.5**	**720.4 e**	**779.1 e**	**860.0 e**	**903.1**	**695.7**	..
35-36	Electricity, gas and water	660.2	664.9	680.9 e	735.1 e	817.7 e	862.6	654.6	..
37-39	Sewerage, waste management and remediation activities	34.4	28.7	39.5 e	44.0 e	42.3 e	40.5	41.1	..
41-43	**CONSTRUCTION**	**165.7**	**185.4**	**183.9 e**	**145.5 e**	**124.6 e**	**153.3**	**161.9**	..
45-99	**TOTAL SERVICES**	**17 527.9**	**17 868.5**	**17 801.1 e**	**17 967.7 e**	**18 153.5 e**	**18 504.6**	**19 642.2**	..
45-82	**Business sector services**	**17 459.1**	**17 798.1**	**17 719.9 e**	**17 890.3 e**	**18 061.8 e**	**18 362.1**	**19 489.4**	..
45-47	**Wholesale and retail trade; motor vehicle and motorcycle repairs**	**1 896.6**	**1 947.4**	**2 057.5 e**	**2 036.9 e**	**2 132.7 e**	**2 519.9**	**2 578.6**	..
49-53	**Transportation and storage**	**62.2**	**59.5**	**57.7 e**	**150.1 e**	**224.4 e**	**194.9**	**212.7**	..
55-56	**Accommodation and food service activities**	**0.5**	**4.4**	**5.3 e**	**3.9 e**	**2.5 e**	**2.3**	**1.5**	..
58-63	**Information and communication**	**3 864.9**	**4 213.0**	**4 556.0 e**	**4 681.9 e**	**4 664.1 e**	**4 812.7**	**5 547.4**	..
58-60	Publishing, audiovisual and broadcasting activities	1 013.7	1 142.7	1 240.3 e	1 272.0 e	1 316.2 e	1 426.2	1 489.8	..
58	Publishing activities	939.4	1 052.5	1 171.1 e	1 215.0 e	1 259.8 e	1 374.9	1 435.5	..
59-60	Motion picture, video and TV programme production; broadcasting activities	74.3	90.2	69.2 e	57.0 e	56.4 e	51.3	54.3	..
59	Motion picture, video and TV programme production; sound and music	63.5	80.1	62.1 e	53.4 e	55.4 e	50.8	51.3	..
60	Programming and broadcasting activities	10.7	10.0	7.1 e	3.5 e	1.0 e	0.5	3.0	..
61	Telecommunications	764.5	914.1	1 052.6 e	1 036.0 e	953.9 e	968.6	1 195.2	..
62-63	IT and other information services	2 086.8	2 156.2	2 263.2 e	2 374.0 e	2 394.1 e	2 417.9	2 862.4	..
62	Computer programming, consultancy and related activities	1 939.9	2 026.2	2 123.3 e	2 222.6 e	2 230.1 e	2 234.5	2 668.5	..
63	Information service activities	146.9	130.0	139.9 e	151.4 e	164.0 e	183.4	193.9	..
64-66	**Financial and insurance activities**	**335.6**	**324.2**	**317.6 e**	**300.0 e**	**302.9 e**	**360.9**	**434.4**	..
68-82	**Real estate; professional, scientific and technical; administrative and support**	**11 299.3**	**11 249.6**	**10 725.8 e**	**10 717.5 e**	**10 735.1 e**	**10 471.5**	**10 714.7**	..
68	Real estate activities	4.6	2.3	2.7 e	0.8 e	1.3 e	7.2	7.0	..
69-75x72	Professional, scientific and technical activities, except scientific R&D	6 443.7	6 344.7	5 963.8 e	5 967.8 e	5 946.6 e	5 645.3	5 706.5	..
72	Scientific research and development	4 675.4	4 698.5	4 509.7 e	4 524.5 e	4 608.2 e	4 619.9	4 751.8	..
77-82	Administrative and support service activities	175.5	204.1	249.5 e	224.3 e	179.0 e	199.1	249.4	..
84-99	Community, social and personal services	68.8	70.4	81.2 e	77.3 e	91.7 e	142.5	152.8	..
84-85	Public administration and defence; compulsory social security and education	5.0	4.8	5.9 e	6.3 e	8.3 e	15.6	30.7	..
86-88	Human health and social work activities	18.2	19.3	25.2 e	26.4 e	30.0 e	42.6	50.3	..
90-93	Arts, entertainment and recreation	4.4	7.4	8.3 e	2.7 e	5.5 e	21.2	12.1	..
94-99	Other services; household-employers; extraterritorial bodies	41.2	38.9	41.9 e	42.0 e	47.9 e	63.1	59.6	..

.. Not available; e Estimated value

Note: Detailed metadata at: *http://metalinks.oecd.org/anberd/20200813/2abe.*

FRANCE

R&D expenditure in industry by industry orientation, current prices
ISIC Rev. 4

Million USD PPP

		2011	2012	2013	2014	2015	2016	2017	2018
	TOTAL BUSINESS ENTERPRISE	**34 290.4**	**35 581.4**	**37 834.5**	**38 551.3**	**39 279.2**	**41 436.6**	**43 100.6**	..
01-03	**AGRICULTURE, FORESTRY AND FISHING**	**496.5**	**532.2**	**624.4**	**666.2 e**	**677.3 e**	**701.6**	**721.4**	..
05-09	**MINING AND QUARRYING**	**281.2**	**295.3**	**297.8**	**296.4 e**	**301.0 e**	**307.0**	**289.6**	..
10-33	**MANUFACTURING**	**26 216.5**	**26 762.7**	**27 918.4**	**28 177.1 e**	**28 568.3 e**	**29 884.8**	**30 578.6**	..
10-12	Food products, beverages and tobacco	721.6	734.8	811.9	835.6 e	832.3 e	843.7	839.8	..
13-15	Textiles, wearing apparel, leather and related products	166.2	149.4	172.9	188.3 e	195.8 e	206.4	213.6	..
13	Textiles	92.9	80.1	88.8	92.8 e	94.3 e	103.8	120.7	..
14	Wearing apparel	66.3	61.7	74.3	85.8 e	92.3 e	92.5	80.1	..
15	Leather and related products, footwear	7.0	7.6	9.7	9.7 e	9.3 e	10.2	12.8	..
16-18	Wood and paper products and printing	116.8	123.2	125.1	116.0 e	108.9 e	118.1	144.5	..
16	Wood and wood products, except furniture	34.3	35.4	34.4	32.8 e	33.5 e	38.0	44.3	..
17	Paper and paper products	73.7	75.3	78.5	70.9 e	60.7 e	60.8	74.7	..
18	Printing and reproduction of recorded media	8.8	12.3	12.2	12.3 e	14.6 e	19.4	25.6	..
19-23	Chemical, rubber, plastic, non-metallic mineral products	7 076.0	7 239.4	7 710.4	7 834.9 e	7 885.9 e	8 128.6	8 178.4	..
19	Coke and refined petroleum products	255.9	238.4	277.1	310.4 e	330.0 e	343.9	335.5	..
20-21	Chemical and pharmaceutical products	5 565.1	5 649.9	6 020.3	6 070.9 e	6 036.9 e	6 183.4	6 256.5	..
20	Chemicals and chemical products	1 831.9	1 940.2	2 185.4	2 255.7 e	2 243.3 e	2 294.8	2 350.3	..
21	Pharmaceuticals, medicinal, chemical and botanical products	3 733.2	3 709.7	3 834.8	3 815.2 e	3 793.7 e	3 888.7	3 906.2	..
22	Rubber and plastic products	887.7	979.6	992.7	1 014.9 e	1 079.8 e	1 145.7	1 107.3	..
23	Other non-metallic mineral products	367.3	371.4	420.4	438.7 e	439.2 e	455.6	479.0	..
24-25	Basic metals, metal products, except machinery and equipment	1 295.3	1 295.2	1 347.9	1 381.1 e	1 435.9 e	1 544.5	1 621.9	..
24	Basic metals	503.5	462.0	484.2	483.3 e	465.9 e	460.9	454.9	..
25	Fabricated metal products, except machinery and equipment	791.9	833.1	863.7	897.8 e	970.0 e	1 083.6	1 167.0	..
26-30	Computer, electronic, optical products; electrical machinery, transport equipment	16 321.0	16 722.7	17 239.0	17 328.7 e	17 642.8 e	18 565.5	19 059.7	..
26	Computer, electronic and optical products	4 586.2	4 781.8	5 062.8	5 065.3 e	5 052.7 e	5 251.2	5 442.4	..
27	Electrical equipment	1 141.1	1 179.1	1 256.3	1 263.7 e	1 275.9 e	1 388.9	1 568.0	..
28	Machinery and equipment n.e.c.	1 214.9	1 302.3	1 363.9	1 383.0 e	1 421.9 e	1 506.3	1 549.4	..
29	Motor vehicles, trailers and semi-trailers	5 592.0	5 324.8	4 877.1	4 756.8 e	5 034.2 e	5 480.0	5 556.1	..
30	Other transport equipment	3 786.8	4 134.8	4 678.9	4 859.9 e	4 858.1 e	4 939.1	4 943.8	..
31-33	Furniture; repair, installation of machinery and equipment	519.7	498.2	511.1	492.3 e	466.7 e	478.1	520.6	..
31	Furniture	28.2	23.1	27.5	27.4 e	23.3 e	22.2	27.4	..
32	Other manufacturing	491.5	475.1	483.6	465.0 e	443.5 e	455.9	493.3	..
33	Repair and installation of machinery and equipment	0.0	0.0	0.0	0.0 e	0.0 e	0.0	0.0	..
35-39	**ELECTRICITY, GAS, WATER AND WASTE MANAGEMENT**	**697.5**	**710.4**	**769.6**	**817.2 e**	**848.5 e**	**862.3**	**801.6**	..
35-36	Electricity, gas and water	652.6	664.2	716.8	761.9 e	794.5 e	810.3	753.4	..
37-39	Sewerage, waste management and remediation activities	44.9	46.2	52.7	55.3 e	54.0 e	52.0	48.2	..
41-43	**CONSTRUCTION**	**128.3**	**138.2**	**128.3**	**122.8 e**	**129.1 e**	**142.3**	**149.1**	..
45-99	**TOTAL SERVICES**	**6 470.5**	**7 142.6**	**8 096.0**	**8 471.6 e**	**8 755.0 e**	**9 538.5**	**10 560.3**	..
45-82	**Business sector services**	**6 434.9**	**7 084.8**	**8 008.3**	**8 366.2 e**	**8 640.0 e**	**9 411.9**	**10 421.3**	..
45-47	**Wholesale and retail trade; motor vehicle and motorcycle repairs**	**0.0**	**0.0**	**0.0**	**0.0 e**	**0.0 e**	**0.0**	**0.0**	..
49-53	**Transportation and storage**	**72.4**	**63.8**	**62.2**	**97.5 e**	**154.5 e**	**209.9**	**235.6**	..
55-56	**Accommodation and food service activities**	**0.0**	**0.0**	**0.0**	**0.0 e**	**0.0 e**	**0.0**	**0.0**	..
58-63	**Information and communication**	**4 233.4**	**4 523.6**	**5 015.1**	**5 203.1 e**	**5 327.6 e**	**5 657.5**	**5 984.1**	..
58-60	Publishing, audiovisual and broadcasting activities	1 063.4	1 132.3	1 302.1	1 410.6 e	1 511.6 e	1 684.3	1 868.3	..
58	Publishing activities	956.2	1 007.5	1 201.8	1 340.9 e	1 451.1 e	1 614.0	1 777.7	..
59-60	Motion picture, video and TV programme production; broadcasting activities	107.2	125.0	100.3	69.7 e	60.5 e	70.3	90.6	..
59	Motion picture, video and TV programme production; sound and music	53.9	67.6	51.5	36.0 e	35.9 e	41.9	44.3	..
60	Programming and broadcasting activities	53.3	57.3	48.7	33.7 e	24.7 e	28.4	46.3	..
61	Telecommunications	959.7	1 097.4	1 215.3	1 203.1 e	1 152.6 e	1 145.9	1 156.2	..
62-63	IT and other information services	2 210.3	2 294.0	2 497.8	2 589.4 e	2 663.3 e	2 827.3	2 959.6	..
62	Computer programming, consultancy and related activities	2 020.0	2 133.1	2 324.4	2 406.0 e	2 473.5 e	2 614.0	2 707.3	..
63	Information service activities	190.3	160.8	173.4	183.3 e	189.9 e	213.3	252.3	..
64-66	**Financial and insurance activities**	**231.9**	**235.8**	**246.3**	**240.7 e**	**235.8 e**	**254.5**	**293.2**	..
68-82	**Real estate; professional, scientific and technical; administrative and support**	**1 897.2**	**2 261.4**	**2 684.7**	**2 825.0 e**	**2 922.0 e**	**3 290.0**	**3 908.4**	..
68	Real estate activities	0.0	0.0	0.0	0.0 e	0.0 e	0.0	0.0	..
69-75x72	Professional, scientific and technical activities, except scientific R&D	1 275.4	1 486.6	1 817.4	1 893.9 e	1 893.4 e	2 103.6	2 566.9	..
72	Scientific research and development	501.8	621.6	699.1	771.9 e	876.9 e	1 021.0	1 141.1	..
77-82	Administrative and support service activities	119.9	153.3	168.2	159.1 e	151.7 e	165.4	200.4	..
84-99	Community, social and personal services	35.6	57.8	87.7	105.4 e	115.0 e	126.6	139.0	..
84-85	Public administration and defence; compulsory social security and education	3.1	4.3 e	4.1	3.4 e	4.3 e	10.6	23.8	..
86-88	Human health and social work activities	23.1	30.1	37.0	51.1 e	57.0 e	62.8	66.3	..
90-93	Arts, entertainment and recreation	2.5	3.6	7.3	13.4 e	16.2 e	16.8	14.6	..
94-99	Other services; household-employers; extraterritorial bodies	6.8	19.8 e	26.2	37.5 e	37.6 e	36.4	34.3	..

.. Not available; e Estimated value

Note: Detailed metadata at: *http://metalinks.oecd.org/anberd/20200813/2abe.*

FRANCE

R&D expenditure in industry by industry orientation, constant prices
ISIC Rev. 4

2010 USD PPP

		2011	2012	2013	2014	2015	2016	2017	2018
	TOTAL BUSINESS ENTERPRISE	**37 007.0**	**38 091.9**	**38 636.6**	**38 946.1**	**39 279.2**	**39 775.5**	**40 462.1**	..
01-03	**AGRICULTURE, FORESTRY AND FISHING**	**535.8**	**569.7**	**637.7**	**673.0 e**	**677.3 e**	**673.5**	**677.2**	..
05-09	**MINING AND QUARRYING**	**303.5**	**316.1**	**304.1**	**299.4 e**	**301.0 e**	**294.6**	**271.9**	..
10-33	**MANUFACTURING**	**28 293.5**	**28 651.0**	**28 510.3**	**28 465.6 e**	**28 568.3 e**	**28 686.8**	**28 706.7**	..
10-12	Food products, beverages and tobacco	778.8	786.7	829.1	844.2 e	832.3 e	809.8	788.4	..
13-15	Textiles, wearing apparel, leather and related products	179.3	159.9	176.5	190.2 e	195.8 e	198.1	200.5	..
13	Textiles	100.3	85.7	90.7	93.7 e	94.3 e	99.6	113.3	..
14	Wearing apparel	71.5	66.1	75.9	86.7 e	92.3 e	88.8	75.2	..
15	Leather and related products, footwear	7.5	8.1	9.9	9.8 e	9.3 e	9.8	12.0	..
16-18	Wood and paper products and printing	126.0	131.9	127.7	117.2 e	108.9 e	113.4	135.7	..
16	Wood and wood products, except furniture	37.0	37.9	35.1	33.1 e	33.5 e	36.4	41.6	..
17	Paper and paper products	79.5	80.6	80.1	71.6 e	60.7 e	58.4	70.1	..
18	Printing and reproduction of recorded media	9.5	13.2	12.5	12.5 e	14.6 e	18.6	24.0	..
19-23	Chemical, rubber, plastic, non-metallic mineral products	7 636.5	7 750.1	7 873.9	7 915.1 e	7 885.9 e	7 802.7	7 677.8	..
19	Coke and refined petroleum products	276.1	255.2	283.0	313.6 e	330.0 e	330.1	315.0	..
20-21	Chemical and pharmaceutical products	6 006.0	6 048.5	6 147.9	6 133.1 e	6 036.9 e	5 935.6	5 873.5	..
20	Chemicals and chemical products	1 977.0	2 077.1	2 231.8	2 278.8 e	2 243.3 e	2 202.8	2 206.5	..
21	Pharmaceuticals, medicinal, chemical and botanical products	4 028.9	3 971.4	3 916.1	3 854.3 e	3 793.7 e	3 732.8	3 667.1	..
22	Rubber and plastic products	958.0	1 048.7	1 013.7	1 025.3 e	1 079.8 e	1 099.7	1 039.5	..
23	Other non-metallic mineral products	396.4	397.6	429.3	443.2 e	439.2 e	437.3	449.7	..
24-25	Basic metals, metal products, except machinery and equipment	1 397.9	1 386.5	1 376.5	1 395.3 e	1 435.9 e	1 482.6	1 522.6	..
24	Basic metals	543.3	494.6	494.5	488.3 e	465.9 e	442.4	427.1	..
25	Fabricated metal products, except machinery and equipment	854.6	891.9	882.0	907.0 e	970.0 e	1 040.2	1 095.6	..
26-30	Computer, electronic, optical products; electrical machinery, transport equipment	17 614.0	17 902.6	17 604.5	17 506.2 e	17 642.8 e	17 821.2	17 892.9	..
26	Computer, electronic and optical products	4 949.6	5 119.2	5 170.2	5 117.2 e	5 052.7 e	5 040.7	5 109.3	..
27	Electrical equipment	1 231.5	1 262.3	1 283.0	1 276.6 e	1 275.9 e	1 333.3	1 472.0	..
28	Machinery and equipment n.e.c.	1 311.2	1 394.1	1 392.8	1 397.2 e	1 421.9 e	1 445.9	1 454.6	..
29	Motor vehicles, trailers and semi-trailers	6 035.0	5 700.5	4 980.5	4 805.5 e	5 034.2 e	5 260.3	5 215.9	..
30	Other transport equipment	4 086.8	4 426.5	4 778.1	4 909.7 e	4 858.1 e	4 741.1	4 641.2	..
31-33	Furniture; repair, installation of machinery and equipment	560.9	533.3	521.9	497.4 e	466.7 e	459.0	488.7	..
31	Furniture	30.5	24.7	28.1	27.7 e	23.3 e	21.3	25.7	..
32	Other manufacturing	530.4	508.6	493.8	469.7 e	443.5 e	437.6	463.1	..
33	Repair and installation of machinery and equipment	0.0	0.0	0.0	0.0 e	0.0 e	0.0	0.0	..
35-39	**ELECTRICITY, GAS, WATER AND WASTE MANAGEMENT**	**752.7**	**760.5**	**785.9**	**825.6 e**	**848.5 e**	**827.7**	**752.5**	..
35-36	Electricity, gas and water	704.3	711.1	732.0	769.7 e	794.5 e	777.8	707.3	..
37-39	Sewerage, waste management and remediation activities	48.5	49.5	53.9	55.9 e	54.0 e	49.9	45.2	..
41-43	**CONSTRUCTION**	**138.4**	**148.0**	**131.0**	**124.1 e**	**129.1 e**	**136.6**	**140.0**	..
45-99	**TOTAL SERVICES**	**6 983.1**	**7 646.5**	**8 267.7**	**8 558.4 e**	**8 755.0 e**	**9 156.1**	**9 913.8**	..
45-82	**Business sector services**	**6 944.7**	**7 584.7**	**8 178.1**	**8 451.9 e**	**8 640.0 e**	**9 034.6**	**9 783.3**	..
45-47	**Wholesale and retail trade; motor vehicle and motorcycle repairs**	**0.0**	**0.0**	**0.0**	**0.0 e**	**0.0 e**	**0.0**	**0.0**	..
49-53	**Transportation and storage**	**78.1**	**68.3**	**63.5**	**98.5 e**	**154.5 e**	**201.5**	**221.2**	..
55-56	**Accommodation and food service activities**	**0.0**	**0.0**	**0.0**	**0.0 e**	**0.0 e**	**0.0**	**0.0**	..
58-63	**Information and communication**	**4 568.8**	**4 842.8**	**5 121.5**	**5 256.4 e**	**5 327.6 e**	**5 430.7**	**5 617.7**	..
58-60	Publishing, audiovisual and broadcasting activities	1 147.7	1 212.2	1 329.7	1 425.0 e	1 511.6 e	1 616.8	1 753.9	..
58	Publishing activities	1 032.0	1 078.5	1 227.2	1 354.6 e	1 451.1 e	1 549.3	1 668.9	..
59-60	Motion picture, video and TV programme production; broadcasting activities	115.7	133.8	102.4	70.4 e	60.5 e	67.5	85.0	..
59	Motion picture, video and TV programme production; sound and music	58.1	72.4	52.6	36.4 e	35.9 e	40.2	41.6	..
60	Programming and broadcasting activities	57.6	61.4	49.7	34.0 e	24.7 e	27.3	43.4	..
61	Telecommunications	1 035.8	1 174.8	1 241.1	1 215.5 e	1 152.6 e	1 099.9	1 085.4	..
62-63	IT and other information services	2 385.4	2 455.8	2 550.7	2 615.9 e	2 663.3 e	2 714.0	2 778.4	..
62	Computer programming, consultancy and related activities	2 180.0	2 283.6	2 373.7	2 430.7 e	2 473.5 e	2 509.3	2 541.6	..
63	Information service activities	205.4	172.2	177.0	185.2 e	189.9 e	204.7	236.8	..
64-66	**Financial and insurance activities**	**250.3**	**252.5**	**251.5**	**243.1 e**	**235.8 e**	**244.3**	**275.2**	..
68-82	**Real estate; professional, scientific and technical; administrative and support**	**2 047.5**	**2 421.0**	**2 741.6**	**2 853.9 e**	**2 922.0 e**	**3 158.1**	**3 669.2**	..
68	Real estate activities	0.0	0.0	0.0	0.0 e	0.0 e	0.0	0.0	..
69-75x72	Professional, scientific and technical activities, except scientific R&D	1 376.4	1 591.4	1 856.0	1 913.3 e	1 893.4 e	2 019.2	2 409.8	..
72	Scientific research and development	541.6	665.4	713.9	779.8 e	876.9 e	980.1	1 071.3	..
77-82	Administrative and support service activities	129.4	164.1	171.7	160.8 e	151.7 e	158.7	188.1	..
84-99	Community, social and personal services	38.4	61.9	89.5	106.5 e	115.0 e	121.6	130.5	..
84-85	Public administration and defence; compulsory social security and education	3.4	4.6 e	4.2	3.4 e	4.3 e	10.1	22.4	..
86-88	Human health and social work activities	24.9	32.2	37.7	51.6 e	57.0 e	60.3	62.2	..
90-93	Arts, entertainment and recreation	2.7	3.8	7.4	13.5 e	16.2 e	16.1	13.7	..
94-99	Other services; household-employers; extraterritorial bodies	7.4	21.2 e	26.8	37.9 e	37.6 e	35.0	32.2	..

.. Not available; e Estimated value

Note: Detailed metadata at: *http://metalinks.oecd.org/anberd/20200813/2abe.*

R&D expenditure in industry by main activity of the enterprise, current prices
ISIC Rev. 4

Million USD PPP

		2011	2012	2013	2014	2015	2016	2017	2018
	TOTAL BUSINESS ENTERPRISE	**64 758.0**	**68 327.0**	**69 136.9**	**74 123.8**	**78 353.2**	**83 469.3**	**92 885.2**	..
01-03	**AGRICULTURE, FORESTRY AND FISHING**	**159.9**	**175.7**	**185.6**	**178.0**	**192.8**	**210.2**	**227.9**	..
05-09	**MINING AND QUARRYING**	**12.7**	**13.6**	**19.9**	**16.1**	**27.0**	**27.2**	**33.5**	..
10-33	**MANUFACTURING**	**55 447.2**	**58 854.9**	**59 434.2**	**64 351.7**	**66 733.7**	**70 891.8**	**78 985.2**	..
10-12	Food products, beverages and tobacco	390.5	400.0	406.2	414.1	408.3	416.1	428.9	..
13-15	Textiles, wearing apparel, leather and related products	151.1	155.4	145.8	149.6	117.0	125.6	137.3	..
13	Textiles	78.7	81.8	72.5	72.0	68.1	77.0 e	75.3	..
14	Wearing apparel	65.4	66.3	66.1	70.1	43.7	43.1 e	55.2	..
15	Leather and related products, footwear	7.0	7.2	7.2	7.4	5.1	5.4 e	6.6	..
16-18	Wood and paper products and printing	231.6	218.4	293.0	291.1	276.4	304.9	334.7	..
16	Wood and wood products, except furniture	28.7	25.2	25.7	25.4	25.7	28.2 e	29.2	..
17	Paper and paper products	77.7	73.8	130.2	133.7	126.0	135.4 e	141.9	..
18	Printing and reproduction of recorded media	125.3	119.4	137.1	132.0	123.4	141.3 e	163.7	..
19-23	Chemical, rubber, plastic, non-metallic mineral products	11 011.9	11 337.5	11 328.3	11 831.8	11 922.9	13 386.0	13 920.4	..
19	Coke and refined petroleum products	119.6	121.9	120.9	154.6	173.5	187.6	195.1	..
20-21	Chemical and pharmaceutical products	9 339.5	9 638.4	9 578.8	9 966.1	9 952.3	11 201.4	11 742.4	..
20	Chemicals and chemical products	4 179.7	4 440.5	4 319.4	4 719.1	4 866.9	5 199.0	5 489.2	..
21	Pharmaceuticals, medicinal, chemical and botanical products	5 159.8	5 197.9	5 259.4	5 247.0	5 085.4	6 002.4	6 253.2	..
22	Rubber and plastic products	1 196.1	1 214.4	1 251.8	1 318.2	1 398.6	1 559.8	1 552.1	..
23	Other non-metallic mineral products	356.8	362.8	376.8	392.9	398.5	437.2	430.8	..
24-25	Basic metals, metal products, except machinery and equipment	1 574.8	1 644.5	1 643.4	1 670.6	1 741.8	1 836.9	2 024.4	..
24	Basic metals	654.5	688.1	683.9	695.4	682.6	716.6	780.4	..
25	Fabricated metal products, except machinery and equipment	920.3	956.4	959.5	975.2	1 059.2	1 120.3	1 244.1	..
26-30	Computer, electronic, optical products; electrical machinery, transport equipment	40 548.1	43 633.5	43 967.2	48 216.6	49 779.3	52 481.5	60 737.1	..
26	Computer, electronic and optical products	8 321.4	9 389.4	9 476.1	9 762.4	9 693.9	10 146.5	10 450.7	..
27	Electrical equipment	2 030.7	2 200.5	2 749.3	2 824.3	2 891.1	3 052.9	3 635.2	..
28	Machinery and equipment n.e.c.	6 215.6	6 583.2	6 954.5	7 348.6	7 017.5	7 509.8	9 609.9	..
29	Motor vehicles, trailers and semi-trailers	20 681.6	22 052.6	22 183.0	25 577.9	27 594.3	29 081.3	34 643.7	..
30	Other transport equipment	3 298.8	3 408.0	2 604.5	2 690.1	2 580.0	2 691.2	2 397.8	..
31-33	Furniture; repair, installation of machinery and equipment	1 539.2	1 465.7	1 650.3	1 778.0	2 488.7	2 341.0	1 402.2	..
31	Furniture	52.9	50.7	48.3	50.7	45.0	43.4	45.5	..
32	Other manufacturing	697.3	667.3	786.0	840.9	804.7	773.9	1 085.9	..
33	Repair and installation of machinery and equipment	789.0	747.8	816.0	886.4	1 639.0	1 523.6	270.7	..
35-39	**ELECTRICITY, GAS, WATER AND WASTE MANAGEMENT**	**250.3**	**236.4**	**269.1**	**254.2**	**207.0**	**205.5**	**238.3**	..
35-36	Electricity, gas and water	235.4	224.3	251.6	237.3	192.8	191.0 e	221.5	..
37-39	Sewerage, waste management and remediation activities	14.8	12.1	17.6	16.9	14.1	14.5 e	17.0	..
41-43	**CONSTRUCTION**	**83.4**	**89.7**	**103.3**	**104.0**	**96.4**	**106.7**	**114.2**	..
45-99	**TOTAL SERVICES**	**8 804.6**	**8 956.7**	**9 124.9**	**9 219.6**	**11 096.4**	**12 027.9**	**13 286.0**	..
45-82	**Business sector services**	**8 773.6**	**8 925.3**	**9 087.6**	**9 183.1**	**11 055.2**	**11 988.6**	**13 280.6**	..
45-47	Wholesale and retail trade; motor vehicle and motorcycle repairs	331.7	360.2	333.6	333.8	339.4	310.8	598.7	..
49-53	**Transportation and storage**	**137.7**	**156.0**	**118.2**	**123.7**	**172.3**	**145.7**	**159.1**	..
55-56	**Accommodation and food service activities**	**0.5**	**0.5**	**0.3**	**0.3**	**0.0**	**0.4**	**0.3**	..
58-63	**Information and communication**	**3 790.4**	**4 033.4**	**4 092.0**	**4 199.4**	**4 094.3**	**4 425.4**	**4 563.7**	..
58-60	Publishing, audiovisual and broadcasting activities	53.5	53.4	34.5	35.1	38.6	44.0 e	46.2	..
58	Publishing activities	..	..	..	..	..	..	43.8	..
59-60	Motion picture, video and TV programme production; broadcasting activities	..	..	..	..	..	..	2.4	..
59	Motion picture, video and TV programme production; sound and music	..	..	..	..	..	..	..	..
60	Programming and broadcasting activities	..	..	..	..	..	..	..	..
61	Telecommunications	723.8	789.0	482.7	495.6	257.1	146.7 e	175.9	..
62-63	IT and other information services	3 013.0	3 189.7	3 574.8	3 668.7	3 798.6	4 234.6 e	4 341.6	..
62	Computer programming, consultancy and related activities	2 893.6	3 065.2	3 449.0	3 540.3	3 668.8	4 095.8 e	4 205.9	..
63	Information service activities	119.4	124.5	125.8	128.4	129.8	138.8 e	135.7	..
64-66	**Financial and insurance activities**	**330.8**	**336.9**	**374.7**	**413.0**	**365.1**	**387.4**	**335.4**	..
68-82	**Real estate; professional, scientific and technical; administrative and support**	**4 182.6**	**4 038.3**	**4 168.8**	**4 112.8**	**6 084.2**	**6 718.9**	**7 623.3**	..
68	Real estate activities	1.0	1.0	0.9	0.9	1.3	1.1	2.0	..
69-75x72	Professional, scientific and technical activities, except scientific R&D	1 967.2	1 837.5	1 956.5	1 808.0	3 233.0	3 660.1	3 610.5	..
72	Scientific research and development	2 168.8	2 150.7	2 174.7	2 267.4	2 789.5	3 002.3	3 942.8	..
77-82	Administrative and support service activities	45.6	49.0	36.7	36.5	60.4	55.4	67.9	..
84-99	Community, social and personal services	30.9	31.4	37.3	36.5	41.1	39.3	5.4	..
84-85	Public administration and defence; compulsory social security and education	2.8	2.8	3.5	3.3	1.3	1.7	0.0	..
86-88	Human health and social work activities	4.6	4.7	8.1	8.2	10.3	9.8	0.0	..
90-93	Arts, entertainment and recreation	1.6	1.7	4.5	4.4	2.6	2.8	0.0	..
94-99	Other services; household-employers; extraterritorial bodies	21.9	22.2	21.2	20.7	25.7	25.1	5.4	..

.. Not available; e Estimated value

Note: Detailed metadata at: http://metalinks.oecd.org/anberd/20200813/2abe.

GERMANY

R&D expenditure in industry by main activity of the enterprise, constant prices
ISIC Rev. 4

2010 USD PPP

		2011	2012	2013	2014	2015	2016	2017	2018
	TOTAL BUSINESS ENTERPRISE	**70 420.2**	**73 067.8**	**71 358.7**	**74 540.5**	**78 353.2**	**79 822.7**	**86 490.9**	..
01-03	**AGRICULTURE, FORESTRY AND FISHING**	173.9	187.9	191.6	179.0	192.8	201.0	212.2	..
05-09	**MINING AND QUARRYING**	13.8	14.5	20.5	16.2	27.0	26.0	31.2	..
10-33	**MANUFACTURING**	60 295.3	62 938.6	61 344.2	64 713.5	66 733.7	67 794.7	73 547.8	..
10-12	Food products, beverages and tobacco	424.6	427.8	419.2	416.4	408.3	397.9	399.3	..
13-15	Textiles, wearing apparel, leather and related products	164.3	166.1	150.5	150.4	117.0	120.1	127.9	..
13	Textiles	85.6	87.5	74.9	72.5	68.1	73.7 e	70.2	..
14	Wearing apparel	71.1	70.9	68.2	70.5	43.7	41.2 e	51.4	..
15	Leather and related products, footwear	7.6	7.7	7.5	7.5	5.1	5.2 e	6.2	..
16-18	Wood and paper products and printing	251.9	233.5	302.4	292.7	276.4	291.6	311.7	..
16	Wood and wood products, except furniture	31.2	26.9	26.5	25.5	25.7	27.0 e	27.2	..
17	Paper and paper products	84.5	78.9	134.4	134.4	126.0	129.5 e	132.1	..
18	Printing and reproduction of recorded media	136.2	127.7	141.5	132.7	123.4	135.1 e	152.4	..
19-23	Chemical, rubber, plastic, non-metallic mineral products	11 974.7	12 124.1	11 692.4	11 898.3	11 922.9	12 801.2	12 962.1	..
19	Coke and refined petroleum products	130.0	130.4	124.8	155.5	173.5	179.4	181.7	..
20-21	Chemical and pharmaceutical products	10 156.1	10 307.2	9 886.6	10 022.1	9 952.3	10 712.0	10 934.1	..
20	Chemicals and chemical products	4 545.2	4 748.6	4 458.2	4 745.6	4 866.9	4 971.9	5 111.3	..
21	Pharmaceuticals, medicinal, chemical and botanical products	5 610.9	5 558.5	5 428.4	5 276.5	5 085.4	5 740.2	5 822.7	..
22	Rubber and plastic products	1 300.7	1 298.6	1 292.1	1 325.6	1 398.6	1 491.6	1 445.2	..
23	Other non-metallic mineral products	388.0	388.0	388.9	395.1	398.5	418.1	401.1	..
24-25	Basic metals, metal products, except machinery and equipment	1 712.5	1 758.6	1 696.2	1 680.0	1 741.8	1 756.6	1 885.0	..
24	Basic metals	711.7	735.8	705.9	699.3	682.6	685.3	726.6	..
25	Fabricated metal products, except machinery and equipment	1 000.8	1 022.7	990.3	980.7	1 059.2	1 071.3	1 158.4	..
26-30	Computer, electronic, optical products; electrical machinery, transport equipment	44 093.5	46 661.0	45 380.1	48 487.7	49 779.3	50 188.7	56 555.9	..
26	Computer, electronic and optical products	9 049.0	10 040.9	9 780.6	9 817.3	9 693.9	9 703.2	9 731.3	..
27	Electrical equipment	2 208.3	2 353.1	2 837.6	2 840.2	2 891.1	2 919.6	3 385.0	..
28	Machinery and equipment n.e.c.	6 759.1	7 040.0	7 177.9	7 389.9	7 017.5	7 181.7	8 948.3	..
29	Motor vehicles, trailers and semi-trailers	22 489.9	23 582.7	22 895.8	25 721.7	27 594.3	27 810.8	32 258.8	..
30	Other transport equipment	3 587.2	3 644.4	2 688.2	2 705.2	2 580.0	2 573.6	2 232.7	..
31-33	Furniture; repair, installation of machinery and equipment	1 673.7	1 567.4	1 703.3	1 788.0	2 488.7	2 238.7	1 305.7	..
31	Furniture	57.5	54.2	49.8	51.0	45.0	41.5	42.4	..
32	Other manufacturing	758.3	713.6	811.3	845.6	804.7	740.1	1 011.2	..
33	Repair and installation of machinery and equipment	858.0	799.7	842.2	891.4	1 639.0	1 457.1	252.1	..
35-39	**ELECTRICITY, GAS, WATER AND WASTE MANAGEMENT**	272.2	252.8	277.8	255.7	207.0	196.6	221.9	..
35-36	Electricity, gas and water	256.0	239.9	259.6	238.7	192.8	182.7 e	206.2	..
37-39	Sewerage, waste management and remediation activities	16.1	12.9	18.1	17.0	14.1	13.9 e	15.8	..
41-43	**CONSTRUCTION**	90.7	95.9	106.6	104.6	96.4	102.0	106.4	..
45-99	**TOTAL SERVICES**	9 574.4	9 578.1	9 418.1	9 271.5	11 096.4	11 502.4	12 371.4	..
45-82	**Business sector services**	9 540.7	9 544.6	9 379.6	9 234.7	11 055.2	11 464.8	12 366.3	..
45-47	**Wholesale and retail trade; motor vehicle and motorcycle repairs**	360.7	385.2	344.4	335.7	339.4	297.2	557.5	..
49-53	**Transportation and storage**	149.7	166.8	122.0	124.4	172.3	139.4	148.1	..
55-56	**Accommodation and food service activities**	0.6	0.5	0.3	0.3	0.0	0.4	0.3	..
58-63	**Information and communication**	4 121.8	4 313.3	4 223.5	4 223.0	4 094.3	4 232.0	4 249.5	..
58-60	Publishing, audiovisual and broadcasting activities	58.2	57.1	35.6	35.3	38.6	42.1 e	43.0	..
58	Publishing activities	..	..	..	..	..	..	40.7	..
59-60	Motion picture, video and TV programme production; broadcasting activities	..	..	..	..	..	..	2.3	..
59	Motion picture, video and TV programme production; sound and music	..	..	..	..	..	..	..	..
60	Programming and broadcasting activities	..	..	..	..	..	..	..	..
61	Telecommunications	787.1	843.7	498.2	498.4	257.1	140.3 e	163.8	..
62-63	IT and other information services	3 276.5	3 411.0	3 689.7	3 689.3	3 798.6	4 049.6 e	4 042.7	..
62	Computer programming, consultancy and related activities	3 146.6	3 277.9	3 559.8	3 560.2	3 668.8	3 916.9 e	3 916.3	..
63	Information service activities	129.9	133.1	129.9	129.1	129.8	132.7 e	126.4	..
64-66	**Financial and insurance activities**	359.7	360.2	386.7	415.4	365.1	370.5	312.3	..
68-82	**Real estate; professional, scientific and technical; administrative and support**	4 548.3	4 318.4	4 302.7	4 135.9	6 084.2	6 425.4	7 098.5	..
68	Real estate activities	1.1	1.1	0.9	0.9	1.3	1.0	1.9	..
69-75x72	Professional, scientific and technical activities, except scientific R&D	2 139.2	1 965.0	2 019.4	1 818.1	3 233.0	3 500.2	3 671.9	..
72	Scientific research and development	2 358.4	2 299.9	2 244.6	2 280.2	2 789.5	2 871.2	3 671.4	..
77-82	Administrative and support service activities	49.6	52.4	37.8	36.7	60.4	53.0	63.2	..
84-99	Community, social and personal services	33.6	33.6	38.5	36.7	41.1	37.6	5.0	..
84-85	Public administration and defence; compulsory social security and education	3.0	3.0	3.6	3.3	1.3	1.7	0.0	..
86-88	Human health and social work activities	5.0	5.0	8.4	8.2	10.3	9.4	0.0	..
90-93	Arts, entertainment and recreation	1.8	1.8	4.7	4.4	2.6	2.7	0.0	..
94-99	Other services; household-employers; extraterritorial bodies	23.9	23.8	21.8	20.8	25.7	24.0	5.0	..

.. Not available; e Estimated value

Note: Detailed metadata at: *http://metalinks.oecd.org/anberd/20200813/2abe*.

GREECE

R&D expenditure in industry by main activity of the enterprise, current prices
ISIC Rev. 4

Million USD PPP

		2011	2012	2013	2014	2015	2016	2017	2018
	TOTAL BUSINESS ENTERPRISE	**681.3**	**669.8**	**774.1**	**825.3**	**922.3**	**1 257.8**	**1 725.6**	..
01-03	**AGRICULTURE, FORESTRY AND FISHING**	**2.0**	**1.5 e**	**1.5**	**2.1 e**	**2.9**	**4.0 e**	**5.2**	..
05-09	**MINING AND QUARRYING**	**0.5**	**2.3 e**	**1.1**	**0.0 e**	**2.1**	**34.6 e**	**85.3**	..
10-33	**MANUFACTURING**	**267.2**	**258.2 e**	**278.5**	**251.3 e**	**245.9**	**345.8 e**	**509.8**	..
10-12	Food products, beverages and tobacco	23.7	36.6 e	47.8 e	40.2 e	32.0	45.4 e	73.0	..
13-15	Textiles, wearing apparel, leather and related products	1.7	1.2 e	1.5	3.0 e	4.5	5.1 e	4.9	..
13	Textiles	..	..	..	..	..	..	4.7	..
14	Wearing apparel	..	..	..	..	..	..	0.1	..
15	Leather and related products, footwear	..	..	..	..	..	..	0.0	..
16-18	Wood and paper products and printing	14.5	7.4 e	3.3	2.6 e	6.3	14.2 e	24.6	..
16	Wood and wood products, except furniture	..	..	..	..	..	..	0.3	..
17	Paper and paper products	..	..	..	..	..	..	19.9	..
18	Printing and reproduction of recorded media	..	..	..	..	..	..	4.4	..
19-23	Chemical, rubber, plastic, non-metallic mineral products	122.6	120.8 e	129.5	110.5 e	103.5	153.5 e	239.3	..
19	Coke and refined petroleum products	7.2 e	8.2 e	7.8 e	3.5 e	10.4	42.5 e	91.9	..
20-21	Chemical and pharmaceutical products	107.2	104.8 e	113.2	98.7 e	84.3	98.8 e	130.1	..
20	Chemicals and chemical products	22.7	20.3 e	20.0	15.8 e	15.0	25.1 e	42.1	..
21	Pharmaceuticals, medicinal, chemical and botanical products	84.6	84.5 e	93.2	82.9 e	69.3	73.7 e	88.0	..
22	Rubber and plastic products	3.0	3.3 e	3.5	2.3 e	1.5	3.3 e	6.8	..
23	Other non-metallic mineral products	5.2	4.4 e	5.0	6.0 e	7.3	8.9 e	10.5	..
24-25	Basic metals, metal products, except machinery and equipment	35.5	37.9 e	44.5	43.5 e	44.7	61.1 e	86.7	..
24	Basic metals	17.7	16.5 e	17.4	15.8 e	15.1	19.6 e	27.3	..
25	Fabricated metal products, except machinery and equipment	17.8	21.4 e	27.0	27.7 e	29.6	41.5 e	59.5	..
26-30	Computer, electronic, optical products; electrical machinery, transport equipment	67.3	52.7 e	49.9	48.3 e	50.8	61.8 e	76.6	..
26	Computer, electronic and optical products	32.3	25.4 e	23.2	20.1 e	19.6	25.3 e	34.5	..
27	Electrical equipment	14.9	12.2 e	11.8	11.1 e	11.7	15.4 e	21.0	..
28	Machinery and equipment n.e.c.	10.4	9.4 e	10.4	11.1 e	12.1	14.7 e	18.0	..
29	Motor vehicles, trailers and semi-trailers	0.6 e	0.4 e	0.3	0.0 e	0.0	0.5 e	1.3	..
30	Other transport equipment	9.0 e	5.3 e	4.2	6.0 e	7.5	5.9 e	1.8	..
31-33	Furniture; repair, installation of machinery and equipment	2.0	1.7 e	2.1	3.2 e	4.1	4.6 e	4.7	..
31	Furniture	..	..	..	..	..	..	0.6	..
32	Other manufacturing	..	..	..	..	..	..	4.1	..
33	Repair and installation of machinery and equipment	..	..	..	..	..	..	0.0	..
35-39	**ELECTRICITY, GAS, WATER AND WASTE MANAGEMENT**	**8.8**	**8.1 e**	**9.7**	**12.4 e**	**16.7**	**24.2 e**	**33.5**	..
35-36	Electricity, gas and water	7.4	6.9 e	8.4	10.9 e	15.0	22.6 e	32.1	..
37-39	Sewerage, waste management and remediation activities	1.4	1.2 e	1.3	1.5 e	1.6	1.6 e	1.4	..
41-43	**CONSTRUCTION**	**7.5**	**5.0 e**	**3.8**	**3.2 e**	**5.1**	**11.1 e**	**19.6**	..
45-99	**TOTAL SERVICES**	**395.2**	**394.7 e**	**479.5**	**556.4 e**	**649.7**	**838.1 e**	**1 072.2**	..
45-82	**Business sector services**	**392.4**	**391.2 e**	**475.4**	**553.1 e**	**645.3**	**827.2 e**	**1 051.1**	..
45-47	**Wholesale and retail trade; motor vehicle and motorcycle repairs**	**41.9**	**65.7 e**	**103.0**	**131.6 e**	**147.9**	**159.9 e**	**166.0**	..
49-53	**Transportation and storage**	**0.3**	**7.2 e**	**7.0**	**0.0 e**	**4.0**	**64.9 e**	**161.8**	..
55-56	**Accommodation and food service activities**	**0.1 e**	**0.6 e**	**1.1**	**1.2 e**	**1.0 e**	**0.6 e**	**0.1**	..
58-63	**Information and communication**	**98.1**	**100.0 e**	**115.7**	**115.5 e**	**126.4**	**178.2 e**	**254.9**	..
58-60	Publishing, audiovisual and broadcasting activities	0.1	6.6 e	11.3	9.3 e	4.9	3.7 e	4.7	..
58	Publishing activities	0.1	5.9 e	10.2	8.5 e	4.4 e	2.8 e	2.8	..
59-60	Motion picture, video and TV programme production; broadcasting activities	0.0	0.7 e	1.1	0.8 e	0.5 e	0.9 e	1.9	..
59	Motion picture, video and TV programme production; sound and music	..	..	..	..	..	..	1.2	..
60	Programming and broadcasting activities	..	..	..	..	..	..	0.8	..
61	Telecommunications	41.0	27.2 e	17.9	9.0 e	14.1	43.1 e	87.7	..
62-63	IT and other information services	56.9	66.2 e	86.5	97.2 e	107.4	131.4 e	162.5	..
62	Computer programming, consultancy and related activities	52.6	63.8 e	85.1	96.0 e	105.6	129.0 e	159.4	..
63	Information service activities	4.3	2.4 e	1.4	1.3 e	1.8	2.4 e	3.1	..
64-66	**Financial and insurance activities**	**143.7**	**131.2 e**	**163.5**	**217.9 e**	**269.3**	**304.7 e**	**322.0**	..
68-82	**Real estate; professional, scientific and technical; administrative and support**	**108.4**	**86.5 e**	**85.1**	**86.8 e**	**96.7**	**118.9 e**	**146.3**	..
68	Real estate activities	0.0 e	0.0 e	0.0	0.0 e	0.0 e	0.0 e	0.0	..
69-75x72	Professional, scientific and technical activities, except scientific R&D	48.2	31.9 e	24.3	21.0 e	25.3	37.7 e	54.4	..
72	Scientific research and development	59.5	53.7 e	60.1	65.7 e	71.3	79.7 e	87.9	..
77-82	Administrative and support service activities	0.7 e	0.8 e	0.7	0.1 e	0.0 e	1.5 e	4.1	..
84-99	Community, social and personal services	2.8	3.6 e	4.1	3.3 e	4.4	10.9 e	21.1	..
84-85	Public administration and defence; compulsory social security and education	1.7	2.0 e	2.0	1.1 e	1.7	6.2 e	13.4	..
86-88	Human health and social work activities	0.5	1.1 e	1.8	2.2 e	2.7	3.9 e	5.5	..
90-93	Arts, entertainment and recreation	0.0	0.0 e	0.0 e	0.0 e	0.0 e	0.1 e	0.2	..
94-99	Other services; household-employers; extraterritorial bodies	0.6	0.5 e	0.3 e	0.0 e	0.0 e	0.8 e	2.0	..

.. Not available; e Estimated value

Note: Detailed metadata at: *http://metalinks.oecd.org/anberd/20200813/2abe.*

R&D expenditure in industry by main activity of the enterprise, constant prices
ISIC Rev. 4

2010 USD PPP

		2011	2012	2013	2014	2015	2016	2017	2018
	TOTAL BUSINESS ENTERPRISE	**759.4**	**719.5**	**785.1**	**825.5**	**922.3**	**1 218.9**	**1 626.7**	..
01-03	**AGRICULTURE, FORESTRY AND FISHING**	**2.3**	**1.6 e**	**1.5**	**2.1 e**	**2.9**	**3.9 e**	**4.9**	..
05-09	**MINING AND QUARRYING**	**0.6**	**2.5 e**	**1.1**	**0.0 e**	**2.1**	**33.6 e**	**80.4**	..
10-33	**MANUFACTURING**	**297.9**	**277.3 e**	**282.5**	**251.3 e**	**245.9**	**335.1 e**	**480.6**	..
10-12	Food products, beverages and tobacco	26.4	39.4 e	48.5 e	40.2 e	32.0	44.0 e	68.8	..
13-15	Textiles, wearing apparel, leather and related products	1.9	1.2 e	1.5	3.0 e	4.5	4.9 e	4.6	..
13	Textiles	..	..	..	..	..	..	4.5	..
14	Wearing apparel	..	..	..	..	..	..	0.1	..
15	Leather and related products, footwear	..	..	..	..	..	..	0.0	..
16-18	Wood and paper products and printing	16.1	7.9 e	3.3	2.6 e	6.3	13.8 e	23.2	..
16	Wood and wood products, except furniture	..	..	..	..	..	..	0.3	..
17	Paper and paper products	..	..	..	..	..	..	18.8	..
18	Printing and reproduction of recorded media	..	..	..	..	..	..	4.1	..
19-23	Chemical, rubber, plastic, non-metallic mineral products	136.7	129.7 e	131.3	110.5 e	103.5	148.8 e	225.6	..
19	Coke and refined petroleum products	8.0 e	8.8 e	7.9 e	3.5 e	10.4	41.2 e	86.6	..
20-21	Chemical and pharmaceutical products	119.5	112.6 e	114.8	98.7 e	84.3	95.7 e	122.6	..
20	Chemicals and chemical products	25.3	21.9 e	20.3	15.8 e	15.0	24.3 e	39.7	..
21	Pharmaceuticals, medicinal, chemical and botanical products	94.3	90.7 e	94.5	82.9 e	69.3	71.4 e	82.9	..
22	Rubber and plastic products	3.3	3.6 e	3.6	2.3 e	1.5	3.2 e	6.4	..
23	Other non-metallic mineral products	5.8	4.8 e	5.0	6.0 e	7.3	8.6 e	9.9	..
24-25	Basic metals, metal products, except machinery and equipment	39.6	40.7 e	45.1	43.5 e	44.7	59.2 e	81.8	..
24	Basic metals	19.8	17.7 e	17.7	15.8 e	15.1	19.0 e	25.7	..
25	Fabricated metal products, except machinery and equipment	19.9	22.9 e	27.4	27.7 e	29.6	40.2 e	56.1	..
26-30	Computer, electronic, optical products; electrical machinery, transport equipment	75.0	56.6 e	50.6	48.3 e	50.8	59.9 e	72.2	..
26	Computer, electronic and optical products	36.0	27.3 e	23.5	20.1 e	19.6	24.5 e	32.6	..
27	Electrical equipment	16.6	13.1 e	12.0	11.1 e	11.7	15.0 e	19.8	..
28	Machinery and equipment n.e.c.	11.6	10.1 e	10.5	11.1 e	12.1	14.2 e	17.0	..
29	Motor vehicles, trailers and semi-trailers	0.7 e	0.5 e	0.3	0.0 e	0.0	0.5 e	1.2	..
30	Other transport equipment	10.1 e	5.6 e	4.3	6.0 e	7.5	5.7 e	1.7	..
31-33	Furniture; repair, installation of machinery and equipment	2.2	1.8 e	2.2	3.2 e	4.1	4.5 e	4.5	..
31	Furniture	..	..	..	..	..	..	0.6	..
32	Other manufacturing	..	..	..	..	..	..	3.9	..
33	Repair and installation of machinery and equipment	..	..	..	..	..	..	0.0	..
35-39	**ELECTRICITY, GAS, WATER AND WASTE MANAGEMENT**	**9.8**	**8.7 e**	**9.8**	**12.4 e**	**16.7**	**23.4 e**	**31.6**	..
35-36	Electricity, gas and water	8.2	7.4 e	8.5	10.9 e	15.0	21.9 e	30.3	..
37-39	Sewerage, waste management and remediation activities	1.5	1.3 e	1.3	1.5 e	1.6	1.5 e	1.3	..
41-43	**CONSTRUCTION**	**8.4**	**5.4 e**	**3.8**	**3.2 e**	**5.1**	**10.7 e**	**18.5**	..
45-99	**TOTAL SERVICES**	**440.5**	**424.0 e**	**486.4**	**556.5 e**	**649.7**	**812.2 e**	**1 010.8**	..
45-82	**Business sector services**	**437.4**	**420.1 e**	**482.2**	**553.2 e**	**645.3**	**801.6 e**	**990.9**	..
45-47	**Wholesale and retail trade; motor vehicle and motorcycle repairs**	**46.7**	**70.5 e**	**104.5**	**131.7 e**	**147.9**	**155.0 e**	**156.5**	..
49-53	**Transportation and storage**	**0.3**	**7.7 e**	**7.1**	**0.0 e**	**4.0**	**62.9 e**	**152.5**	..
55-56	**Accommodation and food service activities**	**0.1 e**	**0.6 e**	**1.1**	**1.2 e**	**1.0 e**	**0.6 e**	**0.1**	..
58-63	**Information and communication**	**109.3**	**107.4 e**	**117.3**	**115.5 e**	**126.4**	**172.7 e**	**240.3**	..
58-60	Publishing, audiovisual and broadcasting activities	0.2	7.1 e	11.5	9.3 e	4.9	3.6 e	4.5	..
58	Publishing activities	0.2	6.4 e	10.3	8.5 e	4.4	2.7 e	2.6	..
59-60	Motion picture, video and TV programme production; broadcasting activities	0.0	0.7 e	1.2	0.8 e	0.5 e	0.9 e	1.8	..
59	Motion picture, video and TV programme production; sound and music	..	..	..	..	..	..	1.1	..
60	Programming and broadcasting activities	..	..	..	..	..	..	0.7	..
61	Telecommunications	45.7	29.2 e	18.1	9.0 e	14.1	41.7 e	82.6	..
62-63	IT and other information services	63.5	71.1 e	87.7	97.3 e	107.4	127.3 e	153.2	..
62	Computer programming, consultancy and related activities	58.7	68.5 e	86.3	96.0 e	105.6	125.0 e	150.3	..
63	Information service activities	4.8	2.6 e	1.4	1.3 e	1.8	2.4 e	2.9	..
64-66	**Financial and insurance activities**	**160.1**	**141.0 e**	**165.8**	**217.9 e**	**269.3**	**295.3 e**	**303.5**	..
68-82	**Real estate; professional, scientific and technical; administrative and support**	**120.9**	**92.9 e**	**86.3**	**86.9 e**	**96.7**	**115.2 e**	**138.0**	..
68	Real estate activities	0.0 e	0.0 e	0.0	0.0 e	0.0 e	0.0 e	0.0	..
69-75x72	Professional, scientific and technical activities, except scientific R&D	53.8	34.3 e	24.6	21.0 e	25.3	36.5 e	51.2	..
72	Scientific research and development	66.3	57.7 e	61.0	65.7 e	71.3	77.2 e	82.8	..
77-82	Administrative and support service activities	0.8 e	0.8 e	0.7	0.1 e	0.0 e	1.5 e	3.9	..
84-99	Community, social and personal services	3.1	3.8 e	4.2	3.3 e	4.4	10.6 e	19.9	..
84-85	Public administration and defence; compulsory social security and education	1.9	2.1 e	2.1	1.1 e	1.7 e	6.0 e	12.6	..
86-88	Human health and social work activities	0.6	1.1 e	1.8	2.2 e	2.7	3.8 e	5.2	..
90-93	Arts, entertainment and recreation	0.0	0.0 e	0.0 e	0.0 e	0.0 e	0.1 e	0.1	..
94-99	Other services; household-employers; extraterritorial bodies	0.7	0.5 e	0.4 e	0.0 e	0.0 e	0.7 e	1.9	..

.. Not available; e Estimated value

Note: Detailed metadata at: *http://metalinks.oecd.org/anberd/20200813/2abe.*

HUNGARY

R&D expenditure in industry by main activity of the enterprise, current prices
ISIC Rev. 4

Million USD PPP

		2011	2012	2013	2014	2015	2016	2017	2018
	TOTAL BUSINESS ENTERPRISE	**1 690.4**	**1 899.9**	**2 333.8**	**2 437.9**	**2 595.8**	**2 398.5**	**2 814.5**	..
01-03	**AGRICULTURE, FORESTRY AND FISHING**	23.7 e	32.2 e	38.3 e	39.8	27.2	19.8	28.2	..
05-09	**MINING AND QUARRYING**	0.0 e	1.8 e	0.8 e	1.1 e	2.9	0.2	0.9	..
10-33	**MANUFACTURING**	939.5 e	1 070.1 e	1 171.2 e	1 091.3	1 052.2	1 158.0	1 318.7	..
10-12	Food products, beverages and tobacco	32.0 e	32.4 e	37.4 e	21.8	21.1	19.0	28.2	..
13-15	Textiles, wearing apparel, leather and related products	..	..	..	..	..	..	1.7	..
13	Textiles	..	..	..	..	..	..	..	..
14	Wearing apparel	..	..	..	..	..	..	..	..
15	Leather and related products, footwear	..	..	..	..	..	..	..	..
16-18	Wood and paper products and printing	9.8 e	12.6 e	31.9 e	29.1	10.5	15.9	51.2	..
16	Wood and wood products, except furniture	2.1 e	0.6 e	4.7 e	2.0	0.5 e	0.2 e	1.4	..
17	Paper and paper products	4.7 e	5.7 e	22.5 e	3.4	0.8 e	12.5	28.0	..
18	Printing and reproduction of recorded media	3.0 e	6.3 e	4.7 e	23.7	9.2	3.2 e	21.8	..
19-23	Chemical, rubber, plastic, non-metallic mineral products	..	..	..	..	..	..	481.8	..
19	Coke and refined petroleum products	..	..	..	..	..	..	..	..
20-21	Chemical and pharmaceutical products	403.4 e	451.7 e	448.5 e	448.3	431.5	425.6	429.8	..
20	Chemicals and chemical products	22.6 e	15.8 e	28.2 e	15.1	24.6	11.1	24.7	..
21	Pharmaceuticals, medicinal, chemical and botanical products	380.8 e	436.0 e	420.3 e	433.2	406.9	414.4	405.1	..
22	Rubber and plastic products	13.1 e	14.5 e	15.7 e	18.7	13.2	16.6	21.4	..
23	Other non-metallic mineral products	5.5 e	13.0 e	5.7 e	5.4	6.3	5.7	..	..
24-25	Basic metals, metal products, except machinery and equipment	16.9 e	42.6 e	39.0 e	46.1	22.2 e	32.6 e	46.7	..
24	Basic metals	1.2 e	1.3 e	2.1 e	3.3	3.9 e	8.1	14.0	..
25	Fabricated metal products, except machinery and equipment	15.7 e	41.3 e	37.0 e	42.9	18.3	24.5	32.7	..
26-30	Computer, electronic, optical products; electrical machinery, transport equipment	401.7 e	433.5 e	509.7 e	450.8	493.9	563.1	657.7	..
26	Computer, electronic and optical products	113.0 e	97.0 e	95.4 e	35.7	37.8	45.8	45.3	..
27	Electrical equipment	51.7 e	48.0 e	68.0 e	64.0	51.6	58.0	81.4	..
28	Machinery and equipment n.e.c.	95.4 e	121.2 e	133.3 e	130.0	119.9	129.1	137.5	..
29	Motor vehicles, trailers and semi-trailers	139.7 e	165.1 e	211.0 e	208.9	274.4	316.9	382.2	..
30	Other transport equipment	1.8 e	2.2 e	2.1 e	12.1	10.1	13.3	11.4	..
31-33	Furniture; repair, installation of machinery and equipment	36.4 e	47.4 e	66.2 e	54.8	37.1	49.9	51.3	..
31	Furniture	3.4 e	3.5 e	13.3 e	5.2	2.8	5.0	5.5	..
32	Other manufacturing	21.0 e	24.4 e	24.2 e	34.6	22.9	32.2	33.1	..
33	Repair and installation of machinery and equipment	11.9 e	19.5 e	28.7 e	15.0	11.4	12.8	12.7	..
35-39	**ELECTRICITY, GAS, WATER AND WASTE MANAGEMENT**	4.6 e	3.4 e	12.7 e	8.5 e	21.6	8.9	5.3	..
35-36	Electricity, gas and water	2.0 e	1.9 e	2.7 e	4.2 e	13.5	4.4	2.7	..
37-39	Sewerage, waste management and remediation activities	2.6 e	1.6 e	10.1 e	4.3	8.1	4.5	2.6	..
41-43	**CONSTRUCTION**	7.9 e	8.2 e	22.2 e	19.8	14.1	10.8	39.3	..
45-99	**TOTAL SERVICES**	714.8 e	784.1 e	1 088.5 e	1 277.2	1 477.7	1 200.8	1 422.2	..
45-82	**Business sector services**	702.4 e	768.5 e	1 074.7 e	1 261.5	1 460.7	1 188.9	1 408.1	..
45-47	**Wholesale and retail trade; motor vehicle and motorcycle repairs**	207.7 e	217.8 e	275.2 e	359.9	360.2	149.9	181.5	..
49-53	**Transportation and storage**	1.0 e	2.9 e	7.5 e	6.5	7.3	5.9 e	8.4	..
55-56	**Accommodation and food service activities**	..	..	..	..	..	..	8.5	..
58-63	**Information and communication**	51.1 e	122.0 e	161.9 e	244.9	208.6	177.6	237.2	..
58-60	Publishing, audiovisual and broadcasting activities	8.8 e	16.5 e	22.6 e	29.7	23.2	22.5	35.9	..
58	Publishing activities	..	..	..	29.5	..	22.5	..	..
59-60	Motion picture, video and TV programme production; broadcasting activities	..	..	..	0.1	..	..	..	..
59	Motion picture, video and TV programme production; sound and music	..	..	..	..	..	..	..	..
60	Programming and broadcasting activities	..	..	..	..	..	..	..	..
61	Telecommunications	..	..	..	3.4	11.7	5.0	5.2	..
62-63	IT and other information services	..	..	..	211.9	173.7	150.1	196.2	..
62	Computer programming, consultancy and related activities	..	..	..	188.0	164.3	139.9	192.3	..
63	Information service activities	..	..	..	23.9	9.4	10.2	3.9	..
64-66	**Financial and insurance activities**	..	..	..	..	..	..	3.1	..
68-82	**Real estate; professional, scientific and technical; administrative and support**	436.8 e	417.6 e	626.0 e	646.5	881.0	854.8	969.2	..
68	Real estate activities	4.0 e	3.5 e	8.8 e	15.1	11.5	4.3	3.9	..
69-75x72	Professional, scientific and technical activities, except scientific R&D	134.1 e	159.9 e	45.9 e	86.4	85.2	52.2	84.5	..
72	Scientific research and development	295.1 e	250.6 e	564.6 e	528.2	755.9	783.9	862.4	..
77-82	Administrative and support service activities	3.5 e	3.6 e	6.7 e	16.8	28.4	14.4	18.4	..
84-99	Community, social and personal services	12.3 e	15.6 e	13.8 e	15.7	17.0	11.9	14.2	..
84-85	Public administration and defence; compulsory social security and education	0.2 e	2.9 e	1.3 e	2.4	3.6	1.3	2.1	..
86-88	Human health and social work activities	3.2 e	4.7 e	2.4 e	3.5	3.6	1.8	5.0	..
90-93	Arts, entertainment and recreation	1.0 e	1.7 e	1.5 e	2.0	2.7	6.0	2.0	..
94-99	Other services; household-employers; extraterritorial bodies	7.9 e	6.4 e	8.6 e	7.9	7.1	2.7	5.1	..

.. Not available; e Estimated value

Note: Detailed metadata at: http://metalinks.oecd.org/anberd/20200813/2abe.

R&D expenditure in industry by main activity of the enterprise, constant prices
ISIC Rev. 4

2010 USD PPP

		2011	2012	2013	2014	2015	2016	2017	2018
	TOTAL BUSINESS ENTERPRISE	**1 788.1**	**1 968.5**	**2 336.1**	**2 439.3**	**2 595.8**	**2 366.9**	**2 725.3**	..
01-03	**AGRICULTURE, FORESTRY AND FISHING**	25.0 e	33.4 e	38.4 e	39.9	27.2	19.6	27.3	..
05-09	**MINING AND QUARRYING**	0.0 e	1.9 e	0.8 e	1.1 e	2.9	0.2	0.9	..
10-33	**MANUFACTURING**	993.8 e	1 108.8 e	1 172.3 e	1 091.9	1 052.2	1 142.7	1 276.9	..
10-12	Food products, beverages and tobacco	33.8 e	33.6 e	37.5 e	21.8	21.1	18.7	27.4	..
13-15	Textiles, wearing apparel, leather and related products	..	..	..	..	..	..	1.6	..
13	Textiles	..	..	..	..	..	..	..	..
14	Wearing apparel	..	..	..	..	..	..	..	..
15	Leather and related products, footwear	..	..	..	..	..	..	..	..
16-18	Wood and paper products and printing	10.3 e	13.0 e	31.9 e	29.1	10.5	15.7	49.6	..
16	Wood and wood products, except furniture	2.2 e	0.6 e	4.7 e	2.0	0.5 e	0.2 e	1.4	..
17	Paper and paper products	5.0 e	5.9 e	22.5 e	3.4	0.8 e	12.3	27.1	..
18	Printing and reproduction of recorded media	3.1 e	6.5 e	4.7 e	23.7	9.2	3.2 e	21.1	..
19-23	Chemical, rubber, plastic, non-metallic mineral products	..	..	..	..	..	..	466.5	..
19	Coke and refined petroleum products	..	..	..	..	..	..	..	..
20-21	Chemical and pharmaceutical products	426.7 e	468.0 e	449.0 e	448.6	431.5	420.0	416.2	..
20	Chemicals and chemical products	23.9 e	16.3 e	28.3 e	15.1	24.6	11.0	23.9	..
21	Pharmaceuticals, medicinal, chemical and botanical products	402.7 e	451.7 e	420.7 e	433.4	406.9	409.0	392.3	..
22	Rubber and plastic products	13.9 e	15.0 e	15.7 e	18.7	13.2	16.4	20.7	..
23	Other non-metallic mineral products	5.8 e	13.5 e	5.7 e	5.4	6.3	5.6	..	..
24-25	Basic metals, metal products, except machinery and equipment	17.9 e	44.1 e	39.1 e	46.2	22.2 e	32.2 e	45.2	..
24	Basic metals	1.2 e	1.4 e	2.1 e	3.3	3.9 e	8.0	13.6	..
25	Fabricated metal products, except machinery and equipment	16.6 e	42.8 e	37.0 e	42.9	18.3	24.2	31.7	..
26-30	Computer, electronic, optical products; electrical machinery, transport equipment	424.9 e	449.2 e	510.2 e	451.0	493.9	555.7	636.9	..
26	Computer, electronic and optical products	119.5 e	100.5 e	95.5 e	35.8	37.8	45.1	43.9	..
27	Electrical equipment	54.7 e	49.7 e	68.0 e	64.1	51.6	57.2	78.8	..
28	Machinery and equipment n.e.c.	100.9 e	125.5 e	133.4 e	130.1	119.9	127.4	133.1	..
29	Motor vehicles, trailers and semi-trailers	147.7 e	171.1 e	211.2 e	209.0	274.4	312.8	370.1	..
30	Other transport equipment	1.9 e	2.3 e	2.1 e	12.1	10.1	13.1	11.0	..
31-33	Furniture; repair, installation of machinery and equipment	38.5 e	49.2 e	66.3 e	54.9	37.1	49.3	49.7	..
31	Furniture	3.6 e	3.7 e	13.3 e	5.2	2.8	4.9	5.3	..
32	Other manufacturing	22.2 e	25.3 e	24.2 e	34.7	22.9	31.8	32.0	..
33	Repair and installation of machinery and equipment	12.6 e	20.2 e	28.8 e	15.0	11.4	12.6	12.3	..
35-39	**ELECTRICITY, GAS, WATER AND WASTE MANAGEMENT**	4.9 e	3.6 e	12.7 e	8.5 e	21.6	8.8	5.1	..
35-36	Electricity, gas and water	2.2 e	1.9 e	2.7 e	4.2 e	13.5	4.3	2.6	..
37-39	Sewerage, waste management and remediation activities	2.7 e	1.6 e	10.1 e	4.3	8.1	4.5	2.5	..
41-43	**CONSTRUCTION**	8.3 e	8.4 e	22.2 e	19.8	14.1	10.7	38.0	..
45-99	**TOTAL SERVICES**	756.0 e	812.4 e	1 089.6 e	1 278.0	1 477.7	1 185.0	1 377.1	..
45-82	**Business sector services**	743.0 e	796.3 e	1 075.8 e	1 262.2	1 460.7	1 173.3	1 363.4	..
45-47	**Wholesale and retail trade; motor vehicle and motorcycle repairs**	219.7 e	225.7 e	275.5 e	360.1	360.2	148.0	175.8	..
49-53	**Transportation and storage**	1.0 e	3.1 e	7.5 e	6.5	7.3	5.9 e	8.2	..
55-56	**Accommodation and food service activities**	..	..	..	..	..	..	8.3	..
58-63	**Information and communication**	54.1 e	126.4 e	162.1 e	245.1	208.6	175.3	229.7	..
58-60	Publishing, audiovisual and broadcasting activities	9.3 e	17.1 e	22.6 e	29.7	23.2	22.2	34.7	..
58	Publishing activities	..	..	..	29.6	..	22.2	..	..
59-60	Motion picture, video and TV programme production; broadcasting activities	..	..	..	0.1	..	..	..	..
59	Motion picture, video and TV programme production; sound and music	..	..	..	..	..	..	..	..
60	Programming and broadcasting activities	..	..	..	..	..	..	..	..
61	Telecommunications	..	..	..	3.4	11.7	4.9	5.0	..
62-63	IT and other information services	..	..	..	212.0	173.7	148.2	190.0	..
62	Computer programming, consultancy and related activities	..	..	..	188.1	164.3	138.1	186.2	..
63	Information service activities	..	..	..	23.9	9.4	10.1	3.8	..
64-66	**Financial and insurance activities**	..	..	..	..	..	..	3.0	..
68-82	Real estate; professional, scientific and technical; administrative and support	462.0 e	432.7 e	626.6 e	646.9	881.0	843.6	938.5	..
68	Real estate activities	4.2 e	3.6 e	8.8 e	15.1	11.5	4.2	3.7	..
69-75x72	Professional, scientific and technical activities, except scientific R&D	141.8 e	165.7 e	46.0 e	86.5	85.2	51.6	81.9	..
72	Scientific research and development	312.2 e	259.6 e	565.1 e	528.5	755.9	773.6	835.1	..
77-82	Administrative and support service activities	3.8 e	3.8 e	6.7 e	16.8	28.4	14.3	17.8	..
84-99	Community, social and personal services	13.0 e	16.2 e	13.8 e	15.7	17.0	11.7	13.7	..
84-85	Public administration and defence; compulsory social security and education	0.3 e	3.0 e	1.3 e	2.4	3.6	1.3	2.0	..
86-88	Human health and social work activities	3.4 e	4.8 e	2.4 e	3.5	3.6	1.8	4.8	..
90-93	Arts, entertainment and recreation	1.1 e	1.8 e	1.5 e	2.0	2.7	5.9	1.9	..
94-99	Other services; household-employers; extraterritorial bodies	8.3 e	6.6 e	8.6 e	7.9	7.1	2.7	4.9	..

.. Not available; e Estimated value

Note: Detailed metadata at: *http://metalinks.oecd.org/anberd/20200813/2abe.*

ICELAND

R&D expenditure in industry by main activity of the enterprise, current prices
ISIC Rev. 4

Million USD PPP

		2011	2012	2013	2014	2015	2016	2017	2018
	TOTAL BUSINESS ENTERPRISE	..	..	135.9	178.1	234.4	243.8	258.3	267.5
01-03	**AGRICULTURE, FORESTRY AND FISHING**	..	..	1.4	1.4	2.4	2.1	5.2	4.3
05-09	**MINING AND QUARRYING**	..	..	0.0	0.0	0.1	0.1	0.0	0.0
10-33	**MANUFACTURING**	..	..	33.7	34.5	49.7	52.1	59.7	71.1
10-12	Food products, beverages and tobacco	..	..	4.0	4.4	3.7	4.2	4.3	4.5
13-15	Textiles, wearing apparel, leather and related products	..	..	0.0	0.0	0.1	0.1	0.1	0.2
13	Textiles	..	..	..	..	0.0	0.0	0.1	0.2
14	Wearing apparel	..	..	..	..	0.0	0.0	0.0	0.0
15	Leather and related products, footwear	..	..	..	..	0.1	0.1	0.0	0.0
16-18	Wood and paper products and printing	..	..	0.1	0.2	0.1	0.1	0.0	0.0
16	Wood and wood products, except furniture	..	..	..	..	..	..	..	..
17	Paper and paper products	..	..	..	..	..	..	..	..
18	Printing and reproduction of recorded media	..	..	..	..	..	..	..	..
19-23	Chemical, rubber, plastic, non-metallic mineral products	..	..	3.1	3.2	7.2	5.8	4.4	6.7
19	Coke and refined petroleum products	..	..	0.1	0.1	3.4	1.4	0.5	1.6
20-21	Chemical and pharmaceutical products	..	..	2.8	2.8	2.9	3.3	3.1	3.9
20	Chemicals and chemical products	..	..	2.4	2.5	1.9	1.9	2.0	2.5
21	Pharmaceuticals, medicinal, chemical and botanical products	..	..	0.4	0.2	1.0	1.4	1.1	1.5
22	Rubber and plastic products	..	..	0.3	0.3	0.6	0.6	0.7	1.1
23	Other non-metallic mineral products	..	..	0.0	0.0	0.4	0.4	0.0	0.0
24-25	Basic metals, metal products, except machinery and equipment	..	..	2.5	2.5	2.3	3.4	5.7	7.2
24	Basic metals	..	..	0.6	0.7	0.4	1.5	2.7	3.9
25	Fabricated metal products, except machinery and equipment	..	..	1.9	1.8	1.8	1.9	2.9	3.3
26-30	Computer, electronic, optical products; electrical machinery, transport equipment	..	..	8.8	9.1	19.0	20.4	22.5	27.0
26	Computer, electronic and optical products	..	..	2.7	2.8	2.4	2.9	3.6	4.4
27	Electrical equipment	..	..	0.0	0.1	1.4	1.8	0.8	1.1
28	Machinery and equipment n.e.c.	..	..	5.9	5.9	15.2	15.7	18.0	21.5
29	Motor vehicles, trailers and semi-trailers	..	..	0.0	0.0	0.0	0.0	0.0	0.0
30	Other transport equipment	..	..	0.2	0.2	0.1	0.0	0.0	0.0
31-33	Furniture; repair, installation of machinery and equipment	..	..	15.1	15.2	17.2	18.0	22.7	25.6
31	Furniture	..	..	0.0	0.0	0.0	0.0	0.2	0.2
32	Other manufacturing	..	..	15.1	14.9	16.1	17.0	21.5	24.3
33	Repair and installation of machinery and equipment	..	..	0.0	0.3	1.1	1.0	1.0	1.0
35-39	**ELECTRICITY, GAS, WATER AND WASTE MANAGEMENT**	..	..	5.8	8.5	7.9	9.8	7.4	6.7
35-36	Electricity, gas and water	..	..	5.5	8.2	7.6	9.5	6.9	6.3
37-39	Sewerage, waste management and remediation activities	..	..	0.3	0.3	0.3	0.3	0.6	0.4
41-43	**CONSTRUCTION**	..	..	0.0	1.1	0.0	0.0	0.0	0.0
45-99	**TOTAL SERVICES**	..	..	95.0	132.5	174.3	179.8	185.9	185.4
45-82	**Business sector services**	..	..	90.3	127.4	169.0	175.4	182.6	181.6
45-47	**Wholesale and retail trade; motor vehicle and motorcycle repairs**	..	..	0.7	0.6	1.3	1.8	1.2	2.5
49-53	**Transportation and storage**	..	..	0.2	0.2	0.1	0.2	0.3	0.4
55-56	**Accommodation and food service activities**	..	..	0.1	0.1	0.7	0.4	0.0	0.0
58-63	**Information and communication**	..	..	24.4	29.9	52.5	57.6	61.9	71.3
58-60	Publishing, audiovisual and broadcasting activities	..	..	..	1.0	2.5	2.9	2.6	3.5
58	Publishing activities	..	..	..	1.0	2.5	2.9	2.6	3.5
59-60	Motion picture, video and TV programme production; broadcasting activities	..	..	..	0.0	0.0	0.0	0.0	0.0
59	Motion picture, video and TV programme production; sound and music	..	..	..	..	..	..	..	..
60	Programming and broadcasting activities	..	..	..	..	..	..	..	..
61	Telecommunications	..	..	..	0.0	0.0	0.0	0.1	0.1
62-63	IT and other information services	..	..	..	28.9	50.8	54.7	59.2	67.7
62	Computer programming, consultancy and related activities	..	..	..	25.1	39.1	45.3	52.3	60.5
63	Information service activities	..	..	..	3.9	11.6	9.4	6.9	7.2
64-66	**Financial and insurance activities**	..	..	0.5	0.5	0.4	0.9	2.0	2.8
68-82	**Real estate; professional, scientific and technical; administrative and support**	..	..	64.3	96.0	113.2	114.5	117.2	104.6
68	Real estate activities	..	..	0.0	0.0	0.0	0.0	0.0	0.0
69-75x72	Professional, scientific and technical activities, except scientific R&D	..	..	9.2	7.4	4.5	6.6	4.5	5.9
72	Scientific research and development	..	..	53.7	87.3	106.8	105.3	109.1	95.5
77-82	Administrative and support service activities	..	..	1.4	1.3	1.9	2.7	3.6	3.3
84-99	Community, social and personal services	..	..	4.7	5.1	5.4	4.4	3.3	3.8
84-85	Public administration and defence; compulsory social security and education	..	..	0.6	0.8	0.7	0.5	0.1	0.1
86-88	Human health and social work activities	..	..	3.0	3.2	4.4	3.5	2.3	2.7
90-93	Arts, entertainment and recreation	..	..	0.8	0.7	0.0	0.1	0.0	0.0
94-99	Other services; household-employers; extraterritorial bodies	..	..	0.3	0.4	0.3	0.2	0.9	1.0

.. Not available

Note: Detailed metadata at: *http://metalinks.oecd.org/anberd/20200813/2abe.*

ICELAND

R&D expenditure in industry by main activity of the enterprise, constant prices
ISIC Rev. 4

2010 USD PPP

		2011	2012	2013	2014	2015	2016	2017	2018
	TOTAL BUSINESS ENTERPRISE	..	..	**143.7**	**183.6**	**234.4**	**236.2**	**244.0**	**246.2**
01-03	**AGRICULTURE, FORESTRY AND FISHING**	..	..	**1.5**	**1.4**	**2.4**	**2.0**	**4.9**	**3.9**
05-09	**MINING AND QUARRYING**	..	..	**0.0**	**0.0**	**0.1**	**0.1**	**0.0**	**0.0**
10-33	**MANUFACTURING**	..	..	**35.6**	**35.6**	**49.7**	**50.4**	**56.4**	**65.5**
10-12	Food products, beverages and tobacco	..	..	4.3	4.5	3.7	4.1	4.1	4.2
13-15	Textiles, wearing apparel, leather and related products	..	..	0.0	0.0	0.1	0.1	0.1	0.1
13	Textiles	..	..	..	..	0.0	0.0	0.1	0.1
14	Wearing apparel	..	..	..	..	0.0	0.0	0.0	0.0
15	Leather and related products, footwear	..	..	..	..	0.1	0.1	0.0	0.0
16-18	Wood and paper products and printing	..	..	0.1	0.2	0.1	0.1	0.0	0.0
16	Wood and wood products, except furniture	..	..	..	..	..	..	..	..
17	Paper and paper products	..	..	..	..	..	..	..	..
18	Printing and reproduction of recorded media	..	..	..	..	..	..	..	..
19-23	Chemical, rubber, plastic, non-metallic mineral products	..	..	3.3	3.3	7.2	5.6	4.2	6.2
19	Coke and refined petroleum products	..	..	0.1	0.1	3.4	1.4	0.5	1.5
20-21	Chemical and pharmaceutical products	..	..	2.9	2.9	2.9	3.2	3.0	3.6
20	Chemicals and chemical products	..	..	2.5	2.6	1.9	1.9	1.9	2.3
21	Pharmaceuticals, medicinal, chemical and botanical products	..	..	0.4	0.2	1.0	1.3	1.0	1.3
22	Rubber and plastic products	..	..	0.3	0.3	0.6	0.6	0.7	1.0
23	Other non-metallic mineral products	..	..	0.0	0.0	0.4	0.4	0.0	0.0
24-25	Basic metals, metal products, except machinery and equipment	..	..	2.7	2.6	2.3	3.3	5.4	6.6
24	Basic metals	..	..	0.7	0.7	0.4	1.5	2.6	3.6
25	Fabricated metal products, except machinery and equipment	..	..	2.0	1.8	1.8	1.8	2.8	3.1
26-30	Computer, electronic, optical products; electrical machinery, transport equipment	..	..	9.3	9.4	19.0	19.7	21.3	24.8
26	Computer, electronic and optical products	..	..	2.9	2.9	2.4	2.8	3.4	4.0
27	Electrical equipment	..	..	0.0	0.1	1.4	1.7	0.8	1.0
28	Machinery and equipment n.e.c.	..	..	6.2	6.1	15.2	15.2	17.0	19.8
29	Motor vehicles, trailers and semi-trailers	..	..	0.0	0.0	0.0	0.0	0.0	0.0
30	Other transport equipment	..	..	0.2	0.2	0.1	0.0	0.0	0.0
31-33	Furniture; repair, installation of machinery and equipment	..	..	16.0	15.7	17.2	17.4	21.4	23.5
31	Furniture	..	..	0.0	0.0	0.0	0.0	0.2	0.2
32	Other manufacturing	..	..	15.9	15.4	16.1	16.5	20.3	22.4
33	Repair and installation of machinery and equipment	..	..	0.0	0.3	1.1	1.0	0.9	0.9
35-39	**ELECTRICITY, GAS, WATER AND WASTE MANAGEMENT**	..	..	**6.1**	**8.8**	**7.9**	**9.5**	**7.0**	**6.2**
35-36	Electricity, gas and water	..	..	5.8	8.5	7.6	9.2	6.5	5.8
37-39	Sewerage, waste management and remediation activities	..	..	0.3	0.3	0.3	0.3	0.5	0.4
41-43	**CONSTRUCTION**	..	..	**0.0**	**1.1**	**0.0**	**0.0**	**0.0**	**0.0**
45-99	**TOTAL SERVICES**	..	..	**100.4**	**136.6**	**174.3**	**174.2**	**175.6**	**170.7**
45-82	**Business sector services**	..	..	**95.4**	**131.3**	**169.0**	**170.0**	**172.5**	**167.2**
45-47	**Wholesale and retail trade; motor vehicle and motorcycle repairs**	..	..	**0.7**	**0.7**	**1.3**	**1.7**	**1.2**	**2.3**
49-53	**Transportation and storage**	..	..	**0.3**	**0.2**	**0.1**	**0.2**	**0.2**	**0.3**
55-56	**Accommodation and food service activities**	..	..	**0.1**	**0.1**	**0.7**	**0.4**	**0.0**	**0.0**
58-63	**Information and communication**	..	..	**25.8**	**30.8**	**52.5**	**55.8**	**58.5**	**65.7**
58-60	Publishing, audiovisual and broadcasting activities	..	..	..	1.0	2.5	2.8	2.4	3.2
58	Publishing activities	..	..	..	1.0	2.5	2.8	2.4	3.2
59-60	Motion picture, video and TV programme production; broadcasting activities	..	..	..	0.0	0.0	0.0	0.0	0.0
59	Motion picture, video and TV programme production; sound and music	..	..	..	..	..	..	..	..
60	Programming and broadcasting activities	..	..	..	..	..	..	..	..
61	Telecommunications	..	..	..	0.0	0.0	0.0	0.1	0.1
62-63	IT and other information services	..	..	..	29.8	50.8	53.0	55.9	62.3
62	Computer programming, consultancy and related activities	..	..	..	25.8	39.1	43.9	49.4	55.7
63	Information service activities	..	..	..	4.0	11.6	9.1	6.5	6.7
64-66	**Financial and insurance activities**	..	..	**0.5**	**0.5**	**0.4**	**0.9**	**1.9**	**2.5**
68-82	**Real estate; professional, scientific and technical; administrative and support**	..	..	**68.0**	**99.0**	**113.2**	**110.9**	**110.7**	**96.3**
68	Real estate activities	..	..	0.0	0.0	0.0	0.0	0.0	0.0
69-75x72	Professional, scientific and technical activities, except scientific R&D	..	..	9.7	7.7	4.5	6.4	4.3	5.4
72	Scientific research and development	..	..	56.8	90.0	106.8	102.0	103.1	87.9
77-82	Administrative and support service activities	..	..	1.5	1.4	1.9	2.6	3.4	3.0
84-99	Community, social and personal services	..	..	5.0	5.2	5.4	4.2	3.1	3.5
84-85	Public administration and defence; compulsory social security and education	..	..	0.6	0.8	0.7	0.5	0.1	0.1
86-88	Human health and social work activities	..	..	3.2	3.3	4.4	3.4	2.1	2.4
90-93	Arts, entertainment and recreation	..	..	0.8	0.7	0.0	0.1	0.0	0.0
94-99	Other services; household-employers; extraterritorial bodies	..	..	0.3	0.4	0.3	0.2	0.8	0.9

.. Not available

Note: Detailed metadata at: *http://metalinks.oecd.org/anberd/20200813/2abe.*

IRELAND

R&D expenditure in industry by main activity of the enterprise, current prices
ISIC Rev. 4

Million USD PPP

		2011	2012	2013	2014	2015	2016	2017	2018
	TOTAL BUSINESS ENTERPRISE	**2 236.4**	**2 383.4**	**2 492.4**	**2 572.3**	**2 758.6**	**2 886.3**	**3 501.7**	..
01-03	**AGRICULTURE, FORESTRY AND FISHING**	2.5	2.2 e	1.5 e	1.5 e	1.2	1.1 e	1.1	..
05-09	**MINING AND QUARRYING**	1.0 e	1.4 e	1.4 e	2.1 e	2.5	2.4 e	2.8	..
10-33	**MANUFACTURING**	864.1	962.9 e	1 047.7	1 043.0 e	1 082.2	1 225.8 e	1 578.0	..
10-12	Food products, beverages and tobacco	88.6 e	94.2 e	98.3	93.4 e	92.7	95.1 e	113.8	..
13-15	Textiles, wearing apparel, leather and related products	3.9	4.6 e	5.3 e	5.6 e	6.2	3.2 e	0.7	..
13	Textiles	..	..	..	..	..	..	0.5	..
14	Wearing apparel	..	..	..	..	..	..	0.3	..
15	Leather and related products, footwear	..	..	..	..	..	..	0.0	..
16-18	Wood and paper products and printing	32.7	38.9 e	44.6	22.4 e	1.2	4.6 e	8.7	..
16	Wood and wood products, except furniture	9.7	..	6.8	..	..	..	1.7	..
17	Paper and paper products	..	..	..	..	..	..	5.7	..
18	Printing and reproduction of recorded media	..	..	..	..	..	..	1.3	..
19-23	Chemical, rubber, plastic, non-metallic mineral products	231.7	265.4 e	295.4	301.6 e	321.2	419.2 e	590.6	..
19	Coke and refined petroleum products	0.0	0.0 e	0.0	0.0 e	0.0	0.0 e	0.0	..
20-21	Chemical and pharmaceutical products	212.8	240.2 e	264.2	276.7 e	301.4	400.5 e	569.7	..
20	Chemicals and chemical products	59.8	61.0 e	61.2	89.7 e	122.3	119.9 e	137.8	..
21	Pharmaceuticals, medicinal, chemical and botanical products	153.0	179.2 e	203.0	186.9 e	179.1	280.6 e	432.0	..
22	Rubber and plastic products	13.1	18.6 e	24.1	19.6 e	16.1	14.8 e	16.1	..
23	Other non-metallic mineral products	5.9	6.5 e	7.1	5.3 e	3.7	3.9 e	4.8	..
24-25	Basic metals, metal products, except machinery and equipment	33.5	36.5 e	39.0	35.4 e	33.4	42.5 e	59.1	..
24	Basic metals	2.8	4.3 e	5.8	5.8 e	6.2	5.4 e	5.5	..
25	Fabricated metal products, except machinery and equipment	30.7	32.2 e	33.3	29.6 e	27.2	37.1 e	53.6	..
26-30	Computer, electronic, optical products; electrical machinery, transport equipment	242.7	289.4 e	332.3	364.9 e	413.9	393.5 e	439.5	..
26	Computer, electronic and optical products	183.8	219.1 e	251.6 e	289.2 e	339.7	313.4 e	339.6	..
27	Electrical equipment	15.3	18.2 e	20.9 e	19.9 e	19.8	23.1 e	30.5	..
28	Machinery and equipment n.e.c.	35.8	42.6 e	49.0 e	48.1 e	49.4	49.5 e	57.9	..
29	Motor vehicles, trailers and semi-trailers	5.7	6.8 e	7.8 e	5.6 e	3.7	6.8 e	11.1	..
30	Other transport equipment	2.2	2.6 e	3.0 e	2.1 e	1.2	0.7 e	0.3	..
31-33	Furniture; repair, installation of machinery and equipment	230.9 e	233.8 e	232.8 e	219.6 e	216.2	267.6 e	365.5	..
31	Furniture	1.6 e	1.8 e	2.1 e	2.2 e	2.5	2.1 e	2.0	..
32	Other manufacturing	220.4	225.0 e	225.8	213.8 e	211.2	263.2 e	361.0	..
33	Repair and installation of machinery and equipment	9.0	7.0 e	4.9	3.6 e	2.5	2.3 e	2.5	..
35-39	**ELECTRICITY, GAS, WATER AND WASTE MANAGEMENT**	**19.8**	**13.9 e**	**7.6**	**8.0 e**	**8.6**	**8.3 e**	**9.3**	..
35-36	Electricity, gas and water	14.5	9.9 e	5.1	4.9 e	4.9	6.1 e	8.3	..
37-39	Sewerage, waste management and remediation activities	5.3	4.0 e	2.5	3.0 e	3.7	2.2 e	1.0	..
41-43	**CONSTRUCTION**	**3.1**	**3.1 e**	**3.1**	**2.1 e**	**1.2**	**2.4 e**	**4.1**	..
45-99	**TOTAL SERVICES**	**1 345.9 e**	**1 399.9 e**	**1 431.2**	**1 515.6 e**	**1 664.1**	**1 646.3 e**	**1 904.0**	..
45-82	**Business sector services**	**1 334.0**	**1 383.0 e**	**1 409.4**	**1 500.7 e**	**1 655.4**	**1 638.2 e**	**1 895.0**	..
45-47	**Wholesale and retail trade; motor vehicle and motorcycle repairs**	212.2	183.2 e	150.3	218.1 e	295.3	260.7 e	269.0	..
49-53	**Transportation and storage**	2.5	2.0 e	1.5	2.5 e	3.7	2.6 e	1.8	..
55-56	**Accommodation and food service activities**	0.7	0.6 e	0.5	0.2 e	0.0	0.0 e	0.0	..
58-63	**Information and communication**	686.9	745.0 e	791.7	793.0 e	827.7	829.5 e	970.2	..
58-60	Publishing, audiovisual and broadcasting activities	211.9	210.1 e	204.6	154.1 e	109.9	110.3 e	129.1	..
58	Publishing activities	211.2	208.6 e	202.4	152.5 e	108.8	109.1 e	127.8 e	..
59-60	Motion picture, video and TV programme production; broadcasting activities	0.7	1.4 e	2.1	1.6 e	1.2 e	1.2 e	1.4 e	..
59	Motion picture, video and TV programme production; sound and music	..	..	2.0	1.5 e	1.1 e	1.1 e	1.3 e	..
60	Programming and broadcasting activities	..	..	0.1	0.1 e	0.1 e	0.1 e	0.1 e	..
61	Telecommunications	13.9	16.0 e	17.9	16.0 e	14.8	15.5 e	18.8	..
62-63	IT and other information services	461.1	518.8 e	569.2	622.9 e	702.9	703.7 e	822.3	..
62	Computer programming, consultancy and related activities	413.3	467.8 e	515.6	567.0 e	642.4	582.3 e	618.4	..
63	Information service activities	47.8	51.1 e	53.6	55.9 e	60.5	121.3 e	203.9	..
64-66	**Financial and insurance activities**	**57.2**	**61.2 e**	**64.3**	**58.1 e**	**54.4**	**48.2 e**	**50.0**	..
68-82	**Real estate; professional, scientific and technical; administrative and support**	**374.4**	**391.0 e**	**401.3**	**428.8 e**	**474.4**	**497.3 e**	**604.0**	..
68	Real estate activities	0.0	0.0 e	0.0	0.0 e	0.0	0.1 e	0.2	..
69-75x72	Professional, scientific and technical activities, except scientific R&D	71.7	95.0 e	117.2	121.9 e	131.0	132.0 e	154.5	..
72	Scientific research and development	279.9	273.4 e	262.1	274.3 e	296.5	333.6 e	425.8	..
77-82	Administrative and support service activities	22.8	22.6 e	21.9	32.6 e	44.5	31.6 e	23.5	..
84-99	Community, social and personal services	11.9 e	16.9 e	21.7	14.9 e	8.6	8.1 e	9.0	..
84-85	Public administration and defence; compulsory social security and education	..	..	..	..	2.5	..	..	..
86-88	Human health and social work activities	2.6	..	3.3	..	3.7	..	..	..
90-93	Arts, entertainment and recreation	2.4	..	5.7	..	2.5	..	..	..
94-99	Other services; household-employers; extraterritorial bodies	..	..	..	..	..	..	..	..

.. Not available; e Estimated value

Note: Detailed metadata at: *http://metalinks.oecd.org/anberd/20200813/2abe.*

IRELAND

R&D expenditure in industry by main activity of the enterprise, constant prices
ISIC Rev. 4

2010 USD PPP

		2011	2012	2013	2014	2015	2016	2017	2018
	TOTAL BUSINESS ENTERPRISE	**2 561.0**	**2 641.3**	**2 689.4**	**2 805.4**	**2 758.6**	**2 841.0**	**3 394.2**	..
01-03	**AGRICULTURE, FORESTRY AND FISHING**	2.9	2.5 e	1.6 e	1.7 e	1.2	1.0 e	1.0	..
05-09	**MINING AND QUARRYING**	1.1 e	1.5 e	1.5 e	2.2 e	2.5	2.4 e	2.7	..
10-33	**MANUFACTURING**	989.5	1 067.1 e	1 130.5	1 137.5 e	1 082.2	1 206.5 e	1 529.6	..
10-12	Food products, beverages and tobacco	101.5 e	104.4 e	106.1	101.9 e	92.7	93.6 e	110.3	..
13-15	Textiles, wearing apparel, leather and related products	4.5	5.1 e	5.7 e	6.1 e	6.2	3.2 e	0.7	..
13	Textiles	..	..	..	..	..	..	0.4	..
14	Wearing apparel	..	..	..	..	..	..	0.3	..
15	Leather and related products, footwear	..	..	..	..	..	..	0.0	..
16-18	Wood and paper products and printing	37.5	43.1 e	48.1	24.5 e	1.2	4.5 e	8.4	..
16	Wood and wood products, except furniture	11.1	..	7.3	..	..	..	1.6	..
17	Paper and paper products	..	..	..	..	..	..	5.6	..
18	Printing and reproduction of recorded media	..	..	..	..	..	..	1.3	..
19-23	Chemical, rubber, plastic, non-metallic mineral products	265.3	294.1 e	318.7	328.9 e	321.2	412.6 e	572.5	..
19	Coke and refined petroleum products	0.0	0.0 e	0.0	0.0 e	0.0	0.0 e	0.0	..
20-21	Chemical and pharmaceutical products	243.7	266.2 e	285.1	301.7 e	301.4	394.2 e	552.2	..
20	Chemicals and chemical products	68.5	67.6 e	66.0	97.8 e	122.3	118.0 e	133.5	..
21	Pharmaceuticals, medicinal, chemical and botanical products	175.2	198.6 e	219.1	203.9 e	179.1	276.2 e	418.7	..
22	Rubber and plastic products	15.0	20.7 e	26.0	21.4 e	16.1	14.6 e	15.6	..
23	Other non-metallic mineral products	6.7	7.2 e	7.7	5.8 e	3.7	3.9 e	4.7	..
24-25	Basic metals, metal products, except machinery and equipment	38.3	40.5 e	42.1	38.6 e	33.4	41.9 e	57.3	..
24	Basic metals	3.2	4.8 e	6.2	6.4 e	6.2	5.3 e	5.3	..
25	Fabricated metal products, except machinery and equipment	35.1	35.7 e	35.9	32.3 e	27.2	36.6 e	52.0	..
26-30	Computer, electronic, optical products; electrical machinery, transport equipment	277.9	320.7 e	358.5	398.0 e	413.9	387.3 e	426.0	..
26	Computer, electronic and optical products	210.4	242.8 e	271.5	315.4 e	339.7	308.5 e	329.2	..
27	Electrical equipment	17.5	20.2 e	22.6	21.7 e	19.8	22.8 e	29.6	..
28	Machinery and equipment n.e.c.	40.9	47.2 e	52.8 e	52.5 e	49.4	48.7 e	56.1	..
29	Motor vehicles, trailers and semi-trailers	6.5	7.5 e	8.4 e	6.1 e	3.7	6.7 e	10.7	..
30	Other transport equipment	2.5	2.9 e	3.3 e	2.3 e	1.2	0.7 e	0.3	..
31-33	Furniture; repair, installation of machinery and equipment	264.4 e	259.1 e	251.2 e	239.5 e	216.2	263.4 e	354.3	..
31	Furniture	1.8 e	2.0 e	2.3 e	2.4 e	2.5	2.0 e	2.0	..
32	Other manufacturing	252.4	249.3 e	243.6	233.2 e	211.2	259.1 e	349.9	..
33	Repair and installation of machinery and equipment	10.3	7.8 e	5.3	3.9 e	2.5	2.3 e	2.4	..
35-39	**ELECTRICITY, GAS, WATER AND WASTE MANAGEMENT**	22.7	15.4 e	8.2	8.7 e	8.6	8.2 e	9.0	..
35-36	Electricity, gas and water	16.6	11.0 e	5.5	5.3 e	4.9	6.0 e	8.1	..
37-39	Sewerage, waste management and remediation activities	6.1	4.4 e	2.7	3.3 e	3.7	2.1 e	1.0	..
41-43	**CONSTRUCTION**	3.5	3.4 e	3.3	2.3 e	1.2	2.4 e	3.9	..
45-99	**TOTAL SERVICES**	1 541.2 e	1 551.4 e	1 544.3	1 653.0 e	1 664.1	1 620.5 e	1 845.5	..
45-82	**Business sector services**	1 527.6	1 532.6 e	1 520.8	1 636.8 e	1 655.4	1 612.5 e	1 836.8	..
45-47	**Wholesale and retail trade; motor vehicle and motorcycle repairs**	243.0	203.0 e	162.1	237.9 e	295.3	256.6 e	260.7	..
49-53	**Transportation and storage**	2.9	2.2 e	1.6	2.8 e	3.7	2.5 e	1.7	..
55-56	**Accommodation and food service activities**	0.8	0.7 e	0.5	0.3 e	0.0	0.0 e	0.0	..
58-63	**Information and communication**	786.6	825.6 e	854.2	864.9 e	827.7	816.4 e	940.4	..
58-60	Publishing, audiovisual and broadcasting activities	242.7	232.8 e	220.7	168.0 e	109.9	108.6 e	125.1	..
58	Publishing activities	241.8	231.2 e	218.4	166.3 e	108.8 e	107.4 e	123.8 e	..
59-60	Motion picture, video and TV programme production; broadcasting activities	0.9	1.6 e	2.3	1.8 e	1.2 e	1.1 e	1.3 e	..
59	Motion picture, video and TV programme production; sound and music	..	..	2.2	1.6 e	1.1 e	1.1 e	1.2 e	..
60	Programming and broadcasting activities	..	..	0.2	0.1 e	0.1 e	0.1 e	0.1 e	..
61	Telecommunications	16.0	17.8 e	19.3	17.5 e	14.8	15.3 e	18.2	..
62-63	IT and other information services	528.0	575.0 e	614.2	679.3 e	702.9	692.6 e	797.1	..
62	Computer programming, consultancy and related activities	473.3	518.4 e	556.4	618.4 e	642.4	573.2 e	599.5	..
63	Information service activities	54.7	56.6 e	57.8	60.9 e	60.5	119.4 e	197.6	..
64-66	**Financial and insurance activities**	65.5	67.8 e	69.3	63.4 e	54.4	47.5 e	48.5	..
68-82	**Real estate; professional, scientific and technical; administrative and support**	428.8	433.3 e	433.0	467.6 e	474.4	489.4 e	585.4	..
68	Real estate activities	0.0	0.0 e	0.0	0.0 e	0.0	0.1 e	0.2	..
69-75x72	Professional, scientific and technical activities, except scientific R&D	82.2	105.3 e	126.5	132.9 e	131.0	129.9 e	149.8	..
72	Scientific research and development	320.5	303.0 e	282.8	299.1 e	296.5	328.4 e	412.7	..
77-82	Administrative and support service activities	26.2	25.0 e	23.7	35.6 e	44.5	31.1 e	22.8	..
84-99	Community, social and personal services	13.6 e	18.7 e	23.5	16.2 e	8.6	8.0 e	8.7	..
84-85	Public administration and defence; compulsory social security and education	..	..	..	..	2.5	..	..	..
86-88	Human health and social work activities	3.0	..	3.5	..	3.7	..	..	..
90-93	Arts, entertainment and recreation	2.8	..	6.1	..	2.5	..	..	..
94-99	Other services; household-employers; extraterritorial bodies	..	..	..	..	..	..	..	..

.. Not available; e Estimated value

Note: Detailed metadata at: *http://metalinks.oecd.org/anberd/20200813/2abe.*

ISRAEL

R&D expenditure in industry by main activity of the enterprise, current prices
ISIC Rev. 4

Million USD PPP

		2011	2012	2013	2014	2015	2016	2017	2018
	TOTAL BUSINESS ENTERPRISE	7 979.6	8 788.5	9 491.4	9 953.1	10 792.0	12 632.7	14 356.8	..
01-03	AGRICULTURE, FORESTRY AND FISHING	..	..	..	..	..	..	..	..
05-09	MINING AND QUARRYING	3.3	5.8	6.5	6.1	4.6	5.3	4.1	
10-33	MANUFACTURING	2 396.1	2 372.1	2 437.5	2 313.4	2 377.2	2 449.9	2 622.0	..
10-12	Food products, beverages and tobacco	20.0	24.1	18.4	16.5	11.8	16.7	16.0	
13-15	Textiles, wearing apparel, leather and related products	21.9 e	22.8 e	20.5	20.8	20.1	20.7	20.8	
13	Textiles	..	..	..	..	..	..	..	
14	Wearing apparel	..	..	..	..	..	..	..	
15	Leather and related products, footwear	..	..	..	..	..	..	..	
16-18	Wood and paper products and printing	3.4 e	3.5 e	3.2	1.2	4.8	4.4	5.9	
16	Wood and wood products, except furniture	..	..	..	..	..	..	..	
17	Paper and paper products	..	..	..	..	..	..	..	
18	Printing and reproduction of recorded media	..	..	..	..	..	..	..	
19-23	Chemical, rubber, plastic, non-metallic mineral products	375.6	401.0	495.8	400.5	488.5	466.2	422.7	
19	Coke and refined petroleum products	45.9	66.0	64.8	75.4	88.9	72.0	76.6	
20-21	Chemical and pharmaceutical products	..	..	..	..	..	..	..	
20	Chemicals and chemical products	..	..	..	..	..	..	..	
21	Pharmaceuticals, medicinal, chemical and botanical products	283.2	286.2	383.2	279.0	349.6	341.7	271.5	
22	Rubber and plastic products	..	..	..	..	..	..	..	
23	Other non-metallic mineral products	..	..	..	..	..	..	..	
24-25	Basic metals, metal products, except machinery and equipment	89.5	54.0	53.8	51.4	54.3	52.6	66.7	
24	Basic metals	..	..	..	..	..	..	..	
25	Fabricated metal products, except machinery and equipment	..	..	..	..	..	..	..	
26-30	Computer, electronic, optical products; electrical machinery, transport equipment	1 855.8 e	1 833.0 e	1 816.1	1 797.5	1 758.4	1 837.4	2 030.9	
26	Computer, electronic and optical products	1 559.4	1 497.9	1 522.2	1 518.7	1 460.6	1 545.7	1 711.7	
27	Electrical equipment	229.2 e	259.1 e	206.5 e	200.0	199.0 e	186.3 e	234.7 e	
28	Machinery and equipment n.e.c.	0.7 e	0.8 e	0.6 e	0.6	0.6 e	0.6 e	0.7 e	
29	Motor vehicles, trailers and semi-trailers	..	..	..	..	..	..	..	
30	Other transport equipment	..	..	..	..	..	..	..	
31-33	Furniture; repair, installation of machinery and equipment	..	..	..	..	..	..	..	
31	Furniture	..	..	..	..	..	..	..	
32	Other manufacturing	29.9 e	33.8 e	29.6	25.6	39.3	51.9	59.1	
33	Repair and installation of machinery and equipment	..	..	..	..	..	..	..	
35-39	**ELECTRICITY, GAS, WATER AND WASTE MANAGEMENT**	..	..	1.1	0.8	0.6	0.6	0.9	..
35-36	Electricity, gas and water	..	..	..	..	..	..	..	
37-39	Sewerage, waste management and remediation activities	..	..	3.0	18.4	18.4	17.3	34.1	
41-43	**CONSTRUCTION**	..	..						..
45-99	**TOTAL SERVICES**	5 506.0	6 354.1	7 043.4	7 614.5	8 391.3	10 159.5	11 695.7	
45-82	**Business sector services**	5 331.7	6 165.2	6 837.4	7 403.6	8 169.9	9 920.1	11 448.8	
45-47	**Wholesale and retail trade; motor vehicle and motorcycle repairs**			5.6	3.3	8.6	9.8	73.3	
49-53	**Transportation and storage**	0.0	0.0	0.0	0.0	0.0	0.0	0.0	
55-56	**Accommodation and food service activities**	0.0	0.0	0.0	0.0	0.0	0.0	0.0	
58-63	**Information and communication**	2 415.9	2 983.6	3 442.3	3 779.3	4 346.5	5 720.0	6 588.3	
58-60	Publishing, audiovisual and broadcasting activities	..	..	..	..	..	..	..	
58	Publishing activities	..	..	..	..	..	..	..	
59-60	Motion picture, video and TV programme production; broadcasting activities	..	..	..	..	..	..	..	
59	Motion picture, video and TV programme production; sound and music	..	..	..	..	..	..	..	
60	Programming and broadcasting activities	..	..	..	..	..	..	..	
61	Telecommunications	..	..	..	..	..	..	..	
62-63	IT and other information services	..	..	..	..	..	..	..	
62	Computer programming, consultancy and related activities	..	..	..	..	..	..	..	
63	Information service activities	..	..	..	..	..	..	..	
64-66	**Financial and insurance activities**	6.4	18.8	23.5	17.3	29.7	39.3	91.8	
68-82	**Real estate; professional, scientific and technical; administrative and support**	2 909.4	3 162.7	3 366.0	3 603.7	3 785.1	4 151.0	4 695.4	
68	Real estate activities	0.0	0.0	0.0	0.0	0.0	0.0	0.0	
69-75x72	Professional, scientific and technical activities, except scientific R&D	..	..	..	..	..	..	..	
72	Scientific research and development	2 909.4	3 162.7	3 356.7	3 593.4	3 764.4	4 131.7	4 627.8	
77-82	Administrative and support service activities	..	..	..	..	..	..	..	
84-99	Community, social and personal services	174.3	188.9	206.0	210.9	221.4	239.4	246.9	
84-85	Public administration and defence; compulsory social security and education	..	..	..	..	..	..	..	
86-88	Human health and social work activities	..	..	..	..	..	..	..	
90-93	Arts, entertainment and recreation	..	..	..	..	..	..	..	
94-99	Other services; household-employers; extraterritorial bodies	..	..	..	..	..	..	..	

.. Not available; e Estimated value

Note: Detailed metadata at: http://metalinks.oecd.org/anberd/20200813/2abe.

Information on data for Israel: http://oe.cd/israel-disclaimer.

ISRAEL

R&D expenditure in industry by main activity of the enterprise, constant prices
ISIC Rev. 4

2010 USD PPP

		2011	2012	2013	2014	2015	2016	2017	2018
	TOTAL BUSINESS ENTERPRISE	**8 815.9**	**9 402.7**	**9 646.3**	**10 277.8**	**10 792.0**	**12 061.4**	**13 523.7**	..
01-03	**AGRICULTURE, FORESTRY AND FISHING**	..	..	..	..	..	..	..	..
05-09	**MINING AND QUARRYING**	**3.6**	**6.2**	**6.6**	**6.3**	**4.6**	**5.1**	**3.8**	..
10-33	**MANUFACTURING**	**2 647.2**	**2 537.9**	**2 477.2**	**2 388.9**	**2 377.2**	**2 339.1**	**2 469.8**	..
10-12	Food products, beverages and tobacco	22.1	25.8	18.7	17.0	11.8	15.9	15.0	..
13-15	Textiles, wearing apparel, leather and related products	24.2 e	24.4 e	20.8	21.4	20.1	19.8	19.6	..
13	Textiles	..	..	..	..	..	..	..	..
14	Wearing apparel	..	..	..	..	..	..	..	..
15	Leather and related products, footwear	..	..	..	..	..	..	..	..
16-18	Wood and paper products and printing	3.8 e	3.8 e	3.2	1.3	4.8	4.2	5.5	..
16	Wood and wood products, except furniture	..	..	..	..	..	..	..	..
17	Paper and paper products	..	..	..	..	..	..	..	..
18	Printing and reproduction of recorded media	..	..	..	..	..	..	..	..
19-23	Chemical, rubber, plastic, non-metallic mineral products	415.0	429.0	503.9	413.5	488.5	445.1	398.1	..
19	Coke and refined petroleum products	50.7	70.6	65.9	77.8	88.9	68.8	72.1	..
20-21	Chemical and pharmaceutical products	..	..	..	..	..	..	..	..
20	Chemicals and chemical products	..	..	..	..	..	..	..	..
21	Pharmaceuticals, medicinal, chemical and botanical products	312.9	306.2	389.4	288.1	349.6	326.3	255.8	..
22	Rubber and plastic products	..	..	..	..	..	..	..	..
23	Other non-metallic mineral products	..	..	..	..	..	..	..	..
24-25	Basic metals, metal products, except machinery and equipment	98.9	57.7	54.7	53.0	54.3	50.3	62.8	..
24	Basic metals	..	..	..	..	..	..	..	..
25	Fabricated metal products, except machinery and equipment	..	..	..	..	..	..	..	..
26-30	Computer, electronic, optical products; electrical machinery, transport equipment	2 050.3 e	1 961.1 e	1 845.8	1 856.1	1 758.4	1 754.3	1 913.1	..
26	Computer, electronic and optical products	1 722.8	1 602.6	1 547.0	1 568.3	1 460.6	1 475.8	1 612.4	..
27	Electrical equipment	253.2 e	277.2 e	209.9 e	206.5	199.0 e	177.9 e	221.1 e	..
28	Machinery and equipment n.e.c.	0.8 e	0.8 e	0.6 e	0.6	0.6 e	0.5 e	0.7 e	..
29	Motor vehicles, trailers and semi-trailers	..	..	..	..	..	..	..	..
30	Other transport equipment	..	..	..	..	..	..	..	..
31-33	Furniture; repair, installation of machinery and equipment	..	..	..	..	..	..	..	..
31	Furniture	..	..	..	..	..	..	..	..
32	Other manufacturing	33.0 e	36.1 e	30.1	26.5	39.3	49.6	55.6	..
33	Repair and installation of machinery and equipment	..	..	..	..	..	..	..	..
35-39	**ELECTRICITY, GAS, WATER AND WASTE MANAGEMENT**	..	..	**1.2**	**0.8**	**0.6**	**0.6**	**0.9**	..
35-36	Electricity, gas and water	..	..	..	..	..	..	..	..
37-39	Sewerage, waste management and remediation activities	..	..	..	..	..	..	..	..
41-43	**CONSTRUCTION**	..	..	**3.0**	**19.0**	**18.4**	**16.5**	**32.1**	..
45-99	**TOTAL SERVICES**	**6 083.1**	**6 798.1**	**7 158.3**	**7 862.9**	**8 391.3**	**9 700.1**	**11 017.1**	..
45-82	**Business sector services**	**5 890.5**	**6 596.1**	**6 948.9**	**7 645.1**	**8 169.9**	**9 471.5**	**10 784.5**	..
45-47	**Wholesale and retail trade; motor vehicle and motorcycle repairs**	..	..	**5.7**	**3.4**	**8.6**	**9.3**	**69.1**	..
49-53	**Transportation and storage**	**0.0**	**0.0**	**0.0**	**0.0**	**0.0**	**0.0**	**0.0**	..
55-56	**Accommodation and food service activities**	**0.0**	**0.0**	**0.0**	**0.0**	**0.0**	**0.0**	**0.0**	..
58-63	**Information and communication**	**2 669.1**	**3 192.1**	**3 498.4**	**3 902.6**	**4 346.5**	**5 461.4**	**6 206.0**	..
58-60	Publishing, audiovisual and broadcasting activities	..	..	..	..	..	..	..	..
58	Publishing activities	..	..	..	..	..	..	..	..
59-60	Motion picture, video and TV programme production; broadcasting activities	..	..	..	..	..	..	..	..
59	Motion picture, video and TV programme production; sound and music	..	..	..	..	..	..	..	..
60	Programming and broadcasting activities	..	..	..	..	..	..	..	..
61	Telecommunications	..	..	..	..	..	..	..	..
62-63	IT and other information services	..	..	..	..	..	..	..	..
62	Computer programming, consultancy and related activities	..	..	..	..	..	..	..	..
63	Information service activities	..	..	..	..	..	..	..	..
64-66	**Financial and insurance activities**	**7.1**	**20.2**	**23.9**	**17.8**	**29.7**	**37.5**	**86.5**	..
68-82	**Real estate; professional, scientific and technical; administrative and support**	**3 214.4**	**3 383.8**	**3 420.9**	**3 721.3**	**3 785.1**	**3 963.3**	**4 422.9**	..
68	Real estate activities	0.0	0.0	0.0	0.0	0.0	0.0	0.0	..
69-75x72	Professional, scientific and technical activities, except scientific R&D	..	..	..	..	..	..	..	..
72	Scientific research and development	3 214.4	3 383.8	3 411.5	3 710.6	3 764.4	3 944.8	4 359.3	..
77-82	Administrative and support service activities	..	..	..	..	..	..	..	..
84-99	Community, social and personal services	192.5	202.1	209.4	217.7	221.4	228.5	232.6	..
84-85	Public administration and defence; compulsory social security and education	..	..	..	..	..	..	..	..
86-88	Human health and social work activities	..	..	..	..	..	..	..	..
90-93	Arts, entertainment and recreation	..	..	..	..	..	..	..	..
94-99	Other services; household-employers; extraterritorial bodies	..	..	..	..	..	..	..	..

.. Not available; e Estimated value

Note: Detailed metadata at: *http://metalinks.oecd.org/anberd/20200813/2abe.*

Information on data for Israel: *http://oe.cd/israel-disclaimer.*

ITALY

R&D expenditure in industry by main activity of the enterprise, current prices
ISIC Rev. 4

Million USD PPP

		2011	2012	2013	2014	2015	2016	2017	2018
	TOTAL BUSINESS ENTERPRISE	**14 268.5**	**14 854.5**	**15 570.9**	**16 688.8**	**17 449.5**	**20 108.3**	**21 615.9**	..
01-03	**AGRICULTURE, FORESTRY AND FISHING**	**4.3**	**4.5**	**6.0**	**9.4**	**12.6**	**15.9**	**8.7**	..
05-09	**MINING AND QUARRYING**	**82.6**	**83.3**	**79.9**	**72.0**	**62.7**	**88.0**	**106.4**	..
10-33	**MANUFACTURING**	**10 501.7**	**11 035.4**	**11 229.0**	**11 810.9**	**12 226.3**	**14 034.5**	**14 788.7**	..
10-12	Food products, beverages and tobacco	198.1	229.5	255.4	270.1	301.6	359.6	376.9	..
13-15	Textiles, wearing apparel, leather and related products	572.6	611.2	651.8	692.7	745.2	852.1	1 012.3	..
13	Textiles	131.9	137.3	150.1	171.2	179.3	198.8	243.8	..
14	Wearing apparel	281.5	301.4	304.5	306.2	349.0	396.2	474.2	..
15	Leather and related products, footwear	159.1	172.4	197.2	215.4	216.9	257.1	294.2	..
16-18	Wood and paper products and printing	95.3	87.1	101.6	106.0	127.0	157.8	201.4	..
16	Wood and wood products, except furniture	17.9	18.3	18.4	18.3	16.9	25.6	42.9	..
17	Paper and paper products	63.7	56.7	69.4	69.7	92.5	94.6	112.9	..
18	Printing and reproduction of recorded media	13.7	12.0	13.7	18.0	17.6	37.6	45.6	..
19-23	Chemical, rubber, plastic, non-metallic mineral products	1 640.7	1 765.1	1 751.9	1 827.2	1 912.0	2 238.8	2 431.2	..
19	Coke and refined petroleum products	16.6	16.4	18.3	23.5	21.9	14.9	16.0	..
20-21	Chemical and pharmaceutical products	1 208.9	1 244.3	1 232.5	1 213.0	1 295.1	1 521.4	1 589.7	..
20	Chemicals and chemical products	446.6	472.8	494.2	521.3	565.5	679.8	716.9	..
21	Pharmaceuticals, medicinal, chemical and botanical products	762.4	771.5	738.2	691.7	729.6	841.6	872.7	..
22	Rubber and plastic products	309.6	375.5	370.1	443.8	416.4	486.9	577.1	..
23	Other non-metallic mineral products	105.6	128.8	131.0	146.9	178.6	215.6	248.4	..
24-25	Basic metals, metal products, except machinery and equipment	494.1	507.3	568.0	534.9	604.9	741.9	763.6	..
24	Basic metals	138.9	134.4	125.6	109.6	119.3	181.5	205.0	..
25	Fabricated metal products, except machinery and equipment	355.2	372.9	442.4	425.4	485.6	560.4	558.6	..
26-30	Computer, electronic, optical products; electrical machinery, transport equipment	7 244.2	7 533.5	7 601.7	8 049.6	8 190.2	9 223.9	9 489.4	..
26	Computer, electronic and optical products	1 902.8	1 828.9	1 757.4	1 771.2	1 857.0	1 391.8	1 502.2	..
27	Electrical equipment	607.1	631.0	655.1	631.4	684.4	843.2	915.7	..
28	Machinery and equipment n.e.c.	1 539.2	1 731.5	1 860.4	1 976.4	2 042.8	2 333.9	2 672.0	..
29	Motor vehicles, trailers and semi-trailers	1 710.5	1 844.0	1 971.2	2 361.9	2 299.1	2 557.4	2 187.7	..
30	Other transport equipment	1 484.8	1 498.0	1 357.8	1 308.6	1 306.8	2 097.5	2 211.8	..
31-33	Furniture; repair, installation of machinery and equipment	256.6	301.8	298.1	330.3	345.4	460.4	514.1	..
31	Furniture	69.2	75.4	77.0	90.6	99.4	127.0	157.5	..
32	Other manufacturing	118.9	146.3	129.1	146.7	154.6	238.9	245.2	..
33	Repair and installation of machinery and equipment	68.5	80.1	92.0	93.0	91.4	94.5	111.4	..
35-39	**ELECTRICITY, GAS, WATER AND WASTE MANAGEMENT**	**28.1**	**37.2**	**43.8**	**212.1**	**138.5**	**93.2**	**147.2**	..
35-36	Electricity, gas and water	20.6	28.0	36.3	194.3	120.7	70.8	118.4	..
37-39	Sewerage, waste management and remediation activities	7.5	9.2	7.5	17.9	17.9	22.5	28.7	..
41-43	**CONSTRUCTION**	**42.0**	**48.7**	**57.1**	**50.9**	**142.2**	**138.4**	**192.5**	..
45-99	**TOTAL SERVICES**	**3 609.7**	**3 645.4**	**4 155.2**	**4 533.3**	**4 867.2**	**5 738.4**	**6 372.4**	..
45-82	**Business sector services**	**3 500.0**	**3 477.1**	**3 913.6**	**4 276.2**	**4 565.1**	**5 393.6**	**5 922.4**	..
45-47	**Wholesale and retail trade; motor vehicle and motorcycle repairs**	**336.9**	**365.2**	**434.4**	**480.8**	**542.7**	**723.1**	**973.0**	..
49-53	**Transportation and storage**	**36.6**	**23.9**	**55.1**	**51.2**	**53.4**	**59.1**	**81.0**	..
55-56	**Accommodation and food service activities**	**3.8**	**3.2**	**2.4**	**3.0**	**2.7**	**4.4**	**9.5**	..
58-63	**Information and communication**	**1 489.9**	**1 515.3**	**1 764.7**	**1 664.2**	**1 847.5**	**2 154.4**	**2 322.3**	..
58-60	Publishing, audiovisual and broadcasting activities	16.3	23.7	21.3	26.4	31.0	33.6	41.5	..
58	Publishing activities	5.9	15.1	12.2	17.6	20.7	27.7	32.5	..
59-60	Motion picture, video and TV programme production; broadcasting activities	10.4	8.6	9.0	8.9	10.2	5.9	9.1	..
59	Motion picture, video and TV programme production; sound and music	..	..	..	..	..	..	..	..
60	Programming and broadcasting activities	..	..	..	..	..	..	..	..
61	Telecommunications	1 090.8	1 088.2	577.9	421.8	436.3	845.8	718.8	..
62-63	IT and other information services	382.8	403.4	1 165.3	1 216.0	1 380.2	1 275.1	1 562.0	..
62	Computer programming, consultancy and related activities	346.8	362.2	661.9	1 162.6	1 330.4	1 177.8	1 454.8	..
63	Information service activities	36.0	41.2	503.5	53.4	49.8	97.3	107.2	..
64-66	**Financial and insurance activities**	**188.4**	**229.4**	**253.2**	**303.5**	**317.4**	**363.1**	**421.3**	..
68-82	**Real estate; professional, scientific and technical; administrative and support**	**1 444.3**	**1 340.1**	**1 403.8**	**1 773.4**	**1 801.4**	**2 089.4**	**2 115.3**	..
68	Real estate activities	7.0	10.3	3.0	4.0	1.5	5.8	3.8	..
69-75x72	Professional, scientific and technical activities, except scientific R&D	495.2	431.8	460.6	487.6	509.5	606.2	674.1	..
72	Scientific research and development	930.2	879.3	929.3	1 242.4	1 216.7	1 356.1	1 310.0	..
77-82	Administrative and support service activities	12.0	18.6	10.9	39.5	73.7	121.4	127.4	..
84-99	Community, social and personal services	109.7	168.4	241.6	257.1	302.1	344.8	450.0	..
84-85	Public administration and defence; compulsory social security and education	2.9	1.9	2.3	2.2	16.9	5.8	8.3	..
86-88	Human health and social work activities	94.4	155.1	216.7	223.7	238.3	290.2	395.0	..
90-93	Arts, entertainment and recreation	2.0	1.3	10.4	19.5	36.4	30.5	29.3	..
94-99	Other services; household-employers; extraterritorial bodies	10.4	10.0	12.1	11.8	10.4	18.2	17.5	..

.. Not available

Note: Detailed metadata at: *http://metalinks.oecd.org/anberd/20200813/2abe.*

R&D expenditure in industry by main activity of the enterprise, constant prices
ISIC Rev. 4

2010 USD PPP

		2011	2012	2013	2014	2015	2016	2017	2018
	TOTAL BUSINESS ENTERPRISE	15 335.3	15 494.9	15 833.8	16 870.5	17 449.5	18 862.5	19 732.9	..
01-03	**AGRICULTURE, FORESTRY AND FISHING**	4.7	4.7	6.1	9.5	12.6	14.9	7.9	..
05-09	**MINING AND QUARRYING**	88.8	86.9	81.2	72.8	62.7	82.5	97.2	..
10-33	**MANUFACTURING**	11 286.9	11 511.1	11 418.6	11 939.5	12 226.3	13 165.0	13 500.5	..
10-12	Food products, beverages and tobacco	212.9	239.4	259.7	273.1	301.6	337.3	344.0	..
13-15	Textiles, wearing apparel, leather and related products	615.4	637.5	662.8	700.3	745.2	799.3	924.1	..
13	Textiles	141.8	143.3	152.7	173.1	179.3	186.5	222.6	..
14	Wearing apparel	302.6	314.4	309.6	309.5	349.0	371.6	432.9	..
15	Leather and related products, footwear	171.0	179.8	200.5	217.7	216.9	241.1	268.6	..
16-18	Wood and paper products and printing	102.4	90.8	103.3	107.2	127.0	148.0	183.8	..
16	Wood and wood products, except furniture	19.3	19.1	18.8	18.5	16.9	24.0	39.1	..
17	Paper and paper products	68.4	59.1	70.6	70.4	92.5	88.7	103.0	..
18	Printing and reproduction of recorded media	14.7	12.6	13.9	18.2	17.6	35.3	41.6	..
19-23	Chemical, rubber, plastic, non-metallic mineral products	1 763.4	1 841.2	1 781.5	1 847.1	1 912.0	2 100.1	2 219.4	..
19	Coke and refined petroleum products	17.8	17.2	18.6	23.7	21.9	13.9	14.6	..
20-21	Chemical and pharmaceutical products	1 299.3	1 297.9	1 253.3	1 226.3	1 295.1	1 427.2	1 451.2	..
20	Chemicals and chemical products	480.0	493.1	502.6	527.0	565.5	637.7	654.5	..
21	Pharmaceuticals, medicinal, chemical and botanical products	819.4	804.8	750.7	699.2	729.6	789.5	796.7	..
22	Rubber and plastic products	332.8	391.7	376.4	448.6	416.4	456.7	526.8	..
23	Other non-metallic mineral products	113.5	134.3	133.2	148.5	178.6	202.2	226.8	..
24-25	Basic metals, metal products, except machinery and equipment	531.1	529.1	577.6	540.8	604.9	696.0	697.1	..
24	Basic metals	149.3	140.2	127.7	110.7	119.3	170.3	187.1	..
25	Fabricated metal products, except machinery and equipment	381.8	388.9	449.9	430.0	485.6	525.7	509.9	..
26-30	Computer, electronic, optical products; electrical machinery, transport equipment	7 785.9	7 858.2	7 730.0	8 137.3	8 190.2	8 652.4	8 662.7	..
26	Computer, electronic and optical products	2 045.0	1 907.7	1 787.0	1 790.5	1 857.0	1 305.6	1 371.3	..
27	Electrical equipment	652.5	658.2	666.2	638.3	684.4	791.0	835.9	..
28	Machinery and equipment n.e.c.	1 654.3	1 806.1	1 891.9	1 997.9	2 042.8	2 189.3	2 439.2	..
29	Motor vehicles, trailers and semi-trailers	1 838.3	1 923.5	2 004.5	2 387.6	2 299.1	2 399.0	1 997.1	..
30	Other transport equipment	1 595.8	1 562.6	1 380.7	1 322.9	1 306.8	1 967.6	2 019.1	..
31-33	Furniture; repair, installation of machinery and equipment	275.8	314.9	303.1	333.9	345.4	431.9	469.3	..
31	Furniture	74.4	78.7	78.3	91.6	99.4	119.2	143.7	..
32	Other manufacturing	127.8	152.6	131.3	148.3	154.6	224.1	223.8	..
33	Repair and installation of machinery and equipment	73.7	83.6	93.5	94.0	91.4	88.6	101.7	..
35-39	**ELECTRICITY, GAS, WATER AND WASTE MANAGEMENT**	30.2	38.8	44.5	214.5	138.5	87.5	134.3	..
35-36	Electricity, gas and water	22.1	29.2	37.0	196.5	120.7	66.4	108.1	..
37-39	Sewerage, waste management and remediation activities	8.1	9.6	7.6	18.1	17.9	21.1	26.2	..
41-43	**CONSTRUCTION**	45.2	50.8	58.1	51.4	142.2	129.8	175.7	..
45-99	**TOTAL SERVICES**	3 879.5	3 802.6	4 225.3	4 582.7	4 867.2	5 382.8	5 817.3	..
45-82	**Business sector services**	3 761.7	3 626.9	3 979.7	4 322.8	4 565.1	5 059.4	5 406.5	..
45-47	**Wholesale and retail trade; motor vehicle and motorcycle repairs**	362.1	381.0	441.8	486.1	542.7	678.3	888.2	..
49-53	**Transportation and storage**	39.4	25.0	56.0	51.7	53.4	55.5	74.0	..
55-56	**Accommodation and food service activities**	4.1	3.3	2.5	3.1	2.7	4.1	8.6	..
58-63	**Information and communication**	1 601.3	1 580.6	1 794.5	1 682.4	1 847.5	2 021.0	2 120.0	..
58-60	Publishing, audiovisual and broadcasting activities	17.6	24.7	21.7	26.7	31.0	31.5	37.9	..
58	Publishing activities	6.4	15.8	12.4	17.8	20.7	26.0	29.6	..
59-60	Motion picture, video and TV programme production; broadcasting activities	11.2	8.9	9.1	9.0	10.2	5.5	8.3	..
59	Motion picture, video and TV programme production; sound and music	..	..	..	..	..	..	..	..
60	Programming and broadcasting activities	..	..	..	..	..	..	..	..
61	Telecommunications	1 172.4	1 135.1	587.7	426.4	436.3	793.4	656.2	..
62-63	IT and other information services	411.4	420.7	1 185.0	1 229.2	1 380.2	1 196.1	1 425.9	..
62	Computer programming, consultancy and related activities	372.7	377.8	673.1	1 175.2	1 330.4	1 104.8	1 328.1	..
63	Information service activities	38.7	43.0	512.0	54.0	49.8	91.3	97.9	..
64-66	**Financial and insurance activities**	202.4	239.2	257.5	306.8	317.4	340.6	384.6	..
68-82	**Real estate; professional, scientific and technical; administrative and support**	1 552.3	1 397.8	1 427.5	1 792.7	1 801.4	1 960.0	1 931.1	..
68	Real estate activities	7.5	10.7	3.0	4.0	1.5	5.4	3.5	..
69-75x72	Professional, scientific and technical activities, except scientific R&D	532.2	450.5	468.4	493.0	509.5	568.7	615.4	..
72	Scientific research and development	999.7	917.2	945.0	1 255.9	1 216.7	1 272.1	1 195.9	..
77-82	Administrative and support service activities	12.9	19.4	11.0	39.9	73.7	113.8	116.3	..
84-99	Community, social and personal services	117.9	175.6	245.6	259.9	302.1	323.4	410.8	..
84-85	Public administration and defence; compulsory social security and education	3.1	2.0	2.3	2.2	16.9	5.5	7.5	..
86-88	Human health and social work activities	101.4	161.8	220.4	226.1	238.3	272.3	360.6	..
90-93	Arts, entertainment and recreation	2.1	1.4	10.6	19.7	36.4	28.6	26.7	..
94-99	Other services; household-employers; extraterritorial bodies	11.2	10.5	12.3	11.9	10.4	17.0	15.9	..

.. Not available

Note: Detailed metadata at: http://metalinks.oecd.org/anberd/20200813/2abe.

ITALY

R&D expenditure in industry by industry orientation, current prices
ISIC Rev. 4

Million USD PPP

		2011	2012	2013	2014	2015	2016	2017	2018
	TOTAL BUSINESS ENTERPRISE	**14 268.5**	**14 854.5**	**15 570.9**	**16 688.8**	**17 449.5**	**20 108.3**	..	..
01-03	**AGRICULTURE, FORESTRY AND FISHING**	119.3	130.4	130.7	155.8	130.0	363.1	..	..
05-09	**MINING AND QUARRYING**	47.3	50.2	82.6	53.0	116.6	124.7	..	..
10-33	**MANUFACTURING**	11 511.1	11 772.1	12 181.1	12 599.6	14 015.5	15 679.9	..	..
10-12	Food products, beverages and tobacco	278.6	324.6	385.5	405.4	518.8	750.4	..	..
13-15	Textiles, wearing apparel, leather and related products	736.0	785.0	939.1	1 397.6	928.8	1 080.2	..	..
13	Textiles	269.5	296.1	353.7	685.4	314.3	401.6	..	..
14	Wearing apparel	295.4	310.7	328.2	454.2	372.4	402.8	..	..
15	Leather and related products, footwear	171.1	178.3	257.2	258.0	242.1	275.8	..	..
16-18	Wood and paper products and printing	171.3	171.2	209.5	314.5	212.9	246.4	..	..
16	Wood and wood products, except furniture	46.0	53.6	64.6	75.0	55.7	75.3	..	..
17	Paper and paper products	95.8	94.3	99.0	193.7	116.9	121.6	..	..
18	Printing and reproduction of recorded media	29.5	23.3	46.0	45.8	40.5	49.4	..	..
19-23	Chemical, rubber, plastic, non-metallic mineral products	2 291.9	2 281.3	2 227.7	2 320.8	2 589.5	2 794.6	..	..
19	Coke and refined petroleum products	130.2	115.5	128.4	56.5	35.3	48.0	..	..
20-21	Chemical and pharmaceutical products	1 609.5	1 551.2	1 504.1	1 507.0	1 721.1	1 888.8	..	..
20	Chemicals and chemical products	439.0	455.2	534.0	541.2	575.0	675.3	..	..
21	Pharmaceuticals, medicinal, chemical and botanical products	1 170.4	1 096.0	970.2	965.8	1 146.1	1 213.5	..	..
22	Rubber and plastic products	419.8	455.0	429.3	592.5	587.0	608.6	..	..
23	Other non-metallic mineral products	132.3	159.5	165.9	164.8	246.0	249.2	..	..
24-25	Basic metals, metal products, except machinery and equipment	622.0	682.1	821.0	710.7	946.4	982.1	..	..
24	Basic metals	280.5	321.9	424.4	321.5	325.5	435.5	..	..
25	Fabricated metal products, except machinery and equipment	341.5	360.2	396.6	389.2	620.9	546.7	..	..
26-30	Computer, electronic, optical products; electrical machinery, transport equipment	7 262.2	7 371.9	7 432.5	7 247.6	8 594.9	9 573.4	..	..
26	Computer, electronic and optical products	2 031.3	1 983.3	1 964.5	1 987.2	2 402.5	2 727.6	..	..
27	Electrical equipment	486.8	504.7	535.2	421.5	561.5	659.4	..	..
28	Machinery and equipment n.e.c.	1 069.6	1 172.6	1 224.6	1 340.5	1 417.2	1 788.9	..	..
29	Motor vehicles, trailers and semi-trailers	2 140.7	2 246.7	2 233.4	2 548.2	2 874.0	3 165.8	..	..
30	Other transport equipment	1 534.0	1 464.3	1 474.8	950.2	1 339.9	1 231.6	..	..
31-33	Furniture; repair, installation of machinery and equipment	149.1	156.1	165.7	203.0	224.2	252.9	..	..
31	Furniture	46.8	43.7	45.6	54.7	62.3	72.1	..	..
32	Other manufacturing	91.1	93.5	93.9	120.5	142.2	152.7	..	..
33	Repair and installation of machinery and equipment	11.2	18.9	26.3	27.7	19.8	28.1	..	..
35-39	**ELECTRICITY, GAS, WATER AND WASTE MANAGEMENT**	328.6	303.1	305.4	429.8	339.1	294.0	..	..
35-36	Electricity, gas and water	277.7	258.6	264.6	380.0	291.8	242.9	..	..
37-39	Sewerage, waste management and remediation activities	50.9	44.4	40.8	49.8	47.4	51.1	..	..
41-43	**CONSTRUCTION**	**64.6**	**145.2**	**70.5**	**77.9**	**87.3**	**61.2**	..	..
45-99	**TOTAL SERVICES**	**2 197.6**	**2 453.6**	**2 800.5**	**3 372.8**	**2 761.0**	**3 585.5**	..	..
45-82	**Business sector services**	**2 021.4**	**2 209.9**	**2 522.0**	**3 123.1**	**2 382.8**	**3 176.3**	..	..
45-47	**Wholesale and retail trade; motor vehicle and motorcycle repairs**	42.6	72.2	169.5	390.4	65.7	41.2	..	..
49-53	**Transportation and storage**	66.4	75.2	70.5	77.8	61.5	97.8	..	..
55-56	**Accommodation and food service activities**	10.4	16.7	8.3	15.2	12.3	17.6	..	..
58-63	**Information and communication**	1 494.0	1 539.6	1 624.7	1 834.4	1 618.2	2 186.4	..	..
58-60	Publishing, audiovisual and broadcasting activities	12.0	14.0	17.1	23.8	14.4	35.9	..	..
58	Publishing activities	0.0	0.0	0.0	0.0	0.0	0.0	..	..
59-60	Motion picture, video and TV programme production; broadcasting activities	12.0	14.0	17.1	23.8	14.4	35.9	..	..
59	Motion picture, video and TV programme production; sound and music	12.0	14.0	17.1	23.8	14.4	35.9	..	..
60	Programming and broadcasting activities	0.0	0.0	0.0	0.0	0.0	0.0	..	..
61	Telecommunications	1 050.9	1 084.5	1 009.8	1 127.0	792.0	1 084.9	..	..
62-63	IT and other information services	431.0	441.1	597.9	683.5	811.8	1 065.6	..	..
62	Computer programming, consultancy and related activities	406.9	414.9	553.5	612.1	729.7	952.3	..	..
63	Information service activities	24.1	26.2	44.4	71.5	82.1	113.3	..	..
64-66	**Financial and insurance activities**	216.4	271.2	315.5	361.7	415.4	513.3	..	..
68-82	**Real estate; professional, scientific and technical; administrative and support**	191.5	235.0	333.5	443.5	209.8	320.1	..	..
68	Real estate activities	0.1	0.1	0.9	1.0	3.1	2.6	..	..
69-75x72	Professional, scientific and technical activities, except scientific R&D	188.6	231.5	328.9	438.8	198.5	271.7	..	..
72	Scientific research and development	0.0	0.0	0.0	0.0	0.0	41.5	..	..
77-82	Administrative and support service activities	2.8	3.3	3.7	3.7	8.1	4.3	..	..
84-99	Community, social and personal services	176.2	243.7	278.4	249.7	378.2	409.2	..	..
84-85	Public administration and defence; compulsory social security and education	44.6	51.8	51.7	41.7	44.0	27.0	..	..
86-88	Human health and social work activities	114.4	176.3	216.6	186.3	285.4	337.1	..	..
90-93	Arts, entertainment and recreation	0.5	3.7	1.9	5.5	9.6	15.6	..	..
94-99	Other services; household-employers; extraterritorial bodies	16.7	11.9	8.3	16.1	39.3	29.5	..	..

.. Not available

Note: Detailed metadata at: *http://metalinks.oecd.org/anberd/20200813/2abe.*

ITALY

R&D expenditure in industry by industry orientation, constant prices
ISIC Rev. 4

2010 USD PPP

		2011	2012	2013	2014	2015	2016	2017	2018
	TOTAL BUSINESS ENTERPRISE	**15 335.3**	**15 494.9**	**15 833.8**	**16 870.5**	**17 449.5**	**18 862.5**	..	..
01-03	**AGRICULTURE, FORESTRY AND FISHING**	**128.2**	**136.0**	**133.0**	**157.4**	**130.0**	**340.6**	..	..
05-09	**MINING AND QUARRYING**	**50.9**	**52.3**	**84.0**	**53.6**	**116.6**	**117.0**	..	..
10-33	**MANUFACTURING**	**12 371.7**	**12 279.6**	**12 386.8**	**12 736.8**	**14 015.5**	**14 708.5**	..	..
10-12	Food products, beverages and tobacco	299.5	338.6	392.0	409.8	518.8	703.9	..	..
13-15	Textiles, wearing apparel, leather and related products	791.0	818.9	955.0	1 412.8	928.8	1 013.2	..	..
13	Textiles	289.7	308.9	359.7	692.9	314.3	376.7	..	..
14	Wearing apparel	317.5	324.1	333.8	459.1	372.4	377.8	..	..
15	Leather and related products, footwear	183.9	186.0	261.5	260.9	242.1	258.7	..	..
16-18	Wood and paper products and printing	184.2	178.6	213.1	318.0	212.9	231.1	..	..
16	Wood and wood products, except furniture	49.4	55.9	65.7	75.8	55.7	70.7	..	..
17	Paper and paper products	103.0	98.3	100.7	195.8	116.9	114.1	..	..
18	Printing and reproduction of recorded media	31.7	24.3	46.8	46.3	40.5	46.4	..	..
19-23	Chemical, rubber, plastic, non-metallic mineral products	2 463.2	2 379.6	2 265.3	2 346.0	2 589.5	2 621.4	..	..
19	Coke and refined petroleum products	140.0	120.5	130.6	57.1	35.3	45.0	..	..
20-21	Chemical and pharmaceutical products	1 729.8	1 618.1	1 529.5	1 523.4	1 721.1	1 771.8	..	..
20	Chemicals and chemical products	471.9	474.9	543.0	547.1	575.0	633.5	..	..
21	Pharmaceuticals, medicinal, chemical and botanical products	1 258.0	1 143.2	986.5	976.3	1 146.1	1 138.3	..	..
22	Rubber and plastic products	451.2	474.6	436.5	599.0	587.0	570.9	..	..
23	Other non-metallic mineral products	142.2	166.4	168.7	166.6	246.0	233.7	..	..
24-25	Basic metals, metal products, except machinery and equipment	668.5	711.5	834.8	718.4	946.4	921.3	..	..
24	Basic metals	301.5	335.8	431.6	325.0	325.5	408.5	..	..
25	Fabricated metal products, except machinery and equipment	367.0	375.7	403.3	393.4	620.9	512.8	..	..
26-30	Computer, electronic, optical products; electrical machinery, transport equipment	7 805.1	7 689.7	7 558.0	7 326.5	8 594.9	8 980.3	..	..
26	Computer, electronic and optical products	2 183.1	2 068.8	1 997.6	2 008.9	2 402.5	2 558.6	..	..
27	Electrical equipment	523.2	526.5	544.2	426.1	561.5	618.5	..	..
28	Machinery and equipment n.e.c.	1 149.6	1 223.2	1 245.3	1 355.1	1 417.2	1 678.1	..	..
29	Motor vehicles, trailers and semi-trailers	2 300.7	2 343.5	2 271.1	2 575.9	2 874.0	2 969.7	..	..
30	Other transport equipment	1 648.7	1 527.4	1 499.7	960.6	1 339.9	1 155.3	..	..
31-33	Furniture; repair, installation of machinery and equipment	160.2	162.8	168.5	205.2	224.2	237.2	..	..
31	Furniture	50.3	45.6	46.3	55.3	62.3	67.7	..	..
32	Other manufacturing	97.9	97.5	95.4	121.9	142.2	143.2	..	..
33	Repair and installation of machinery and equipment	12.0	19.7	26.8	28.0	19.8	26.4	..	..
35-39	**ELECTRICITY, GAS, WATER AND WASTE MANAGEMENT**	**353.2**	**316.1**	**310.6**	**434.5**	**339.1**	**275.7**	..	..
35-36	Electricity, gas and water	298.5	269.8	269.1	384.2	291.8	227.8	..	..
37-39	Sewerage, waste management and remediation activities	54.7	46.3	41.5	50.3	47.4	47.9	..	..
41-43	**CONSTRUCTION**	**69.4**	**151.5**	**71.7**	**78.7**	**87.3**	**57.4**	..	..
45-99	**TOTAL SERVICES**	**2 361.9**	**2 559.3**	**2 847.8**	**3 409.5**	**2 761.0**	**3 363.3**	..	..
45-82	**Business sector services**	**2 172.5**	**2 305.2**	**2 564.6**	**3 157.2**	**2 382.8**	**2 979.5**	..	..
45-47	**Wholesale and retail trade; motor vehicle and motorcycle repairs**	**45.8**	**75.3**	**172.4**	**394.7**	**65.7**	**38.6**	..	..
49-53	**Transportation and storage**	**71.4**	**78.4**	**71.7**	**78.6**	**61.5**	**91.7**	..	..
55-56	**Accommodation and food service activities**	**11.2**	**17.4**	**8.4**	**15.4**	**12.3**	**16.5**	..	..
58-63	**Information and communication**	**1 605.7**	**1 606.0**	**1 652.1**	**1 854.4**	**1 618.2**	**2 050.9**	..	..
58-60	Publishing, audiovisual and broadcasting activities	12.9	14.6	17.4	24.1	14.4	33.7	..	..
58	Publishing activities	0.0	0.0	0.0	0.0	0.0	0.0	..	..
59-60	Motion picture, video and TV programme production; broadcasting activities	12.9	14.6	17.4	24.1	14.4	33.7	..	..
59	Motion picture, video and TV programme production; sound and music	12.9	14.6	17.4	24.1	14.4	33.7	..	..
60	Programming and broadcasting activities	0.0	0.0	0.0	0.0	0.0	0.0	..	..
61	Telecommunications	1 129.5	1 131.2	1 026.8	1 139.3	792.0	1 017.7	..	..
62-63	IT and other information services	463.2	460.1	608.0	691.0	811.8	999.6	..	..
62	Computer programming, consultancy and related activities	437.3	432.7	562.9	618.7	729.7	893.3	..	..
63	Information service activities	25.9	27.3	45.1	72.2	82.1	106.3	..	..
64-66	**Financial and insurance activities**	**232.6**	**282.9**	**320.8**	**365.7**	**415.4**	**481.5**	..	..
68-82	**Real estate; professional, scientific and technical; administrative and support**	**205.8**	**245.1**	**339.1**	**448.4**	**209.8**	**300.3**	..	..
68	Real estate activities	0.1	0.1	1.0	1.0	3.1	2.4	..	..
69-75x72	Professional, scientific and technical activities, except scientific R&D	202.7	241.5	334.5	443.5	198.5	254.9	..	..
72	Scientific research and development	0.0	0.0	0.0	0.0	0.0	39.0	..	..
77-82	Administrative and support service activities	3.0	3.5	3.7	3.8	8.1	4.0	..	..
84-99	Community, social and personal services	189.4	254.2	283.2	252.4	378.2	383.8	..	..
84-85	Public administration and defence; compulsory social security and education	47.9	54.0	52.5	42.1	44.0	25.3	..	..
86-88	Human health and social work activities	123.0	183.9	220.3	188.4	285.4	316.2	..	..
90-93	Arts, entertainment and recreation	0.6	3.9	1.9	5.6	9.6	14.6	..	..
94-99	Other services; household-employers; extraterritorial bodies	18.0	12.4	8.4	16.3	39.3	27.7	..	..

.. Not available

Note: Detailed metadata at: http://metalinks.oecd.org/anberd/20200813/2abe.

R&D expenditure in industry by main activity of the enterprise, current prices
ISIC Rev. 4

Million USD PPP

		2011	2012	2013	2014	2015	2016	2017	2018
	TOTAL BUSINESS ENTERPRISE	114 204.6	116 716.3	125 287.5	131 839.8	132 293.7	126 236.6	130 945.5	136 044.5
01-03	**AGRICULTURE, FORESTRY AND FISHING**	27.6	17.8	21.2	18.4	20.7	24.1	19.4	24.3
05-09	**MINING AND QUARRYING**	30.3	29.0	43.1	36.6	39.5	38.3	33.4	34.4
10-33	**MANUFACTURING**	100 352.8	102 653.6	111 166.7	114 069.5	114 684.6	109 710.9	113 701.8	117 724.3
10-12	Food products, beverages and tobacco	2 085.7	2 113.7	2 306.8	2 034.5	2 122.1	2 148.7	2 612.9	2 567.5
13-15	Textiles, wearing apparel, leather and related products	1 266.2	1 305.1	1 366.3	1 320.1	1 332.7	1 352.0	1 700.4	1 798.6
13	Textiles	1 191.3	1 240.0	1 297.4	1 244.3	1 267.6	1 303.6	1 650.5	1 713.2
14	Wearing apparel	40.9	29.6	30.8	41.0	27.5	18.8	20.5	51.9
15	Leather and related products, footwear	34.0	35.4	38.0	34.8	37.5	29.7	29.4	33.6
16-18	Wood and paper products and printing	734.3	677.2	579.6	590.3	568.4	605.2	625.4	645.7
16	Wood and wood products, except furniture	86.0	101.3	91.6	83.3	82.0	82.4	79.9	72.5
17	Paper and paper products	319.8	240.5	203.3	282.0	268.7	278.4	291.3	316.6
18	Printing and reproduction of recorded media	328.5	335.4	284.8	225.0	217.7	244.3	254.2	256.6
19-23	Chemical, rubber, plastic, non-metallic mineral products	22 802.7	24 183.4	26 445.0	26 988.8	27 063.5	25 956.5	27 311.4	26 929.6
19	Coke and refined petroleum products	447.7	440.0	462.4	408.4	427.8	430.0	448.3	444.7
20-21	Chemical and pharmaceutical products	18 371.2	19 688.5	21 608.5	21 821.4	21 984.6	20 861.5	21 994.8	21 428.2
20	Chemicals and chemical products	6 925.1	7 162.5	7 422.7	7 310.9	7 893.5	8 050.8	8 089.8	8 000.5
21	Pharmaceuticals, medicinal, chemical and botanical products	11 446.1	12 526.0	14 185.8	14 510.5	14 091.1	12 810.8	13 905.0	13 427.6
22	Rubber and plastic products	2 594.7	2 638.7	2 916.5	3 281.8	3 310.2	3 309.1	3 372.0	3 539.4
23	Other non-metallic mineral products	1 389.0	1 416.3	1 457.6	1 477.1	1 340.9	1 355.8	1 496.3	1 517.4
24-25	Basic metals, metal products, except machinery and equipment	2 865.7	2 658.2	2 747.4	2 975.0	2 835.3	2 692.0	2 791.3	2 794.3
24	Basic metals	2 360.2	2 166.9	2 256.9	2 459.5	2 372.7	2 222.4	2 231.2	2 235.1
25	Fabricated metal products, except machinery and equipment	505.5	491.4	490.5	515.5	462.6	469.7	560.1	559.2
26-30	Computer, electronic, optical products; electrical machinery, transport equipment	68 596.4	69 587.1	75 291.2	77 941.2	78 954.0	75 239.7	76 790.3	80 466.8
26	Computer, electronic and optical products	29 244.8	28 387.1	28 750.8	28 017.8	27 883.9	24 905.7	25 331.6	26 477.0
27	Electrical equipment	3 221.7	3 267.6	3 467.5	3 428.3	3 418.5	3 418.5	3 556.8	3 689.4
28	Machinery and equipment n.e.c.	10 211.0	10 414.6	12 315.0	12 440.8	12 610.7	12 737.5	12 708.7	13 625.9
29	Motor vehicles, trailers and semi-trailers	25 408.9	26 930.1	29 995.1	33 184.4	33 977.3	33 120.1	33 977.6	35 466.1
30	Other transport equipment	510.1	587.7	762.7	869.9	1 063.5	1 058.0	1 215.6	1 208.4
31-33	Furniture; repair, installation of machinery and equipment	2 002.0	2 128.9	2 430.4	2 219.7	1 808.6	1 716.8	1 870.0	2 521.8
31	Furniture	106.8	98.0	97.4	108.8	106.4	136.1	124.9	139.9
32	Other manufacturing	1 895.2	2 030.9	2 333.0	2 110.9	1 702.2	1 580.7	1 745.1	2 381.9
33	Repair and installation of machinery and equipment	..	..	..	..	..	..	..	..
35-39	**ELECTRICITY, GAS, WATER AND WASTE MANAGEMENT**	505.6	503.7	512.4	464.3	468.3	384.2	558.0	513.7
35-36	Electricity, gas and water	..	..	..	..	..	..	..	..
37-39	Sewerage, waste management and remediation activities	..	..	..	..	..	..	..	..
41-43	**CONSTRUCTION**	1 024.1	1 066.6	1 061.3	951.1	1 035.7	1 183.9	1 179.9	1 442.1
45-99	**TOTAL SERVICES**	12 264.2	12 445.6	12 482.7	16 299.8	16 044.8	14 895.1	15 453.1	16 305.7
45-82	**Business sector services**	12 264.2	12 445.6	12 482.7	16 299.8	16 044.8	14 895.1	15 453.1	16 305.7
45-47	Wholesale and retail trade; motor vehicle and motorcycle repairs	313.1	463.2	489.0	641.1	723.1	714.3	696.9	853.5
49-53	Transportation and storage	326.9	425.8	519.2	561.5	439.1	434.5	520.7	536.9
55-56	Accommodation and food service activities	..	..	..	..	..	..	..	..
58-63	Information and communication	5 237.9	5 181.1	4 587.8	6 680.2	6 238.2	5 551.0	5 752.4	5 744.7
58-60	Publishing, audiovisual and broadcasting activities	8.7	9.5	18.9	16.3	15.7	28.1	30.8	24.8
58	Publishing activities	4.6	6.3	8.6	9.4	5.6	17.3	15.8	15.0
59-60	Motion picture, video and TV programme production; broadcasting activities	4.1	3.2	10.3	6.9	10.0	10.9	15.0	9.8
59	Motion picture, video and TV programme production; sound and music	0.7	0.7	1.8	1.9	2.2	3.5	4.9	3.4
60	Programming and broadcasting activities	3.5	2.5	8.5	5.0	7.9	7.4	10.1	6.4
61	Telecommunications	2 779.8	2 832.9	2 764.9	3 686.0	3 669.8	3 196.3	2 697.6	2 612.3
62-63	IT and other information services	2 449.5	2 338.7	1 804.0	2 977.9	2 552.8	2 326.5	3 024.0	3 107.6
62	Computer programming, consultancy and related activities	2 142.3	2 093.0	1 592.3	2 685.3	2 249.5	2 037.6	2 765.8	2 830.7
63	Information service activities	307.1	245.7	211.8	292.6	303.3	289.0	258.2	276.9
64-66	**Financial and insurance activities**	30.5	17.6	21.6	31.8	35.7	28.7	43.9	84.8
68-82	**Real estate; professional, scientific and technical; administrative and support**	6 355.8	6 357.8	6 865.0	8 385.2	8 608.6	8 166.6	8 439.1	9 085.7
68	Real estate activities	..	..	..	..	..	..	..	..
69-75x72	Professional, scientific and technical activities, except scientific R&D	342.0	588.2	711.0	725.6	577.0	653.4	593.5	656.3
72	Scientific research and development	5 958.0	5 713.5	6 101.3	7 602.0	7 952.3	7 433.5	7 773.8	8 334.5
77-82	Administrative and support service activities	55.7	56.1	52.7	57.7	79.3	79.8	71.8	94.9
84-99	Community, social and personal services	..	..	..	..	..	..	..	..
84-85	Public administration and defence; compulsory social security and education	..	..	..	..	..	..	..	..
86-88	Human health and social work activities	..	..	..	..	..	..	..	..
90-93	Arts, entertainment and recreation	..	..	..	..	..	..	..	..
94-99	Other services; household-employers; extraterritorial bodies	..	..	..	..	..	..	..	..

.. Not available

Note: Detailed metadata at: http://metalinks.oecd.org/anberd/20200813/2abe.

R&D expenditure in industry by main activity of the enterprise, constant prices
ISIC Rev. 4

2010 USD PPP

		2011	2012	2013	2014	2015	2016	2017	2018
	TOTAL BUSINESS ENTERPRISE	121 938.8	121 860.2	127 506.5	134 150.6	132 293.7	128 398.1	133 324.9	137 623.7
01-03	AGRICULTURE, FORESTRY AND FISHING	29.5	18.6	21.6	18.7	20.7	24.6	19.7	24.6
05-09	MINING AND QUARRYING	32.4	30.3	43.8	37.2	39.5	39.0	34.0	34.8
10-33	MANUFACTURING	107 148.9	107 177.7	113 135.7	116 068.9	114 684.6	111 589.4	115 767.9	119 090.9
10-12	Food products, beverages and tobacco	2 226.9	2 206.8	2 347.6	2 070.2	2 122.1	2 185.5	2 660.4	2 597.3
13-15	Textiles, wearing apparel, leather and related products	1 351.9	1 362.6	1 390.5	1 343.2	1 332.7	1 375.2	1 731.3	1 819.5
13	Textiles	1 271.9	1 294.7	1 320.4	1 266.1	1 267.6	1 325.9	1 680.5	1 733.1
14	Wearing apparel	43.7	30.9	31.3	41.7	27.5	19.1	20.9	52.5
15	Leather and related products, footwear	36.3	37.0	38.7	35.4	37.5	30.2	30.0	34.0
16-18	Wood and paper products and printing	784.0	707.1	589.9	600.6	568.4	615.6	636.8	653.2
16	Wood and wood products, except furniture	91.8	105.8	93.2	84.7	82.0	83.9	81.4	73.3
17	Paper and paper products	341.4	251.1	206.9	286.9	268.7	283.2	296.6	320.3
18	Printing and reproduction of recorded media	350.8	350.2	289.8	228.9	217.7	248.5	258.8	259.6
19-23	Chemical, rubber, plastic, non-metallic mineral products	24 346.9	25 249.2	26 913.4	27 461.9	27 063.5	26 400.9	27 807.7	27 242.2
19	Coke and refined petroleum products	478.0	459.3	470.6	415.6	427.8	437.3	456.4	449.9
20-21	Chemical and pharmaceutical products	19 615.4	20 556.2	21 991.2	22 203.9	21 984.6	21 218.7	22 394.5	21 676.9
20	Chemicals and chemical products	7 394.1	7 478.2	7 554.2	7 439.1	7 893.5	8 188.6	8 236.8	8 093.4
21	Pharmaceuticals, medicinal, chemical and botanical products	12 221.3	13 078.0	14 437.0	14 764.8	14 091.1	13 030.1	14 157.7	13 583.5
22	Rubber and plastic products	2 770.4	2 755.0	2 968.2	3 339.4	3 310.2	3 365.8	3 433.3	3 580.5
23	Other non-metallic mineral products	1 483.1	1 478.7	1 483.4	1 503.0	1 340.9	1 379.1	1 523.5	1 535.0
24-25	Basic metals, metal products, except machinery and equipment	3 059.7	2 775.4	2 796.1	3 027.1	2 835.3	2 738.1	2 842.1	2 826.8
24	Basic metals	2 520.0	2 262.4	2 296.9	2 502.6	2 372.7	2 260.4	2 271.8	2 261.1
25	Fabricated metal products, except machinery and equipment	539.7	513.0	499.2	524.5	462.6	477.7	570.3	565.7
26-30	Computer, electronic, optical products; electrical machinery, transport equipment	73 241.9	72 653.9	76 624.7	79 307.3	78 954.0	76 528.0	78 185.7	81 400.8
26	Computer, electronic and optical products	31 225.3	29 638.2	29 260.0	28 508.8	27 883.9	25 332.2	25 791.9	26 784.3
27	Electrical equipment	3 439.9	3 411.6	3 528.9	3 488.4	3 418.5	3 477.0	3 621.4	3 732.2
28	Machinery and equipment n.e.c.	10 902.5	10 873.6	12 533.2	12 658.9	12 610.7	12 955.6	12 939.7	13 784.0
29	Motor vehicles, trailers and semi-trailers	27 129.6	28 117.0	30 526.4	33 766.1	33 977.3	33 687.2	34 595.0	35 877.8
30	Other transport equipment	544.6	613.6	776.2	885.1	1 063.5	1 076.1	1 237.7	1 222.4
31-33	Furniture; repair, installation of machinery and equipment	2 137.6	2 222.7	2 473.4	2 258.6	1 808.6	1 746.2	1 904.0	2 551.1
31	Furniture	114.0	102.3	99.1	110.7	106.4	138.4	127.2	141.5
32	Other manufacturing	2 023.5	2 120.4	2 374.4	2 147.9	1 702.2	1 607.8	1 776.8	2 409.6
33	Repair and installation of machinery and equipment	..	..	..	..	..	..	..	..
35-39	ELECTRICITY, GAS, WATER AND WASTE MANAGEMENT	539.9	526.0	521.5	472.5	468.3	390.8	568.1	519.7
35-36	Electricity, gas and water	..	..	..	..	..	..	..	..
37-39	Sewerage, waste management and remediation activities	..	..	..	..	..	..	..	..
41-43	CONSTRUCTION	1 093.4	1 113.6	1 080.1	967.8	1 035.7	1 204.2	1 201.4	1 458.8
45-99	TOTAL SERVICES	13 094.7	12 994.1	12 703.8	16 585.5	16 044.8	15 150.2	15 733.9	16 495.0
45-82	Business sector services	13 094.7	12 994.1	12 703.8	16 585.5	16 044.8	15 150.2	15 733.9	16 495.0
45-47	Wholesale and retail trade; motor vehicle and motorcycle repairs	334.3	483.6	497.7	652.4	723.1	726.6	709.6	863.4
49-53	Transportation and storage	349.0	444.6	528.4	571.3	439.1	442.0	530.2	543.2
55-56	Accommodation and food service activities	..	..	..	..	..	..	..	..
58-63	Information and communication	5 592.6	5 409.4	4 669.1	6 797.3	6 238.2	5 646.0	5 856.9	5 811.4
58-60	Publishing, audiovisual and broadcasting activities	9.3	9.9	19.3	16.6	15.7	28.6	31.3	25.1
58	Publishing activities	4.9	6.6	8.8	9.5	5.6	17.6	16.0	15.2
59-60	Motion picture, video and TV programme production; broadcasting activities	4.4	3.3	10.5	7.0	10.0	11.0	15.3	9.9
59	Motion picture, video and TV programme production; sound and music	0.7	0.7	1.8	2.0	2.2	3.5	5.0	3.5
60	Programming and broadcasting activities	3.7	2.6	8.7	5.1	7.9	7.5	10.3	6.5
61	Telecommunications	2 968.0	2 957.7	2 813.8	3 750.7	3 669.8	3 251.0	2 746.6	2 642.6
62-63	IT and other information services	2 615.3	2 441.8	1 836.0	3 030.1	2 552.8	2 366.4	3 079.0	3 143.7
62	Computer programming, consultancy and related activities	2 287.4	2 185.2	1 620.5	2 732.4	2 249.5	2 072.5	2 816.1	2 863.5
63	Information service activities	327.9	256.5	215.5	297.7	303.3	293.9	262.9	280.2
64-66	Financial and insurance activities	32.6	18.4	22.0	32.4	35.7	29.2	44.7	85.8
68-82	Real estate; professional, scientific and technical; administrative and support	6 786.2	6 638.0	6 986.6	8 532.2	8 608.6	8 306.5	8 592.5	9 191.2
68	Real estate activities	..	..	..	..	..	..	..	..
69-75x72	Professional, scientific and technical activities, except scientific R&D	365.2	614.1	723.6	738.3	577.0	664.6	604.3	663.9
72	Scientific research and development	6 361.5	5 965.3	6 209.4	7 735.2	7 952.3	7 560.8	7 915.1	8 431.3
77-82	Administrative and support service activities	59.5	58.6	53.6	58.7	79.3	81.1	73.1	96.0
84-99	Community, social and personal services	..	..	..	..	..	..	..	..
84-85	Public administration and defence; compulsory social security and education	..	..	..	..	..	..	..	..
86-88	Human health and social work activities	..	..	..	..	..	..	..	..
90-93	Arts, entertainment and recreation	..	..	..	..	..	..	..	..
94-99	Other services; household-employers; extraterritorial bodies	..	..	..	..	..	..	..	..

.. Not available

Note: Detailed metadata at: http://metalinks.oecd.org/anberd/20200813/2abe.

KOREA

R&D expenditure in industry by main activity of the enterprise, current prices
ISIC Rev. 4

Million USD PPP

		2011	2012	2013	2014	2015	2016	2017	2018
	TOTAL BUSINESS ENTERPRISE	**44 680.5**	**50 559.8**	**53 573.7**	**57 180.5**	**59 643.5**	..	..	..
01-03	**AGRICULTURE, FORESTRY AND FISHING**	42.3	31.2	30.2	33.0	36.5	..	..	..
05-09	**MINING AND QUARRYING**	25.7	41.1	29.1	23.2	27.3	..	..	..
10-33	**MANUFACTURING**	39 112.9	44 404.0	47 468.5	50 842.2	53 445.5	..	..	..
10-12	Food products, beverages and tobacco	472.0	550.9	532.2	560.8	1 169.8	..	..	..
13-15	Textiles, wearing apparel, leather and related products	334.1	376.0	418.6	423.4	471.4	..	..	..
13	Textiles	142.2	135.5	142.5	148.3	180.5	..	..	..
14	Wearing apparel	164.3	203.9	231.8	226.9	234.0	..	..	..
15	Leather and related products, footwear	27.6	36.6	44.3	48.2	56.9	..	..	..
16-18	Wood and paper products and printing	106.4	141.0	119.4	124.8	160.3	..	..	..
16	Wood and wood products, except furniture	18.8	15.1	15.5	15.1	27.1	..	..	..
17	Paper and paper products	55.6	88.2	63.5	67.3	73.1	..	..	..
18	Printing and reproduction of recorded media	31.9	37.7	40.5	42.4	60.2	..	..	..
19-23	Chemical, rubber, plastic, non-metallic mineral products	5 042.5	5 225.5	5 837.0	5 441.6	6 225.8	..	..	..
19	Coke and refined petroleum products	395.4	317.7	335.3	273.5	294.7	..	..	..
20-21	Chemical and pharmaceutical products	3 739.1	3 893.4	4 303.0	4 012.0	4 712.1	..	..	..
20	Chemicals and chemical products	2 729.0	2 671.6	3 057.1	2 724.9	3 135.7	..	..	..
21	Pharmaceuticals, medicinal, chemical and botanical products	1 010.1	1 221.9	1 245.9	1 287.1	1 576.4	..	..	..
22	Rubber and plastic products	631.0	634.2	834.0	882.9	953.9	..	..	..
23	Other non-metallic mineral products	277.1	380.1	364.7	273.3	265.0	..	..	..
24-25	Basic metals, metal products, except machinery and equipment	1 346.8	1 442.1	1 344.0	1 325.5	1 474.0	..	..	..
24	Basic metals	721.8	858.4	712.9	744.0	760.2	..	..	..
25	Fabricated metal products, except machinery and equipment	625.0	583.7	631.1	581.5	713.9	..	..	..
26-30	Computer, electronic, optical products; electrical machinery, transport equipment	31 402.7	36 303.2	38 848.2	42 530.6	43 391.0	..	..	..
26	Computer, electronic and optical products	21 873.9	25 237.8	27 676.6	30 402.1	29 892.6	..	..	..
27	Electrical equipment	1 076.2	1 265.4	1 188.4	1 277.7	1 621.7	..	..	..
28	Machinery and equipment n.e.c.	2 413.7	3 184.4	3 066.3	3 238.9	3 315.5	..	..	..
29	Motor vehicles, trailers and semi-trailers	5 309.3	5 724.1	6 071.2	6 739.8	7 549.8	..	..	..
30	Other transport equipment	729.5	891.5	845.7	872.1	1 011.4	..	..	..
31-33	Furniture; repair, installation of machinery and equipment	408.6	365.2	369.0	435.4	553.1	..	..	..
31	Furniture	62.7	66.3	74.7	99.3	100.4	..	..	..
32	Other manufacturing	345.9	298.9	294.3	336.1	452.7	..	..	..
33	Repair and installation of machinery and equipment	..	..	..	..	..	..	..	..
35-39	**ELECTRICITY, GAS, WATER AND WASTE MANAGEMENT**	**481.1**	**509.2**	**409.8**	**422.4**	**456.4**	..	..	..
35-36	Electricity, gas and water	444.1	476.5	371.3	382.8	395.2	..	..	..
37-39	Sewerage, waste management and remediation activities	37.0	32.7	38.4	39.6	61.3	..	..	..
41-43	**CONSTRUCTION**	**1 063.2**	**1 156.1**	**1 104.8**	**1 137.6**	**875.5**	..	..	..
45-99	**TOTAL SERVICES**	**3 955.3**	**4 418.3**	**4 531.4**	**4 722.2**	**4 802.3**	..	..	..
45-82	**Business sector services**	**3 912.0**	**4 379.9**	**4 491.4**	**4 679.8**	**4 750.2**	..	..	..
45-47	Wholesale and retail trade; motor vehicle and motorcycle repairs	719.9	788.8	813.8	857.9	722.1	..	..	..
49-53	Transportation and storage	144.8	81.6	127.7	45.8	46.5	..	..	..
55-56	Accommodation and food service activities	7.7	1.4	10.0	8.8	16.2	..	..	..
58-63	Information and communication	1 978.6	2 378.6	2 247.3	2 457.4	2 470.2	..	..	..
58-60	Publishing, audiovisual and broadcasting activities	1 111.1	1 559.1	1 436.0	1 627.1	1 654.5	..	..	..
58	Publishing activities	1 079.0	1 527.5	1 396.0	1 588.3	1 619.5	..	..	..
59-60	Motion picture, video and TV programme production; broadcasting activities	32.0	31.6	40.0	38.8	35.0	..	..	..
59	Motion picture, video and TV programme production; sound and music	15.4	12.7	9.5	13.7	18.7	..	..	..
60	Programming and broadcasting activities	16.7	18.9	30.6	25.1	16.3	..	..	..
61	Telecommunications	402.6	452.1	468.1	492.5	438.9	..	..	..
62-63	IT and other information services	465.0	367.4	343.2	337.7	376.7	..	..	..
62	Computer programming, consultancy and related activities	319.3	246.7	206.8	222.9	255.3	..	..	..
63	Information service activities	145.7	120.7	136.4	114.8	121.4	..	..	..
64-66	**Financial and insurance activities**	**1.2**	**2.1**	**2.0**	**5.2**	**6.5**	..	..	..
68-82	**Real estate; professional, scientific and technical; administrative and support**	**1 059.8**	**1 127.4**	**1 290.6**	**1 304.8**	**1 488.7**	..	..	..
68	Real estate activities	3.5	1.9	1.6	3.7	6.8	..	..	..
69-75x72	Professional, scientific and technical activities, except scientific R&D	679.4	768.7	790.8	865.8	989.3	..	..	..
72	Scientific research and development	305.3	274.8	406.8	342.1	401.6	..	..	..
77-82	Administrative and support service activities	71.7	82.0	91.4	93.2	91.0	..	..	..
84-99	Community, social and personal services	43.3	38.4	40.0	42.4	52.2	..	..	..
84-85	Public administration and defence; compulsory social security and education	19.2	14.6	16.6	16.2	20.1	..	..	..
86-88	Human health and social work activities	0.3	1.1	5.0	5.6	13.8	..	..	..
90-93	Arts, entertainment and recreation	3.2	3.2	3.0	2.2	3.5	..	..	..
94-99	Other services; household-employers; extraterritorial bodies	20.6	19.5	15.4	18.4	14.8	..	..	..

.. Not available

Note: Detailed metadata at: *http://metalinks.oecd.org/anberd/20200813/2abe.*

R&D expenditure in industry by main activity of the enterprise, constant prices
ISIC Rev. 4

2010 USD PPP

		2011	2012	2013	2014	2015	2016	2017	2018
	TOTAL BUSINESS ENTERPRISE	**47 429.6**	**53 025.9**	**56 543.8**	**60 000.6**	**59 643.5**	..	..	..
01-03	**AGRICULTURE, FORESTRY AND FISHING**	**44.9**	**32.7**	**31.8**	**34.6**	**36.5**	..	..	..
05-09	**MINING AND QUARRYING**	**27.2**	**43.1**	**30.7**	**24.4**	**27.3**	..	..	..
10-33	**MANUFACTURING**	**41 519.6**	**46 569.8**	**50 100.1**	**53 349.7**	**53 445.5**	..	..	..
10-12	Food products, beverages and tobacco	501.0	577.8	561.7	588.5	1 169.8	..	..	..
13-15	Textiles, wearing apparel, leather and related products	354.6	394.3	441.9	444.2	471.4	..	..	..
13	Textiles	150.9	142.1	150.4	155.6	180.5	..	..	..
14	Wearing apparel	174.4	213.8	244.7	238.0	234.0	..	..	..
15	Leather and related products, footwear	29.3	38.4	46.8	50.6	56.9	..	..	..
16-18	Wood and paper products and printing	112.9	147.9	126.1	131.0	160.3	..	..	..
16	Wood and wood products, except furniture	19.9	15.9	16.3	15.8	27.1	..	..	..
17	Paper and paper products	59.1	92.5	67.0	70.7	73.1	..	..	..
18	Printing and reproduction of recorded media	33.9	39.5	42.7	44.5	60.2	..	..	..
19-23	Chemical, rubber, plastic, non-metallic mineral products	5 352.8	5 480.4	6 160.6	5 710.0	6 225.8	..	..	..
19	Coke and refined petroleum products	419.7	333.2	353.9	287.0	294.7	..	..	..
20-21	Chemical and pharmaceutical products	3 969.1	4 083.3	4 541.6	4 209.9	4 712.1	..	..	..
20	Chemicals and chemical products	2 896.9	2 801.9	3 226.6	2 859.3	3 135.7	..	..	..
21	Pharmaceuticals, medicinal, chemical and botanical products	1 072.2	1 281.5	1 314.9	1 350.6	1 576.4	..	..	..
22	Rubber and plastic products	669.8	665.2	880.3	926.4	953.9	..	..	..
23	Other non-metallic mineral products	294.1	398.7	384.9	286.8	265.0	..	..	..
24-25	Basic metals, metal products, except machinery and equipment	1 429.7	1 512.5	1 418.5	1 390.9	1 474.0	..	..	..
24	Basic metals	766.2	900.3	752.4	780.7	760.2	..	..	..
25	Fabricated metal products, except machinery and equipment	663.5	612.2	666.1	610.2	713.9	..	..	..
26-30	Computer, electronic, optical products; electrical machinery, transport equipment	33 334.9	38 073.9	41 001.9	44 628.2	43 391.0	..	..	..
26	Computer, electronic and optical products	23 219.8	26 468.8	29 211.0	31 901.5	29 892.6	..	..	..
27	Electrical equipment	1 142.4	1 327.1	1 254.2	1 340.7	1 621.7	..	..	..
28	Machinery and equipment n.e.c.	2 562.2	3 339.7	3 236.3	3 398.7	3 315.5	..	..	..
29	Motor vehicles, trailers and semi-trailers	5 636.0	6 003.3	6 407.8	7 072.2	7 549.8	..	..	..
30	Other transport equipment	774.4	934.9	892.5	915.1	1 011.4	..	..	..
31-33	Furniture; repair, installation of machinery and equipment	433.7	383.0	389.5	456.9	553.1	..	..	..
31	Furniture	66.5	69.6	78.9	104.2	100.4	..	..	..
32	Other manufacturing	367.2	313.5	310.6	352.7	452.7	..	..	..
33	Repair and installation of machinery and equipment	..	..	..	..	..	..	..	..
35-39	**ELECTRICITY, GAS, WATER AND WASTE MANAGEMENT**	**510.7**	**534.0**	**432.5**	**443.2**	**456.4**	..	..	..
35-36	Electricity, gas and water	471.4	499.7	391.9	401.6	395.2	..	..	..
37-39	Sewerage, waste management and remediation activities	39.3	34.3	40.6	41.6	61.3	..	..	..
41-43	**CONSTRUCTION**	**1 128.6**	**1 212.5**	**1 166.0**	**1 193.7**	**875.5**	..	..	..
45-99	**TOTAL SERVICES**	**4 198.7**	**4 633.8**	**4 782.6**	**4 955.1**	**4 802.3**	..	..	..
45-82	**Business sector services**	**4 152.7**	**4 593.5**	**4 740.4**	**4 910.6**	**4 750.2**	..	..	..
45-47	**Wholesale and retail trade; motor vehicle and motorcycle repairs**	**764.2**	**827.2**	**858.9**	**900.2**	**722.1**	..	..	..
49-53	**Transportation and storage**	**153.7**	**85.6**	**134.8**	**48.0**	**46.5**	..	..	..
55-56	**Accommodation and food service activities**	**8.2**	**1.4**	**10.5**	**9.3**	**16.2**	..	..	..
58-63	**Information and communication**	**2 100.4**	**2 494.6**	**2 371.9**	**2 578.6**	**2 470.2**	..	..	..
58-60	Publishing, audiovisual and broadcasting activities	1 179.5	1 635.1	1 515.6	1 707.4	1 654.5	..	..	..
58	Publishing activities	1 145.4	1 602.0	1 473.4	1 666.6	1 619.5	..	..	..
59-60	Motion picture, video and TV programme production; broadcasting activities	34.0	33.2	42.3	40.7	35.0	..	..	..
59	Motion picture, video and TV programme production; sound and music	16.3	13.3	10.0	14.4	18.7	..	..	..
60	Programming and broadcasting activities	17.7	19.9	32.3	26.3	16.3	..	..	..
61	Telecommunications	427.3	474.1	494.0	516.8	438.9	..	..	..
62-63	IT and other information services	493.6	385.3	362.2	354.4	376.7	..	..	..
62	Computer programming, consultancy and related activities	338.9	258.7	218.2	233.9	255.3	..	..	..
63	Information service activities	154.7	126.6	144.0	120.5	121.4	..	..	..
64-66	**Financial and insurance activities**	**1.2**	**2.2**	**2.1**	**5.4**	**6.5**	..	..	..
68-82	**Real estate; professional, scientific and technical; administrative and support**	**1 125.0**	**1 182.4**	**1 362.2**	**1 369.1**	**1 488.7**	..	..	..
68	Real estate activities	3.7	2.0	1.6	3.9	6.8	..	..	..
69-75x72	Professional, scientific and technical activities, except scientific R&D	721.1	806.2	834.7	908.5	989.3	..	..	..
72	Scientific research and development	324.1	288.2	429.4	359.0	401.6	..	..	..
77-82	Administrative and support service activities	76.1	86.0	96.5	97.8	91.0	..	..	..
84-99	Community, social and personal services	46.0	40.2	42.2	44.5	52.2	..	..	..
84-85	Public administration and defence; compulsory social security and education	20.4	15.4	17.6	17.0	20.1	..	..	..
86-88	Human health and social work activities	0.3	1.2	5.3	5.9	13.8	..	..	..
90-93	Arts, entertainment and recreation	3.4	3.3	3.2	2.3	3.5	..	..	..
94-99	Other services; household-employers; extraterritorial bodies	21.9	20.4	16.2	19.3	14.8	..	..	..

.. Not available

Note: Detailed metadata at: http://metalinks.oecd.org/anberd/20200813/2abe.

LITHUANIA

R&D expenditure in industry by main activity of the enterprise, current prices
ISIC Rev. 4

Million USD PPP

		2011	2012	2013	2014	2015	2016	2017	2018
	TOTAL BUSINESS ENTERPRISE	**164.0**	**177.5**	**190.9**	**262.8**	**239.5**	**261.3**	**315.6**	..
01-03	**AGRICULTURE, FORESTRY AND FISHING**	0.0 e	0.0	0.1	0.1	0.4	0.0	0.1	..
05-09	**MINING AND QUARRYING**	0.3	0.2	0.2	0.1	0.0 e	0.0 e	0.0 e	..
10-33	**MANUFACTURING**	50.8	59.2	70.8	112.8	84.1	86.1	106.5	..
10-12	Food products, beverages and tobacco	4.4	1.7	5.9	3.7	5.6	8.2	19.1	..
13-15	Textiles, wearing apparel, leather and related products	1.0	0.5	0.6	0.8	0.7	0.8	1.2	..
13	Textiles	0.5	0.0	0.1	0.1	0.2 e	0.1 e	0.3 e	..
14	Wearing apparel	0.3	0.3	0.4	0.6	0.5	0.6	0.7	..
15	Leather and related products, footwear	0.2	0.1	0.1	0.0	0.1 e	0.1 e	0.1 e	..
16-18	Wood and paper products and printing	0.5	0.3	0.4	1.7	1.0	17.5	1.0	..
16	Wood and wood products, except furniture	0.0	0.0	0.0	0.6	0.1	2.3	0.1	..
17	Paper and paper products	0.4	0.2	0.2	0.4	0.3 e	0.5 e	0.7	..
18	Printing and reproduction of recorded media	0.1	0.1	0.2	0.7	0.6 e	14.6 e	0.2	..
19-23	Chemical, rubber, plastic, non-metallic mineral products	13.9 e	30.2	19.6	45.7	17.7 e	15.5 e	16.7 e	..
19	Coke and refined petroleum products	0.0 e	0.7	0.2	0.2	0.2 e	0.0 e	0.1 e	..
20-21	Chemical and pharmaceutical products	11.8	27.9	16.1	42.5	15.9	11.0 e	13.8 e	..
20	Chemicals and chemical products	5.1	21.9	10.5	25.5	10.9	9.8	12.2	..
21	Pharmaceuticals, medicinal, chemical and botanical products	6.7	6.0	5.6	17.1	5.0	1.2 e	1.6 e	..
22	Rubber and plastic products	0.4	1.0	2.8	2.0	1.0	1.4	2.5	..
23	Other non-metallic mineral products	1.7	0.6	0.5	1.0	0.6	3.0	0.4	..
24-25	Basic metals, metal products, except machinery and equipment	3.3 e	0.9	0.9	7.7	1.0 e	1.0 e	3.6 e	..
24	Basic metals	0.0 e	0.1	0.0	0.0	0.0 e	0.0 e	0.0 e	..
25	Fabricated metal products, except machinery and equipment	3.3	0.8	0.9	7.7	0.9	1.0	3.6	..
26-30	Computer, electronic, optical products; electrical machinery, transport equipment	22.1	22.9	23.7	30.8	37.5	36.5	52.4	..
26	Computer, electronic and optical products	11.5	12.3	12.8	17.8	18.2	18.9	35.2	..
27	Electrical equipment	1.8	1.8	2.4	2.6	3.6	2.1	3.3	..
28	Machinery and equipment n.e.c.	6.5	6.4	4.1	5.2	6.8	6.9	5.3	..
29	Motor vehicles, trailers and semi-trailers	2.2	2.3	4.1	5.0	8.5	8.5	8.4	..
30	Other transport equipment	0.1	0.1	0.2	0.2	0.4	0.1	0.2	..
31-33	Furniture; repair, installation of machinery and equipment	5.6	2.8	19.6	22.4	20.6	6.7	12.5	..
31	Furniture	2.9	1.2	12.1	12.0	2.2	2.2	6.9	..
32	Other manufacturing	1.1	0.7	1.2	9.2	17.3	3.4	2.2	..
33	Repair and installation of machinery and equipment	1.5	0.8	6.3	1.2	1.1	1.1	3.4	..
35-39	**ELECTRICITY, GAS, WATER AND WASTE MANAGEMENT**	0.1	7.9	4.8	0.9	0.4	0.8	1.0	..
35-36	Electricity, gas and water	..	7.2	4.6	0.6	0.1	0.3	0.7	..
37-39	Sewerage, waste management and remediation activities	..	0.7	0.2	0.3	0.3	0.5	0.2	..
41-43	**CONSTRUCTION**	2.5	1.0	0.5	3.1	1.7	1.0	3.1	..
45-99	**TOTAL SERVICES**	110.4 e	109.2	114.6	145.8	152.9	173.3 e	204.9	..
45-82	**Business sector services**	96.5	100.9	113.1	143.5	150.3	171.3	202.0	..
45-47	Wholesale and retail trade; motor vehicle and motorcycle repairs	5.0	4.0	6.1	13.7	13.1	11.0	13.0	..
49-53	Transportation and storage	0.1	0.1	0.2	1.4	0.8	4.4	6.9	..
55-56	Accommodation and food service activities	0.0	0.0	0.0	0.2	0.0	0.0	0.0	..
58-63	Information and communication	56.9	24.9	32.6	40.9	28.8	20.7	56.9	..
58-60	Publishing, audiovisual and broadcasting activities	0.6	0.6	0.5	2.1	0.3 e	2.2 e	3.3	..
58	Publishing activities	..	..	..	..	..	1.7	2.1	..
59-60	Motion picture, video and TV programme production; broadcasting activities	..	..	..	..	..	0.5	1.3	..
59	Motion picture, video and TV programme production; sound and music	..	..	..	..	..	..	0.4	..
60	Programming and broadcasting activities	..	..	..	..	..	..	0.9	..
61	Telecommunications	40.6	8.0	12.3	11.0	1.7 e	0.2 e	0.3 e	..
62-63	IT and other information services	15.6	16.3	19.8	27.8	26.8	18.3	53.2	..
62	Computer programming, consultancy and related activities	13.6	14.1	18.2	25.1	23.6	13.4	48.6	..
63	Information service activities	2.1	2.2	1.6	2.7	3.2	4.9	4.6	..
64-66	**Financial and insurance activities**	11.5	10.6	10.7	6.6	7.8	11.1	11.8	..
68-82	**Real estate; professional, scientific and technical; administrative and support**	22.9	61.3	63.4	80.6	99.7	124.0	113.5	..
68	Real estate activities	0.0	0.0	5.2	0.4	0.1	0.7	0.8	..
69-75x72	Professional, scientific and technical activities, except scientific R&D	5.8	2.7	8.2	13.1	14.6	7.7	14.3	..
72	Scientific research and development	16.7	58.5	49.9	65.7	83.9	114.8	96.5	..
77-82	Administrative and support service activities	0.5	0.1	0.2	1.4	1.1	0.9	1.8	..
84-99	Community, social and personal services	13.9 e	8.3	1.5	2.3	2.6	2.1	2.9	..
84-85	Public administration and defence; compulsory social security and education	0.3	0.1	0.4	0.3	0.4	0.8	1.4	..
86-88	Human health and social work activities	13.3	8.2	0.8	1.4	1.0	1.1	1.1	..
90-93	Arts, entertainment and recreation	0.3	0.0	0.0	0.2	0.6	0.1	0.2	..
94-99	Other services; household-employers; extraterritorial bodies	0.0 e	0.0	0.3	0.4	0.6	0.1 e	0.2	..

.. Not available; e Estimated value

Note: Detailed metadata at: *http://metalinks.oecd.org/anberd/20200813/2abe.*

LITHUANIA

R&D expenditure in industry by main activity of the enterprise, constant prices
ISIC Rev. 4

2010 USD PPP

		2011	2012	2013	2014	2015	2016	2017	2018
	TOTAL BUSINESS ENTERPRISE	**175.0**	**184.5**	**191.8**	**261.2**	**239.5**	**252.9**	**295.4**	..
01-03	**AGRICULTURE, FORESTRY AND FISHING**	**0.0 e**	**0.0**	**0.1**	**0.1**	**0.4**	**0.0**	**0.1**	..
05-09	**MINING AND QUARRYING**	**0.3**	**0.2**	**0.2**	**0.1**	**0.0 e**	**0.0 e**	**0.0 e**	..
10-33	**MANUFACTURING**	**54.2**	**61.5**	**71.1**	**112.1**	**84.1**	**83.4**	**99.7**	..
10-12	Food products, beverages and tobacco	4.6	1.7	6.0	3.7	5.6	7.9	17.9	..
13-15	Textiles, wearing apparel, leather and related products	1.1	0.5	0.6	0.8	0.7	0.7	1.1	..
13	Textiles	0.5	0.0	0.1	0.1	0.2 e	0.1 e	0.3 e	..
14	Wearing apparel	0.3	0.4	0.4	0.6	0.5	0.5	0.7	..
15	Leather and related products, footwear	0.2	0.1	0.1	0.0	0.1 e	0.1 e	0.1 e	..
16-18	Wood and paper products and printing	0.5	0.3	0.4	1.6	1.0	16.9	0.9	..
16	Wood and wood products, except furniture	0.0	0.0	0.0	0.6	0.1	2.2	0.1	..
17	Paper and paper products	0.5	0.2	0.2	0.4	0.3 e	0.5 e	0.7	..
18	Printing and reproduction of recorded media	0.1	0.1	0.2	0.7	0.6 e	14.2 e	0.2	..
19-23	Chemical, rubber, plastic, non-metallic mineral products	14.8 e	31.4	19.7	45.4	17.7 e	15.0 e	15.6 e	..
19	Coke and refined petroleum products	0.0 e	0.7	0.2	0.2	0.2 e	0.0 e	0.1 e	..
20-21	Chemical and pharmaceutical products	12.6	29.0	16.2	42.3	15.9	10.6 e	12.9 e	..
20	Chemicals and chemical products	5.5	22.7	10.6	25.3	10.9	9.5	11.4	..
21	Pharmaceuticals, medicinal, chemical and botanical products	7.1	6.2	5.6	16.9	5.0	1.1 e	1.5 e	..
22	Rubber and plastic products	0.4	1.1	2.8	2.0	1.0	1.4	2.3	..
23	Other non-metallic mineral products	1.8	0.6	0.5	0.9	0.6	2.9	0.3	..
24-25	Basic metals, metal products, except machinery and equipment	3.6 e	1.0	0.9	7.7	1.0 e	1.0 e	3.4 e	..
24	Basic metals	0.0 e	0.1	0.0	0.0	0.0 e	0.0 e	0.0 e	..
25	Fabricated metal products, except machinery and equipment	3.6	0.8	0.9	7.6	0.9	0.9	3.4	..
26-30	Computer, electronic, optical products; electrical machinery, transport equipment	23.6	23.8	23.8	30.7	37.5	35.4	49.0	..
26	Computer, electronic and optical products	12.2	12.8	12.9	17.7	18.2	18.3	33.0	..
27	Electrical equipment	1.9	1.9	2.4	2.6	3.6	2.0	3.1	..
28	Machinery and equipment n.e.c.	7.0	6.7	4.2	5.2	6.8	6.6	5.0	..
29	Motor vehicles, trailers and semi-trailers	2.4	2.4	4.2	4.9	8.5	8.3	7.8	..
30	Other transport equipment	0.1	0.1	0.2	0.2	0.4	0.1	0.2	..
31-33	Furniture; repair, installation of machinery and equipment	5.9	2.9	19.7	22.3	20.6	6.5	11.7	..
31	Furniture	3.1	1.2	12.2	11.9	2.2	2.1	6.4	..
32	Other manufacturing	1.2	0.8	1.2	9.2	17.3	3.3	2.1	..
33	Repair and installation of machinery and equipment	1.6	0.9	6.3	1.2	1.1	1.1	3.2	..
35-39	**ELECTRICITY, GAS, WATER AND WASTE MANAGEMENT**	**0.1**	**8.2**	**4.9**	**0.9**	**0.4**	**0.8**	**0.9**	..
35-36	Electricity, gas and water	..	7.5	4.6	0.6	0.1	0.3	0.7	..
37-39	Sewerage, waste management and remediation activities	..	0.8	0.2	0.3	0.3	0.5	0.2	..
41-43	**CONSTRUCTION**	**2.7**	**1.0**	**0.5**	**3.1**	**1.7**	**1.0**	**2.9**	..
45-99	**TOTAL SERVICES**	**117.7 e**	**113.6**	**115.1**	**144.9**	**152.9**	**167.8 e**	**191.7**	..
45-82	**Business sector services**	**102.9**	**104.9**	**113.7**	**142.6**	**150.3**	**165.8**	**189.1**	..
45-47	**Wholesale and retail trade; motor vehicle and motorcycle repairs**	**5.3**	**4.1**	**6.1**	**13.6**	**13.1**	**10.7**	**12.2**	..
49-53	**Transportation and storage**	**0.1**	**0.1**	**0.2**	**1.4**	**0.8**	**4.3**	**6.4**	..
55-56	**Accommodation and food service activities**	**0.0**	**0.0**	**0.0**	**0.2**	**0.0**	**0.0**	**0.0**	..
58-63	**Information and communication**	**60.7**	**25.9**	**32.8**	**40.6**	**28.8**	**20.1**	**53.2**	..
58-60	Publishing, audiovisual and broadcasting activities	0.7	0.6	0.5	2.1	0.3 e	2.1 e	3.1	..
58	Publishing activities	..	..	..	..	..	1.6	1.9	..
59-60	Motion picture, video and TV programme production; broadcasting activities	..	..	..	..	..	0.5	1.2	..
59	Motion picture, video and TV programme production; sound and music	..	..	..	..	..	..	0.3	..
60	Programming and broadcasting activities	..	..	..	..	..	..	0.9	..
61	Telecommunications	43.3	8.3	12.3	10.9	1.7 e	0.2 e	0.3 e	..
62-63	IT and other information services	16.7	17.0	19.9	27.6	26.8	17.7	49.8	..
62	Computer programming, consultancy and related activities	14.5	14.7	18.3	25.0	23.6	13.0	45.5	..
63	Information service activities	2.2	2.3	1.6	2.6	3.2	4.7	4.3	..
64-66	**Financial and insurance activities**	**12.3**	**11.1**	**10.8**	**6.6**	**7.8**	**10.7**	**11.0**	..
68-82	**Real estate; professional, scientific and technical; administrative and support**	**24.5**	**63.7**	**63.7**	**80.1**	**99.7**	**120.1**	**106.2**	..
68	Real estate activities	0.0	0.0	5.2	0.4	0.1	0.7	0.8	..
69-75x72	Professional, scientific and technical activities, except scientific R&D	6.2	2.8	8.2	13.0	14.6	7.4	13.4	..
72	Scientific research and development	17.8	60.8	50.1	65.3	83.9	111.1	90.3	..
77-82	Administrative and support service activities	0.5	0.1	0.2	1.4	1.1	0.8	1.7	..
84-99	Community, social and personal services	14.8 e	8.6	1.5	2.3	2.6	2.0	2.7	..
84-85	Public administration and defence; compulsory social security and education	0.3	0.1	0.4	0.3	0.4	0.8	1.3	..
86-88	Human health and social work activities	14.2	8.5	0.8	1.4	1.0	1.1	1.0	..
90-93	Arts, entertainment and recreation	0.3	0.0	0.0	0.2	0.6	0.1	0.2	..
94-99	Other services; household-employers; extraterritorial bodies	0.0 e	0.0	0.3	0.4	0.6	0.1 e	0.2	..

.. Not available; e Estimated value

Note: Detailed metadata at: *http://metalinks.oecd.org/anberd/20200813/2abe.*

R&D expenditure in industry by main activity of the enterprise, current prices
ISIC Rev. 4

Million USD PPP

		2011	2012	2013	2014	2015	2016	2017	2018
	TOTAL BUSINESS ENTERPRISE	3 143.7	2 268.6	2 233.6	1 688.1	1 781.7	2 053.6	1 824.4	1 780.8
01-03	**AGRICULTURE, FORESTRY AND FISHING**	0.0	0.0	0.0	0.0	0.0	0.0	0.0	0.0
05-09	**MINING AND QUARRYING**	46.9	4.6	19.6	6.1	18.1	11.5	10.2	9.9
10-33	**MANUFACTURING**	1 843.9	1 028.4	1 204.4	1 021.1	1 103.5	1 262.0	1 121.1	1 094.3
10-12	Food products, beverages and tobacco	159.5	117.1	141.2	42.4	43.2	87.6	77.8	75.9
13-15	Textiles, wearing apparel, leather and related products	38.4	19.2	19.4	7.1	20.5	20.8	18.5	18.1
13	Textiles	..	..	..	..	..	..	..	..
14	Wearing apparel	..	..	..	..	..	..	..	..
15	Leather and related products, footwear	..	..	..	..	..	..	..	..
16-18	Wood and paper products and printing	20.5	19.5	21.7	7.6	18.8	23.9	21.2	20.7
16	Wood and wood products, except furniture	..	..	..	..	..	..	..	..
17	Paper and paper products	..	..	..	..	..	..	..	..
18	Printing and reproduction of recorded media	..	..	..	..	..	..	..	..
19-23	Chemical, rubber, plastic, non-metallic mineral products	733.0	244.4	286.8	345.7	341.9	350.7	311.6	304.1
19	Coke and refined petroleum products	..	..	..	..	..	..	..	..
20-21	Chemical and pharmaceutical products	..	..	..	..	..	..	..	..
20	Chemicals and chemical products	..	..	..	..	..	..	..	..
21	Pharmaceuticals, medicinal, chemical and botanical products	..	..	..	..	..	..	..	..
22	Rubber and plastic products	..	..	..	..	..	..	..	..
23	Other non-metallic mineral products	..	..	..	..	..	..	..	..
24-25	Basic metals, metal products, except machinery and equipment	..	..	..	..	..	..	..	..
24	Basic metals	..	..	..	..	..	..	..	..
25	Fabricated metal products, except machinery and equipment	..	..	..	..	..	..	..	..
26-30	Computer, electronic, optical products; electrical machinery, transport equipment	..	..	..	..	..	..	..	..
26	Computer, electronic and optical products	..	..	..	..	..	..	..	..
27	Electrical equipment	..	..	..	..	..	..	..	..
28	Machinery and equipment n.e.c.	..	..	..	..	..	..	..	..
29	Motor vehicles, trailers and semi-trailers	..	..	..	..	..	..	..	..
30	Other transport equipment	..	..	..	..	..	..	..	..
31-33	Furniture; repair, installation of machinery and equipment	1.5	1.9	2.9	0.5	0.9	1.6	1.4	1.3
31	Furniture	..	..	..	..	..	..	..	..
32	Other manufacturing	..	..	..	..	..	..	..	..
33	Repair and installation of machinery and equipment	..	..	..	..	..	..	..	..
35-39	**ELECTRICITY, GAS, WATER AND WASTE MANAGEMENT**	0.0	8.1	11.9	0.0	0.0	0.0	0.0	0.0
35-36	Electricity, gas and water	..	..	..	..	..	..	..	..
37-39	Sewerage, waste management and remediation activities	..	..	..	..	..	..	..	..
41-43	**CONSTRUCTION**	1.4	4.9	8.5	6.0	9.8	44.4	39.4	38.5
45-99	**TOTAL SERVICES**	1 251.5	1 222.5	989.2	655.0	650.3	735.8	653.7	638.0
45-82	**Business sector services**	..	..	..	..	..	..	..	..
45-47	**Wholesale and retail trade; motor vehicle and motorcycle repairs**	..	..	..	..	..	..	..	..
49-53	**Transportation and storage**	..	..	..	..	..	..	..	..
55-56	**Accommodation and food service activities**	..	..	..	..	..	..	..	..
58-63	**Information and communication**	..	..	..	..	..	..	..	..
58-60	Publishing, audiovisual and broadcasting activities	..	..	..	..	..	..	..	..
58	Publishing activities	..	..	..	..	..	..	..	..
59-60	Motion picture, video and TV programme production; broadcasting activities	..	..	..	..	..	..	..	..
59	Motion picture, video and TV programme production; sound and music	..	..	..	..	..	..	..	..
60	Programming and broadcasting activities	..	..	..	..	..	..	..	..
61	Telecommunications	..	..	..	..	..	..	..	..
62-63	IT and other information services	..	..	..	..	..	..	..	..
62	Computer programming, consultancy and related activities	..	..	..	..	..	..	..	..
63	Information service activities	..	..	..	..	..	..	..	..
64-66	**Financial and insurance activities**	..	..	..	..	..	..	..	..
68-82	**Real estate; professional, scientific and technical; administrative and support**	..	..	..	..	..	..	..	..
68	Real estate activities	..	..	..	..	..	..	..	..
69-75x72	Professional, scientific and technical activities, except scientific R&D	..	..	..	..	..	..	..	..
72	Scientific research and development	..	..	..	..	..	..	..	..
77-82	Administrative and support service activities	..	..	..	..	..	..	..	..
84-99	Community, social and personal services	..	..	..	..	..	..	..	..
84-85	Public administration and defence; compulsory social security and education	..	..	..	..	..	..	..	..
86-88	Human health and social work activities	..	..	..	..	..	..	..	..
90-93	Arts, entertainment and recreation	..	..	..	..	..	..	..	..
94-99	Other services; household-employers; extraterritorial bodies	..	..	..	..	..	..	..	..

.. Not available

Note: Detailed metadata at: *http://metalinks.oecd.org/anberd/20200813/2abe.*

R&D expenditure in industry by main activity of the enterprise, constant prices
ISIC Rev. 4

2010 USD PPP

		2011	2012	2013	2014	2015	2016	2017	2018
	TOTAL BUSINESS ENTERPRISE	**3 285.6**	**2 333.5**	**2 270.2**	**1 676.7**	**1 781.7**	**1 976.8**	**1 729.5**	**1 654.7**
01-03	**AGRICULTURE, FORESTRY AND FISHING**	**0.0**	**0.0**	**0.0**	**0.0**	**0.0**	**0.0**	**0.0**	**0.0**
05-09	**MINING AND QUARRYING**	**49.0**	**4.8**	**19.9**	**6.1**	**18.1**	**11.0**	**9.6**	**9.2**
10-33	**MANUFACTURING**	**1 927.2**	**1 057.8**	**1 224.2**	**1 014.1**	**1 103.5**	**1 214.8**	**1 062.8**	**1 016.8**
10-12	Food products, beverages and tobacco	166.7	120.5	143.5	42.1	43.2	84.3	73.7	70.5
13-15	Textiles, wearing apparel, leather and related products	40.1	19.7	19.7	7.1	20.5	20.0	17.5	16.8
13	Textiles	..	..	..	..	..	..	..	..
14	Wearing apparel	..	..	..	..	..	..	..	..
15	Leather and related products, footwear	..	..	..	..	..	..	..	..
16-18	Wood and paper products and printing	21.5	20.1	22.0	7.5	18.8	23.0	20.1	19.3
16	Wood and wood products, except furniture	..	..	..	..	..	..	..	..
17	Paper and paper products	..	..	..	..	..	..	..	..
18	Printing and reproduction of recorded media	..	..	..	..	..	..	..	..
19-23	Chemical, rubber, plastic, non-metallic mineral products	766.1	251.4	291.5	343.4	341.9	337.6	295.4	282.6
19	Coke and refined petroleum products	..	..	..	..	..	..	..	..
20-21	Chemical and pharmaceutical products	..	..	..	..	..	..	..	..
20	Chemicals and chemical products	..	..	..	..	..	..	..	..
21	Pharmaceuticals, medicinal, chemical and botanical products	..	..	..	..	..	..	..	..
22	Rubber and plastic products	..	..	..	..	..	..	..	..
23	Other non-metallic mineral products	..	..	..	..	..	..	..	..
24-25	Basic metals, metal products, except machinery and equipment	..	..	..	..	..	..	..	..
24	Basic metals	..	..	..	..	..	..	..	..
25	Fabricated metal products, except machinery and equipment	..	..	..	..	..	..	..	..
26-30	Computer, electronic, optical products; electrical machinery, transport equipment	..	..	..	..	..	..	..	..
26	Computer, electronic and optical products	..	..	..	..	..	..	..	..
27	Electrical equipment	..	..	..	..	..	..	..	..
28	Machinery and equipment n.e.c.	..	..	..	..	..	..	..	..
29	Motor vehicles, trailers and semi-trailers	..	..	..	..	..	..	..	..
30	Other transport equipment	..	..	..	..	..	..	..	..
31-33	Furniture; repair, installation of machinery and equipment	1.6	1.9	2.9	0.5	0.9	1.5	1.3	1.3
31	Furniture	..	..	..	..	..	..	..	..
32	Other manufacturing	..	..	..	..	..	..	..	..
33	Repair and installation of machinery and equipment	..	..	..	..	..	..	..	..
35-39	**ELECTRICITY, GAS, WATER AND WASTE MANAGEMENT**	**0.0**	**8.3**	**12.1**	**0.0**	**0.0**	**0.0**	**0.0**	**0.0**
35-36	Electricity, gas and water	..	..	..	..	..	..	..	..
37-39	Sewerage, waste management and remediation activities	..	..	..	..	..	..	..	..
41-43	**CONSTRUCTION**	**1.5**	**5.0**	**8.6**	**5.9**	**9.8**	**42.7**	**37.4**	**35.8**
45-99	**TOTAL SERVICES**	**1 308.0**	**1 257.5**	**1 005.5**	**650.5**	**650.3**	**708.3**	**619.7**	**592.9**
45-82	**Business sector services**	..	..	..	..	..	..	..	..
45-47	**Wholesale and retail trade; motor vehicle and motorcycle repairs**	..	..	..	..	..	..	..	..
49-53	**Transportation and storage**	..	..	..	..	..	..	..	..
55-56	**Accommodation and food service activities**	..	..	..	..	..	..	..	..
58-63	**Information and communication**	..	..	..	..	..	..	..	..
58-60	Publishing, audiovisual and broadcasting activities	..	..	..	..	..	..	..	..
58	Publishing activities	..	..	..	..	..	..	..	..
59-60	Motion picture, video and TV programme production; broadcasting activities	..	..	..	..	..	..	..	..
59	Motion picture, video and TV programme production; sound and music	..	..	..	..	..	..	..	..
60	Programming and broadcasting activities	..	..	..	..	..	..	..	..
61	Telecommunications	..	..	..	..	..	..	..	..
62-63	IT and other information services	..	..	..	..	..	..	..	..
62	Computer programming, consultancy and related activities	..	..	..	..	..	..	..	..
63	Information service activities	..	..	..	..	..	..	..	..
64-66	**Financial and insurance activities**	..	..	..	..	..	..	..	..
68-82	**Real estate; professional, scientific and technical; administrative and support**	..	..	..	..	..	..	..	..
68	Real estate activities	..	..	..	..	..	..	..	..
69-75x72	Professional, scientific and technical activities, except scientific R&D	..	..	..	..	..	..	..	..
72	Scientific research and development	..	..	..	..	..	..	..	..
77-82	Administrative and support service activities	..	..	..	..	..	..	..	..
84-99	Community, social and personal services	..	..	..	..	..	..	..	..
84-85	Public administration and defence; compulsory social security and education	..	..	..	..	..	..	..	..
86-88	Human health and social work activities	..	..	..	..	..	..	..	..
90-93	Arts, entertainment and recreation	..	..	..	..	..	..	..	..
94-99	Other services; household-employers; extraterritorial bodies	..	..	..	..	..	..	..	..

.. Not available

Note: Detailed metadata at: *http://metalinks.oecd.org/anberd/20200813/2abe.*

NETHERLANDS

R&D expenditure in industry by main activity of the enterprise, current prices
ISIC Rev. 4

Million USD PPP

		2011	2012	2013	2014	2015	2016	2017	2018
	TOTAL BUSINESS ENTERPRISE	8 278.9	8 585.1	8 888.9	9 190.7	9 470.7	10 363.2	10 927.6	..
01-03	**AGRICULTURE, FORESTRY AND FISHING**	210.7	173.7	175.7	212.6	266.0	305.6	341.7	..
05-09	**MINING AND QUARRYING**	34.9	70.7	72.5	85.1	18.0	13.1	12.8	..
10-33	**MANUFACTURING**	4 708.0	4 911.0	5 196.4	5 426.3	5 369.4	5 800.2	6 177.4	..
10-12	Food products, beverages and tobacco	456.5	483.7	489.7	465.0	393.3	468.4	418.8	..
13-15	Textiles, wearing apparel, leather and related products	14.2	23.4	23.8	22.3	27.3	28.0	37.3	..
13	Textiles	13.0	19.3	16.9	16.7	18.2	18.4	27.0	..
14	Wearing apparel	0.6	0.5	1.0	1.1	0.6	0.5	0.0	..
15	Leather and related products, footwear	0.7	3.7	5.9	4.4	8.5	9.1	9.0	..
16-18	Wood and paper products and printing	25.6	29.8	29.0	38.9	51.4	80.9	60.4	..
16	Wood and wood products, except furniture	2.3	3.5	2.1	3.0	7.9	7.1	5.1	..
17	Paper and paper products	6.9	18.2	20.4	28.1	29.9	60.2	45.0	..
18	Printing and reproduction of recorded media	16.3	8.1	6.5	7.9	13.6	13.5	10.3	..
19-23	Chemical, rubber, plastic, non-metallic mineral products	1 325.0	1 363.0	1 387.2	1 396.8	1 361.6	1 321.8	1 397.6	..
19	Coke and refined petroleum products	128.9	282.7	295.6	311.3	280.1	210.3	232.5	..
20-21	Chemical and pharmaceutical products	1 048.6	948.7	960.8	975.9	958.1	974.1	1 018.6	..
20	Chemicals and chemical products	664.1	630.7	655.6	659.2	639.5	677.9	697.5	..
21	Pharmaceuticals, medicinal, chemical and botanical products	384.5	318.0	305.2	316.7	318.6	296.2	321.1	..
22	Rubber and plastic products	117.4	102.5	106.9	88.9	100.4	114.2	125.9	..
23	Other non-metallic mineral products	30.0	29.1	23.9	20.6	23.0	23.2	20.6	..
24-25	Basic metals, metal products, except machinery and equipment	188.9	173.8	206.8	185.5	235.2	271.7	310.9	..
24	Basic metals	95.2	90.1	100.7	82.3	100.3	106.1	120.7	..
25	Fabricated metal products, except machinery and equipment	93.8	83.7	106.1	103.2	135.0	165.6	190.1	..
26-30	Computer, electronic, optical products; electrical machinery, transport equipment	2 538.5	2 751.1	2 977.5	3 224.4	3 200.6	3 510.9	3 810.0	..
26	Computer, electronic and optical products	697.1	742.5	818.2	848.5	761.0	814.2	872.2	..
27	Electrical equipment	576.2	580.8	651.5	576.5	569.0	617.4	666.7	..
28	Machinery and equipment n.e.c.	979.1	1 136.3	1 196.3	1 487.5	1 541.1	1 724.6	1 907.5	..
29	Motor vehicles, trailers and semi-trailers	170.4	168.9	183.0	186.9	204.5	209.7	246.6	..
30	Other transport equipment	115.7	122.7	128.6	125.0	125.1	145.0	116.9	..
31-33	Furniture; repair, installation of machinery and equipment	159.2	86.2	82.5	93.5	100.0	118.5	141.3	..
31	Furniture	105.3	14.7	8.1	14.1	14.1	23.2	18.0	..
32	Other manufacturing	26.6	37.6	35.5	32.2	37.9	49.8	65.5	..
33	Repair and installation of machinery and equipment	27.3	33.9	38.8	47.3	48.0	45.5	57.8	..
35-39	**ELECTRICITY, GAS, WATER AND WASTE MANAGEMENT**	49.1	37.9	27.2	51.1	59.6	56.3	84.8	..
35-36	Electricity, gas and water	25.7	18.9	14.4	27.0	30.5	43.5	71.9	..
37-39	Sewerage, waste management and remediation activities	23.4	18.9	12.8	24.1	29.1	12.9	14.1	..
41-43	**CONSTRUCTION**	124.2	158.9	133.5	138.4	130.7	143.2	109.2	..
45-99	**TOTAL SERVICES**	3 152.1	3 232.9	3 283.5	3 277.1	3 627.0	4 044.8	4 201.7	..
45-82	**Business sector services**	3 138.2	3 196.8	3 247.0	3 247.6	3 549.0	3 969.8	4 123.4	..
45-47	**Wholesale and retail trade; motor vehicle and motorcycle repairs**	465.5	513.6	495.3	518.4	627.5	760.8	684.7	..
49-53	**Transportation and storage**	140.7	142.1	122.0	129.8	157.2	139.2	120.7	..
55-56	**Accommodation and food service activities**	13.1	2.7	2.2	1.5	1.8	2.2	2.6	..
58-63	**Information and communication**	944.7	929.2	925.6	995.6	1 123.2	1 317.9	1 320.5	..
58-60	Publishing, audiovisual and broadcasting activities	28.8	34.6	24.8	31.5	34.3	29.9	28.3	..
58	Publishing activities	17.6	20.2	16.5	..	..	..	..	..
59-60	Motion picture, video and TV programme production; broadcasting activities	11.3	14.4	8.2	..	..	..	..	..
59	Motion picture, video and TV programme production; sound and music	9.3	14.1	7.9	..	..	..	..	..
60	Programming and broadcasting activities	2.0	0.3	0.3	..	..	..	..	..
61	Telecommunications	76.1	61.4	38.9	59.9	53.0	57.2	62.9	..
62-63	IT and other information services	839.7	833.1	861.9	904.2	1 035.9	1 230.7	1 229.3	..
62	Computer programming, consultancy and related activities	769.3	794.7	814.6	825.9	986.2	1 185.2	1 175.4	..
63	Information service activities	70.4	38.4	47.3	78.3	49.7	45.5	54.0	..
64-66	**Financial and insurance activities**	240.7	329.0	321.9	242.6	309.8	320.8	384.1	..
68-82	**Real estate; professional, scientific and technical; administrative and support**	1 333.5	1 280.2	1 380.1	1 359.5	1 329.5	1 428.8	1 610.8	..
68	Real estate activities	8.1	5.1	5.9	7.3	2.8	2.7	2.6	..
69-75x72	Professional, scientific and technical activities, except scientific R&D	756.2	633.4	621.8	582.5	550.9	536.4	583.2	..
72	Scientific research and development	453.3	537.5	603.5	623.7	695.4	801.5	913.3	..
77-82	Administrative and support service activities	115.8	104.2	148.9	146.0	80.5	88.3	111.8	..
84-99	Community, social and personal services	13.9	36.1	36.4	29.6	78.0	75.0	78.4	..
84-85	Public administration and defence; compulsory social security and education	..	..	..	..	..	..	..	..
86-88	Human health and social work activities	..	..	..	..	..	..	..	..
90-93	Arts, entertainment and recreation	..	..	..	..	..	..	..	..
94-99	Other services; household-employers; extraterritorial bodies	..	..	..	..	..	..	..	..

.. Not available

Note: Detailed metadata at: *http://metalinks.oecd.org/anberd/20200813/2abe.*

NETHERLANDS

R&D expenditure in industry by main activity of the enterprise, constant prices
ISIC Rev. 4

2010 USD PPP

		2011	2012	2013	2014	2015	2016	2017	2018
	TOTAL BUSINESS ENTERPRISE	**8 872.8**	**8 943.3**	**8 851.6**	**9 250.7**	**9 470.7**	**10 135.0**	**10 327.8**	..
01-03	**AGRICULTURE, FORESTRY AND FISHING**	225.8	181.0	175.0	214.0	266.0	298.9	322.9	..
05-09	**MINING AND QUARRYING**	37.4	73.6	72.2	85.7	18.0	12.8	12.1	..
10-33	**MANUFACTURING**	5 045.7	5 115.9	5 174.6	5 461.8	5 369.4	5 672.5	5 838.3	..
10-12	Food products, beverages and tobacco	489.2	503.9	487.7	468.0	393.3	458.1	395.8	..
13-15	Textiles, wearing apparel, leather and related products	15.3	24.4	23.7	22.4	27.3	27.4	35.2	..
13	Textiles	13.9	20.1	16.8	16.8	18.2	18.0	25.5	..
14	Wearing apparel	0.6	0.5	1.0	1.1	0.6	0.5	0.0	..
15	Leather and related products, footwear	0.8	3.8	5.8	4.4	8.5	8.9	8.5	..
16-18	Wood and paper products and printing	27.4	31.0	28.8	39.2	51.4	79.1	57.1	..
16	Wood and wood products, except furniture	2.5	3.6	2.1	3.0	7.9	6.9	4.9	..
17	Paper and paper products	7.4	19.0	20.3	28.3	29.9	58.9	42.5	..
18	Printing and reproduction of recorded media	17.5	8.5	6.4	7.9	13.6	13.2	9.7	..
19-23	Chemical, rubber, plastic, non-metallic mineral products	1 420.0	1 419.8	1 381.4	1 405.9	1 361.6	1 292.6	1 320.9	..
19	Coke and refined petroleum products	138.2	294.5	294.3	313.3	280.1	205.7	219.7	..
20-21	Chemical and pharmaceutical products	1 123.8	988.3	956.8	982.3	958.1	952.6	962.7	..
20	Chemicals and chemical products	711.8	657.0	652.8	663.5	639.5	663.0	659.2	..
21	Pharmaceuticals, medicinal, chemical and botanical products	412.1	331.3	304.0	318.8	318.6	289.7	303.5	..
22	Rubber and plastic products	125.9	106.7	106.5	89.5	100.4	111.6	119.0	..
23	Other non-metallic mineral products	32.2	30.3	23.8	20.8	23.0	22.7	19.4	..
24-25	Basic metals, metal products, except machinery and equipment	202.5	181.1	205.9	186.7	235.2	265.8	293.8	..
24	Basic metals	102.0	93.9	100.3	82.8	100.3	103.8	114.1	..
25	Fabricated metal products, except machinery and equipment	100.5	87.2	105.7	103.9	135.0	162.0	179.7	..
26-30	Computer, electronic, optical products; electrical machinery, transport equipment	2 720.6	2 865.9	2 965.0	3 245.4	3 200.6	3 433.6	3 600.8	..
26	Computer, electronic and optical products	747.1	773.5	814.7	854.0	761.0	796.3	824.3	..
27	Electrical equipment	617.6	605.0	648.7	580.2	569.0	603.8	630.1	..
28	Machinery and equipment n.e.c.	1 049.4	1 183.7	1 191.3	1 497.3	1 541.1	1 686.6	1 802.8	..
29	Motor vehicles, trailers and semi-trailers	182.6	175.9	182.2	188.2	204.5	205.1	233.1	..
30	Other transport equipment	124.0	127.8	128.0	125.8	125.1	141.8	110.5	..
31-33	Furniture; repair, installation of machinery and equipment	170.6	89.8	82.1	94.2	100.0	115.9	133.5	..
31	Furniture	112.9	15.3	8.1	14.1	14.1	22.7	17.0	..
32	Other manufacturing	28.5	39.2	35.4	32.4	37.9	48.7	61.9	..
33	Repair and installation of machinery and equipment	29.3	35.3	38.7	47.6	48.0	44.5	54.6	..
35-39	**ELECTRICITY, GAS, WATER AND WASTE MANAGEMENT**	52.6	39.4	27.1	51.5	59.6	55.1	80.1	..
35-36	Electricity, gas and water	27.5	19.7	14.3	27.2	30.5	42.5	68.0	..
37-39	Sewerage, waste management and remediation activities	25.1	19.7	12.8	24.3	29.1	12.6	13.4	..
41-43	**CONSTRUCTION**	133.1	165.5	132.9	139.3	130.7	140.1	103.2	..
45-99	**TOTAL SERVICES**	3 378.2	3 367.8	3 269.7	3 298.5	3 627.0	3 955.7	3 971.1	..
45-82	**Business sector services**	3 363.3	3 330.2	3 233.5	3 268.8	3 549.0	3 882.3	3 897.1	..
45-47	**Wholesale and retail trade; motor vehicle and motorcycle repairs**	498.9	535.0	493.2	521.8	627.5	744.1	647.1	..
49-53	**Transportation and storage**	150.8	148.0	121.5	130.6	157.2	136.1	114.1	..
55-56	**Accommodation and food service activities**	14.0	2.9	2.2	1.6	1.8	2.2	2.4	..
58-63	**Information and communication**	1 012.4	967.9	921.7	1 002.1	1 123.2	1 288.8	1 248.0	..
58-60	Publishing, audiovisual and broadcasting activities	30.9	36.1	24.7	31.7	34.3	29.3	26.7	..
58	Publishing activities	18.8	21.1	16.5	..	..	..	..	..
59-60	Motion picture, video and TV programme production; broadcasting activities	12.1	15.0	8.2	..	..	..	..	..
59	Motion picture, video and TV programme production; sound and music	9.9	14.7	7.9	..	..	..	..	..
60	Programming and broadcasting activities	2.1	0.3	0.3	..	..	..	..	..
61	Telecommunications	81.6	64.0	38.7	60.3	53.0	55.9	59.5	..
62-63	IT and other information services	899.9	867.8	858.3	910.2	1 035.9	1 203.6	1 161.8	..
62	Computer programming, consultancy and related activities	824.5	827.8	811.2	831.3	986.2	1 159.1	1 110.8	..
63	Information service activities	75.4	40.0	47.1	78.8	49.7	44.5	51.0	..
64-66	**Financial and insurance activities**	258.0	342.7	320.5	244.2	309.8	313.8	363.0	..
68-82	**Real estate; professional, scientific and technical; administrative and support**	1 429.2	1 333.6	1 374.3	1 368.4	1 329.5	1 397.4	1 522.4	..
68	Real estate activities	8.7	5.3	5.9	7.4	2.8	2.6	2.4	..
69-75x72	Professional, scientific and technical activities, except scientific R&D	810.5	659.8	619.2	586.3	550.9	524.6	551.2	..
72	Scientific research and development	485.9	560.0	601.0	627.8	695.4	783.8	863.2	..
77-82	Administrative and support service activities	124.1	108.6	148.3	147.0	80.5	86.3	105.6	..
84-99	Community, social and personal services	14.9	37.6	36.3	29.8	78.0	73.3	74.1	..
84-85	Public administration and defence; compulsory social security and education	..	..	..	..	..	..	..	..
86-88	Human health and social work activities	..	..	..	..	..	..	..	..
90-93	Arts, entertainment and recreation	..	..	..	..	..	..	..	..
94-99	Other services; household-employers; extraterritorial bodies	..	..	..	..	..	..	..	..

.. Not available

Note: Detailed metadata at: *http://metalinks.oecd.org/anberd/20200813/2abe.*

R&D expenditure in industry by main activity of the enterprise, current prices
ISIC Rev. 4

Million USD PPP

		2011	2012	2013	2014	2015	2016	2017	2018
	TOTAL BUSINESS ENTERPRISE	802.9	796.1 e	861.7	979.0 e	1 085.8	..	..	..
01-03	**AGRICULTURE, FORESTRY AND FISHING**	84.1	75.0 e	63.6	61.7 e	65.1	..	..	..
05-09	**MINING AND QUARRYING**	..	..	..	..	..	..	..	..
10-33	**MANUFACTURING**	360.7	346.1 e	361.0	406.7 e	454.8	..	..	..
10-12	Food products, beverages and tobacco	76.7	68.2 e	61.5	67.4 e	79.3			
13-15	Textiles, wearing apparel, leather and related products	4.7	5.9 e	7.6	6.8 e	4.1			
13	Textiles	..	..	..	..	..			
14	Wearing apparel	..	..	..	..	..			
15	Leather and related products, footwear	..	..	..	..	..			
16-18	Wood and paper products and printing	..	..	..	..	..			..
16	Wood and wood products, except furniture	..	..	..	..	..			..
17	Paper and paper products	..	..	..	..	..			..
18	Printing and reproduction of recorded media	..	..	..	..	..			..
19-23	Chemical, rubber, plastic, non-metallic mineral products	51.1	57.6 e	65.7	63.9 e	53.5	..	..	..
19	Coke and refined petroleum products	..	..	..	..	..	..	..	..
20-21	Chemical and pharmaceutical products	..	..	..	..	..	..	..	..
20	Chemicals and chemical products	..	..	..	..	..	..	..	..
21	Pharmaceuticals, medicinal, chemical and botanical products	..	..	..	..	..	..	..	..
22	Rubber and plastic products	..	..	..	..	..			..
23	Other non-metallic mineral products	2.7	2.0 e	1.4	1.5 e	2.0	..	..	..
24-25	Basic metals, metal products, except machinery and equipment	20.9	17.2 e	19.4	30.6 e	45.4	..	..	..
24	Basic metals	..	..	..	..	..			
25	Fabricated metal products, except machinery and equipment	..	..	..	..	..			..
26-30	Computer, electronic, optical products; electrical machinery, transport equipment	177.7	171.5 e	179.1	199.7 e	220.3	..	..	..
26	Computer, electronic and optical products	..	..	..	..	..	..	..	..
27	Electrical equipment	..	..	..	..	..	..	..	..
28	Machinery and equipment n.e.c.	..	..	..	..	..			..
29	Motor vehicles, trailers and semi-trailers	..	..	..	..	..	..	..	..
30	Other transport equipment	..	..	..	..	..	..	..	..
31-33	Furniture; repair, installation of machinery and equipment	..	..	..	..	..	..	..	..
31	Furniture	..	..	..	..	..			..
32	Other manufacturing	..	..	..	..	..	..	..	..
33	Repair and installation of machinery and equipment	..	..	..	..	..	..	..	..
35-39	**ELECTRICITY, GAS, WATER AND WASTE MANAGEMENT**	..	..	..	..	..	..	..	..
35-36	Electricity, gas and water	..	..	..	..	..			..
37-39	Sewerage, waste management and remediation activities	..	..	..	..	..			..
41-43	**CONSTRUCTION**	..	..	..	..	..	..	..	..
45-99	**TOTAL SERVICES**	358.0	375.0 e	437.1	510.6 e	565.9	..	..	..
45-82	**Business sector services**	..	..	..	..	..	..	..	..
45-47	**Wholesale and retail trade; motor vehicle and motorcycle repairs**	59.9	62.5 e	66.4	71.7 e	75.2	..	..	..
49-53	**Transportation and storage**	..	..	..	..	..	..	..	..
55-56	**Accommodation and food service activities**	..	..	..	..	..	..	..	..
58-63	**Information and communication**	..	..	..	..	..	..	..	..
58-60	Publishing, audiovisual and broadcasting activities	..	..	..	..	..	..	..	..
58	Publishing activities	..	..	..	..	..	..	..	..
59-60	Motion picture, video and TV programme production; broadcasting activities	..	..	..	..	..	..	..	..
59	Motion picture, video and TV programme production; sound and music	..	..	..	..	..	..	..	..
60	Programming and broadcasting activities	..	..	..	..	..	..	..	..
61	Telecommunications	..	..	..	..	..	..	..	..
62-63	IT and other information services	148.7	169.6 e	215.1	262.0 e	295.5	..	..	..
62	Computer programming, consultancy and related activities	..	..	..	..	..	..	..	..
63	Information service activities	..	..	..	..	..	..	..	..
64-66	**Financial and insurance activities**	..	..	..	..	..	..	..	..
68-82	**Real estate; professional, scientific and technical; administrative and support**	..	..	..	..	..	..	..	..
68	Real estate activities	..	..	..	..	..	..	..	..
69-75x72	Professional, scientific and technical activities, except scientific R&D	..	..	..	..	..	..	..	..
72	Scientific research and development	34.3	34.7 e	39.4	45.7 e	50.8	..	..	..
77-82	Administrative and support service activities	..	..	..	..	..	..	..	..
84-99	Community, social and personal services	..	..	..	..	..	..	..	..
84-85	Public administration and defence; compulsory social security and education	..	..	..	..	..	..	..	..
86-88	Human health and social work activities	..	..	..	..	..	..	..	..
90-93	Arts, entertainment and recreation	..	..	..	..	..	..	..	..
94-99	Other services; household-employers; extraterritorial bodies	..	..	..	..	..	..	..	..

.. Not available; e Estimated value

Note: Detailed metadata at: *http://metalinks.oecd.org/anberd/20200813/2abe.*

NEW ZEALAND

R&D expenditure in industry by main activity of the enterprise, constant prices
ISIC Rev. 4

2010 USD PPP

		2011	2012	2013	2014	2015	2016	2017	2018
	TOTAL BUSINESS ENTERPRISE	**854.2**	**856.9 e**	**855.1**	**962.7 e**	**1 085.8**	..	..	..
01-03	**AGRICULTURE, FORESTRY AND FISHING**	89.5	80.7 e	63.1	60.7 e	65.1	..	..	..
05-09	**MINING AND QUARRYING**	..	..	..	..	..	..	..	..
10-33	**MANUFACTURING**	**383.8**	**372.5 e**	**358.3**	**399.9 e**	**454.8**	..	..	..
10-12	Food products, beverages and tobacco	81.6	73.4 e	61.1	66.3 e	79.3	..	..	..
13-15	Textiles, wearing apparel, leather and related products	5.0	6.4 e	7.5	6.7 e	4.1	..	..	..
13	Textiles	..	..	..	..	..	..	..	..
14	Wearing apparel	..	..	..	..	..	..	..	..
15	Leather and related products, footwear	..	..	..	..	..	..	..	..
16-18	Wood and paper products and printing	..	..	..	..	..	..	..	..
16	Wood and wood products, except furniture	..	..	..	..	..	..	..	..
17	Paper and paper products	..	..	..	..	..	..	..	..
18	Printing and reproduction of recorded media	..	..	..	..	..	..	..	..
19-23	Chemical, rubber, plastic, non-metallic mineral products	54.4	62.0 e	65.2	62.8 e	53.5	..	..	..
19	Coke and refined petroleum products	..	..	..	..	..	..	..	..
20-21	Chemical and pharmaceutical products	..	..	..	..	..	..	..	..
20	Chemicals and chemical products	..	..	..	..	..	..	..	..
21	Pharmaceuticals, medicinal, chemical and botanical products	..	..	..	..	..	..	..	..
22	Rubber and plastic products	..	..	..	..	..	..	..	..
23	Other non-metallic mineral products	2.9	2.2 e	1.4	1.5 e	2.0	..	..	..
24-25	Basic metals, metal products, except machinery and equipment	22.2	18.5 e	19.2	30.1 e	45.4	..	..	..
24	Basic metals	..	..	..	..	..	..	..	..
25	Fabricated metal products, except machinery and equipment	..	..	..	..	..	..	..	..
26-30	Computer, electronic, optical products; electrical machinery, transport equipment	189.0	184.6 e	177.8	196.4 e	220.3	..	..	..
26	Computer, electronic and optical products	..	..	..	..	..	..	..	..
27	Electrical equipment	..	..	..	..	..	..	..	..
28	Machinery and equipment n.e.c.	..	..	..	..	..	..	..	..
29	Motor vehicles, trailers and semi-trailers	..	..	..	..	..	..	..	..
30	Other transport equipment	..	..	..	..	..	..	..	..
31-33	Furniture; repair, installation of machinery and equipment	..	..	..	..	..	..	..	..
31	Furniture	..	..	..	..	..	..	..	..
32	Other manufacturing	..	..	..	..	..	..	..	..
33	Repair and installation of machinery and equipment	..	..	..	..	..	..	..	..
35-39	**ELECTRICITY, GAS, WATER AND WASTE MANAGEMENT**	..	..	..	..	..	..	..	..
35-36	Electricity, gas and water	..	..	..	..	..	..	..	..
37-39	Sewerage, waste management and remediation activities	..	..	..	..	..	..	..	..
41-43	**CONSTRUCTION**	..	..	..	..	..	..	..	..
45-99	**TOTAL SERVICES**	**380.9**	**403.7 e**	**433.7**	**502.2 e**	**565.9**	..	..	..
45-82	**Business sector services**	..	..	..	..	..	..	..	..
45-47	**Wholesale and retail trade; motor vehicle and motorcycle repairs**	63.7	67.2 e	65.9	70.5 e	75.2	..	..	..
49-53	**Transportation and storage**	..	..	..	..	..	..	..	..
55-56	**Accommodation and food service activities**	..	..	..	..	..	..	..	..
58-63	**Information and communication**	..	..	..	..	..	..	..	..
58-60	Publishing, audiovisual and broadcasting activities	..	..	..	..	..	..	..	..
58	Publishing activities	..	..	..	..	..	..	..	..
59-60	Motion picture, video and TV programme production; broadcasting activities	..	..	..	..	..	..	..	..
59	Motion picture, video and TV programme production; sound and music	..	..	..	..	..	..	..	..
60	Programming and broadcasting activities	..	..	..	..	..	..	..	..
61	Telecommunications	..	..	..	..	..	..	..	..
62-63	IT and other information services	158.2	182.6 e	213.4	257.7 e	295.5	..	..	..
62	Computer programming, consultancy and related activities	..	..	..	..	..	..	..	..
63	Information service activities	..	..	..	..	..	..	..	..
64-66	**Financial and insurance activities**	..	..	..	..	..	..	..	..
68-82	**Real estate; professional, scientific and technical; administrative and support**	..	..	..	..	..	..	..	..
68	Real estate activities	..	..	..	..	..	..	..	..
69-75x72	Professional, scientific and technical activities, except scientific R&D	..	..	..	..	..	..	..	..
72	Scientific research and development	36.5	37.4 e	39.1	45.0 e	50.8	..	..	..
77-82	Administrative and support service activities	..	..	..	..	..	..	..	..
84-99	Community, social and personal services	..	..	..	..	..	..	..	..
84-85	Public administration and defence; compulsory social security and education	..	..	..	..	..	..	..	..
86-88	Human health and social work activities	..	..	..	..	..	..	..	..
90-93	Arts, entertainment and recreation	..	..	..	..	..	..	..	..
94-99	Other services; household-employers; extraterritorial bodies	..	..	..	..	..	..	..	..

.. Not available; e Estimated value

Note: Detailed metadata at: *http://metalinks.oecd.org/anberd/20200813/2abe.*

NORWAY

R&D expenditure in industry by main activity of the enterprise, current prices
ISIC Rev. 4

Million USD PPP

		2011	2012	2013	2014	2015	2016	2017	2018
	TOTAL BUSINESS ENTERPRISE	**2 610.4**	**2 779.1**	**2 949.9**	**3 118.9**	**3 267.4**	**3 359.9**	**3 667.9**	..
01-03	**AGRICULTURE, FORESTRY AND FISHING**	32.3	32.9	35.3	56.4	74.0	76.6	107.1	..
05-09	**MINING AND QUARRYING**	135.0	177.7	229.6	210.0	177.0	187.3	174.5	..
10-33	**MANUFACTURING**	853.6	892.6	921.4	987.6	1 017.9	1 003.4	1 066.0	..
10-12	Food products, beverages and tobacco	63.9	72.2	69.6	79.2	106.5	126.1	127.1	..
13-15	Textiles, wearing apparel, leather and related products	8.7	7.9	6.8	7.5	7.9	8.9	12.5	..
13	Textiles	5.5	5.6	5.4	5.9	6.4	6.4	7.3	..
14	Wearing apparel	..	..	..	..	..	..	..	..
15	Leather and related products, footwear	..	..	..	..	..	..	..	..
16-18	Wood and paper products and printing	30.3	24.4	23.4	23.8	25.6	30.7	38.3	..
16	Wood and wood products, except furniture	6.8	7.2	7.3	6.1	8.7	10.6	18.5	..
17	Paper and paper products	20.7	13.7	12.4	13.7	12.5	12.6	12.2	..
18	Printing and reproduction of recorded media	2.8	3.4	3.7	4.0	4.5	7.5	7.6	..
19-23	Chemical, rubber, plastic, non-metallic mineral products	194.5	167.1	168.1	165.4	154.1	158.2	179.5	..
19	Coke and refined petroleum products	..	..	..	..	..	..	..	..
20-21	Chemical and pharmaceutical products	..	..	..	..	..	*	..	..
20	Chemicals and chemical products	..	..	..	..	..	..	..	..
21	Pharmaceuticals, medicinal, chemical and botanical products	79.3	43.4	42.5	36.8	33.3	35.5	40.8	..
22	Rubber and plastic products	9.7	13.8	14.4	15.3	15.4	15.9	19.7	..
23	Other non-metallic mineral products	12.9	12.2	12.6	11.5	10.0	11.5	12.5	..
24-25	Basic metals, metal products, except machinery and equipment	126.1	150.0	150.6	161.7	188.6	181.4	176.9	..
24	Basic metals	24.7	33.2	34.0	33.0	51.8	45.9	49.1	..
25	Fabricated metal products, except machinery and equipment	101.4	116.8	116.6	128.7	136.8	135.5	127.8	..
26-30	Computer, electronic, optical products; electrical machinery, transport equipment	388.6	421.4	452.4	499.2	475.8	436.6	463.3	..
26	Computer, electronic and optical products	183.6	182.5	180.9	195.6	196.7	188.6	192.6	..
27	Electrical equipment	41.4	46.1	51.8	60.6	53.5	53.6	55.0	..
28	Machinery and equipment n.e.c.	100.0	112.1	138.2	150.9	136.6	132.1	135.1	..
29	Motor vehicles, trailers and semi-trailers	22.8	23.8	25.8	30.2	17.1	18.9	23.7	..
30	Other transport equipment	40.9	56.8	55.7	61.9	71.9	43.4 e	56.9 e	..
31-33	Furniture; repair, installation of machinery and equipment	41.5	49.5	50.4	50.7	59.4	61.4	68.5	..
31	Furniture	12.8	14.6	16.5	16.9	14.5	16.1	18.3	..
32	Other manufacturing	11.9	14.2	12.5	13.9	16.5	16.3	20.3	..
33	Repair and installation of machinery and equipment	16.8	20.7	21.4	19.9	28.5	29.1	30.0	..
35-39	**ELECTRICITY, GAS, WATER AND WASTE MANAGEMENT**	22.3	25.5	24.5	24.5	30.4	38.3	37.9	..
35-36	Electricity, gas and water	16.3 e	16.3 e	15.9 e	15.2	17.4	20.1	28.0	..
37-39	Sewerage, waste management and remediation activities	5.9	9.2	8.7	9.3	13.0	18.3	9.9	..
41-43	**CONSTRUCTION**	12.4	12.6	19.0	22.2	24.3	25.7	34.0	..
45-99	**TOTAL SERVICES**	**1 554.7**	**1 637.9**	**1 720.1**	**1 818.2**	**1 943.7**	**2 028.5**	**2 248.1**	..
45-82	**Business sector services**	**1 554.7 e**	**1 637.9 e**	**1 720.1 e**	**1 818.2 e**	**1 943.7 e**	**2 028.5 e**	**2 248.1 e**	..
45-47	**Wholesale and retail trade; motor vehicle and motorcycle repairs**	62.6	58.1	75.8	81.9	79.2	102.6	93.9	..
49-53	**Transportation and storage**	16.2	21.2	20.0	21.9	38.7	36.1	41.8	..
55-56	**Accommodation and food service activities**	..	..	..	..	..	..	..	..
58-63	**Information and communication**	556.7	616.0	672.1	717.0	803.0	905.5	1 022.6	..
58-60	Publishing, audiovisual and broadcasting activities	165.6	160.9	158.5	207.8	250.6	250.8	299.0	..
58	Publishing activities	164.4	159.3	155.3	204.4	248.0	244.5	294.1	..
59-60	Motion picture, video and TV programme production; broadcasting activities	1.2	1.6	3.2	3.4	2.6	6.3	4.8	..
59	Motion picture, video and TV programme production; sound and music	1.2 e	1.6 e	3.2 e	3.4 e	2.6	4.1 e	2.2	..
60	Programming and broadcasting activities	0.0 e	0.0 e	0.0 e	0.0 e	0.0	2.3 e	2.7	..
61	Telecommunications	78.1	79.2	79.3	88.4	99.2	127.0	111.8	..
62-63	IT and other information services	313.0	375.9	434.3	420.8	453.1	527.7	611.8	..
62	Computer programming, consultancy and related activities	298.3	344.3	407.2	388.9	423.4	496.3	577.8	..
63	Information service activities	14.6	31.6	27.0	31.9	29.7	31.4	34.0	..
64-66	**Financial and insurance activities**	145.9	138.5	151.1	149.6	141.5	111.4	159.9	..
68-82	**Real estate; professional, scientific and technical; administrative and support**	773.4	804.2	801.1	847.9	881.3	873.0	929.9	..
68	Real estate activities	0.0	0.0	0.0	0.0	0.0	0.0	0.0	..
69-75x72	Professional, scientific and technical activities, except scientific R&D	306.6	287.1	280.1	331.2	340.4	359.2	378.2	..
72	Scientific research and development	448.3	502.1	506.8	510.4	532.0	504.8	540.2	..
77-82	Administrative and support service activities	18.5	15.0	14.2	6.3	8.9	9.0	11.4	..
84-99	Community, social and personal services	..	..	..	..	..	..	..	..
84-85	Public administration and defence; compulsory social security and education	..	..	..	..	..	..	..	..
86-88	Human health and social work activities	..	..	..	..	..	..	..	..
90-93	Arts, entertainment and recreation	..	..	..	..	..	..	..	..
94-99	Other services; household-employers; extraterritorial bodies	..	..	..	..	..	..	..	..

.. Not available; e Estimated value

Note: Detailed metadata at: *http://metalinks.oecd.org/anberd/20200813/2abe.*

R&D expenditure in industry by main activity of the enterprise, constant prices
ISIC Rev. 4

2010 USD PPP

		2011	2012	2013	2014	2015	2016	2017	2018
	TOTAL BUSINESS ENTERPRISE	**2 630.7**	**2 718.6**	**2 808.3**	**2 973.1**	**3 267.4**	**3 334.5**	**3 516.7**	..
01-03	**AGRICULTURE, FORESTRY AND FISHING**	**32.6**	**32.2**	**33.6**	**53.7**	**74.0**	**76.0**	**103.0**	..
05-09	**MINING AND QUARRYING**	**136.1**	**173.8**	**218.6**	**200.2**	**177.0**	**185.9**	**167.3**	..
10-33	**MANUFACTURING**	**860.3**	**873.1**	**877.2**	**941.4**	**1 017.9**	**995.8**	**1 022.1**	..
10-12	Food products, beverages and tobacco	64.4	70.7	66.3	75.5	106.5	125.2	121.9	..
13-15	Textiles, wearing apparel, leather and related products	8.7	7.8	6.5	7.2	7.9	8.8	11.9	..
13	Textiles	5.5	5.5	5.1	5.7	6.4	6.4	7.0	..
14	Wearing apparel	..	..	..	..	..	..	..	..
15	Leather and related products, footwear	..	..	..	..	..	..	..	..
16-18	Wood and paper products and printing	30.5	23.9	22.3	22.7	25.6	30.5	36.7	..
16	Wood and wood products, except furniture	6.9	7.1	6.9	5.8	8.7	10.5	17.8	..
17	Paper and paper products	20.9	13.4	11.9	13.0	12.5	12.5	11.7	..
18	Printing and reproduction of recorded media	2.8	3.3	3.5	3.8	4.5	7.5	7.3	..
19-23	Chemical, rubber, plastic, non-metallic mineral products	196.0	163.5	160.0	157.7	154.1	157.0	172.1	..
19	Coke and refined petroleum products	..	..	..	..	..	..	..	..
20-21	Chemical and pharmaceutical products	..	..	..	..	..	..	..	..
20	Chemicals and chemical products	..	..	..	..	..	..	..	..
21	Pharmaceuticals, medicinal, chemical and botanical products	79.9	42.4	40.4	35.1	33.3	35.2	39.1	..
22	Rubber and plastic products	9.8	13.5	13.7	14.6	15.4	15.8	18.9	..
23	Other non-metallic mineral products	13.0	12.0	12.0	10.9	10.0	11.4	12.0	..
24-25	Basic metals, metal products, except machinery and equipment	127.1	146.7	143.4	154.1	188.6	180.1	169.6	..
24	Basic metals	24.9	32.5	32.4	31.5	51.8	45.6	47.1	..
25	Fabricated metal products, except machinery and equipment	102.2	114.3	111.0	122.7	136.8	134.5	122.5	..
26-30	Computer, electronic, optical products; electrical machinery, transport equipment	391.7	412.2	430.7	475.9	475.8	433.3	444.2	..
26	Computer, electronic and optical products	185.0	178.5	172.2	186.5	196.7	187.2	184.7	..
27	Electrical equipment	41.7	45.1	49.3	57.7	53.5	53.2	52.7	..
28	Machinery and equipment n.e.c.	100.8	109.7	131.6	143.9	136.6	131.1	129.5	..
29	Motor vehicles, trailers and semi-trailers	23.0	23.3	24.6	28.7	17.1	18.8	22.7	..
30	Other transport equipment	41.2	55.6	53.0	59.0	71.9	43.0 e	54.6 e	..
31-33	Furniture; repair, installation of machinery and equipment	41.8	48.4	48.0	48.3	59.4	61.0	65.7	..
31	Furniture	12.9	14.3	15.7	16.1	14.5	15.9	17.5	..
32	Other manufacturing	12.0	13.9	11.9	13.3	16.5	16.1	19.4	..
33	Repair and installation of machinery and equipment	16.9	20.3	20.4	18.9	28.5	28.9	28.7	..
35-39	**ELECTRICITY, GAS, WATER AND WASTE MANAGEMENT**	**22.5**	**25.0**	**23.3**	**23.3**	**30.4**	**38.0**	**36.3**	..
35-36	Electricity, gas and water	16.5 e	16.0 e	15.1 e	14.5	17.4	19.9	26.8	..
37-39	Sewerage, waste management and remediation activities	6.0	9.0	8.2	8.8	13.0	18.1	9.5	..
41-43	**CONSTRUCTION**	**12.5**	**12.3**	**18.1**	**21.2**	**24.3**	**25.5**	**32.6**	..
45-99	**TOTAL SERVICES**	**1 566.8**	**1 602.2**	**1 637.5**	**1 733.3**	**1 943.7**	**2 013.2**	**2 155.4**	..
45-82	**Business sector services**	**1 566.8 e**	**1 602.2 e**	**1 637.5 e**	**1 733.3 e**	**1 943.7 e**	**2 013.2 e**	**2 155.4 e**	..
45-47	**Wholesale and retail trade; motor vehicle and motorcycle repairs**	**63.1**	**56.8**	**72.2**	**78.1**	**79.2**	**101.8**	**90.1**	..
49-53	**Transportation and storage**	**16.3**	**20.7**	**19.0**	**20.8**	**38.7**	**35.8**	**40.1**	..
55-56	**Accommodation and food service activities**	..	..	..	..	..	..	..	..
58-63	**Information and communication**	**561.0**	**602.6**	**639.8**	**683.5**	**803.0**	**898.7**	**980.4**	..
58-60	Publishing, audiovisual and broadcasting activities	166.9	157.4	150.9	198.1	250.6	248.9	286.6	..
58	Publishing activities	165.7	155.9	147.8	194.8	248.0	242.6	282.0	..
59-60	Motion picture, video and TV programme production; broadcasting activities	1.2	1.6	3.0	3.2	2.6	6.3	4.6	..
59	Motion picture, video and TV programme production; sound and music	1.2 e	1.5 e	3.0 e	3.2 e	2.6	4.1 e	2.1	..
60	Programming and broadcasting activities	0.0 e	0.0 e	0.0 e	0.0 e	0.0	2.2 e	2.6	..
61	Telecommunications	78.7	77.5	75.5	84.2	99.2	126.0	107.2	..
62-63	IT and other information services	315.4	367.7	413.4	401.2	453.1	523.7	586.6	..
62	Computer programming, consultancy and related activities	300.6	336.8	387.7	370.8	423.4	492.5	554.0	..
63	Information service activities	14.8	30.9	25.7	30.4	29.7	31.2	32.6	..
64-66	**Financial and insurance activities**	**147.1**	**135.4**	**143.9**	**142.6**	**141.5**	**110.5**	**153.3**	..
68-82	**Real estate; professional, scientific and technical; administrative and support**	**779.4**	**786.6**	**762.7**	**808.3**	**881.3**	**866.4**	**891.5**	..
68	Real estate activities	0.0	0.0	0.0	0.0	0.0	0.0	0.0	..
69-75x72	Professional, scientific and technical activities, except scientific R&D	309.0	280.8	266.6	315.7	340.4	356.5	362.6	..
72	Scientific research and development	451.8	491.1	482.5	486.5	532.0	500.9	517.9	..
77-82	Administrative and support service activities	18.6	14.7	13.6	6.0	8.9	9.0	10.9	..
84-99	Community, social and personal services	..	..	..	..	..	..	..	..
84-85	Public administration and defence; compulsory social security and education	..	..	..	..	..	..	..	..
86-88	Human health and social work activities	..	..	..	..	..	..	..	..
90-93	Arts, entertainment and recreation	..	..	..	..	..	..	..	..
94-99	Other services; household-employers; extraterritorial bodies	..	..	..	..	..	..	..	..

.. Not available; e Estimated value

Note: Detailed metadata at: *http://metalinks.oecd.org/anberd/20200813/2abe.*

POLAND

R&D expenditure in industry by main activity of the enterprise, current prices
ISIC Rev. 4

Million USD PPP

		2011	2012	2013	2014	2015	2016	2017	2018
	TOTAL BUSINESS ENTERPRISE	1 954.9	2 973.6	3 570.4	4 262.3	4 766.6	6 798.8	7 639.1	..
01-03	**AGRICULTURE, FORESTRY AND FISHING**	15.0	18.5	17.7	19.2	25.1	..	33.7	..
05-09	**MINING AND QUARRYING**	..	..	..	..	..	..	7.3	
10-33	**MANUFACTURING**	960.9	1 429.5	1 572.9	1 944.4	2 113.3	2 293.6 e	3 042.5	..
10-12	Food products, beverages and tobacco	35.4	33.3	79.3	231.8	79.3	69.4	147.1	..
13-15	Textiles, wearing apparel, leather and related products	9.1	12.6	14.8	21.3	32.3	10.6	59.7	..
13	Textiles	7.5	7.6	12.3	17.9	27.2 e	6.0	57.4	..
14	Wearing apparel	1.1 e	3.7	2.0	2.5 e	3.8 e	3.2 e	1.0	..
15	Leather and related products, footwear	0.5 e	1.3	0.5	0.9 e	1.2	1.3 e	1.4	..
16-18	Wood and paper products and printing	19.5	24.7	40.2	29.8	47.8	53.9 e	96.3	..
16	Wood and wood products, except furniture	6.3 e	8.7	13.0	7.3	23.9	36.2	51.4	..
17	Paper and paper products	8.3	3.2	3.6	10.4	6.0	6.8 e	26.0	..
18	Printing and reproduction of recorded media	4.9 e	12.7	23.6	12.1	18.0	10.9	18.9	..
19-23	Chemical, rubber, plastic, non-metallic mineral products	240.9	322.0	322.4	360.5	512.0	457.8	695.5	..
19	Coke and refined petroleum products	2.4	5.0	10.4 e	6.2 e	31.0	19.4	77.5	..
20-21	Chemical and pharmaceutical products	162.9	222.9	227.6	232.5	360.0	293.4	460.1	..
20	Chemicals and chemical products	70.1	78.7	104.8 e	81.8	144.1	113.5	196.5	..
21	Pharmaceuticals, medicinal, chemical and botanical products	92.9	144.1	122.8	150.7	216.0	179.9	263.6	..
22	Rubber and plastic products	57.1	62.2	57.8	88.1	73.4	108.4	102.8	..
23	Other non-metallic mineral products	18.4	31.9	26.7	33.8 e	47.6	36.6	55.1	..
24-25	Basic metals, metal products, except machinery and equipment	119.1	174.3	212.9	247.5	240.6	231.9	368.9	..
24	Basic metals	16.3	19.5	16.9	85.3	53.5	46.8	110.7	..
25	Fabricated metal products, except machinery and equipment	102.8	154.7	196.0	162.2	187.1	185.1	258.2	..
26-30	Computer, electronic, optical products; electrical machinery, transport equipment	480.0	751.2	830.6	958.7	1 073.1	1 275.4	1 510.1	..
26	Computer, electronic and optical products	74.0	89.0	84.5	94.7	115.3	125.7	175.3	..
27	Electrical equipment	118.7	264.3	186.8	166.0	198.9	264.4	274.1	..
28	Machinery and equipment n.e.c.	95.5	160.7	123.5	173.6	176.1	187.2	245.6	..
29	Motor vehicles, trailers and semi-trailers	101.2	125.8	310.3	388.7	391.9	536.0 e	624.7	..
30	Other transport equipment	90.4	111.3	125.5	135.8	190.9	162.1 e	190.5	..
31-33	Furniture; repair, installation of machinery and equipment	57.1	111.3	72.8	94.7	128.1	194.7	164.9	..
31	Furniture	11.8	31.6	26.8	29.0	34.0	86.8	50.8	..
32	Other manufacturing	17.3	36.8	24.6	31.0	30.8	58.5	52.7	..
33	Repair and installation of machinery and equipment	28.0	43.0	21.3	34.7	63.4	49.3	61.5	..
35-39	**ELECTRICITY, GAS, WATER AND WASTE MANAGEMENT**	..	..	..	..	..	41.9	51.2	..
35-36	Electricity, gas and water	..	..	69.4	23.0	..	31.0	29.0	
37-39	Sewerage, waste management and remediation activities	11.7	34.4	..	..	..	10.8	22.2	
41-43	**CONSTRUCTION**	31.3	30.4	71.9	31.7	30.5	47.3	64.5	..
45-99	**TOTAL SERVICES**	925.0	1 332.8	1 647.7	2 130.2	2 473.1	4 371.5 e	4 439.9	
45-82	**Business sector services**	895.2	1 320.1	1 631.6	2 110.9	2 439.6	4 328.1	4 398.6	
45-47	**Wholesale and retail trade; motor vehicle and motorcycle repairs**	127.7	209.8	288.8	325.4	362.7	301.2	383.9	..
49-53	**Transportation and storage**	..	..	..	..	8.2	..	5.1	..
55-56	**Accommodation and food service activities**	..	..	..	..	..	2.0	0.6	..
58-63	**Information and communication**	514.4	604.9	681.8	807.6	1 024.3	..	1 801.5	..
58-60	Publishing, audiovisual and broadcasting activities	100.5	27.8	28.6	39.8	72.9	..	74.4	..
58	Publishing activities	..	..	27.4	38.5	69.8	..	71.6	..
59-60	Motion picture, video and TV programme production; broadcasting activities	..	..	1.2	1.2	3.1	3.9	2.8	..
59	Motion picture, video and TV programme production; sound and music	..	..	..	..	..	..	2.3	..
60	Programming and broadcasting activities	..	..	..	..	..	..	0.5	..
61	Telecommunications	..	..	..	..	..	..	..	..
62-63	IT and other information services	..	..	..	..	..	1 380.5	..	..
62	Computer programming, consultancy and related activities	231.8	369.6	408.6	445.5	557.4	1 347.0	1 149.3	..
63	Information service activities	..	..	..	..	..	33.6	..	..
64-66	**Financial and insurance activities**	5.9	18.3	46.3	128.5	..	457.2	237.3	..
68-82	**Real estate; professional, scientific and technical; administrative and support**	233.2	483.2	596.4	833.9	..	..	1 970.4	..
68	Real estate activities	0.0	28.9	42.3	35.6	..	..	5.0	..
69-75x72	Professional, scientific and technical activities, except scientific R&D	30.3	122.3	107.5	233.3	316.6	290.2	356.2	..
72	Scientific research and development	202.7	327.7	439.7	555.2	568.3	1 377.8	1 583.5	..
77-82	Administrative and support service activities	0.3	4.3	6.8	9.7	11.1	56.5	25.7	..
84-99	Community, social and personal services	29.9	12.7	16.1	19.3	33.5	43.4 e	41.3	..
84-85	Public administration and defence; compulsory social security and education	0.7 e	0.7	0.9	1.4	0.9	1.4	1.7	..
86-88	Human health and social work activities	21.1 e	10.5	8.8	10.5	19.4	22.2	35.1	..
90-93	Arts, entertainment and recreation	6.9	0.3	0.3	0.7	0.6	1.7	0.8	..
94-99	Other services; household-employers; extraterritorial bodies	1.2	1.2	6.1	6.7	12.7	18.1 e	3.7	..

.. Not available; e Estimated value

Note: Detailed metadata at: *http://metalinks.oecd.org/anberd/20200813/2abe.*

POLAND

R&D expenditure in industry by main activity of the enterprise, constant prices
ISIC Rev. 4

2010 USD PPP

		2011	2012	2013	2014	2015	2016	2017	2018
	TOTAL BUSINESS ENTERPRISE	**2 074.6**	**3 074.2**	**3 610.6**	**4 301.2**	**4 766.6**	**6 656.4**	**7 361.0**	..
01-03	**AGRICULTURE, FORESTRY AND FISHING**	16.0	19.2	17.9	19.4	25.1	..	32.4	..
05-09	**MINING AND QUARRYING**	..	..	..	..	..	..	7.0	..
10-33	**MANUFACTURING**	**1 019.7**	**1 477.8**	**1 590.6**	**1 962.2**	**2 113.3**	**2 245.6 e**	**2 931.7**	..
10-12	Food products, beverages and tobacco	37.5	34.5	80.2	234.0	79.3	68.0	141.7	..
13-15	Textiles, wearing apparel, leather and related products	9.7	13.1	14.9	21.5	32.3	10.3	57.6	..
13	Textiles	8.0	7.8	12.4	18.1	27.2 e	5.9	55.3	..
14	Wearing apparel	1.1 e	3.8	2.0	2.5 e	3.8 e	3.2 e	0.9	..
15	Leather and related products, footwear	0.5 e	1.4	0.5	0.9 e	1.2	1.3 e	1.3	..
16-18	Wood and paper products and printing	20.7	25.6	40.6	30.1	47.8	52.8 e	92.8	..
16	Wood and wood products, except furniture	6.7 e	9.0	13.1	7.4	23.9	35.5	49.5	..
17	Paper and paper products	8.8	3.3	3.6	10.5	6.0	6.6 e	25.1	..
18	Printing and reproduction of recorded media	5.2 e	13.2	23.9	12.2	18.0	10.7	18.2	..
19-23	Chemical, rubber, plastic, non-metallic mineral products	255.6	332.9	326.0	363.8	512.0	448.2	670.2	..
19	Coke and refined petroleum products	2.5	5.2	10.5 e	6.2 e	31.0	19.0	74.7	..
20-21	Chemical and pharmaceutical products	172.9	230.4	230.1	234.6	360.0	287.2	443.4	..
20	Chemicals and chemical products	74.3	81.4	106.0 e	82.5	144.1	111.1	189.3	..
21	Pharmaceuticals, medicinal, chemical and botanical products	98.6	149.0	124.2	152.1	216.0	176.1	254.0	..
22	Rubber and plastic products	60.6	64.3	58.4	88.9	73.4	106.1	99.1	..
23	Other non-metallic mineral products	19.6	33.0	27.0	34.1 e	47.6	35.9	53.1	..
24-25	Basic metals, metal products, except machinery and equipment	126.4	180.2	215.3	249.7	240.6	227.0	355.5	..
24	Basic metals	17.3	20.2	17.1	86.1	53.5	45.8	106.7	..
25	Fabricated metal products, except machinery and equipment	109.1	160.0	198.2	163.7	187.1	181.2	248.8	..
26-30	Computer, electronic, optical products; electrical machinery, transport equipment	509.3	776.6	840.0	967.5	1 073.1	1 248.7	1 455.1	..
26	Computer, electronic and optical products	78.5	92.0	85.5	95.5	115.3	123.0	168.9	..
27	Electrical equipment	126.0	273.3	188.9	167.5	198.9	258.9	264.1	..
28	Machinery and equipment n.e.c.	101.4	166.1	124.9	175.1	176.1	183.3	236.7	..
29	Motor vehicles, trailers and semi-trailers	107.4	130.1	313.8	392.2	391.9	524.8 e	601.9	..
30	Other transport equipment	96.0	115.1	126.9	137.1	190.9	158.7 e	183.6	..
31-33	Furniture; repair, installation of machinery and equipment	60.6	115.1	73.6	95.6	128.1	190.6	158.9	..
31	Furniture	12.5	32.6	27.1	29.3	34.0	85.0	48.9	..
32	Other manufacturing	18.3	38.0	24.9	31.2	30.8	57.3	50.7	..
33	Repair and installation of machinery and equipment	29.7	44.4	21.5	35.1	63.4	48.3	59.2	..
35-39	**ELECTRICITY, GAS, WATER AND WASTE MANAGEMENT**	..	..	..	..	..	41.1	49.3	..
35-36	Electricity, gas and water	..	..	70.1	23.2	..	30.4	27.9	..
37-39	Sewerage, waste management and remediation activities	12.4	35.5	..	..	..	10.6	21.4	..
41-43	**CONSTRUCTION**	**33.2**	**31.4**	**72.7**	**32.0**	**30.5**	**46.3**	**62.2**	..
45-99	**TOTAL SERVICES**	**981.7**	**1 377.9**	**1 666.2**	**2 149.7**	**2 473.1**	**4 279.9 e**	**4 278.2**	..
45-82	**Business sector services**	**950.0**	**1 364.7**	**1 650.0**	**2 130.2**	**2 439.6**	**4 237.4**	**4 238.4**	..
45-47	Wholesale and retail trade; motor vehicle and motorcycle repairs	135.5	216.9	292.0	328.4	362.7	294.9	369.9	..
49-53	**Transportation and storage**	..	..	..	..	8.2	..	4.9	..
55-56	**Accommodation and food service activities**	..	..	..	..	..	1.9	0.6	..
58-63	**Information and communication**	**545.9**	**625.4**	**689.4**	**814.9**	**1 024.3**	..	**1 735.9**	..
58-60	Publishing, audiovisual and broadcasting activities	106.7	28.8	28.9	40.1	72.9	..	71.7	..
58	Publishing activities	..	..	27.7	38.8	69.8	..	69.0	..
59-60	Motion picture, video and TV programme production; broadcasting activities	..	..	1.3	1.3	3.1	3.8	2.7	..
59	Motion picture, video and TV programme production; sound and music	..	..	..	..	..	..	2.2	..
60	Programming and broadcasting activities	..	..	..	..	..	..	0.5	..
61	Telecommunications	..	..	..	..	..	..	..	..
62-63	IT and other information services	..	..	..	..	..	1 351.6	..	..
62	Computer programming, consultancy and related activities	246.0	382.1	413.2	449.5	557.4	1 318.7	1 107.4	..
63	Information service activities	..	..	..	..	..	32.9	..	..
64-66	**Financial and insurance activities**	**6.3**	**18.9**	**46.8**	**129.6**	..	**447.6**	**228.6**	..
68-82	**Real estate; professional, scientific and technical; administrative and support**	**247.5**	**499.5**	**603.1**	**841.5**	..	..	**1 898.6**	..
68	Real estate activities	0.0	29.9	42.8	35.9	..	..	4.8	..
69-75x72	Professional, scientific and technical activities, except scientific R&D	32.1	126.5	108.8	235.4	316.6	284.1	343.2	..
72	Scientific research and development	215.1	338.8	444.7	560.3	568.3	1 349.0	1 525.8	..
77-82	Administrative and support service activities	0.3	4.4	6.8	9.8	11.1	55.3	24.7	..
84-99	Community, social and personal services	31.7	13.2	16.2	19.5	33.5	42.5 e	39.8	..
84-85	Public administration and defence; compulsory social security and education	0.8 e	0.7	0.9	1.4	0.9	1.4	1.6	..
86-88	Human health and social work activities	22.4 e	10.9	8.9	10.6	19.4	21.8	33.8	..
90-93	Arts, entertainment and recreation	7.3	0.3	0.3	0.7	0.6	1.6	0.8	..
94-99	Other services; household-employers; extraterritorial bodies	1.2	1.3	6.2	6.7	12.7	17.7 e	3.6	..

.. Not available; e Estimated value

Note: Detailed metadata at: http://metalinks.oecd.org/anberd/20200813/2abe.

R&D expenditure in industry by main activity of the enterprise, current prices
ISIC Rev. 4

Million USD PPP

		2011	2012	2013	2014	2015	2016	2017	2018
	TOTAL BUSINESS ENTERPRISE	**1 952.1**	**1 905.1**	**1 838.4**	**1 789.6**	**1 772.5**	**2 023.7**	**2 267.1**	..
01-03	**AGRICULTURE, FORESTRY AND FISHING**	4.6	7.9	11.6	7.9	8.5	15.8	19.6	..
05-09	**MINING AND QUARRYING**	6.4	4.4	6.5	5.9	12.4	9.1	14.0	..
10-33	**MANUFACTURING**	692.7	781.3	727.3	742.4	705.5	846.6	897.7	..
10-12	Food products, beverages and tobacco	66.4	117.3	101.0	96.9	77.1	85.6	87.8	..
13-15	Textiles, wearing apparel, leather and related products	33.2	38.4	38.9	44.0	46.0	49.8	51.7	..
13	Textiles	20.0	23.0	19.0	23.3	26.7	28.5	27.3	..
14	Wearing apparel	5.0	5.8	4.4	5.7	5.6	7.3	8.6	..
15	Leather and related products, footwear	8.3	9.6	15.5	15.0	13.8	14.0	15.8	..
16-18	Wood and paper products and printing	54.8	58.9	61.6	56.4	55.1	58.8	72.3	..
16	Wood and wood products, except furniture	15.3	16.0	14.5	15.0	18.4	18.6	26.8	..
17	Paper and paper products	21.1	25.7	26.3	19.4	16.8	19.6	23.7	..
18	Printing and reproduction of recorded media	18.4	17.1	20.7	22.0	19.9	20.6	21.7	..
19-23	Chemical, rubber, plastic, non-metallic mineral products	259.7	297.8 e	269.5	259.0 e	258.8 e	317.5 e	343.4 e	..
19	Coke and refined petroleum products	8.7	7.1 e	5.8	3.7 e	5.6 e	7.4 e	7.6 e	..
20-21	Chemical and pharmaceutical products	169.4	188.6	186.8	171.6	173.2	210.2	225.5	..
20	Chemicals and chemical products	29.1	40.8	41.9	41.9	45.7	56.2	51.6	..
21	Pharmaceuticals, medicinal, chemical and botanical products	140.4	147.8	144.9	129.7	127.5	154.1	173.9	..
22	Rubber and plastic products	34.8	38.9	35.6	36.6	38.7	63.0	58.0	..
23	Other non-metallic mineral products	46.8	63.1	41.3	47.0	41.4	36.8	52.3	..
24-25	Basic metals, metal products, except machinery and equipment	61.3	57.7	59.4	77.7	51.4	65.1	77.2	..
24	Basic metals	19.2	19.2	22.0	33.0	12.9	18.1	21.0	..
25	Fabricated metal products, except machinery and equipment	42.1	38.5	37.5	44.7	38.5	47.0	56.2	..
26-30	Computer, electronic, optical products; electrical machinery, transport equipment	200.9	195.4	177.3	189.4	197.1	245.3	240.8	..
26	Computer, electronic and optical products	42.5	43.0	41.0	49.8	53.1	64.1	63.8	..
27	Electrical equipment	70.8	62.9	59.9	52.6	45.1	53.1	54.6	..
28	Machinery and equipment n.e.c.	25.8	34.6	31.7	32.5	36.4	44.0	46.4	..
29	Motor vehicles, trailers and semi-trailers	55.4	47.3	40.9	50.0	55.4	68.4	63.7	..
30	Other transport equipment	6.5	7.6	3.8	4.5	7.0	15.8	12.3	..
31-33	Furniture; repair, installation of machinery and equipment	16.4	15.8 e	19.5	19.0 e	20.0 e	24.4 e	24.4 e	..
31	Furniture	6.4	7.3	7.8	8.0	6.2	5.3	8.4	..
32	Other manufacturing	4.9	4.1 e	4.7	3.0 e	4.5 e	6.0 e	6.2 e	..
33	Repair and installation of machinery and equipment	5.0	4.4	7.0	8.1	9.3	13.1	9.9	..
35-39	**ELECTRICITY, GAS, WATER AND WASTE MANAGEMENT**	24.3	33.9	17.0	16.1	21.5	23.5	16.4	..
35-36	Electricity, gas and water	17.8	15.2	9.1	8.8	14.4	16.8	10.1	..
37-39	Sewerage, waste management and remediation activities	6.5	18.7	7.8	7.3	7.1	6.7	6.3	..
41-43	**CONSTRUCTION**	16.6	8.5	13.1	14.1	13.8	10.9	18.6	..
45-99	**TOTAL SERVICES**	**1 207.6**	**1 069.1**	**1 062.8**	**1 003.2**	**1 010.7**	**1 117.8**	**1 300.8**	..
45-82	**Business sector services**	**1 183.6**	**1 046.5**	**1 039.2**	**972.6**	**978.1**	**1 089.0**	**1 264.5**	..
45-47	**Wholesale and retail trade; motor vehicle and motorcycle repairs**	138.1	129.0	81.4	96.0	85.9	91.5	107.3	..
49-53	**Transportation and storage**	41.7	19.4	23.1	23.1	19.7	18.8	34.2	..
55-56	**Accommodation and food service activities**	0.3	0.2	0.1	0.1	0.1	0.7	1.3	..
58-63	**Information and communication**	532.4	449.1	412.3	336.5	312.9	374.1	450.1	..
58-60	Publishing, audiovisual and broadcasting activities	29.4	25.7	23.6	26.7	20.7	21.6	28.7	..
58	Publishing activities	22.6	19.6	22.3	25.6 e	20.3	20.4	28.2	..
59-60	Motion picture, video and TV programme production; broadcasting activities	6.9	6.0	1.3	1.0 e	0.4	1.1	0.5	..
59	Motion picture, video and TV programme production; sound and music	0.2	0.5	0.1 e	..	..	0.6	0.5	..
60	Programming and broadcasting activities	6.7	5.6	1.2 e	..	..	0.6	0.0	..
61	Telecommunications	339.1	225.2	184.0	85.8	78.6	102.9	124.6	..
62-63	IT and other information services	163.9	198.2	204.8	224.1	213.5	249.6	296.8	..
62	Computer programming, consultancy and related activities	158.6	188.9	197.2	215.5	200.7	232.8	255.7	..
63	Information service activities	5.2	9.3	7.6	8.6	12.9	16.8	41.1	..
64-66	**Financial and insurance activities**	244.1	246.6	271.9	258.4	284.4	291.3	237.9	..
68-82	**Real estate; professional, scientific and technical; administrative and support**	227.0	202.1	250.2	258.5	275.1	312.5	433.8	..
68	Real estate activities	0.0	0.0	0.0	0.0	0.0	0.0	0.0	..
69-75x72	Professional, scientific and technical activities, except scientific R&D	138.1	95.2	97.4	89.5	108.1	128.6	225.2	..
72	Scientific research and development	73.4	89.0	136.9	148.7	145.5	160.7	183.3	..
77-82	Administrative and support service activities	15.5	17.9	15.9	20.3	21.4	23.2	25.3	..
84-99	Community, social and personal services	24.0	22.6	23.7	30.6	32.6	28.7	36.3	..
84-85	Public administration and defence; compulsory social security and education	2.2	1.5	4.0	3.9	1.0	0.4	0.5 e	..
86-88	Human health and social work activities	7.3	6.9	7.7	8.1	9.6	13.3	17.7 e	..
90-93	Arts, entertainment and recreation	1.1	0.6	3.8	1.4	2.8	2.3	3.0	..
94-99	Other services; household-employers; extraterritorial bodies	13.3	13.6	8.1	17.2	19.2	12.8	15.1	..

.. Not available; e Estimated value

Note: Detailed metadata at: *http://metalinks.oecd.org/anberd/20200813/2abe.*

PORTUGAL

R&D expenditure in industry by main activity of the enterprise, constant prices
ISIC Rev. 4

2010 USD PPP

		2011	2012	2013	2014	2015	2016	2017	2018
	TOTAL BUSINESS ENTERPRISE	**2 176.5**	**2 071.8**	**1 884.9**	**1 807.3**	**1 772.5**	**1 944.2**	**2 158.7**	..
01-03	**AGRICULTURE, FORESTRY AND FISHING**	**5.1**	**8.6**	**11.9**	**7.9**	**8.5**	**15.2**	**18.7**	..
05-09	**MINING AND QUARRYING**	**7.1**	**4.8**	**6.7**	**6.0**	**12.4**	**8.8**	**13.4**	..
10-33	**MANUFACTURING**	**772.3**	**849.7**	**745.7**	**749.7**	**705.5**	**813.3**	**854.8**	..
10-12	Food products, beverages and tobacco	74.0	127.6	103.6	97.9	77.1	82.2	83.6	..
13-15	Textiles, wearing apparel, leather and related products	37.0	41.7	39.9	44.4	46.0	47.9	49.2	..
13	Textiles	22.3	25.0	19.4	23.5	26.7	27.4	26.0	..
14	Wearing apparel	5.5	6.3	4.5	5.8	5.6	7.0	8.2	..
15	Leather and related products, footwear	9.2	10.5	15.9	15.1	13.8	13.4	15.0	..
16-18	Wood and paper products and printing	61.1	64.0	63.2	57.0	55.1	56.5	68.8	..
16	Wood and wood products, except furniture	17.0	17.4	14.9	15.2	18.4	17.9	25.5	..
17	Paper and paper products	23.6	28.0	27.0	19.6	16.8	18.8	22.6	..
18	Printing and reproduction of recorded media	20.5	18.6	21.3	22.2	19.9	19.8	20.7	..
19-23	Chemical, rubber, plastic, non-metallic mineral products	289.5	323.9 e	276.3	261.5 e	258.8 e	305.0 e	327.0 e	..
19	Coke and refined petroleum products	9.7	7.8 e	5.9	3.8 e	5.6 e	7.1 e	7.3 e	..
20-21	Chemical and pharmaceutical products	188.9	205.1	191.5	173.3	173.2	202.0	214.7	..
20	Chemicals and chemical products	32.4	44.4	43.0	42.3	45.7	54.0	49.2	..
21	Pharmaceuticals, medicinal, chemical and botanical products	156.5	160.8	148.6	131.0	127.5	148.0	165.5	..
22	Rubber and plastic products	38.8	42.3	36.5	37.0	38.7	60.6	55.3	..
23	Other non-metallic mineral products	52.1	68.6	42.4	47.5	41.4	35.4	49.8	..
24-25	Basic metals, metal products, except machinery and equipment	68.4	62.8	60.9	78.5	51.4	62.6	73.5	..
24	Basic metals	21.4	20.9	22.5	33.3	12.9	17.4	20.0	..
25	Fabricated metal products, except machinery and equipment	46.9	41.9	38.4	45.1	38.5	45.1	53.5	..
26-30	Computer, electronic, optical products; electrical machinery, transport equipment	224.0	212.5	181.8	191.3	197.1	235.7	229.3	..
26	Computer, electronic and optical products	47.4	46.8	42.0	50.2	53.1	61.6	60.8	..
27	Electrical equipment	78.9	68.4	61.4	53.1	45.1	51.0	52.0	..
28	Machinery and equipment n.e.c.	28.8	37.6	32.5	32.9	36.4	42.3	44.2	..
29	Motor vehicles, trailers and semi-trailers	61.8	51.5	41.9	50.5	55.4	65.7	60.7	..
30	Other transport equipment	7.3	8.3	3.9	4.6	7.0	15.2	11.7	..
31-33	Furniture; repair, installation of machinery and equipment	18.2	17.2 e	20.0	19.2 e	20.0 e	23.4 e	23.2 e	..
31	Furniture	7.1	8.0	8.0	8.0	6.2	5.1	8.0	..
32	Other manufacturing	5.5	4.4 e	4.8	3.0 e	4.5 e	5.7 e	5.9 e	..
33	Repair and installation of machinery and equipment	5.6	4.8	7.2	8.1	9.3	12.6	9.4	..
35-39	**ELECTRICITY, GAS, WATER AND WASTE MANAGEMENT**	**27.1**	**36.9**	**17.4**	**16.3**	**21.5**	**22.6**	**15.6**	..
35-36	Electricity, gas and water	19.9	16.5	9.4	8.9	14.4	16.2	9.6	..
37-39	Sewerage, waste management and remediation activities	7.2	20.3	8.0	7.4	7.1	6.4	6.0	..
41-43	**CONSTRUCTION**	**18.5**	**9.3**	**13.5**	**14.2**	**13.8**	**10.5**	**17.7**	..
45-99	**TOTAL SERVICES**	**1 346.4**	**1 162.6**	**1 089.7**	**1 013.1**	**1 010.7**	**1 073.9**	**1 238.6**	..
45-82	**Business sector services**	**1 319.6**	**1 138.0**	**1 065.5**	**982.2**	**978.1**	**1 046.3**	**1 204.1**	..
45-47	**Wholesale and retail trade; motor vehicle and motorcycle repairs**	**153.9**	**140.3**	**83.5**	**96.9**	**85.9**	**87.9**	**102.1**	..
49-53	**Transportation and storage**	**46.5**	**21.1**	**23.7**	**23.4**	**19.7**	**18.1**	**32.5**	..
55-56	**Accommodation and food service activities**	**0.3**	**0.3**	**0.1**	**0.1**	**0.1**	**0.7**	**1.3**	..
58-63	**Information and communication**	**593.6**	**488.4**	**422.8**	**339.9**	**312.9**	**359.4**	**428.6**	..
58-60	Publishing, audiovisual and broadcasting activities	32.8	27.9	24.2	26.9	20.7	20.7	27.3	..
58	Publishing activities	25.2	21.3	22.9	25.9 e	20.3	19.6	26.8	..
59-60	Motion picture, video and TV programme production; broadcasting activities	7.7	6.6	1.3	1.0 e	0.4	1.1	0.5	..
59	Motion picture, video and TV programme production; sound and music	0.2	0.5	0.1 e	..	..	0.5	0.5	..
60	Programming and broadcasting activities	7.5	6.1	1.2 e	..	..	0.6	0.0	..
61	Telecommunications	378.1	244.9	188.6	86.7	78.6	98.9	118.6	..
62-63	IT and other information services	182.7	215.6	209.9	226.3	213.5	239.8	282.6	..
62	Computer programming, consultancy and related activities	176.9	205.5	202.1	217.6	200.7	223.7	243.5	..
63	Information service activities	5.8	10.1	7.8	8.7	12.9	16.1	39.1	..
64-66	**Financial and insurance activities**	**272.1**	**268.2**	**278.8**	**261.0**	**284.4**	**279.9**	**226.5**	..
68-82	**Real estate; professional, scientific and technical; administrative and support**	**253.1**	**219.8**	**256.6**	**261.0**	**275.1**	**300.3**	**413.1**	..
68	Real estate activities	0.0	0.0	0.0	0.0	0.0	0.0	0.0	..
69-75x72	Professional, scientific and technical activities, except scientific R&D	154.0	103.5	99.9	90.4	108.1	123.5	214.5	..
72	Scientific research and development	81.9	96.8	140.4	150.2	145.5	154.4	174.6	..
77-82	Administrative and support service activities	17.3	19.5	16.3	20.5	21.4	22.3	24.1	..
84-99	Community, social and personal services	26.7	24.6	24.3	30.9	32.6	27.6	34.5	..
84-85	Public administration and defence; compulsory social security and education	2.5	1.7	4.1	3.9	1.0	0.4	0.4 e	..
86-88	Human health and social work activities	8.1	7.5	7.9	8.2	9.6	12.8	16.9 e	..
90-93	Arts, entertainment and recreation	1.3	0.6	3.9	1.4	2.8	2.2	2.9	..
94-99	Other services; household-employers; extraterritorial bodies	14.9	14.8	8.3	17.4	19.2	12.3	14.4	..

.. Not available; e Estimated value

Note: Detailed metadata at: *http://metalinks.oecd.org/anberd/20200813/2abe.*

PORTUGAL

R&D expenditure in industry by industry orientation, current prices
ISIC Rev. 4

Million USD PPP

		2011	2012	2013	2014	2015	2016	2017	2018
	TOTAL BUSINESS ENTERPRISE	1 952.1	1 905.1	1 838.4	1 789.6	1 772.5	2 023.7	2 267.1	..
01-03	**AGRICULTURE, FORESTRY AND FISHING**	18.5	27.3	26.2	23.1	23.8	26.7	36.5	..
05-09	**MINING AND QUARRYING**	23.8	13.0	12.9	13.3	24.9	16.7	20.5	..
10-33	**MANUFACTURING**	752.5	844.8	804.2	840.1	826.2	981.0	1 063.2	..
10-12	Food products, beverages and tobacco	63.8	109.0	89.7	90.7	70.1	85.3	88.6	..
13-15	Textiles, wearing apparel, leather and related products	35.9	40.9	40.8	45.5	52.4	56.5	58.0	..
13	Textiles	20.4	24.3	23.1	28.5	32.7	32.9	31.8	..
14	Wearing apparel	6.9	5.1	3.7	3.7	7.9	9.9	9.8	..
15	Leather and related products, footwear	8.6	11.5	14.1	13.3	11.8	13.7	16.3	..
16-18	Wood and paper products and printing	37.3	44.6	46.7	40.5	39.9	44.6	58.3	..
16	Wood and wood products, except furniture	11.9	15.6	14.1	13.8	15.2	15.1	23.1	..
17	Paper and paper products	25.3	28.2	31.9	25.8	23.7	27.8	33.4	..
18	Printing and reproduction of recorded media	0.1	0.9	0.7	1.0	1.0	1.6	1.8	..
19-23	Chemical, rubber, plastic, non-metallic mineral products	267.7	313.3	283.5 e	276.5	276.2	309.5	350.5	..
19	Coke and refined petroleum products	0.3	5.9	3.2 e	2.9	5.6	5.6	7.7	..
20-21	Chemical and pharmaceutical products	195.4	215.4	208.3	199.1	201.1	235.7	257.1	..
20	Chemicals and chemical products	36.7	46.9	44.9	46.7	50.0	60.2	55.3	..
21	Pharmaceuticals, medicinal, chemical and botanical products	158.7	168.5	163.4	152.4	151.1	175.5	201.8	..
22	Rubber and plastic products	26.2	26.5	27.8	28.3	28.3	31.5	33.1	..
23	Other non-metallic mineral products	45.7	65.5	44.2	46.2	41.1	36.7	52.6	..
24-25	Basic metals, metal products, except machinery and equipment	54.8	49.8	53.9	69.0	47.8	57.3	69.0	..
24	Basic metals	21.5	19.8	22.6	34.0	11.7	17.5	20.7	..
25	Fabricated metal products, except machinery and equipment	33.3	30.0	31.3	35.0	36.1	39.9	48.3	..
26-30	Computer, electronic, optical products; electrical machinery, transport equipment	265.5	258.8	262.6	289.3	308.8	383.6	394.1	..
26	Computer, electronic and optical products	62.5	43.5	65.3	81.6	94.6	105.8	99.1	..
27	Electrical equipment	61.3	53.9	56.8	54.9	49.9	56.8	62.7	..
28	Machinery and equipment n.e.c.	44.9	45.6	40.8	44.2	40.4	50.1	56.5	..
29	Motor vehicles, trailers and semi-trailers	77.2	90.1	75.1	83.2	91.5	128.7	125.0	..
30	Other transport equipment	19.6	25.8	24.5	25.4	32.3	42.1	50.8	..
31-33	Furniture; repair, installation of machinery and equipment	27.4	28.4	27.0 e	28.7	31.0	44.2	44.7	..
31	Furniture	5.8	7.1	8.2	8.0	6.8	6.9	10.0	..
32	Other manufacturing	16.6	14.7	12.2	14.1	16.1	24.9	24.0	..
33	Repair and installation of machinery and equipment	5.0	6.5	6.6 e	6.5	8.2	12.3	10.6	..
35-39	**ELECTRICITY, GAS, WATER AND WASTE MANAGEMENT**	31.9	38.4	21.3	23.7	22.5	24.5	20.7	..
35-36	Electricity, gas and water	18.8	15.0	8.1	10.7	14.1	16.8	12.1	..
37-39	Sewerage, waste management and remediation activities	13.1	23.3	13.2	13.0	.8.4	7.8	8.6	..
41-43	**CONSTRUCTION**	13.7	7.5	12.7	13.2	16.2	17.2	21.2	..
45-99	**TOTAL SERVICES**	1 111.7	974.0	961.1	876.1	858.8	957.6	1 105.0	..
45-82	**Business sector services**	1 098.6	963.9	941.8	842.1	838.3	933.5	1 071.2	..
45-47	**Wholesale and retail trade; motor vehicle and motorcycle repairs**	57.5	71.7	69.8	77.7	67.9	67.4	85.6	..
49-53	**Transportation and storage**	34.2	12.3	17.6	16.5	16.4	15.4	16.5	..
55-56	**Accommodation and food service activities**	0.9	6.2	6.2	1.4	1.7	1.7	1.9 e	..
58-63	**Information and communication**	702.2	605.0	543.2	460.9	425.6	488.3	644.5	..
58-60	Publishing, audiovisual and broadcasting activities	75.7	90.0	112.0	104.2	107.0	136.0	150.0	..
58	Publishing activities	70.6	87.1	109.9	103.8	106.6	135.5	142.9	..
59-60	Motion picture, video and TV programme production; broadcasting activities	5.1	2.9	2.0	0.4	0.4	0.4	7.1	..
59	Motion picture, video and TV programme production; sound and music	2.1	0.8	0.8	0.4	..	..	..	..
60	Programming and broadcasting activities	3.0	2.1	1.3	0.0	..	..	..	..
61	Telecommunications	447.6	328.3	248.4	146.7	140.8	145.7	208.8	..
62-63	IT and other information services	178.9	186.7	182.8	210.0	177.9	206.7	285.6	..
62	Computer programming, consultancy and related activities	131.6	157.5	156.9	182.3	146.7	161.8	206.5	..
63	Information service activities	47.4	29.3	25.8	27.6	31.1	44.9	79.2	..
64-66	**Financial and insurance activities**	146.7	148.9	151.6	135.0	161.4	194.6	141.5	..
68-82	**Real estate; professional, scientific and technical; administrative and support**	157.1	119.7	153.3	150.6	165.3	166.1	181.2	..
68	Real estate activities	1.3	0.9	1.6	1.9	1.4	1.9	2.1 e	..
69-75x72	Professional, scientific and technical activities, except scientific R&D	118.2	73.2	83.1	72.5	83.9	91.8	102.4	..
72	Scientific research and development	33.2	38.6	60.9	69.6	71.3	63.5	70.3	..
77-82	Administrative and support service activities	4.4	7.0	7.7	6.6	8.7	8.8	6.4	..
84-99	Community, social and personal services	13.1	10.2	19.3	34.0	20.5	24.1	33.8	..
84-85	Public administration and defence; compulsory social security and education	0.6	1.2	1.4	1.9	2.5	2.5	1.7	..
86-88	Human health and social work activities	10.2	7.9	14.2	27.5	14.0	18.4	29.3	..
90-93	Arts, entertainment and recreation	0.6	0.5	0.6	1.4	2.8	1.1	0.7	..
94-99	Other services; household-employers; extraterritorial bodies	1.7	0.6	3.1	3.2	1.2	2.2	2.1	..

.. Not available; e Estimated value

Note: Detailed metadata at: *http://metalinks.oecd.org/anberd/20200813/2abe.*

R&D expenditure in industry by industry orientation, constant prices
ISIC Rev. 4

2010 USD PPP

		2011	2012	2013	2014	2015	2016	2017	2018
	TOTAL BUSINESS ENTERPRISE	**2 176.5**	**2 071.8**	**1 884.9**	**1 807.3**	**1 772.5**	**1 944.2**	**2 158.7**	..
01-03	**AGRICULTURE, FORESTRY AND FISHING**	**20.6**	**29.7**	**26.9**	**23.4**	**23.8**	**25.6**	**34.7**	..
05-09	**MINING AND QUARRYING**	**26.5**	**14.2**	**13.3**	**13.5**	**24.9**	**16.0**	**19.5**	..
10-33	**MANUFACTURING**	**839.0**	**918.7**	**824.6**	**848.4**	**826.2**	**942.4**	**1 012.4**	..
10-12	Food products, beverages and tobacco	71.2	118.5	91.9	91.6	70.1	81.9	84.4	..
13-15	Textiles, wearing apparel, leather and related products	40.0	44.5	41.9	45.9	52.4	54.3	55.2	..
13	Textiles	22.8	26.4	23.6	28.7	32.7	31.6	30.3	..
14	Wearing apparel	7.7	5.6	3.8	3.8	7.9	9.5	9.4	..
15	Leather and related products, footwear	9.5	12.5	14.5	13.4	11.8	13.1	15.5	..
16-18	Wood and paper products and printing	41.6	48.5	47.9	40.9	39.9	42.8	55.5	..
16	Wood and wood products, except furniture	13.3	16.9	14.5	13.9	15.2	14.5	22.0	..
17	Paper and paper products	28.2	30.6	32.7	26.0	23.7	26.7	31.8	..
18	Printing and reproduction of recorded media	0.1	1.0	0.7	1.0	1.0	1.6	1.7	..
19-23	Chemical, rubber, plastic, non-metallic mineral products	298.4	340.7	290.6 e	279.2	276.2	297.4	333.8	..
19	Coke and refined petroleum products	0.3	6.4	3.2 e	3.0	5.6	5.4	7.4	..
20-21	Chemical and pharmaceutical products	217.9	234.2	213.6	201.1	201.1	226.5	244.8	..
20	Chemicals and chemical products	40.9	51.0	46.1	47.2	50.0	57.8	52.6	..
21	Pharmaceuticals, medicinal, chemical and botanical products	177.0	183.2	167.5	153.9	151.1	168.6	192.2	..
22	Rubber and plastic products	29.2	28.9	28.5	28.6	28.3	30.3	31.6	..
23	Other non-metallic mineral products	51.0	71.2	45.3	46.6	41.1	35.3	50.0	..
24-25	Basic metals, metal products, except machinery and equipment	61.1	54.1	55.3	69.7	47.8	55.1	65.7	..
24	Basic metals	24.0	21.6	23.2	34.4	11.7	16.8	19.7	..
25	Fabricated metal products, except machinery and equipment	37.1	32.6	32.1	35.3	36.1	38.3	46.0	..
26-30	Computer, electronic, optical products; electrical machinery, transport equipment	296.1	281.5	269.2	292.1	308.8	368.6	375.3	..
26	Computer, electronic and optical products	69.7	47.3	67.0	82.4	94.6	101.7	94.4	..
27	Electrical equipment	68.4	58.6	58.3	55.4	49.9	54.6	59.7	..
28	Machinery and equipment n.e.c.	50.1	49.6	41.8	44.6	40.4	48.2	53.8	..
29	Motor vehicles, trailers and semi-trailers	86.1	97.9	77.0	84.1	91.5	123.6	119.0	..
30	Other transport equipment	21.9	28.0	25.1	25.7	32.3	40.5	48.4	..
31-33	Furniture; repair, installation of machinery and equipment	30.6	30.9	27.7 e	28.9	31.0	42.4	42.5	..
31	Furniture	6.5	7.8	8.4	8.0	6.8	6.7	9.5	..
32	Other manufacturing	18.5	16.0	12.5	14.3	16.1	23.9	22.9	..
33	Repair and installation of machinery and equipment	5.6	7.1	6.8 e	6.6	8.2	11.8	10.1	..
35-39	**ELECTRICITY, GAS, WATER AND WASTE MANAGEMENT**	**35.6**	**41.8**	**21.9**	**24.0**	**22.5**	**23.6**	**19.7**	..
35-36	Electricity, gas and water	21.0	16.4	8.4	10.8	14.1	16.1	11.5	..
37-39	Sewerage, waste management and remediation activities	14.6	25.4	13.5	13.1	8.4	7.5	8.2	..
41-43	**CONSTRUCTION**	**15.3**	**8.2**	**13.0**	**13.4**	**16.2**	**16.6**	**20.2**	..
45-99	**TOTAL SERVICES**	**1 239.5**	**1 059.3**	**985.4**	**884.7**	**858.8**	**920.0**	**1 052.2**	..
45-82	**Business sector services**	**1 224.9**	**1 048.2**	**965.6**	**850.4**	**838.3**	**896.8**	**1 020.0**	..
45-47	**Wholesale and retail trade; motor vehicle and motorcycle repairs**	**64.1**	**78.0**	**71.5**	**78.5**	**67.9**	**64.7**	**81.5**	..
49-53	**Transportation and storage**	**38.1**	**13.4**	**18.1**	**16.7**	**16.4**	**14.8**	**15.7**	..
55-56	**Accommodation and food service activities**	**1.0**	**6.7**	**6.3**	**1.4**	**1.7**	**1.7**	**1.8 e**	..
58-63	**Information and communication**	**782.9**	**658.0**	**557.0**	**465.5**	**425.6**	**469.1**	**613.7**	..
58-60	Publishing, audiovisual and broadcasting activities	84.4	97.9	114.8	105.2	107.0	130.6	142.9	..
58	Publishing activities	78.7	94.7	112.7	104.8	106.6	130.2	136.1	..
59-60	Motion picture, video and TV programme production; broadcasting activities	5.7	3.2	2.1	0.4	0.4	0.4	6.8	..
59	Motion picture, video and TV programme production; sound and music	2.4	0.9	0.8	0.4	..	..	..	..
60	Programming and broadcasting activities	3.3	2.3	1.3	0.0	..	..	..	..
61	Telecommunications	499.0	357.0	254.7	148.2	140.8	140.0	198.8	..
62-63	IT and other information services	199.5	203.1	187.4	212.1	177.9	198.5	272.0	..
62	Computer programming, consultancy and related activities	146.7	171.3	160.9	184.1	146.7	155.4	196.6	..
63	Information service activities	52.8	31.8	26.5	27.9	31.1	43.1	75.4	..
64-66	**Financial and insurance activities**	**163.6**	**162.0**	**155.5**	**136.3**	**161.4**	**186.9**	**134.8**	..
68-82	**Real estate; professional, scientific and technical; administrative and support**	**175.1**	**130.2**	**157.2**	**152.1**	**165.3**	**159.6**	**172.5**	..
68	Real estate activities	1.4	1.0	1.7	1.9	1.4	1.9	2.0 e	..
69-75x72	Professional, scientific and technical activities, except scientific R&D	131.7	79.6	85.2	73.2	83.9	88.2	97.5	..
72	Scientific research and development	37.0	42.0	62.5	70.2	71.3	61.0	67.0	..
77-82	Administrative and support service activities	4.9	7.6	7.9	6.7	8.7	8.5	6.1	..
84-99	Community, social and personal services	14.6	11.1	19.8	34.3	20.5	23.1	32.2	..
84-85	Public administration and defence; compulsory social security and education	0.6	1.3	1.4	1.9	2.5	2.4	1.6	..
86-88	Human health and social work activities	11.4	8.6	14.6	27.8	14.0	17.6	27.9	..
90-93	Arts, entertainment and recreation	0.6	0.5	0.6	1.5	2.8	1.0	0.7	..
94-99	Other services; household-employers; extraterritorial bodies	1.9	0.7	3.1	3.2	1.2	2.1	2.0	..

.. Not available; e Estimated value

Note: Detailed metadata at: *http://metalinks.oecd.org/anberd/20200813/2abe.*

SLOVAK REPUBLIC

R&D expenditure in industry by main activity of the enterprise, current prices
ISIC Rev. 4

Million USD PPP

		2011	2012	2013	2014	2015	2016	2017	2018
	TOTAL BUSINESS ENTERPRISE	343.9	479.6	575.4	508.2	527.4	641.3	806.2	804.1
01-03	**AGRICULTURE, FORESTRY AND FISHING**	2.9	1.9	1.5	1.3	1.5	1.1	1.1	1.3
05-09	**MINING AND QUARRYING**	0.0 e	0.0 e	0.0 e	0.0 e	0.0 e	0.0	0.0	0.0 e
10-33	**MANUFACTURING**	210.0	257.7	330.5	342.3	347.2	429.3	570.3	560.7
10-12	Food products, beverages and tobacco	2.3	2.3	1.4	1.9	2.2	1.5	1.8	4.4
13-15	Textiles, wearing apparel, leather and related products	..	2.5	0.9	0.5	..	0.6	..	..
13	Textiles	..	..	..	..	..	..	..	..
14	Wearing apparel	..	..	..	..	..	..	..	..
15	Leather and related products, footwear	..	..	..	..	..	..	..	..
16-18	Wood and paper products and printing	..	..	..	..	..	..	..	..
16	Wood and wood products, except furniture	..	..	..	..	..	..	..	..
17	Paper and paper products	..	..	..	..	..	..	..	..
18	Printing and reproduction of recorded media	..	..	..	..	..	..	..	..
19-23	Chemical, rubber, plastic, non-metallic mineral products	..	52.6	50.0	57.1	..	..	..	..
19	Coke and refined petroleum products	..	5.5	6.8	6.2	..	..	..	..
20-21	Chemical and pharmaceutical products	32.4	24.4	14.1	14.8	12.2	17.8	16.7	12.1
20	Chemicals and chemical products	7.1	5.8	9.9	6.1	5.9	7.1	10.7	6.9
21	Pharmaceuticals, medicinal, chemical and botanical products	25.3	18.6	4.2	8.7	6.3	10.7	6.0	5.2
22	Rubber and plastic products	11.4	20.3	28.3	32.9	40.1	43.4	61.2	43.6
23	Other non-metallic mineral products	2.1	2.4	0.8	3.2	4.2	3.2	3.8	4.2
24-25	Basic metals, metal products, except machinery and equipment	13.9	17.4	10.7	10.2	33.4	..	..	33.0
24	Basic metals	7.2	7.3	6.2	6.0	5.7			8.2
25	Fabricated metal products, except machinery and equipment	6.7	10.2	4.5	4.2	27.7	16.8	19.1	24.8
26-30	Computer, electronic, optical products; electrical machinery, transport equipment	123.7	163.4	252.0	257.5	233.6	319.8	438.1	437.2
26	Computer, electronic and optical products	5.5	7.2	7.8	7.2	9.0	12.2	12.1	14.0
27	Electrical equipment	35.3	34.5	23.7	35.7	45.0	45.0	46.5	95.5
28	Machinery and equipment n.e.c.	25.6	30.1	29.4	31.2	51.9	55.9	71.0	76.1
29	Motor vehicles, trailers and semi-trailers	47.6	79.4	173.5	152.8	108.0	193.3	286.4	233.4
30	Other transport equipment	9.6	12.3	17.6	30.6	19.6	13.4	22.2	18.2
31-33	Furniture; repair, installation of machinery and equipment	..	..	..	..	..	..	..	..
31	Furniture	..	..	..	..	..	..	..	..
32	Other manufacturing	..	..	..	..	2.1	3.0	3.3	4.3
33	Repair and installation of machinery and equipment	16.5	16.4	..	..	12.0	11.4	12.1	12.9
35-39	**ELECTRICITY, GAS, WATER AND WASTE MANAGEMENT**	0.0 e	..	..	..	..	..	0.0	0.0
35-36	Electricity, gas and water	..	..	..	..	..	..	..	..
37-39	Sewerage, waste management and remediation activities	..	..	..	..	..	..	..	..
41-43	**CONSTRUCTION**	1.1	2.4	2.5	..	..	..	1.8	..
45-99	**TOTAL SERVICES**	129.9 e	217.6	240.2	162.7	169.8	187.9	232.9	240.8
45-82	**Business sector services**	124.9	212.4	237.4	162.3	168.4	187.1	232.1	240.0
45-47	**Wholesale and retail trade; motor vehicle and motorcycle repairs**	2.5	0.6	10.3	7.1	4.7	26.6	30.6	34.1
49-53	**Transportation and storage**	..	..	..	..	..	..	..	0.0
55-56	**Accommodation and food service activities**	..	..	..	..	..	..	..	0.0
58-63	**Information and communication**	11.7	61.2	64.8	65.4	81.0	83.7	108.6	108.1
58-60	Publishing, audiovisual and broadcasting activities	..	..	..	..	..	..	..	..
58	Publishing activities	..	..	..	..	..	..	..	..
59-60	Motion picture, video and TV programme production; broadcasting activities	..	..	..	..	..	..	..	..
59	Motion picture, video and TV programme production; sound and music	..	..	..	..	..	..	..	..
60	Programming and broadcasting activities	..	..	..	..	..	..	..	..
61	Telecommunications	..	..	..	..	..	..	..	..
62-63	IT and other information services	..	..	..	..	..	..	..	..
62	Computer programming, consultancy and related activities	9.6	59.2	62.0	64.1	80.9	..	108.5	104.3
63	Information service activities	..	..	..	..	..	..	..	..
64-66	**Financial and insurance activities**	..	63.5	..	..	..	4.3	..	..
68-82	**Real estate; professional, scientific and technical; administrative and support**	..	..	..	..	..	..	..	..
68	Real estate activities	..	..	..	..	..	..	..	..
69-75x72	Professional, scientific and technical activities, except scientific R&D	17.4	23.8	31.5	29.6	17.6	..	20.9	20.7
72	Scientific research and development	51.1	53.4	52.2	52.1	58.8	52.7	58.2	64.3
77-82	Administrative and support service activities	4.2	3.3	..	..	..	..	6.9	7.8
84-99	Community, social and personal services	5.0 e	5.2	2.8	0.4	1.3	0.8	0.8	0.8
84-85	Public administration and defence; compulsory social security and education	..	..	..	..	..	..	..	..
86-88	Human health and social work activities	..	1.6	0.9	0.4	1.3	0.8	0.8	0.8
90-93	Arts, entertainment and recreation	..	..	..	..	..	..	..	..
94-99	Other services; household-employers; extraterritorial bodies	..	..	..	..	..	..	..	..

.. Not available; e Estimated value

Note: Detailed metadata at: *http://metalinks.oecd.org/anberd/20200813/2abe.*

SLOVAK REPUBLIC

R&D expenditure in industry by main activity of the enterprise, constant prices
ISIC Rev. 4

2010 USD PPP

		2011	2012	2013	2014	2015	2016	2017	2018
	TOTAL BUSINESS ENTERPRISE	359.2	492.9	572.7	500.9	527.4	660.1	819.1	804.2
01-03	**AGRICULTURE, FORESTRY AND FISHING**	3.1	2.0	1.5	1.3	1.5	1.2	1.2	1.3
05-09	**MINING AND QUARRYING**	0.0 e	0.0 e	0.0 e	0.0 e	0.0 e	0.0	0.0	0.0 e
10-33	**MANUFACTURING**	219.3	264.8	328.9	337.4	347.2	441.8	579.4	560.7
10-12	Food products, beverages and tobacco	2.4	2.4	1.4	1.8	2.2	1.5	1.8	4.4
13-15	Textiles, wearing apparel, leather and related products	..	2.6	0.9	0.5	..	0.6	..	..
13	Textiles	..	..	..	..	..	..	..	..
14	Wearing apparel	..	..	..	..	..	..	..	..
15	Leather and related products, footwear	..	..	..	..	..	..	..	..
16-18	Wood and paper products and printing	..	..	..	..	..	..	..	..
16	Wood and wood products, except furniture	..	..	..	..	..	..	..	..
17	Paper and paper products	..	..	..	..	..	..	..	..
18	Printing and reproduction of recorded media	..	..	..	..	..	..	..	..
19-23	Chemical, rubber, plastic, non-metallic mineral products	..	54.1	49.8	56.3	..	..	..	..
19	Coke and refined petroleum products	..	5.7	6.8	6.1	..	..	..	..
20-21	Chemical and pharmaceutical products	33.8	25.0	14.0	14.6	12.2	18.3	16.9	12.1
20	Chemicals and chemical products	7.4	5.9	9.8	6.0	5.9	7.3	10.8	6.9
21	Pharmaceuticals, medicinal, chemical and botanical products	26.4	19.1	4.2	8.6	6.3	11.0	6.1	5.2
22	Rubber and plastic products	11.9	20.9	28.2	32.4	40.1	44.7	62.1	43.6
23	Other non-metallic mineral products	2.2	2.5	0.8	3.2	4.2	3.3	3.9	4.2
24-25	Basic metals, metal products, except machinery and equipment	14.5	17.9	10.6	10.1	33.4	..	..	33.0
24	Basic metals	7.5	7.5	6.1	5.9	5.7			8.2
25	Fabricated metal products, except machinery and equipment	7.0	10.4	4.5	4.2	27.7	17.3	19.4	24.8
26-30	Computer, electronic, optical products; electrical machinery, transport equipment	129.2	167.9	250.8	253.8	233.6	329.2	445.1	437.2
26	Computer, electronic and optical products	5.7	7.3	7.7	7.1	9.0	12.5	12.3	14.0
27	Electrical equipment	36.9	35.4	23.6	35.2	45.0	46.4	47.2	95.5
28	Machinery and equipment n.e.c.	26.7	30.9	29.3	30.8	51.9	57.5	72.1	76.1
29	Motor vehicles, trailers and semi-trailers	49.7	81.6	172.7	150.6	108.0	199.0	291.0	233.4
30	Other transport equipment	10.1	12.6	17.5	30.1	19.6	13.8	22.5	18.2
31-33	Furniture; repair, installation of machinery and equipment	..	..	..	..	..	..	..	..
31	Furniture	..	..	..	..	..	..	..	..
32	Other manufacturing	..	..	..	..	2.1	3.1	3.3	4.3
33	Repair and installation of machinery and equipment	17.2	16.8	..	..	12.0	11.7	12.3	12.9
35-39	**ELECTRICITY, GAS, WATER AND WASTE MANAGEMENT**	0.0 e	..	..	..	..	..	0.0	0.0
35-36	Electricity, gas and water	..	..	..	..	..	..	..	..
37-39	Sewerage, waste management and remediation activities	..	..	..	..	..	..	..	..
41-43	**CONSTRUCTION**	1.1	2.4	2.5	..	..	..	1.8	..
45-99	**TOTAL SERVICES**	135.7 e	223.6	239.1	160.3	169.8	193.4	236.6	240.9
45-82	**Business sector services**	130.5	218.3	236.3	159.9	168.4	192.6	235.8	240.0
45-47	**Wholesale and retail trade; motor vehicle and motorcycle repairs**	2.6	0.6	10.2	7.0	4.7	27.3	31.1	34.1
49-53	**Transportation and storage**	..	..	..	..	..	..	..	0.0
55-56	**Accommodation and food service activities**	..	..	..	..	..	..	..	0.0
58-63	**Information and communication**	12.3	62.9	64.5	64.4	81.0	86.1	110.4	108.1
58-60	Publishing, audiovisual and broadcasting activities	..	..	..	..	..	..	..	..
58	Publishing activities	..	..	..	..	..	..	..	..
59-60	Motion picture, video and TV programme production; broadcasting activities	..	..	..	..	..	..	..	..
59	Motion picture, video and TV programme production; sound and music	..	..	..	..	..	..	..	..
60	Programming and broadcasting activities	..	..	..	..	..	..	..	..
61	Telecommunications	..	..	..	..	..	..	..	..
62-63	IT and other information services	..	..	..	..	..	..	..	..
62	Computer programming, consultancy and related activities	10.1	60.8	61.7	63.2	80.9	..	110.2	104.3
63	Information service activities	..	..	..	..	..	..	..	..
64-66	**Financial and insurance activities**	..	65.3	..	..	..	4.5	..	..
68-82	**Real estate; professional, scientific and technical; administrative and support**	..	..	..	..	..	..	..	..
68	Real estate activities	..	..	..	..	..	..	..	..
69-75x72	Professional, scientific and technical activities, except scientific R&D	18.1	24.4	31.3	29.2	17.6	..	21.2	20.7
72	Scientific research and development	53.3	54.9	51.9	51.4	58.8	54.3	59.1	64.3
77-82	Administrative and support service activities	4.4	3.4	..	..	..	..	7.1	7.8
84-99	Community, social and personal services	5.2 e	5.4	2.8	0.4	1.3	0.8	0.8	0.8
84-85	Public administration and defence; compulsory social security and education	..	..	..	..	..	..	..	..
86-88	Human health and social work activities	..	1.7	0.9	0.4	1.3	0.8	0.8	0.8
90-93	Arts, entertainment and recreation	..	..	..	..	..	..	..	..
94-99	Other services; household-employers; extraterritorial bodies	..	..	..	..	..	..	..	..

.. Not available; e Estimated value

Note: Detailed metadata at: *http://metalinks.oecd.org/anberd/20200813/2abe.*

SLOVENIA

R&D expenditure in industry by main activity of the enterprise, current prices
ISIC Rev. 4

Million USD PPP

		2011	2012	2013	2014	2015	2016	2017	2018
	TOTAL BUSINESS ENTERPRISE	**1 058.5**	**1 158.7**	**1 211.9**	**1 164.5**	**1 093.2**	**1 065.0**	**1 057.0**	..
01-03	**AGRICULTURE, FORESTRY AND FISHING**	**0.7**	**0.9**	**0.0**	**0.0**	**0.9**	**0.1**	..	..
05-09	**MINING AND QUARRYING**	**9.2**	**7.4**	**7.8**	**5.8**	**5.1**	**6.8**	..	..
10-33	**MANUFACTURING**	**722.9**	**712.0**	**788.5**	**769.5**	**769.1**	**797.7**	**783.6**	..
10-12	Food products, beverages and tobacco	5.8	6.0	10.8	10.8	13.0	10.7	..	..
13-15	Textiles, wearing apparel, leather and related products	10.5	12.5	13.6	10.8	9.9	10.7	10.6	..
13	Textiles	8.5	8.7	9.7	5.9	5.7	6.6	5.6	..
14	Wearing apparel	0.4	2.3	2.4	2.1	2.2	2.3	3.5	..
15	Leather and related products, footwear	1.6	1.4	1.5	2.7	2.0	1.8	1.5	..
16-18	Wood and paper products and printing	7.0	5.3	4.9	5.8	7.4	10.5	12.8	..
16	Wood and wood products, except furniture	2.9	2.0	1.2	1.6	2.0	6.4	9.1	..
17	Paper and paper products	3.0	2.2	2.5	2.6	4.2	3.3	..	..
18	Printing and reproduction of recorded media	1.2	1.2	1.3	1.7	1.2	0.9	..	..
19-23	Chemical, rubber, plastic, non-metallic mineral products	316.3	329.9	345.7	340.6	369.4	375.1	..	..
19	Coke and refined petroleum products	0.0	0.0	0.0	0.0	0.0	0.0	0.0	..
20-21	Chemical and pharmaceutical products	295.4	304.1	305.2	306.7	338.8	342.6	..	..
20	Chemicals and chemical products	32.1	33.1	32.3	31.3	30.8	31.0	25.1	..
21	Pharmaceuticals, medicinal, chemical and botanical products	263.4	271.0	272.9	275.4	308.0	311.6	..	..
22	Rubber and plastic products	16.4	16.2	16.2	23.4	19.6	19.3	18.2	..
23	Other non-metallic mineral products	4.5	9.6	24.3	10.5	10.9	13.2	..	..
24-25	Basic metals, metal products, except machinery and equipment	54.2	72.7	69.4	66.7	44.8	32.8	31.1	..
24	Basic metals	13.6	9.1	15.2	16.9	12.8	10.2	8.2	..
25	Fabricated metal products, except machinery and equipment	40.5	63.6	54.2	49.8	32.0	22.5	22.9	..
26-30	Computer, electronic, optical products; electrical machinery, transport equipment	307.0	268.8	325.5	317.1	313.0	337.6	319.7	..
26	Computer, electronic and optical products	61.1	62.8	67.8	69.1	66.5	57.1	59.9	..
27	Electrical equipment	107.0	77.5	147.6	129.6	151.8	186.2	151.1	..
28	Machinery and equipment n.e.c.	51.6	23.5	33.1	33.5	37.4	37.1	43.7	..
29	Motor vehicles, trailers and semi-trailers	77.8	102.1	68.1	81.8	53.7	55.1	54.8	..
30	Other transport equipment	9.6	3.0	9.0	3.1	3.6	2.1	10.2	..
31-33	Furniture; repair, installation of machinery and equipment	22.2	16.8	18.6	17.7	11.7	20.4	..	..
31	Furniture	4.5	1.9	3.1	2.7	1.4	1.8	..	..
32	Other manufacturing	10.7	11.6	6.2	6.2	7.7	9.4	18.0	..
33	Repair and installation of machinery and equipment	7.0	3.3	9.3	8.8	2.6	9.2	10.8	..
35-39	**ELECTRICITY, GAS, WATER AND WASTE MANAGEMENT**	**4.2**	**6.9**	**4.7**	**4.5**	**3.6**	**2.1**	**2.5**	..
35-36	Electricity, gas and water	4.0	6.7	3.0	2.8	2.5	1.4	1.9	..
37-39	Sewerage, waste management and remediation activities	0.3	0.2	1.7	1.7	1.1	0.6	0.5	..
41-43	**CONSTRUCTION**	**2.1**	**2.5**	**2.9**	**3.8**	**3.9**	**3.0**	**2.8**	..
45-99	**TOTAL SERVICES**	**319.4**	**429.0**	**408.1**	**380.9**	**310.5**	**255.3**	**261.7**	..
45-82	**Business sector services**	**314.5**	**423.6**	**404.9**	**378.1**	**308.1**	**249.3**	**261.0**	..
45-47	Wholesale and retail trade; motor vehicle and motorcycle repairs	9.9	9.5	12.5	15.4	10.4	10.6	8.0	..
49-53	Transportation and storage	3.3	1.3	0.3	0.3	0.4	0.1	1.2	..
55-56	Accommodation and food service activities	0.0	0.0	0.0	0.1	0.0	0.0	0.0	..
58-63	Information and communication	69.2	73.7	55.8	79.5	85.3	63.8	75.2	..
58-60	Publishing, audiovisual and broadcasting activities	6.2	21.7	6.6	5.9	7.3	6.1	0.8	..
58	Publishing activities	6.1	6.5	6.6	5.9	7.1	6.0	..	..
59-60	Motion picture, video and TV programme production; broadcasting activities	0.1	15.1	0.0	0.0	0.1	0.1	..	..
59	Motion picture, video and TV programme production; sound and music	0.1	0.0	0.0	0.0	0.1	0.1	..	..
60	Programming and broadcasting activities	0.0	15.1	0.0	0.0	0.0	0.0	..	..
61	Telecommunications	4.5	2.8	2.7	11.8	12.7	3.4	3.8	..
62-63	IT and other information services	58.5	49.3	46.5	61.8	65.3	54.3	70.6	..
62	Computer programming, consultancy and related activities	54.5	44.6	42.8	56.7	58.5	52.2	67.3	..
63	Information service activities	4.0	4.7	3.7	5.1	6.8	2.1	3.3	..
64-66	**Financial and insurance activities**	**19.8**	**10.5**	**16.7**	**6.5**	**1.6**	**0.9**	..	..
68-82	**Real estate; professional, scientific and technical; administrative and support**	**212.3**	**328.6**	**319.7**	**276.3**	**210.4**	**174.0**	..	..
68	Real estate activities	0.0	0.0	1.0	1.5	0.9	1.7	..	..
69-75x72	Professional, scientific and technical activities, except scientific R&D	68.8	57.7	52.8	58.9	56.3	49.0	50.2	..
72	Scientific research and development	143.4	270.8	264.7	215.0	151.9	121.3	121.3	..
77-82	Administrative and support service activities	0.1	0.1	1.2	1.0	1.2	2.0	2.4	..
84-99	Community, social and personal services	5.0	5.4	3.1	2.8	2.4	6.0	0.7	..
84-85	Public administration and defence; compulsory social security and education	0.5	0.6	0.4	1.0	1.2	0.9	0.7	..
86-88	Human health and social work activities	2.7	2.2	0.5	0.2	0.2	0.2	0.0	..
90-93	Arts, entertainment and recreation	0.0	0.0	0.0	0.0	0.0	3.6	0.0	..
94-99	Other services; household-employers; extraterritorial bodies	1.8	2.6	2.2	1.6	1.0	1.3	..	..

.. Not available

Note: Detailed metadata at: *http://metalinks.oecd.org/anberd/20200813/2abe.*

SLOVENIA

R&D expenditure in industry by main activity of the enterprise, constant prices
ISIC Rev. 4

2010 USD PPP

		2011	2012	2013	2014	2015	2016	2017	2018
	TOTAL BUSINESS ENTERPRISE	**1 149.6**	**1 217.9**	**1 219.9**	**1 168.5**	**1 093.2**	**1 025.1**	**985.0**	**..**
01-03	**AGRICULTURE, FORESTRY AND FISHING**	0.7	1.0	0.0	0.0	0.9	0.1	..	..
05-09	**MINING AND QUARRYING**	10.0	7.7	7.9	5.8	5.1	6.5	..	..
10-33	**MANUFACTURING**	785.0	748.4	793.7	772.2	769.1	767.9	730.3	..
10-12	Food products, beverages and tobacco	6.3	6.4	10.9	10.8	13.0	10.3	..	..
13-15	Textiles, wearing apparel, leather and related products	11.4	13.1	13.7	10.9	9.9	10.3	9.8	..
13	Textiles	9.3	9.2	9.8	6.0	5.7	6.3	5.2	..
14	Wearing apparel	0.4	2.4	2.4	2.1	2.2	2.2	3.3	..
15	Leather and related products, footwear	1.7	1.5	1.5	2.8	2.0	1.8	1.4	..
16-18	Wood and paper products and printing	7.6	5.6	5.0	5.8	7.4	10.1	11.9	..
16	Wood and wood products, except furniture	3.1	2.1	1.2	1.6	2.0	6.1	8.5	..
17	Paper and paper products	3.2	2.3	2.5	2.6	4.2	3.1	..	..
18	Printing and reproduction of recorded media	1.3	1.2	1.3	1.7	1.2	0.8	..	..
19-23	Chemical, rubber, plastic, non-metallic mineral products	343.5	346.8	348.0	341.7	369.4	361.1	..	..
19	Coke and refined petroleum products	0.0	0.0	0.0	0.0	0.0	0.0	0.0	..
20-21	Chemical and pharmaceutical products	320.8	319.6	307.2	307.7	338.8	329.8	..	..
20	Chemicals and chemical products	34.8	34.8	32.5	31.4	30.8	29.8	23.4	..
21	Pharmaceuticals, medicinal, chemical and botanical products	286.0	284.8	274.7	276.3	308.0	299.9	..	..
22	Rubber and plastic products	17.8	17.1	16.3	23.4	19.6	18.6	17.0	..
23	Other non-metallic mineral products	4.9	10.1	24.5	10.6	10.9	12.7	..	..
24-25	Basic metals, metal products, except machinery and equipment	58.8	76.4	69.8	66.9	44.8	31.5	29.0	..
24	Basic metals	14.8	9.5	15.3	17.0	12.8	9.9	7.6	..
25	Fabricated metal products, except machinery and equipment	44.0	66.8	54.5	50.0	32.0	21.7	21.3	..
26-30	Computer, electronic, optical products; electrical machinery, transport equipment	333.4	282.5	327.7	318.2	313.0	324.9	297.9	..
26	Computer, electronic and optical products	66.3	66.0	68.2	69.3	66.5	54.9	55.8	..
27	Electrical equipment	116.2	81.4	148.6	130.1	151.8	179.2	140.8	..
28	Machinery and equipment n.e.c.	56.0	24.7	33.3	33.6	37.4	35.8	40.8	..
29	Motor vehicles, trailers and semi-trailers	84.5	107.3	68.5	82.1	53.7	53.0	51.1	..
30	Other transport equipment	10.4	3.2	9.0	3.2	3.6	2.0	9.5	..
31-33	Furniture; repair, installation of machinery and equipment	24.1	17.7	18.7	17.8	11.7	19.6	..	..
31	Furniture	4.9	2.0	3.1	2.8	1.4	1.8	..	..
32	Other manufacturing	11.6	12.2	6.2	6.3	7.7	9.1	16.8	..
33	Repair and installation of machinery and equipment	7.6	3.5	9.3	8.8	2.6	8.8	10.1	..
35-39	**ELECTRICITY, GAS, WATER AND WASTE MANAGEMENT**	4.6	7.2	4.8	4.5	3.6	2.0	2.3	..
35-36	Electricity, gas and water	4.3	7.0	3.0	2.8	2.5	1.4	1.8	..
37-39	Sewerage, waste management and remediation activities	0.3	0.2	1.7	1.7	1.1	0.6	0.5	..
41-43	**CONSTRUCTION**	**2.3**	**2.6**	**2.9**	**3.8**	**3.9**	**2.9**	**2.6**	**..**
45-99	**TOTAL SERVICES**	**346.9**	**451.0**	**410.8**	**382.2**	**310.5**	**245.7**	**243.9**	**..**
45-82	**Business sector services**	**341.5**	**445.3**	**407.6**	**379.4**	**308.1**	**240.0**	**243.2**	**..**
45-47	**Wholesale and retail trade; motor vehicle and motorcycle repairs**	10.7	10.0	12.6	15.5	10.4	10.2	7.4	..
49-53	**Transportation and storage**	3.6	1.4	0.3	0.3	0.4	0.1	1.1	..
55-56	**Accommodation and food service activities**	0.0	0.0	0.0	0.1	0.0	0.0	0.0	..
58-63	**Information and communication**	75.2	77.5	56.1	79.8	85.3	61.4	70.1	..
58-60	Publishing, audiovisual and broadcasting activities	6.7	22.8	6.6	5.9	7.3	5.9	0.7	..
58	Publishing activities	6.6	6.9	6.6	5.9	7.1	5.8	..	..
59-60	Motion picture, video and TV programme production; broadcasting activities	0.1	15.9	0.0	0.0	0.1	0.1	..	..
59	Motion picture, video and TV programme production; sound and music	0.1	0.0	0.0	0.0	0.1	0.1	..	..
60	Programming and broadcasting activities	0.0	15.9	0.0	0.0	0.0	0.0	..	..
61	Telecommunications	4.9	2.9	2.7	11.8	12.7	3.3	3.6	..
62-63	IT and other information services	63.6	51.8	46.8	62.1	65.3	52.3	65.8	..
62	Computer programming, consultancy and related activities	59.2	46.9	43.0	56.9	58.5	50.3	62.7	..
63	Information service activities	4.4	4.9	3.8	5.2	6.8	2.0	3.1	..
64-66	**Financial and insurance activities**	21.5	11.1	16.8	6.6	1.6	0.8	..	..
68-82	**Real estate; professional, scientific and technical; administrative and support**	230.5	345.4	321.8	277.3	210.4	167.4	..	..
68	Real estate activities	0.0	0.0	1.0	1.5	0.9	1.6	..	..
69-75x72	Professional, scientific and technical activities, except scientific R&D	74.7	60.7	53.1	59.1	56.3	47.2	46.8	..
72	Scientific research and development	155.7	284.7	266.4	215.7	151.9	116.7	113.0	..
77-82	Administrative and support service activities	0.1	0.1	1.2	1.0	1.2	1.9	2.3	..
84-99	Community, social and personal services	5.4	5.7	3.1	2.8	2.4	5.7	0.6	..
84-85	Public administration and defence; compulsory social security and education	0.6	0.6	0.4	1.0	1.2	0.8	0.6	..
86-88	Human health and social work activities	2.9	2.3	0.5	0.2	0.2	0.2	0.0	..
90-93	Arts, entertainment and recreation	0.0	0.0	0.0	0.0	0.0	3.4	0.0	..
94-99	Other services; household-employers; extraterritorial bodies	1.9	2.7	2.2	1.6	1.0	1.3	..	..

.. Not available

Note: Detailed metadata at: *http://metalinks.oecd.org/anberd/20200813/2abe.*

SPAIN

R&D expenditure in industry by main activity of the enterprise, current prices
ISIC Rev. 4

Million USD PPP

		2011	2012	2013	2014	2015	2016	2017	2018
	TOTAL BUSINESS ENTERPRISE	**10 357.2**	**10 208.0**	**10 234.7**	**10 242.7**	**10 412.9**	**11 087.4**	**12 266.7**	..
01-03	**AGRICULTURE, FORESTRY AND FISHING**	**74.6**	**76.8**	**78.7**	**88.2**	**90.5**	**106.9**	**135.0**	..
05-09	**MINING AND QUARRYING**	**27.4**	**24.1**	**20.5**	**18.4**	**19.8**	**21.6**	**26.7**	..
10-33	**MANUFACTURING**	**4 789.7**	**4 611.5**	**4 595.7**	**4 674.0**	**4 732.0**	**5 141.7**	**5 654.9**	..
10-12	Food products, beverages and tobacco	272.0	269.4	275.7	279.1	272.8	320.5	368.3	..
13-15	Textiles, wearing apparel, leather and related products	113.9	134.7	149.5	208.4	208.8	162.8	140.9	..
13	Textiles	45.4	42.7	41.8	42.9	34.3	36.8	37.8	..
14	Wearing apparel	51.9	75.7	88.3	145.1	152.0	100.5	75.9	..
15	Leather and related products, footwear	16.5	16.2	19.3	20.3	22.5	25.5	27.2	..
16-18	Wood and paper products and printing	65.7	53.7	48.2	52.3	51.0	63.0	66.9	..
16	Wood and wood products, except furniture	17.7	13.5	12.5	13.5	11.6	15.5	14.6	..
17	Paper and paper products	34.9	23.5	20.7	19.5	21.5	23.2	23.3	..
18	Printing and reproduction of recorded media	13.1	16.7	14.9	19.2	17.9	24.4	29.0	..
19-23	Chemical, rubber, plastic, non-metallic mineral products	1 567.0	1 518.2	1 543.3	1 556.3	1 562.2	1 683.6	1 854.6	..
19	Coke and refined petroleum products	96.1	99.3	101.8	104.8	102.8	95.6	80.9	..
20-21	Chemical and pharmaceutical products	1 229.2	1 182.1	1 196.5	1 225.5	1 239.4	1 354.3	1 533.5	..
20	Chemicals and chemical products	339.2	337.6	354.7	352.5	346.6	372.0	426.1	..
21	Pharmaceuticals, medicinal, chemical and botanical products	890.0	844.5	841.8	873.0	892.8	982.3	1 107.4	..
22	Rubber and plastic products	143.0	154.1	153.8	143.8	145.7	159.8	165.2	..
23	Other non-metallic mineral products	98.7	82.7	91.1	82.3	74.3	73.9	75.0	..
24-25	Basic metals, metal products, except machinery and equipment	323.3	280.0	261.6	257.1	243.9	243.6	317.3	..
24	Basic metals	128.3	92.9	81.3	78.0	67.9	67.6	113.5	..
25	Fabricated metal products, except machinery and equipment	195.0	187.0	180.4	179.0	175.9	176.0	203.8	..
26-30	Computer, electronic, optical products; electrical machinery, transport equipment	2 322.8	2 237.2	2 192.3	2 198.0	2 277.1	2 528.3	2 756.9	..
26	Computer, electronic and optical products	291.4	258.5	260.4	257.0	246.2	263.7	305.3	..
27	Electrical equipment	273.5	301.1	281.3	289.2	319.4	340.1	298.1	..
28	Machinery and equipment n.e.c.	314.3	327.2	323.2	319.0	334.5	356.1	384.1	..
29	Motor vehicles, trailers and semi-trailers	500.5	490.4	486.3	566.3	551.7	684.6	806.8	..
30	Other transport equipment	943.1	859.9	841.1	766.5	825.4	883.7	962.6	..
31-33	Furniture; repair, installation of machinery and equipment	124.9	118.4	125.1	122.9	116.2	140.0	150.1	..
31	Furniture	26.5	22.9	22.7	27.1	22.2	23.3	23.0	..
32	Other manufacturing	80.0	77.2	83.7	76.0	78.3	95.8	103.6	..
33	Repair and installation of machinery and equipment	18.4	18.3	18.8	19.8	15.7	20.9	23.5	..
35-39	**ELECTRICITY, GAS, WATER AND WASTE MANAGEMENT**	**260.8**	**291.3**	**250.3**	**226.1**	**234.9**	**240.8**	**265.3**	..
35-36	Electricity, gas and water	219.7	262.8	221.1	193.7	203.7	204.1	223.9	..
37-39	Sewerage, waste management and remediation activities	41.1	28.5	29.2	32.4	31.2	36.6	41.4	..
41-43	**CONSTRUCTION**	**218.0**	**197.6**	**182.5**	**196.2**	**155.2**	**148.8**	**177.1**	..
45-99	**TOTAL SERVICES**	**4 986.7**	**5 006.6**	**5 107.1**	**5 039.8**	**5 180.6**	**5 427.7**	**6 007.7**	..
45-82	**Business sector services**	**4 823.8**	**4 835.0**	**4 925.7**	**4 849.9**	**5 001.1**	**5 271.5**	**5 842.3**	..
45-47	**Wholesale and retail trade; motor vehicle and motorcycle repairs**	**309.1**	**308.5**	**301.4**	**264.7**	**306.9**	**390.9**	**457.9**	..
49-53	**Transportation and storage**	**85.0**	**85.9**	**67.3**	**71.1**	**54.5**	**89.0**	**109.7**	..
55-56	**Accommodation and food service activities**	**2.9**	**11.5**	**6.9**	**5.9**	**5.6**	**4.3**	**8.2**	..
58-63	**Information and communication**	**1 229.5**	**1 223.5**	**1 253.3**	**1 291.2**	**1 195.7**	**1 300.8**	**1 288.5**	..
58-60	Publishing, audiovisual and broadcasting activities	78.7	74.7	61.2	66.3	57.8	49.8	61.2	..
58	Publishing activities	55.2	48.1	42.6	52.5	36.8	34.5	43.6	..
59-60	Motion picture, video and TV programme production; broadcasting activities	23.5	26.6	18.6	13.8	21.0	15.3	17.6	..
59	Motion picture, video and TV programme production; sound and music	18.1	19.9	12.7	10.8	15.6	8.9	10.2 e	..
60	Programming and broadcasting activities	5.4	6.7	5.9	3.0	5.4	6.4	7.4 e	..
61	Telecommunications	240.1	221.4	221.7	224.9	205.8	231.2	206.7	..
62-63	IT and other information services	910.7	927.5	970.4	1 000.0	932.1	1 019.8	1 020.6	..
62	Computer programming, consultancy and related activities	836.4	858.1	915.8	943.8	870.6	934.9	936.0	..
63	Information service activities	74.3	69.4	54.6	56.2	61.5	84.9	84.6	..
64-66	**Financial and insurance activities**	**213.3**	**134.8**	**131.8**	**126.3**	**204.4**	**239.9**	**373.5**	..
68-82	**Real estate; professional, scientific and technical; administrative and support**	**2 984.0**	**3 070.8**	**3 165.0**	**3 090.6**	**3 234.0**	**3 246.6**	**3 604.6**	..
68	Real estate activities	8.9	8.7	3.2	8.0	7.4	8.3	17.4	..
69-75x72	Professional, scientific and technical activities, except scientific R&D	894.8	869.2	915.6	850.1	851.3	787.2	852.8	..
72	Scientific research and development	2 031.8	2 123.4	2 175.4	2 172.5	2 317.2	2 393.6	2 672.2	..
77-82	Administrative and support service activities	48.5	69.5	70.8	59.8	58.0	57.4	62.1	..
84-99	Community, social and personal services	162.9	171.6	181.5	189.9	179.5	156.1	165.3	..
84-85	Public administration and defence; compulsory social security and education	20.1	19.6	15.1	16.9	10.4	10.0	11.4	..
86-88	Human health and social work activities	104.3	120.7	134.9	141.5	135.3	121.0	125.1	..
90-93	Arts, entertainment and recreation	5.3	5.1	7.1	7.6	9.3	8.6	10.5	..
94-99	Other services; household-employers; extraterritorial bodies	33.1	26.3	24.3	24.0	24.4	16.5	18.4	..

.. Not available; e Estimated value

Note: Detailed metadata at: *http://metalinks.oecd.org/anberd/20200813/2abe.*

SPAIN

R&D expenditure in industry by main activity of the enterprise, constant prices
ISIC Rev. 4

2010 USD PPP

		2011	2012	2013	2014	2015	2016	2017	2018
	TOTAL BUSINESS ENTERPRISE	**11 197.1**	**10 752.1**	**10 425.8**	**10 264.4**	**10 412.9**	**10 688.3**	**11 435.2**	..
01-03	**AGRICULTURE, FORESTRY AND FISHING**	**80.6**	**80.9**	**80.1**	**88.3**	**90.5**	**103.0**	**125.8**	..
05-09	**MINING AND QUARRYING**	**29.6**	**25.4**	**20.8**	**18.4**	**19.8**	**20.8**	**24.9**	..
10-33	**MANUFACTURING**	**5 178.1**	**4 857.3**	**4 681.5**	**4 683.9**	**4 732.0**	**4 956.7**	**5 271.6**	..
10-12	Food products, beverages and tobacco	294.1	283.8	280.8	279.7	272.8	309.0	343.3	..
13-15	Textiles, wearing apparel, leather and related products	123.1	141.8	152.2	208.8	208.8	156.9	131.4	..
13	Textiles	49.1	45.0	42.6	43.0	34.3	35.5	35.3	..
14	Wearing apparel	56.2	79.7	89.9	145.4	152.0	96.8	70.7	..
15	Leather and related products, footwear	17.8	17.1	19.7	20.3	22.5	24.6	25.4	..
16-18	Wood and paper products and printing	71.1	56.6	49.1	52.4	51.0	60.7	62.3	..
16	Wood and wood products, except furniture	19.2	14.2	12.8	13.5	11.6	14.9	13.6	..
17	Paper and paper products	37.7	24.8	21.1	19.6	21.5	22.3	21.7	..
18	Printing and reproduction of recorded media	14.2	17.6	15.2	19.3	17.9	23.5	27.0	..
19-23	Chemical, rubber, plastic, non-metallic mineral products	1 694.0	1 599.1	1 572.1	1 559.6	1 562.2	1 623.0	1 728.9	..
19	Coke and refined petroleum products	103.9	104.6	103.7	105.0	102.8	92.2	75.4	..
20-21	Chemical and pharmaceutical products	1 328.8	1 245.1	1 218.9	1 228.1	1 239.4	1 305.5	1 429.5	..
20	Chemicals and chemical products	366.7	355.6	361.3	353.2	346.6	358.6	397.2	..
21	Pharmaceuticals, medicinal, chemical and botanical products	962.1	889.5	857.6	874.8	892.8	946.9	1 032.3	..
22	Rubber and plastic products	154.6	162.3	156.7	144.1	145.7	154.1	154.0	..
23	Other non-metallic mineral products	106.7	87.1	92.8	82.4	74.3	71.2	69.9	..
24-25	Basic metals, metal products, except machinery and equipment	349.5	294.9	266.5	257.6	243.9	234.8	295.8	..
24	Basic metals	138.8	97.9	82.8	78.2	67.9	65.2	105.8	..
25	Fabricated metal products, except machinery and equipment	210.8	197.0	183.7	179.4	175.9	169.6	190.0	..
26-30	Computer, electronic, optical products; electrical machinery, transport equipment	2 511.2	2 356.4	2 233.3	2 202.6	2 277.1	2 437.3	2 570.0	..
26	Computer, electronic and optical products	315.1	272.3	265.3	257.5	246.2	254.2	284.6	..
27	Electrical equipment	295.7	317.2	286.5	289.8	319.4	327.9	277.9	..
28	Machinery and equipment n.e.c.	339.8	344.6	329.2	319.6	334.5	343.3	358.1	..
29	Motor vehicles, trailers and semi-trailers	541.1	516.6	495.4	567.5	551.7	659.9	752.1	..
30	Other transport equipment	1 019.5	905.8	856.8	768.1	825.4	851.9	897.4	..
31-33	Furniture; repair, installation of machinery and equipment	135.1	124.7	127.5	123.2	116.2	134.9	139.9	..
31	Furniture	28.7	24.1	23.1	27.2	22.2	22.4	21.4	..
32	Other manufacturing	86.5	81.3	85.2	76.2	78.3	92.4	96.5	..
33	Repair and installation of machinery and equipment	19.9	19.3	19.1	19.8	15.7	20.1	21.9	..
35-39	**ELECTRICITY, GAS, WATER AND WASTE MANAGEMENT**	**281.9**	**306.8**	**255.0**	**226.6**	**234.9**	**232.1**	**247.3**	..
35-36	Electricity, gas and water	237.5	276.8	225.2	194.1	203.7	196.8	208.7	..
37-39	Sewerage, waste management and remediation activities	44.4	30.0	29.7	32.5	31.2	35.3	38.6	..
41-43	**CONSTRUCTION**	**235.7**	**208.1**	**185.9**	**196.6**	**155.2**	**143.4**	**165.1**	..
45-99	**TOTAL SERVICES**	**5 391.1**	**5 273.5**	**5 202.4**	**5 050.5**	**5 180.6**	**5 232.3**	**5 600.5**	..
45-82	**Business sector services**	**5 215.0**	**5 092.7**	**5 017.6**	**4 860.1**	**5 001.1**	**5 081.8**	**5 446.3**	..
45-47	**Wholesale and retail trade; motor vehicle and motorcycle repairs**	**334.2**	**325.0**	**307.0**	**265.3**	**306.9**	**376.8**	**426.8**	..
49-53	**Transportation and storage**	**91.9**	**90.5**	**68.6**	**71.3**	**54.5**	**85.8**	**102.3**	..
55-56	**Accommodation and food service activities**	**3.1**	**12.1**	**7.0**	**5.9**	**5.6**	**4.2**	**7.7**	..
58-63	**Information and communication**	**1 329.2**	**1 288.7**	**1 276.7**	**1 293.9**	**1 195.7**	**1 254.0**	**1 201.2**	..
58-60	Publishing, audiovisual and broadcasting activities	85.1	78.6	62.4	66.5	57.8	48.0	57.1	..
58	Publishing activities	59.7	50.6	43.4	52.6	36.8	33.3	40.7	..
59-60	Motion picture, video and TV programme production; broadcasting activities	25.4	28.0	19.0	13.8	21.0	14.7	16.4	..
59	Motion picture, video and TV programme production; sound and music	19.6	21.0	13.0	10.8	15.6	8.6	9.5 e	..
60	Programming and broadcasting activities	5.8	7.1	6.0	3.0	5.4	6.2	6.9 e	..
61	Telecommunications	259.5	233.2	225.8	225.4	205.8	222.9	192.6	..
62-63	IT and other information services	984.6	976.9	988.5	1 002.1	932.1	983.1	951.4	..
62	Computer programming, consultancy and related activities	904.2	903.8	932.9	945.8	870.6	901.2	872.6	..
63	Information service activities	80.4	73.1	55.7	56.3	61.5	81.9	78.8	..
64-66	**Financial and insurance activities**	**230.6**	**142.0**	**134.3**	**126.6**	**204.4**	**231.3**	**348.2**	..
68-82	**Real estate; professional, scientific and technical; administrative and support**	**3 226.0**	**3 234.5**	**3 224.0**	**3 097.1**	**3 234.0**	**3 129.7**	**3 360.2**	..
68	Real estate activities	9.6	9.1	3.3	8.1	7.4	8.0	16.2	..
69-75x72	Professional, scientific and technical activities, except scientific R&D	967.4	915.5	932.7	851.9	851.3	758.9	795.0	..
72	Scientific research and development	2 196.6	2 236.6	2 216.0	2 177.2	2 317.2	2 307.5	2 491.1	..
77-82	Administrative and support service activities	52.4	73.2	72.1	60.0	58.0	55.4	57.9	..
84-99	Community, social and personal services	176.1	180.8	184.8	190.3	179.5	150.5	154.1	..
84-85	Public administration and defence; compulsory social security and education	21.8	20.7	15.4	16.9	10.4	9.6	10.6	..
86-88	Human health and social work activities	112.8	127.1	137.5	141.8	135.3	116.7	116.6	..
90-93	Arts, entertainment and recreation	5.7	5.3	7.2	7.6	9.3	8.3	9.8	..
94-99	Other services; household-employers; extraterritorial bodies	35.8	27.7	24.8	24.1	24.4	15.9	17.1	..

.. Not available; e Estimated value

Note: Detailed metadata at: *http://metalinks.oecd.org/anberd/20200813/2abe.*

SWEDEN

R&D expenditure in industry by main activity of the enterprise, current prices
ISIC Rev. 4

Million USD PPP

		2011	2012	2013	2014	2015	2016	2017	2018
	TOTAL BUSINESS ENTERPRISE	**9 279.2**	**9 470.3**	**9 995.0**	**9 514.1**	**10 797.1**	**11 306.3**	**12 722.5**	..
01-03	**AGRICULTURE, FORESTRY AND FISHING**	**22.7**	**22.8 e**	**23.7 e**	**20.5 e**	**21.2 e**	**21.6 e**	**23.7 e**	..
05-09	**MINING AND QUARRYING**	**18.9**	**19.0 e**	**19.7 e**	**17.0 e**	**17.6 e**	**17.9 e**	**19.7 e**	..
10-33	**MANUFACTURING**	**6 592.8**	**6 700.4 e**	**7 043.3**	**6 635.0 e**	**7 458.8**	**6 908.1 e**	**6 898.4 e**	..
10-12	Food products, beverages and tobacco	46.8	47.2 e	49.2	46.5 e	52.3 e	50.1 e	51.7 e	..
13-15	Textiles, wearing apparel, leather and related products	5.2	5.5 e	5.9	5.6 e	6.3 e	6.5 e	7.2 e	..
13	Textiles	..	..	..	..	..	..	..	..
14	Wearing apparel	..	..	..	..	..	..	..	..
15	Leather and related products, footwear	..	..	..	..	..	..	..	..
16-18	Wood and paper products and printing	107.1	124.0 e	145.7	137.6 e	155.0 e	159.4 e	176.5 e	..
16	Wood and wood products, except furniture	..	..	..	..	..	..	..	..
17	Paper and paper products	102.8	..	136.8	..	..	..	149.7	..
18	Printing and reproduction of recorded media	..	..	..	..	..	..	..	..
19-23	Chemical, rubber, plastic, non-metallic mineral products	1 107.5	1 080.6 e	1 090.3	1 001.9 e	1 100.4 e	1 096.1 e	1 178.8 e	..
19	Coke and refined petroleum products	..	..	..	..	..	..	..	..
20-21	Chemical and pharmaceutical products	..	..	..	..	..	..	..	..
20	Chemicals and chemical products	..	..	..	..	..	..	..	..
21	Pharmaceuticals, medicinal, chemical and botanical products	876.5	829.4 e	809.6	764.4 e	861.1 e	828.2 e	860.7 e	..
22	Rubber and plastic products	24.0	26.5 e	30.0	39.7 e	56.5	71.5 e	92.4	..
23	Other non-metallic mineral products	14.6	15.2 e	16.4	15.5 e	17.4 e	16.1 e	16.1	..
24-25	Basic metals, metal products, except machinery and equipment	261.0	306.8 e	364.5	312.9 e	320.3	326.6 e	359.0	..
24	Basic metals	168.4	205.3 e	250.4	224.2 e	239.9	207.3 e	190.6	..
25	Fabricated metal products, except machinery and equipment	92.6	101.5 e	114.1	88.7 e	80.3	119.3 e	168.4	..
26-30	Computer, electronic, optical products; electrical machinery, transport equipment	4 894.0	4 970.5 e	5 221.2	4 990.9 e	5 685.2	5 142.8 e	5 001.2	..
26	Computer, electronic and optical products	2 149.1	2 059.7 e	2 039.0	1 949.4 e	2 220.9	1 200.1 e	259.3	..
27	Electrical equipment	273.5	296.8 e	331.0	336.7 e	404.2	403.4 e	434.7	..
28	Machinery and equipment n.e.c.	682.3	700.5 e	743.5	689.4 e	763.8	822.1 e	946.6	..
29	Motor vehicles, trailers and semi-trailers	1 075.1	1 149.8 e	1 266.5 e	1 211.0 e	1 379.8 e	1 632.8 e	2 019.4 e	..
30	Other transport equipment	714.0	763.7 e	841.2 e	804.3 e	916.5 e	1 084.5 e	1 341.2 e	..
31-33	Furniture; repair, installation of machinery and equipment	171.2	165.9 e	166.2	139.6 e	139.4 e	126.7 e	124.0 e	..
31	Furniture	9.7	13.4 e	17.6	14.6 e	14.5 e	13.1 e	12.7 e	..
32	Other manufacturing	120.0	126.8 e	138.2	115.1 e	113.8 e	102.9 e	100.1 e	..
33	Repair and installation of machinery and equipment	41.5	25.8 e	10.5	9.9 e	11.1 e	10.7 e	11.1 e	..
35-39	**ELECTRICITY, GAS, WATER AND WASTE MANAGEMENT**	**10.6**	**23.9 e**	**38.4**	**54.8 e**	**80.9**	**84.9 e**	**95.6**	..
35-36	Electricity, gas and water	..	..	..	..	..	..	..	..
37-39	Sewerage, waste management and remediation activities	..	..	..	..	..	..	..	..
41-43	**CONSTRUCTION**	**17.6**	**22.6 e**	**28.5**	**31.6 e**	**40.3**	**37.1 e**	**36.7 e**	..
45-99	**TOTAL SERVICES**	**2 616.6**	**2 681.6 e**	**2 841.5**	**2 755.2 e**	**3 178.3**	**4 236.7 e**	**5 648.2**	..
45-82	**Business sector services**	**2 604.6**	**2 665.2 e**	**2 819.9**	**2 734.9 e**	**3 155.3 e**	**4 210.9 e**	**5 617.4 e**	..
45-47	**Wholesale and retail trade; motor vehicle and motorcycle repairs**	**542.5**	**569.0 e**	**613.7**	**579.0 e**	**649.8 e**	**701.5 e**	**809.7 e**	..
49-53	**Transportation and storage**	**16.7**	**26.6 e**	**37.6**	**34.4 e**	**37.5**	**32.9 e**	**30.7**	..
55-56	**Accommodation and food service activities**	**0.0 e**	**0.0 e**	**0.0 e**	**0.0 e**	**0.0 e**	**0.0 e**	**0.0 e**	..
58-63	**Information and communication**	**380.4**	**445.4 e**	**526.0**	**565.4 e**	**705.6**	**1 538.9 e**	**2 507.3**	..
58-60	Publishing, audiovisual and broadcasting activities	80.2	..	130.4	..	225.6	..	211.8	..
58	Publishing activities	..	..	..	..	..	..	..	..
59-60	Motion picture, video and TV programme production; broadcasting activities	..	..	..	..	..	..	..	..
59	Motion picture, video and TV programme production; sound and music	..	..	..	..	..	..	..	..
60	Programming and broadcasting activities	..	..	..	..	..	..	..	..
61	Telecommunications	..	..	..	..	..	..	..	..
62-63	IT and other information services	..	..	..	..	..	..	..	..
62	Computer programming, consultancy and related activities	..	..	..	..	..	..	..	..
63	Information service activities	..	..	..	..	..	..	..	..
64-66	**Financial and insurance activities**	**91.8**	**95.4 e**	**102.0**	**107.6 e**	**132.4**	**132.5 e**	**143.1**	..
68-82	**Real estate; professional, scientific and technical; administrative and support**	**1 572.8**	**1 528.8 e**	**1 530.4**	**1 448.5 e**	**1 630.0 e**	**1 805.2 e**	**2 126.6 e**	..
68	Real estate activities	0.0 e	0.0 e	0.0 e	0.0 e	0.0 e	0.0 e	0.0 e	..
69-75x72	Professional, scientific and technical activities, except scientific R&D	315.5	383.7 e	465.6	460.7 e	539.0	580.4 e	668.6	..
72	Scientific research and development	1 245.5	1 116.2 e	1 017.5	945.7 e	1 046.5	1 179.0 e	1 407.3	..
77-82	Administrative and support service activities	12.0	29.0 e	47.3	42.0 e	44.4 e	45.7 e	50.7 e	..
84-99	Community, social and personal services	12.0 e	16.4 e	21.5 e	20.4 e	23.0 e	25.8 e	30.8 e	..
84-85	Public administration and defence; compulsory social security and education	..	..	..	..	..	..	..	..
86-88	Human health and social work activities	..	..	..	..	..	..	..	..
90-93	Arts, entertainment and recreation	..	..	..	..	..	..	..	..
94-99	Other services; household-employers; extraterritorial bodies	..	..	..	..	..	..	..	..

.. Not available; e Estimated value

Note: Detailed metadata at: *http://metalinks.oecd.org/anberd/20200813/2abe.*

SWEDEN

R&D expenditure in industry by main activity of the enterprise, constant prices
ISIC Rev. 4

2010 USD PPP

		2011	2012	2013	2014	2015	2016	2017	2018
	TOTAL BUSINESS ENTERPRISE	**9 826.0**	**9 716.8**	**10 093.4**	**9 585.8**	**10 797.1**	**11 103.8**	**12 083.4**	..
01-03	**AGRICULTURE, FORESTRY AND FISHING**	24.1	23.4 e	23.9 e	20.7 e	21.2 e	21.2 e	22.5 e	..
05-09	**MINING AND QUARRYING**	20.0	19.4 e	19.9 e	17.2 e	17.6 e	17.6 e	18.7 e	..
10-33	**MANUFACTURING**	**6 981.3**	**6 874.8 e**	**7 112.7**	**6 685.0 e**	**7 458.8**	**6 784.4 e**	**6 552.0 e**	..
10-12	Food products, beverages and tobacco	49.6	48.4 e	49.7	46.8 e	52.3 e	49.2 e	49.1 e	..
13-15	Textiles, wearing apparel, leather and related products	5.5	5.6 e	6.0	5.6 e	6.3 e	6.4 e	6.8 e	..
13	Textiles	..	..	..	..	..	..	..	..
14	Wearing apparel	..	..	..	..	..	..	..	..
15	Leather and related products, footwear	..	..	..	..	..	..	..	..
16-18	Wood and paper products and printing	113.4	127.2 e	147.2	138.6 e	155.0 e	156.5 e	167.7 e	..
16	Wood and wood products, except furniture	..	..	..	..	..	..	..	..
17	Paper and paper products	108.8		138.1				142.1	..
18	Printing and reproduction of recorded media	..	..	..	..	..	..	..	..
19-23	Chemical, rubber, plastic, non-metallic mineral products	1 172.8	1 108.7 e	1 101.0	1 009.5 e	1 100.4 e	1 076.4 e	1 119.6 e	..
19	Coke and refined petroleum products	..	..	..	..	..	..	..	..
20-21	Chemical and pharmaceutical products	..	..	..	..	..	..	..	..
20	Chemicals and chemical products	..	..	..	..	..	..	..	..
21	Pharmaceuticals, medicinal, chemical and botanical products	928.2	851.0 e	817.6	770.2 e	861.1 e	813.4 e	817.5 e	..
22	Rubber and plastic products	25.4	27.2 e	30.3	40.0 e	56.5	70.2 e	87.8	..
23	Other non-metallic mineral products	15.4	15.6 e	16.6	15.6 e	17.4 e	15.8 e	15.2	..
24-25	Basic metals, metal products, except machinery and equipment	276.3	314.8 e	368.1	315.2 e	320.3	320.7 e	340.9	..
24	Basic metals	178.3	210.6 e	252.9	225.9 e	239.9	203.6 e	181.0	..
25	Fabricated metal products, except machinery and equipment	98.1	104.1 e	115.2	89.4 e	80.3	117.2 e	159.9	..
26-30	Computer, electronic, optical products; electrical machinery, transport equipment	5 182.4	5 099.8 e	5 272.6	5 028.6 e	5 685.2	5 050.7 e	4 750.0	..
26	Computer, electronic and optical products	2 275.8	2 113.3 e	2 059.1	1 964.1 e	2 220.9	1 178.6 e	246.3	..
27	Electrical equipment	289.6	304.5 e	334.3	339.3 e	404.2	396.2 e	412.8	..
28	Machinery and equipment n.e.c.	722.5	718.7 e	750.8	694.6 e	763.8	807.3 e	899.1	..
29	Motor vehicles, trailers and semi-trailers	1 138.4	1 179.7 e	1 279.0 e	1 220.1 e	1 379.8 e	1 603.5 e	1 918.0 e	..
30	Other transport equipment	756.1	783.6 e	849.5 e	810.4 e	916.5 e	1 065.0 e	1 273.9 e	..
31-33	Furniture; repair, installation of machinery and equipment	181.3	170.2 e	167.8	140.6 e	139.4 e	124.5 e	117.8 e	..
31	Furniture	10.3	13.7 e	17.7	14.7 e	14.5 e	12.8 e	12.1 e	..
32	Other manufacturing	127.0	130.1 e	139.5	115.9 e	113.8 e	101.1 e	95.1 e	..
33	Repair and installation of machinery and equipment	43.9	26.4 e	10.6	10.0 e	11.1 e	10.5 e	10.6 e	..
35-39	**ELECTRICITY, GAS, WATER AND WASTE MANAGEMENT**	11.3	24.5 e	38.8	55.2 e	80.9	83.3 e	90.8	..
35-36	Electricity, gas and water	..	..	..	..	..	..	..	..
37-39	Sewerage, waste management and remediation activities	..	..	..	..	..	..	..	..
41-43	**CONSTRUCTION**	18.7	23.2 e	28.8	31.8 e	40.3	36.4 e	34.9 e	..
45-99	**TOTAL SERVICES**	**2 770.7**	**2 751.4 e**	**2 869.4**	**2 776.0 e**	**3 178.3**	**4 160.8 e**	**5 364.5**	..
45-82	**Business sector services**	**2 758.1**	**2 734.6 e**	**2 847.7**	**2 755.5 e**	**3 155.3 e**	**4 135.5 e**	**5 335.3 e**	..
45-47	**Wholesale and retail trade; motor vehicle and motorcycle repairs**	574.5	583.8 e	619.7	583.4 e	649.8 e	688.9 e	769.0 e	..
49-53	**Transportation and storage**	17.7	27.3 e	37.9	34.7 e	37.5	32.3 e	29.2	..
55-56	**Accommodation and food service activities**	0.0 e	0.0 e	0.0 e	0.0 e	0.0 e	0.0 e	0.0 e	..
58-63	**Information and communication**	402.8	457.0 e	531.1	569.6 e	705.6	1 511.3 e	2 381.3	..
58-60	Publishing, audiovisual and broadcasting activities	84.9	..	131.7	..	225.6	..	201.2	..
58	Publishing activities	..	..	..	..	..	..	..	..
59-60	Motion picture, video and TV programme production; broadcasting activities	..	..	..	..	..	..	..	..
59	Motion picture, video and TV programme production; sound and music	..	..	..	..	..	..	..	..
60	Programming and broadcasting activities	..	..	..	..	..	..	..	..
61	Telecommunications	..	..	..	..	..	..	..	..
62-63	IT and other information services	..	..	..	..	..	..	..	..
62	Computer programming, consultancy and related activities	..	..	..	..	..	..	..	..
63	Information service activities	..	..	..	..	..	..	..	..
64-66	**Financial and insurance activities**	97.2	97.9 e	103.0	108.4 e	132.4	130.1 e	135.9	..
68-82	**Real estate; professional, scientific and technical; administrative and support**	1 665.5	1 568.6 e	1 545.5	1 459.4 e	1 630.0 e	1 772.8 e	2 019.8 e	..
68	Real estate activities	0.0 e	0.0 e	0.0 e	0.0 e	0.0 e	0.0 e	0.0 e	..
69-75x72	Professional, scientific and technical activities, except scientific R&D	334.1	393.6 e	470.2	464.2 e	539.0	570.0 e	635.0	..
72	Scientific research and development	1 318.9	1 145.2 e	1 027.5	952.9 e	1 046.5	1 157.9 e	1 336.6	..
77-82	Administrative and support service activities	12.7	29.7 e	47.8	42.3 e	44.4 e	44.9 e	48.1 e	..
84-99	Community, social and personal services	12.7 e	16.8 e	21.7 e	20.5 e	23.0 e	25.4 e	29.2 e	..
84-85	Public administration and defence; compulsory social security and education	..	..	..	..	..	..	..	..
86-88	Human health and social work activities	..	..	..	..	..	..	..	..
90-93	Arts, entertainment and recreation	..	..	..	..	..	..	..	..
94-99	Other services; household-employers; extraterritorial bodies	..	..	..	..	..	..	..	..

.. Not available; e Estimated value

Note: Detailed metadata at: *http://metalinks.oecd.org/anberd/20200813/2abe.*

R&D expenditure in industry by main activity of the enterprise, current prices
ISIC Rev. 4

Million USD PPP

		2011	2012	2013	2014	2015	2016	2017	2018
	TOTAL BUSINESS ENTERPRISE	9 815.8 e	10 542.8	11 266.9 e	11 939.2 e	12 675.6	13 004.3 e	13 262.8	..
01-03	**AGRICULTURE, FORESTRY AND FISHING**	..	..	..	..	..	..	..	..
05-09	**MINING AND QUARRYING**	..	..	..	..	..	..	..	..
10-33	**MANUFACTURING**	6 981.2 e	7 378.7	7 756.2 e	8 121.8 e	8 609.4	8 939.5 e	9 299.5	..
10-12	Food products, beverages and tobacco	37.5 e	45.3	51.2 e	54.8 e	58.0	60.2 e	62.6	..
13-15	Textiles, wearing apparel, leather and related products	..	..	..	..	..	..	..	..
13	Textiles	..	..	..	..	..	..	..	..
14	Wearing apparel	..	..	..	..	..	..	..	..
15	Leather and related products, footwear	..	..	..	..	..	..	..	..
16-18	Wood and paper products and printing	..	..	..	..	..	..	..	..
16	Wood and wood products, except furniture	..	..	..	..	..	..	..	..
17	Paper and paper products	..	..	..	..	..	..	..	..
18	Printing and reproduction of recorded media	..	..	..	..	..	..	..	..
19-23	Chemical, rubber, plastic, non-metallic mineral products	3 845.1 e	4 066.2	4 352.7 e	4 659.8 e	4 991.1	5 126.6 e	5 209.2	..
19	Coke and refined petroleum products	..	..	..	..	..	..	..	..
20-21	Chemical and pharmaceutical products	..	..	..	..	..	..	..	..
20	Chemicals and chemical products	..	..	..	..	..	..	..	..
21	Pharmaceuticals, medicinal, chemical and botanical products	3 494.5 e	3 692.0	3 935.8 e	4 194.0 e	4 481.9	4 610.9 e	4 703.7	..
22	Rubber and plastic products	..	..	..	..	..	..	..	..
23	Other non-metallic mineral products	..	..	..	..	..	..	..	..
24-25	Basic metals, metal products, except machinery and equipment	329.1 e	336.9	301.6 e	257.8 e	258.5	333.3 e	461.4	..
24	Basic metals	..	..	..	..	..	..	..	..
25	Fabricated metal products, except machinery and equipment	..	..	..	..	..	..	..	..
26-30	Computer, electronic, optical products; electrical machinery, transport equipment	2 500.0 e	2 677.4	2 834.1 e	2 954.5 e	3 063.6	3 045.3 e	2 991.5	..
26	Computer, electronic and optical products	1 421.6 e	1 526.1	1 632.9 e	1 718.7 e	1 777.1	1 724.8 e	1 627.2	..
27	Electrical equipment	..	..	..	..	..	..	..	..
28	Machinery and equipment n.e.c.	..	..	..	..	..	..	..	..
29	Motor vehicles, trailers and semi-trailers	..	..	..	..	..	..	..	..
30	Other transport equipment	..	..	..	..	..	..	..	..
31-33	Furniture; repair, installation of machinery and equipment	..	..	..	..	..	..	..	..
31	Furniture	..	..	..	..	..	..	..	..
32	Other manufacturing	..	..	..	..	..	..	..	..
33	Repair and installation of machinery and equipment	..	..	..	..	..	..	..	..
35-39	**ELECTRICITY, GAS, WATER AND WASTE MANAGEMENT**	..	..	..	..	..	..	..	..
35-36	Electricity, gas and water	..	..	..	..	..	..	..	..
37-39	Sewerage, waste management and remediation activities	..	..	..	..	..	..	..	..
41-43	**CONSTRUCTION**	..	..	..	..	..	..	..	..
45-99	**TOTAL SERVICES**	2 834.5 e	3 164.1	3 510.7 e	3 817.5 e	4 066.2	4 064.8 e	3 963.4	..
45-82	**Business sector services**	..	..	..	..	..	..	..	..
45-47	**Wholesale and retail trade; motor vehicle and motorcycle repairs**	..	..	..	..	..	..	..	..
49-53	**Transportation and storage**	..	..	..	..	..	..	..	..
55-56	**Accommodation and food service activities**	..	..	..	..	..	..	..	..
58-63	**Information and communication**	..	..	..	..	..	..	..	..
58-60	Publishing, audiovisual and broadcasting activities	..	..	..	..	..	..	..	..
58	Publishing activities	..	..	..	..	..	..	..	..
59-60	Motion picture, video and TV programme production; broadcasting activities	..	..	..	..	..	..	..	..
59	Motion picture, video and TV programme production; sound and music	..	..	..	..	..	..	..	..
60	Programming and broadcasting activities	..	..	..	..	..	..	..	..
61	Telecommunications	..	..	..	..	..	..	..	..
62-63	IT and other information services	..	..	..	..	..	..	..	..
62	Computer programming, consultancy and related activities	..	..	..	..	..	..	..	..
63	Information service activities	..	..	..	..	..	..	..	..
64-66	**Financial and insurance activities**	..	..	..	..	..	..	..	..
68-82	**Real estate; professional, scientific and technical; administrative and support**	..	..	..	..	..	..	..	..
68	Real estate activities	..	..	..	..	..	..	..	..
69-75x72	Professional, scientific and technical activities, except scientific R&D	..	..	..	..	..	..	..	..
72	Scientific research and development	1 168.6 e	1 412.1	1 649.1 e	1 841.8 e	1 977.2	1 960.4 e	1 876.4	..
77-82	Administrative and support service activities	..	..	..	..	..	..	..	..
84-99	Community, social and personal services	..	..	..	..	..	..	..	..
84-85	Public administration and defence; compulsory social security and education	..	..	..	..	..	..	..	..
86-88	Human health and social work activities	..	..	..	..	..	..	..	..
90-93	Arts, entertainment and recreation	..	..	..	..	..	..	..	..
94-99	Other services; household-employers; extraterritorial bodies	..	..	..	..	..	..	..	..

.. Not available; e Estimated value

Note: Detailed metadata at: *http://metalinks.oecd.org/anberd/20200813/2abe*.

R&D expenditure in industry by main activity of the enterprise, constant prices
ISIC Rev. 4

2010 USD PPP

		2011	2012	2013	2014	2015	2016	2017	2018
	TOTAL BUSINESS ENTERPRISE	10 948.3 e	11 413.7	11 820.0 e	12 309.1 e	12 675.6	12 730.0 e	12 817.2	..
01-03	**AGRICULTURE, FORESTRY AND FISHING**	..	..	..	..	..	..	..	..
05-09	**MINING AND QUARRYING**	..	..	..	..	..	..	..	..
10-33	**MANUFACTURING**	7 786.7 e	7 988.3	8 136.9 e	8 373.4 e	8 609.4	8 750.9 e	8 987.0	..
10-12	Food products, beverages and tobacco	41.8 e	49.0	53.7 e	56.5 e	58.0	58.9 e	60.5	..
13-15	Textiles, wearing apparel, leather and related products	..	..	..	..	..	..	..	..
13	Textiles	..	..	..	..	..	..	..	..
14	Wearing apparel	..	..	..	..	..	..	..	..
15	Leather and related products, footwear	..	..	..	..	..	..	..	..
16-18	Wood and paper products and printing	..	..	..	..	..	..	..	..
16	Wood and wood products, except furniture	..	..	..	..	..	..	..	..
17	Paper and paper products	..	..	..	..	..	..	..	..
18	Printing and reproduction of recorded media	..	..	..	..	..	..	..	..
19-23	Chemical, rubber, plastic, non-metallic mineral products	4 288.8 e	4 402.1	4 566.4 e	4 804.2 e	4 991.1	5 018.5 e	5 034.2	..
19	Coke and refined petroleum products	..	..	..	..	..	..	..	..
20-21	Chemical and pharmaceutical products	..	..	..	..	..	..	..	..
20	Chemicals and chemical products	..	..	..	..	..	..	..	..
21	Pharmaceuticals, medicinal, chemical and botanical products	3 897.7 e	3 997.0	4 128.9 e	4 324.0 e	4 481.9	4 513.6 e	4 545.7	..
22	Rubber and plastic products	..	..	..	..	..	..	..	..
23	Other non-metallic mineral products	..	..	..	..	..	..	..	..
24-25	Basic metals, metal products, except machinery and equipment	367.1 e	364.7	316.4 e	265.8 e	258.5	326.2 e	445.9	..
24	Basic metals	..	..	..	..	..	..	..	..
25	Fabricated metal products, except machinery and equipment	..	..	..	..	..	..	..	..
26-30	Computer, electronic, optical products; electrical machinery, transport equipment	2 788.4 e	2 898.5	2 973.2 e	3 046.0 e	3 063.6	2 981.1 e	2 891.0	..
26	Computer, electronic and optical products	1 585.6 e	1 652.2	1 713.1 e	1 771.9 e	1 777.1	1 688.4 e	1 572.6	..
27	Electrical equipment	..	..	..	..	..	..	..	..
28	Machinery and equipment n.e.c.	..	..	..	..	..	..	..	..
29	Motor vehicles, trailers and semi-trailers	..	..	..	..	..	..	..	..
30	Other transport equipment	..	..	..	..	..	..	..	..
31-33	Furniture; repair, installation of machinery and equipment	..	..	..	..	..	..	..	..
31	Furniture	..	..	..	..	..	..	..	..
32	Other manufacturing	..	..	..	..	..	..	..	..
33	Repair and installation of machinery and equipment	..	..	..	..	..	..	..	..
35-39	**ELECTRICITY, GAS, WATER AND WASTE MANAGEMENT**	..	..	..	..	..	..	..	..
35-36	Electricity, gas and water	..	..	..	..	..	..	..	..
37-39	Sewerage, waste management and remediation activities	..	..	..	..	..	..	..	..
41-43	**CONSTRUCTION**	..	..	..	..	..	..	..	..
45-99	**TOTAL SERVICES**	3 161.6 e	3 425.4	3 683.1 e	3 935.7 e	4 066.2	3 979.1 e	3 830.2	..
45-82	**Business sector services**	..	..	..	..	..	..	..	..
45-47	**Wholesale and retail trade; motor vehicle and motorcycle repairs**	..	..	..	..	..	..	..	..
49-53	**Transportation and storage**	..	..	..	..	..	..	..	..
55-56	**Accommodation and food service activities**	..	..	..	..	..	..	..	..
58-63	**Information and communication**	..	..	..	..	..	..	..	..
58-60	Publishing, audiovisual and broadcasting activities	..	..	..	..	..	..	..	..
58	Publishing activities	..	..	..	..	..	..	..	..
59-60	Motion picture, video and TV programme production; broadcasting activities	..	..	..	..	..	..	..	..
59	Motion picture, video and TV programme production; sound and music	..	..	..	..	..	..	..	..
60	Programming and broadcasting activities	..	..	..	..	..	..	..	..
61	Telecommunications	..	..	..	..	..	..	..	..
62-63	IT and other information services	..	..	..	..	..	..	..	..
62	Computer programming, consultancy and related activities	..	..	..	..	..	..	..	..
63	Information service activities	..	..	..	..	..	..	..	..
64-66	**Financial and insurance activities**	..	..	..	..	..	..	..	..
68-82	**Real estate; professional, scientific and technical; administrative and support**	..	..	..	..	..	..	..	..
68	Real estate activities	..	..	..	..	..	..	..	..
69-75x72	Professional, scientific and technical activities, except scientific R&D	..	..	..	..	..	..	..	..
72	Scientific research and development	1 303.4 e	1 528.8	1 730.1 e	1 898.9 e	1 977.2	1 919.1 e	1 813.3	..
77-82	Administrative and support service activities	..	..	..	..	..	..	..	..
84-99	Community, social and personal services	..	..	..	..	..	..	..	..
84-85	Public administration and defence; compulsory social security and education	..	..	..	..	..	..	..	..
86-88	Human health and social work activities	..	..	..	..	..	..	..	..
90-93	Arts, entertainment and recreation	..	..	..	..	..	..	..	..
94-99	Other services; household-employers; extraterritorial bodies	..	..	..	..	..	..	..	..

.. Not available; e Estimated value

Note: Detailed metadata at: *http://metalinks.oecd.org/anberd/20200813/2abe.*

TURKEY

R&D expenditure in industry by main activity of the enterprise, current prices
ISIC Rev. 4

Million USD PPP

		2011	2012	2013	2014	2015	2016	2017	2018
	TOTAL BUSINESS ENTERPRISE	**4 985.9**	**5 776.5**	**6 569.7**	**7 931.2**	**8 870.5**	**10 763.2**	**12 367.3**	..
01-03	**AGRICULTURE, FORESTRY AND FISHING**	**13.3**	**12.4**	**16.9**	**18.6**	**21.4**	**13.7**	**38.5**	..
05-09	**MINING AND QUARRYING**	**19.8**	**17.1**	**30.6**	**18.2**	**25.1**	**40.2**	**30.3**	..
10-33	**MANUFACTURING**	**2 659.4**	**3 063.3**	**3 373.5**	**4 111.5**	**4 456.1**	**6 164.4**	**7 240.3**	..
10-12	Food products, beverages and tobacco	78.4	80.8	115.6	118.9	103.0	135.0	177.4	
13-15	Textiles, wearing apparel, leather and related products	99.3	106.8	92.9	118.7	129.7	148.4	150.2	
13	Textiles	83.0	88.6	73.2	94.8	109.2	117.6	114.2	
14	Wearing apparel	13.7	15.3	16.3	18.4	16.6	27.4	32.9	
15	Leather and related products, footwear	2.6	2.9	3.4	5.5	3.8	3.4	3.1	
16-18	Wood and paper products and printing	11.3	12.5	11.9	17.6	14.9	36.7	39.1	
16	Wood and wood products, except furniture	3.5	3.2	1.8	3.6	3.0	4.0	4.2	
17	Paper and paper products	4.5	5.7	4.7	5.0	5.8	22.9	29.0	
18	Printing and reproduction of recorded media	3.3	3.6	5.4	8.9	6.0	9.8	5.8	
19-23	Chemical, rubber, plastic, non-metallic mineral products	550.3	601.2	722.8	682.9	644.6	673.7	749.7	
19	Coke and refined petroleum products	16.4 e	19.2 e	29.5 e	26.3 e	23.7 e	23.5 e	19.6 e	
20-21	Chemical and pharmaceutical products	387.6 e	406.1 e	531.2 e	496.6 e	471.0 e	444.1 e	451.0 e	
20	Chemicals and chemical products	186.6 e	218.3 e	334.7 e	298.2 e	269.4 e	267.2 e	222.2 e	
21	Pharmaceuticals, medicinal, chemical and botanical products	201.0	187.8	196.5	198.4	201.6	176.8	228.7	
22	Rubber and plastic products	80.1	98.2	80.5	86.3	70.7	80.2	190.9	
23	Other non-metallic mineral products	66.1	77.7	81.6	73.7	79.2	125.8	88.2	
24-25	Basic metals, metal products, except machinery and equipment	206.7	246.3	252.7	382.4	315.1	569.6	376.4	
24	Basic metals	55.0	59.4	55.7	97.0	74.0	70.8	85.9	
25	Fabricated metal products, except machinery and equipment	151.6	187.0	197.0	285.5	241.1	498.7	290.5	
26-30	Computer, electronic, optical products; electrical machinery, transport equipment	1 654.4	1 945.1	2 108.4	2 711.6	3 179.1	4 496.6	5 583.1	
26	Computer, electronic and optical products	153.7	196.5	263.9	237.1	292.8	1 408.1	1 903.2	
27	Electrical equipment	322.7	328.8	344.0	420.9	438.3	534.1	614.5	
28	Machinery and equipment n.e.c.	242.4	295.6	313.6	309.9	333.4	456.7	535.2	
29	Motor vehicles, trailers and semi-trailers	676.7	773.4	908.9	1 390.6	1 542.0	1 345.6	1 456.4	
30	Other transport equipment	258.9	350.8	277.9	353.1	572.6	752.1	1 073.8	
31-33	Furniture; repair, installation of machinery and equipment	59.1	70.6	69.2	79.5	69.8	104.4	164.5	
31	Furniture	15.9	13.6	14.7	12.9	15.3	24.2	48.2	
32	Other manufacturing	26.8	36.9	28.8	41.2	34.8	52.1	54.2	
33	Repair and installation of machinery and equipment	16.4	20.2	25.8	25.4	19.7	28.2	62.1	
35-39	**ELECTRICITY, GAS, WATER AND WASTE MANAGEMENT**	**17.5**	**30.1**	**34.3**	**38.6**	**59.2**	**44.3**	**35.7**	..
35-36	Electricity, gas and water	12.8	25.0	30.6	34.3	55.4	41.2	32.1	
37-39	Sewerage, waste management and remediation activities	4.7	5.1	3.8	4.3	3.8	3.2	3.6	
41-43	**CONSTRUCTION**	**30.3**	**41.6**	**25.3**	**27.2**	**30.9**	**27.0**	**95.2**	..
45-99	**TOTAL SERVICES**	**2 245.6**	**2 612.1**	**3 089.0**	**3 717.1**	**4 277.8**	**4 473.5**	**4 927.1**	..
45-82	**Business sector services**	**2 230.6**	**2 590.2**	**3 073.0**	**3 695.4**	**4 258.3**	**4 399.7**	**4 857.4**	
45-47	**Wholesale and retail trade; motor vehicle and motorcycle repairs**	**183.4**	**153.6**	**180.7**	**197.6**	**243.8**	**443.1**	**378.2**	
49-53	**Transportation and storage**	**10.3**	**17.6**	**25.8**	**30.1**	**31.4**	**43.1**	**89.1**	
55-56	**Accommodation and food service activities**	**0.0**	**0.5**	**0.4**	**0.6**	**0.6**	**4.9**	**0.3**	
58-63	**Information and communication**	**1 176.8**	**1 449.5**	**1 653.9**	**2 096.5**	**2 479.2**	**3 217.6**	**3 541.4**	..
58-60	Publishing, audiovisual and broadcasting activities	68.1 e	22.7	30.0	55.6	53.8	17.7	32.0	
58	Publishing activities	..	21.1	28.3	52.6	52.2	15.2	29.1	
59-60	Motion picture, video and TV programme production; broadcasting activities	..	1.7	1.7	3.0	1.6	2.5	2.9	
59	Motion picture, video and TV programme production; sound and music	..	..	..	..	..	..	..	
60	Programming and broadcasting activities	..	..	..	..	..	..	..	
61	Telecommunications	215.9 e	310.1	332.8	463.4	512.6	132.7	101.3	
62-63	IT and other information services	892.8	1 116.6	1 291.1	1 577.6	1 912.8	3 067.2	3 408.1	
62	Computer programming, consultancy and related activities	881.8	1 100.2	1 282.6	1 568.5	1 898.7	3 022.7	3 349.7	
63	Information service activities	11.0	16.4	8.5	9.1	14.1	44.5	58.4	
64-66	**Financial and insurance activities**	**96.9**	**93.9**	**130.6**	**121.1**	**71.3**	**61.2**	**98.1**	..
68-82	**Real estate; professional, scientific and technical; administrative and support**	**763.1**	**875.1**	**1 081.5**	**1 249.5**	**1 432.1**	**629.8**	**750.2**	..
68	Real estate activities	0.0	0.0	0.0	0.0	0.0	0.0	16.5	
69-75x72	Professional, scientific and technical activities, except scientific R&D	28.4	31.7	37.2	41.0	46.6	118.3	107.8	
72	Scientific research and development	732.5	840.8	1 039.5	1 200.1	1 375.8	495.4	591.1	
77-82	Administrative and support service activities	2.2	2.6	4.8	8.4	9.7	16.2	34.9	
84-99	Community, social and personal services	15.0	21.9	16.1	21.7	19.5	73.7	69.7	
84-85	Public administration and defence; compulsory social security and education	8.5	15.0	12.0	13.8	11.6	54.8	59.8	
86-88	Human health and social work activities	3.4	3.8	2.2	6.4	5.7	15.2	7.6	
90-93	Arts, entertainment and recreation	..	..	..	..	..	..	..	
94-99	Other services; household-employers; extraterritorial bodies	..	..	..	..	..	..	..	..

.. Not available; e Estimated value

Note: Detailed metadata at: *http://metalinks.oecd.org/anberd/20200813/2abe.*

R&D expenditure in industry by main activity of the enterprise, constant prices
ISIC Rev. 4

2010 USD PPP

		2011	2012	2013	2014	2015	2016	2017	2018
	TOTAL BUSINESS ENTERPRISE	**5 480.8**	**6 239.8**	**7 008.3**	**8 127.8**	**8 870.5**	**10 634.0**	**12 181.9**	..
01-03	**AGRICULTURE, FORESTRY AND FISHING**	**14.6**	**13.4**	**18.1**	**19.0**	**21.4**	**13.5**	**37.9**	..
05-09	**MINING AND QUARRYING**	**21.8**	**18.4**	**32.6**	**18.6**	**25.1**	**39.8**	**29.9**	..
10-33	**MANUFACTURING**	**2 923.4**	**3 309.0**	**3 598.7**	**4 213.4**	**4 456.1**	**6 090.4**	**7 131.8**	..
10-12	Food products, beverages and tobacco	86.2	87.3	123.3	121.8	103.0	133.4	174.8	..
13-15	Textiles, wearing apparel, leather and related products	109.2	115.3	99.1	121.6	129.7	146.6	148.0	..
13	Textiles	91.2	95.7	78.1	97.1	109.2	116.1	112.5	..
14	Wearing apparel	15.1	16.5	17.4	18.9	16.6	27.1	32.4	..
15	Leather and related products, footwear	2.8	3.1	3.6	5.6	3.8	3.4	3.1	..
16-18	Wood and paper products and printing	12.5	13.5	12.7	18.0	14.9	36.3	38.5	..
16	Wood and wood products, except furniture	3.9	3.5	1.9	3.7	3.0	4.0	4.2	..
17	Paper and paper products	5.0	6.1	5.0	5.1	5.8	22.6	28.6	..
18	Printing and reproduction of recorded media	3.6	3.8	5.8	9.2	6.0	9.7	5.8	..
19-23	Chemical, rubber, plastic, non-metallic mineral products	604.9	649.4	771.0	699.8	644.6	665.6	738.5	..
19	Coke and refined petroleum products	18.1 e	20.8 e	31.5 e	26.9 e	23.7 e	23.3 e	19.3 e	..
20-21	Chemical and pharmaceutical products	426.1 e	438.6 e	566.6 e	508.9 e	471.0 e	438.7 e	444.2 e	..
20	Chemicals and chemical products	205.1 e	235.8 e	357.0 e	305.6 e	269.4 e	264.0 e	218.9 e	..
21	Pharmaceuticals, medicinal, chemical and botanical products	221.0	202.8	209.6	203.3	201.6	174.7	225.3	..
22	Rubber and plastic products	88.0	106.1	85.9	88.4	70.7	79.3	188.1	..
23	Other non-metallic mineral products	72.7	83.9	87.0	75.6	79.2	124.3	86.9	..
24-25	Basic metals, metal products, except machinery and equipment	227.2	266.1	269.6	391.9	315.1	562.7	370.8	..
24	Basic metals	60.5	64.1	59.4	99.4	74.0	70.0	84.6	..
25	Fabricated metal products, except machinery and equipment	166.7	202.0	210.2	292.5	241.1	492.8	286.2	..
26-30	Computer, electronic, optical products; electrical machinery, transport equipment	1 818.6	2 101.1	2 249.1	2 778.8	3 179.1	4 442.7	5 499.4	..
26	Computer, electronic and optical products	169.0	212.3	281.6	243.0	292.8	1 391.2	1 874.7	..
27	Electrical equipment	354.7	355.1	367.0	431.3	438.3	527.7	605.3	..
28	Machinery and equipment n.e.c.	266.5	319.3	334.6	317.6	333.4	451.2	527.2	..
29	Motor vehicles, trailers and semi-trailers	743.9	835.4	969.6	1 425.1	1 542.0	1 329.4	1 434.6	..
30	Other transport equipment	284.6	378.9	296.4	361.8	572.6	743.1	1 057.7	..
31-33	Furniture; repair, installation of machinery and equipment	65.0	76.3	73.9	81.5	69.8	103.2	162.0	..
31	Furniture	17.5	14.7	15.6	13.2	15.3	23.9	47.5	..
32	Other manufacturing	29.4	39.8	30.7	42.2	34.8	51.5	53.4	..
33	Repair and installation of machinery and equipment	18.0	21.8	27.5	26.0	19.7	27.8	61.2	..
35-39	**ELECTRICITY, GAS, WATER AND WASTE MANAGEMENT**	**19.2**	**32.5**	**36.6**	**39.6**	**59.2**	**43.8**	**35.2**	..
35-36	Electricity, gas and water	14.1	27.0	32.6	35.2	55.4	40.7	31.6	..
37-39	Sewerage, waste management and remediation activities	5.2	5.5	4.0	4.4	3.8	3.1	3.5	..
41-43	**CONSTRUCTION**	**33.3**	**44.9**	**26.9**	**27.9**	**30.9**	**26.7**	**93.8**	..
45-99	**TOTAL SERVICES**	**2 468.5**	**2 821.6**	**3 295.2**	**3 809.3**	**4 277.8**	**4 419.8**	**4 853.2**	..
45-82	**Business sector services**	**2 452.0**	**2 797.9**	**3 278.1**	**3 787.0**	**4 258.3**	**4 346.9**	**4 784.6**	..
45-47	**Wholesale and retail trade; motor vehicle and motorcycle repairs**	**201.6**	**166.0**	**192.8**	**202.5**	**243.8**	**437.8**	**372.5**	..
49-53	**Transportation and storage**	**11.4**	**19.0**	**27.5**	**30.9**	**31.4**	**42.6**	**87.8**	..
55-56	**Accommodation and food service activities**	**0.0**	**0.5**	**0.4**	**0.6**	**0.6**	**4.9**	**0.3**	..
58-63	**Information and communication**	**1 293.6**	**1 565.7**	**1 764.4**	**2 148.5**	**2 479.2**	**3 179.0**	**3 488.3**	..
58-60	Publishing, audiovisual and broadcasting activities	74.9 e	24.6	32.0	56.9	53.8	17.5	31.5	..
58	Publishing activities	..	22.8	30.2	53.9	52.2	15.0	28.6	..
59-60	Motion picture, video and TV programme production; broadcasting activities	..	1.8	1.8	3.0	1.6	2.4	2.9	..
59	Motion picture, video and TV programme production; sound and music	..	..	..	..	..	..	..	..
60	Programming and broadcasting activities	..	..	..	..	..	..	..	..
61	Telecommunications	237.3 e	335.0	355.0	474.9	512.6	131.2	99.8	..
62-63	IT and other information services	981.4	1 206.2	1 377.3	1 616.7	1 912.8	3 030.4	3 357.0	..
62	Computer programming, consultancy and related activities	969.3	1 188.4	1 368.2	1 607.4	1 898.7	2 986.4	3 299.5	..
63	Information service activities	12.1	17.8	9.1	9.3	14.1	43.9	57.5	..
64-66	**Financial and insurance activities**	**106.5**	**101.4**	**139.4**	**124.1**	**71.3**	**60.5**	**96.7**	..
68-82	**Real estate; professional, scientific and technical; administrative and support**	**838.9**	**945.3**	**1 153.6**	**1 280.5**	**1 432.1**	**622.3**	**739.0**	..
68	Real estate activities	0.0	0.0	0.0	0.0	0.0	0.0	16.2	..
69-75x72	Professional, scientific and technical activities, except scientific R&D	31.2	34.2	39.6	42.0	46.6	116.8	106.2	..
72	Scientific research and development	805.2	908.3	1 108.9	1 229.9	1 375.8	489.4	582.2	..
77-82	Administrative and support service activities	2.4	2.8	5.1	8.6	9.7	16.0	34.4	..
84-99	Community, social and personal services	16.5	23.6	17.1	22.3	19.5	72.9	68.6	..
84-85	Public administration and defence; compulsory social security and education	9.4	16.2	12.8	14.1	11.6	54.1	58.9	..
86-88	Human health and social work activities	3.7	4.1	2.3	6.6	5.7	15.0	7.5	..
90-93	Arts, entertainment and recreation	..	..	..	..	..	..	..	..
94-99	Other services; household-employers; extraterritorial bodies	..	..	..	..	..	..	..	..

.. Not available; e Estimated value

Note: Detailed metadata at: *http://metalinks.oecd.org/anberd/20200813/2abe.*

R&D expenditure in industry by main activity of the enterprise, current prices
ISIC Rev. 4

Million USD PPP

		2011	2012	2013	2014	2015	2016	2017	2018
	TOTAL BUSINESS ENTERPRISE	**24 655.7**	**24 381.2**	**26 534.1**	**28 541.9**	**30 165.0**	**32 271.5**	..	..
01-03	**AGRICULTURE, FORESTRY AND FISHING**	17.6	20.0	14.8	19.2	22.1	31.5	..	..
05-09	**MINING AND QUARRYING**	**245.0**	**243.7**	**273.9**	**261.3**	**229.2**	**241.3**	..	..
10-33	**MANUFACTURING**	**9 097.9**	**9 745.8**	**10 529.0**	**11 144.8**	**11 845.5**	**13 356.9**	..	..
10-12	Food products, beverages and tobacco	393.2	391.7	471.1	472.5	372.5	453.2	..	..
13-15	Textiles, wearing apparel, leather and related products	36.0	45.5	31.6	32.1	27.7	30.6	..	..
13	Textiles	32.4	38.9	23.7	23.8	20.8	25.6	..	..
14	Wearing apparel	1.7	3.8	4.2	4.9	3.9	2.3	..	..
15	Leather and related products, footwear	1.8	2.7	3.7	3.4	3.0	2.8	..	..
16-18	Wood and paper products and printing	21.4	31.2	51.3	57.6	63.4	70.9	..	..
16	Wood and wood products, except furniture	2.0	4.0 e	9.5	8.9	8.8	13.6	..	..
17	Paper and paper products	12.5	11.4 e	15.1	17.6	16.8	17.3	..	..
18	Printing and reproduction of recorded media	6.9	15.8	26.8	31.1	38.0	39.9	..	..
19-23	Chemical, rubber, plastic, non-metallic mineral products	1 350.5	1 310.1	1 390.4	1 370.9	1 394.8	1 578.3	..	..
19	Coke and refined petroleum products	26.8	31.6	27.5	47.8	129.1	61.3	..	..
20-21	Chemical and pharmaceutical products	1 151.0	1 093.2	1 177.6	1 096.4	1 011.0	1 254.0	..	..
20	Chemicals and chemical products	402.4	374.6	519.1	523.9	450.6	698.0	..	..
21	Pharmaceuticals, medicinal, chemical and botanical products	748.7	718.6	658.5	572.6	560.4	556.0	..	..
22	Rubber and plastic products	115.1	140.4	136.8	158.4	194.0	188.2	..	..
23	Other non-metallic mineral products	57.5	44.9	48.6	68.3	60.7	74.8	..	..
24-25	Basic metals, metal products, except machinery and equipment	903.9	796.1	802.4	861.1	776.5	764.7	..	..
24	Basic metals	123.5	90.2	63.9	101.4	85.6	95.0	..	..
25	Fabricated metal products, except machinery and equipment	780.4	705.9	738.6	759.7	690.8	669.7	..	..
26-30	Computer, electronic, optical products; electrical machinery, transport equipment	6 048.1	6 853.0	7 377.4	7 934.2	8 674.8	9 957.3	..	..
26	Computer, electronic and optical products	1 384.5	1 391.9	1 468.3	1 440.9	1 422.7	1 582.6	..	..
27	Electrical equipment	215.7	242.1	230.7	259.6	274.1	254.0	..	..
28	Machinery and equipment n.e.c.	897.4	1 106.3	1 078.9	1 069.5	1 254.8	1 206.5	..	..
29	Motor vehicles, trailers and semi-trailers	1 834.9	2 106.7	2 508.0	2 887.4	3 407.0	4 281.3	..	..
30	Other transport equipment	1 715.6	2 006.0	2 091.5	2 276.9	2 316.1	2 632.7	..	..
31-33	Furniture; repair, installation of machinery and equipment	344.9	318.3	404.7	416.5	535.8	502.1	..	..
31	Furniture	70.8	51.6	73.1	55.8	57.5	62.7	..	..
32	Other manufacturing	166.0	147.7	181.5	177.1	250.0	225.5	..	..
33	Repair and installation of machinery and equipment	108.1	119.0	150.2	183.6	228.3	213.9	..	..
35-39	**ELECTRICITY, GAS, WATER AND WASTE MANAGEMENT**	**46.6**	**118.6**	**162.8**	**155.8**	**199.9**	**183.1**	..	..
35-36	Electricity, gas and water	37.1	102.8	141.0	139.2	175.6	140.1	..	..
37-39	Sewerage, waste management and remediation activities	9.5	15.8	21.9	16.6	24.3	43.1	..	..
41-43	**CONSTRUCTION**	**53.1**	**85.8**	**100.3**	**150.3**	**128.4**	**183.4**	..	..
45-99	**TOTAL SERVICES**	**15 195.6**	**14 167.4**	**15 453.3**	**16 810.5**	**17 739.9**	**18 275.2**	..	..
45-82	**Business sector services**	**14 852.7**	**13 816.3**	**15 010.0**	**16 499.3**	**17 373.5**	**17 694.5**	..	..
45-47	**Wholesale and retail trade; motor vehicle and motorcycle repairs**	**1 084.8**	**996.8**	**993.5**	**1 004.1**	**1 317.4**	**1 234.4**	..	..
49-53	**Transportation and storage**	**41.9**	**14.0**	**43.9**	**66.0**	**82.0**	**61.9**	..	..
55-56	**Accommodation and food service activities**	**36.0**	**41.6**	**23.2**	**41.8**	**55.2**	**90.3**	..	..
58-63	**Information and communication**	**3 317.3**	**3 450.7**	**3 784.4**	**4 202.3**	**4 175.5**	**4 638.6**	..	..
58-60	Publishing, audiovisual and broadcasting activities	120.4	98.1	174.2	281.9	368.3	898.4	..	..
58	Publishing activities	87.0	73.5	126.7	118.4	117.9	119.7	..	..
59-60	Motion picture, video and TV programme production; broadcasting activities	33.4	24.5	47.5	163.5	250.4	778.7	..	..
59	Motion picture, video and TV programme production; sound and music	24.8	15.0	31.9	110.0 e	168.5 e	523.9 e	..	..
60	Programming and broadcasting activities	8.6	9.5	15.5	53.5 e	82.0 e	254.9 e	..	..
61	Telecommunications	1 018.1	999.8	1 053.0	1 139.7	1 029.2	1 086.4	..	..
62-63	IT and other information services	2 178.9	2 352.9	2 557.2	2 780.8	2 778.2	2 653.7	..	..
62	Computer programming, consultancy and related activities	2 116.3	2 228.9	2 319.2	2 340.6	2 489.6	2 387.5	..	..
63	Information service activities	62.6	124.0	238.0	440.1	288.6	266.2	..	..
64-66	**Financial and insurance activities**	**430.0**	**380.3**	**475.8**	**536.5**	**568.9**	**580.1**	..	..
68-82	**Real estate; professional, scientific and technical; administrative and support**	**9 942.8**	**8 933.0**	**9 689.3**	**10 648.5**	**11 174.6**	**11 089.3**	..	..
68	Real estate activities	14.0	16.0	23.7	31.1	29.2	21.1	..	..
69-75x72	Professional, scientific and technical activities, except scientific R&D	1 377.1	1 821.9	2 275.4	2 850.2	2 795.9	2 655.0	..	..
72	Scientific research and development	8 276.0	6 681.7	6 992.5	7 123.0	7 677.7	7 735.3	..	..
77-82	Administrative and support service activities	275.6	413.5	397.7	644.3	671.8	678.0	..	..
84-99	Community, social and personal services	342.9	351.0	443.3	311.3	366.4	580.7	..	..
84-85	Public administration and defence; compulsory social security and education	11.0	27.2	47.6	22.2	14.7	13.9	..	..
86-88	Human health and social work activities	24.8	23.9	45.3	57.0	76.3	89.0	..	..
90-93	Arts, entertainment and recreation	272.1	264.5	304.1	194.7	232.8	432.9	..	..
94-99	Other services; household-employers; extraterritorial bodies	35.0	35.3	46.3	37.4	42.6	44.9	..	..

.. Not available; e Estimated value

Note: Detailed metadata at: *http://metalinks.oecd.org/anberd/20200813/2abe.*

UNITED KINGDOM

R&D expenditure in industry by main activity of the enterprise, constant prices
ISIC Rev. 4

2010 USD PPP

		2011	2012	2013	2014	2015	2016	2017	2018
	TOTAL BUSINESS ENTERPRISE	**26 675.1**	**25 784.6**	**27 288.7**	**28 959.7**	**30 165.0**	**31 426.8**	..	..
01-03	**AGRICULTURE, FORESTRY AND FISHING**	**19.0**	**21.1**	**15.2**	**19.5**	**22.1**	**30.7**	..	..
05-09	**MINING AND QUARRYING**	**265.1**	**257.7**	**281.6**	**265.1**	**229.2**	**235.0**	..	..
10-33	**MANUFACTURING**	**9 843.1**	**10 306.8**	**10 828.5**	**11 307.9**	**11 845.5**	**13 007.2**	..	..
10-12	Food products, beverages and tobacco	425.4	414.2	484.5	479.4	372.5	441.3	..	..
13-15	Textiles, wearing apparel, leather and related products	38.9	48.1	32.5	32.5	27.7	29.8	..	..
13	Textiles	35.1	41.1	24.4	24.1	20.8	24.9	..	..
14	Wearing apparel	1.8	4.1	4.3	4.9	3.9	2.3	..	..
15	Leather and related products, footwear	2.0	2.9	3.8	3.5	3.0	2.7	..	..
16-18	Wood and paper products and printing	23.1	33.0	52.8	58.4	63.4	69.0	..	..
16	Wood and wood products, except furniture	2.1	4.3 e	9.8	9.0	8.8	13.3	..	..
17	Paper and paper products	13.5	12.0 e	15.5	17.9	16.8	16.8	..	..
18	Printing and reproduction of recorded media	7.5	16.7	27.5	31.5	38.0	38.9	..	..
19-23	Chemical, rubber, plastic, non-metallic mineral products	1 461.1	1 385.5	1 430.0	1 391.0	1 394.8	1 536.9	..	..
19	Coke and refined petroleum products	29.0	33.5	28.3	48.5	129.1	59.7	..	..
20-21	Chemical and pharmaceutical products	1 245.3	1 156.1	1 211.1	1 112.5	1 011.0	1 221.2	..	..
20	Chemicals and chemical products	435.3	396.1	533.9	531.5	450.6	679.7	..	..
21	Pharmaceuticals, medicinal, chemical and botanical products	810.0	760.0	677.2	580.9	560.4	541.4	..	..
22	Rubber and plastic products	124.6	148.5	140.7	160.7	194.0	183.3	..	..
23	Other non-metallic mineral products	62.2	47.5	50.0	69.3	60.7	72.8	..	..
24-25	Basic metals, metal products, except machinery and equipment	977.9	842.0	825.3	873.7	776.5	744.6	..	..
24	Basic metals	133.6	95.4	65.7	102.9	85.6	92.5	..	..
25	Fabricated metal products, except machinery and equipment	844.3	746.6	759.6	770.8	690.8	652.2	..	..
26-30	Computer, electronic, optical products; electrical machinery, transport equipment	6 543.5	7 247.5	7 587.2	8 050.4	8 674.8	9 696.6	..	..
26	Computer, electronic and optical products	1 497.9	1 472.0	1 510.0	1 462.0	1 422.7	1 541.2	..	..
27	Electrical equipment	233.4	256.1	237.3	263.4	274.1	247.3	..	..
28	Machinery and equipment n.e.c.	970.9	1 170.0	1 109.6	1 085.2	1 254.8	1 174.9	..	..
29	Motor vehicles, trailers and semi-trailers	1 985.1	2 227.9	2 579.4	2 929.7	3 407.0	4 169.2	..	..
30	Other transport equipment	1 856.1	2 121.5	2 151.0	2 310.3	2 316.1	2 563.8	..	..
31-33	Furniture; repair, installation of machinery and equipment	373.1	336.6	416.3	422.6	535.8	489.0	..	..
31	Furniture	76.6	54.6	75.1	56.7	57.5	61.1	..	..
32	Other manufacturing	179.6	156.2	186.7	179.7	250.0	219.6	..	..
33	Repair and installation of machinery and equipment	116.9	125.9	154.4	186.2	228.3	208.3	..	..
35-39	**ELECTRICITY, GAS, WATER AND WASTE MANAGEMENT**	**50.4**	**125.4**	**167.4**	**158.1**	**199.9**	**178.3**	..	..
35-36	Electricity, gas and water	40.1	108.7	145.0	141.2	175.6	136.5	..	..
37-39	Sewerage, waste management and remediation activities	10.3	16.7	22.5	16.9	24.3	42.0	..	..
41-43	**CONSTRUCTION**	**57.5**	**90.7**	**103.1**	**152.5**	**128.4**	**178.6**	..	..
45-99	**TOTAL SERVICES**	**16 440.2**	**14 982.8**	**15 892.8**	**17 056.6**	**17 739.9**	**17 796.8**	..	..
45-82	**Business sector services**	**16 069.2**	**14 611.6**	**15 436.9**	**16 740.8**	**17 373.5**	**17 231.3**	..	..
45-47	**Wholesale and retail trade; motor vehicle and motorcycle repairs**	**1 173.6**	**1 054.2**	**1 021.7**	**1 018.8**	**1 317.4**	**1 202.1**	..	..
49-53	**Transportation and storage**	**45.4**	**14.8**	**45.1**	**67.0**	**82.0**	**60.2**	..	..
55-56	**Accommodation and food service activities**	**38.9**	**44.0**	**23.8**	**42.4**	**55.2**	**88.0**	..	..
58-63	**Information and communication**	**3 589.0**	**3 649.3**	**3 892.0**	**4 263.9**	**4 175.5**	**4 517.2**	..	..
58-60	Publishing, audiovisual and broadcasting activities	130.2	103.7	179.1	286.0	368.3	874.9	..	..
58	Publishing activities	94.1	77.8	130.3	120.1	117.9	116.5	..	..
59-60	Motion picture, video and TV programme production; broadcasting activities	36.2	25.9	48.8	165.9	250.4	758.4	..	..
59	Motion picture, video and TV programme production; sound and music	26.8	15.8	32.8	111.6 e	168.5 e	510.2 e	..	..
60	Programming and broadcasting activities	9.3	10.1	16.0	54.3 e	82.0 e	248.2 e	..	..
61	Telecommunications	1 101.4	1 057.4	1 083.0	1 156.4	1 029.2	1 058.0	..	..
62-63	IT and other information services	2 357.3	2 488.4	2 629.9	2 821.5	2 778.2	2 584.2	..	..
62	Computer programming, consultancy and related activities	2 289.6	2 357.2	2 385.1	2 374.9	2 489.6	2 325.0	..	..
63	Information service activities	67.7	131.1	244.8	446.6	288.6	259.2	..	..
64-66	**Financial and insurance activities**	**465.2**	**402.1**	**489.3**	**544.3**	**568.9**	**564.9**	..	..
68-82	**Real estate; professional, scientific and technical; administrative and support**	**10 757.1**	**9 447.2**	**9 964.9**	**10 804.4**	**11 174.6**	**10 799.0**	..	..
68	Real estate activities	15.2	16.9	24.4	31.5	29.2	20.5	..	..
69-75x72	Professional, scientific and technical activities, except scientific R&D	1 489.9	1 926.8	2 340.2	2 891.9	2 795.9	2 585.5	..	..
72	Scientific research and development	8 953.9	7 066.3	7 191.3	7 227.3	7 677.7	7 532.8	..	..
77-82	Administrative and support service activities	298.2	437.3	409.0	653.7	671.8	660.2	..	..
84-99	Community, social and personal services	371.0	371.2	455.9	315.8	366.4	565.5	..	..
84-85	Public administration and defence; compulsory social security and education	12.0	28.8	49.0	22.5	14.7	13.6	..	..
86-88	Human health and social work activities	26.8	25.3	46.6	57.8	76.3	86.7	..	..
90-93	Arts, entertainment and recreation	294.4	279.8	312.7	197.6	232.8	421.5	..	..
94-99	Other services; household-employers; extraterritorial bodies	37.8	37.4	47.6	37.9	42.6	43.7	..	..

.. Not available; e Estimated value

Note: Detailed metadata at: *http://metalinks.oecd.org/anberd/20200813/2abe.*

UNITED KINGDOM

R&D expenditure in industry by industry orientation, current prices
ISIC Rev. 4

Million USD PPP

		2011	2012	2013	2014	2015	2016	2017	2018
	TOTAL BUSINESS ENTERPRISE	**24 655.7**	**24 381.2**	**26 534.1**	**28 541.9**	**30 165.0**	..	..	..
01-03	**AGRICULTURE, FORESTRY AND FISHING**	**188.2**	**188.7**	**177.8**	**170.8**	**200.6**	..	..	..
05-09	**MINING AND QUARRYING**	**275.3**	**306.0**	**323.9**	**451.4**	**298.1**	..	..	..
10-33	**MANUFACTURING**	**17 778.0**	**17 438.2**	**18 439.3**	**19 081.7**	**21 014.8**	..	..	..
10-12	Food products, beverages and tobacco	495.9	509.2	610.6	615.5	610.4	..	..	..
13-15	Textiles, wearing apparel, leather and related products	18.6	28.8	31.8	32.1	27.7	..	..	..
13	Textiles	..	..	..	..	..	..	..	..
14	Wearing apparel	..	..	..	..	..	..	..	..
15	Leather and related products, footwear	..	..	..	..	..	..	..	..
16-18	Wood and paper products and printing	30.3	39.6	70.3	68.7	69.9	..	..	..
16	Wood and wood products, except furniture	2.8 e	5.1 e	13.0 e	10.6 e	9.7 e	..	..	..
17	Paper and paper products	17.7 e	14.4 e	20.7 e	21.0 e	18.4 e	..	..	..
18	Printing and reproduction of recorded media	9.8 e	20.1 e	36.6 e	37.1 e	41.8 e	..	..	..
19-23	Chemical, rubber, plastic, non-metallic mineral products	8 168.2	7 168.6	7 070.6	6 991.4	7 761.1	..	..	..
19	Coke and refined petroleum products	102.3	108.5	100.0	123.8	257.7	..	..	..
20-21	Chemical and pharmaceutical products	7 844.7	6 836.0	6 757.6	6 595.4	7 227.1	..	..	..
20	Chemicals and chemical products	975.7	841.6	888.2	976.9	1 193.2	..	..	..
21	Pharmaceuticals, medicinal, chemical and botanical products	6 869.0	5 994.4	5 869.4	5 618.5	6 034.0	..	..	..
22	Rubber and plastic products	136.8	159.8	144.8	184.4	197.7	..	..	..
23	Other non-metallic mineral products	84.4	64.3	68.2	87.8	78.6	..	..	..
24-25	Basic metals, metal products, except machinery and equipment	338.8	275.6	292.8	338.8	321.1	..	..	..
24	Basic metals	171.0	138.0	125.6	181.4	145.3	..	..	..
25	Fabricated metal products, except machinery and equipment	167.8	137.7	167.3	157.3	175.8	..	..	..
26-30	Computer, electronic, optical products; electrical machinery, transport equipment	8 518.2	9 218.6	10 119.3	10 748.9	11 949.0	..	..	..
26	Computer, electronic and optical products	1 820.0	2 105.4	2 296.2	2 456.7	2 833.6	..	..	..
27	Electrical equipment	720.5	663.9	562.4	659.0	686.1	..	..	..
28	Machinery and equipment n.e.c.	1 374.0	1 423.0	1 494.3	1 420.6	1 501.7	..	..	..
29	Motor vehicles, trailers and semi-trailers	2 160.0	2 468.8	2 963.0	3 297.9	3 903.9	..	..	..
30	Other transport equipment	2 443.7	2 557.6	2 803.5	2 914.6	3 023.8	..	..	..
31-33	Furniture; repair, installation of machinery and equipment	208.1	197.7	243.9	286.4	275.6	..	..	..
31	Furniture	..	..	..	..	..	..	..	..
32	Other manufacturing	..	..	..	..	..	..	..	..
33	Repair and installation of machinery and equipment	..	..	..	..	..	..	..	..
35-39	**ELECTRICITY, GAS, WATER AND WASTE MANAGEMENT**	**95.2**	**168.6**	**199.4**	**206.5**	**265.9**	..	..	..
35-36	Electricity, gas and water	80.3	151.5	175.2	190.0	223.3	..	..	..
37-39	Sewerage, waste management and remediation activities	14.9	17.1	24.2	16.5	42.6	..	..	..
41-43	**CONSTRUCTION**	**31.3**	**83.2**	**103.4**	**189.3**	**211.0**	..	..	..
45-99	**TOTAL SERVICES**	**6 287.6**	**6 196.5**	**7 290.3**	**8 442.2**	**8 174.6**	..	..	..
45-82	**Business sector services**	**6 193.5**	**6 099.6**	**7 138.5**	**8 302.3**	**8 048.6**	..	..	..
45-47	**Wholesale and retail trade; motor vehicle and motorcycle repairs**	**334.5**	**261.7**	**240.5**	**350.4**	**311.3**	..	..	..
49-53	**Transportation and storage**	**25.9**	**30.1**	**50.2**	**54.7**	**70.9**	..	..	..
55-56	**Accommodation and food service activities**	..	..	..	..	..	..	..	..
58-63	**Information and communication**	**4 103.7**	**4 060.1**	**4 206.7**	**4 826.2**	**4 723.4**	..	..	..
58-60	Publishing, audiovisual and broadcasting activities	37.7	42.5	92.1	..	..	..	..	..
58	Publishing activities	..	..	..	..	..	..	..	..
59-60	Motion picture, video and TV programme production; broadcasting activities	..	..	..	..	..	..	..	..
59	Motion picture, video and TV programme production; sound and music	..	..	..	..	..	..	..	..
60	Programming and broadcasting activities	..	..	..	..	..	..	..	..
61	Telecommunications	1 489.1	1 267.6	1 208.9	1 370.6	..	..	..	..
62-63	IT and other information services	2 576.9	2 750.0	2 905.7	..	..	..	..	..
62	Computer programming, consultancy and related activities	..	..	..	..	..	..	..	..
63	Information service activities	..	..	..	..	..	..	..	..
64-66	**Financial and insurance activities**	**191.2**	**59.7**	**181.8**	**249.1**	**246.3**	..	..	..
68-82	**Real estate; professional, scientific and technical; administrative and support**	**1 538.1**	**1 688.1**	**2 459.3**	**2 822.0**	**2 696.8**	..	..	..
68	Real estate activities	14.0	0.0	0.0	31.1	29.2	..	..	..
69-75x72	Professional, scientific and technical activities, except scientific R&D	..	..	..	..	..	..	..	..
72	Scientific research and development	965.8	872.1	1 335.8	1 178.8	1 440.9	..	..	..
77-82	Administrative and support service activities	..	..	..	..	..	..	..	..
84-99	Community, social and personal services	94.2	96.9	151.9	139.9	125.9	..	..	..
84-85	Public administration and defence; compulsory social security and education	..	..	..	..	..	..	..	..
86-88	Human health and social work activities	..	..	..	..	..	..	..	..
90-93	Arts, entertainment and recreation	..	..	..	..	..	..	..	..
94-99	Other services; household-employers; extraterritorial bodies	..	..	..	..	..	..	..	..

.. Not available; e Estimated value

Note: Detailed metadata at: *http://metalinks.oecd.org/anberd/20200813/2abe.*

R&D expenditure in industry by industry orientation, constant prices
ISIC Rev. 4

2010 USD PPP

		2011	2012	2013	2014	2015	2016	2017	2018
	TOTAL BUSINESS ENTERPRISE	**26 675.1**	**25 784.6**	**27 288.7**	**28 959.7**	**30 165.0**	..	..	..
01-03	**AGRICULTURE, FORESTRY AND FISHING**	**203.6**	**199.6**	**182.8**	**173.3**	**200.6**	..	..	..
05-09	**MINING AND QUARRYING**	**297.9**	**323.6**	**333.1**	**458.0**	**298.1**	..	..	..
10-33	**MANUFACTURING**	**19 234.1**	**18 441.9**	**18 963.7**	**19 361.1**	**21 014.8**	..	..	..
10-12	Food products, beverages and tobacco	536.5	538.6	627.9	624.5	610.4	..	..	..
13-15	Textiles, wearing apparel, leather and related products	20.1	30.4	32.7	32.5	27.7	..	..	..
13	Textiles	..	..	..	..	..	..	..	..
14	Wearing apparel	..	..	..	..	..	..	..	..
15	Leather and related products, footwear	..	..	..	..	..	..	..	..
16-18	Wood and paper products and printing	32.8	41.9	72.3	69.7	69.9	..	..	..
16	Wood and wood products, except furniture	3.0 e	5.4 e	13.4 e	10.8 e	9.7 e	..	..	..
17	Paper and paper products	19.1 e	15.3 e	21.3 e	21.3 e	18.4 e	..	..	..
18	Printing and reproduction of recorded media	10.6 e	21.2 e	37.7 e	37.6 e	41.8 e	..	..	..
19-23	Chemical, rubber, plastic, non-metallic mineral products	8 837.2	7 581.2	7 271.6	7 093.8	7 761.1	..	..	..
19	Coke and refined petroleum products	110.6	114.7	102.8	125.7	257.7	..	..	..
20-21	Chemical and pharmaceutical products	8 487.3	7 229.5	6 949.8	6 691.9	7 227.1	..	..	..
20	Chemicals and chemical products	1 055.6	890.0	913.4	991.2	1 193.2	..	..	..
21	Pharmaceuticals, medicinal, chemical and botanical products	7 431.6	6 339.5	6 036.3	5 700.7	6 034.0	..	..	..
22	Rubber and plastic products	148.0	169.0	149.0	187.1	197.7	..	..	..
23	Other non-metallic mineral products	91.3	68.0	70.1	89.1	78.6	..	..	..
24-25	Basic metals, metal products, except machinery and equipment	366.5	291.5	301.2	343.7	321.1	..	..	..
24	Basic metals	185.0	145.9	129.1	184.1	145.3	..	..	..
25	Fabricated metal products, except machinery and equipment	181.6	145.6	172.0	159.7	175.8	..	..	..
26-30	Computer, electronic, optical products; electrical machinery, transport equipment	9 215.9	9 749.2	10 407.0	10 906.3	11 949.0	..	..	..
26	Computer, electronic and optical products	1 969.0	2 226.6	2 361.5	2 492.7	2 833.6	..	..	..
27	Electrical equipment	779.5	702.1	578.4	668.7	686.1	..	..	..
28	Machinery and equipment n.e.c.	1 486.5	1 504.9	1 536.8	1 441.4	1 501.7	..	..	..
29	Motor vehicles, trailers and semi-trailers	2 337.0	2 610.9	3 047.2	3 346.2	3 903.9	..	..	..
30	Other transport equipment	2 643.9	2 704.8	2 883.2	2 957.3	3 023.8	..	..	..
31-33	Furniture; repair, installation of machinery and equipment	225.1	209.1	250.9	290.5	275.6	..	..	..
31	Furniture	..	..	..	..	..	..	..	..
32	Other manufacturing	..	..	..	..	..	..	..	..
33	Repair and installation of machinery and equipment	..	..	..	..	..	..	..	..
35-39	**ELECTRICITY, GAS, WATER AND WASTE MANAGEMENT**	**103.0**	**178.3**	**205.0**	**209.5**	**265.9**	..	..	..
35-36	Electricity, gas and water	86.9	160.2	180.2	192.8	223.3	..	..	..
37-39	Sewerage, waste management and remediation activities	16.1	18.1	24.9	16.7	42.6	..	..	..
41-43	**CONSTRUCTION**	**33.9**	**88.0**	**106.4**	**192.0**	**211.0**	..	..	..
45-99	**TOTAL SERVICES**	**6 802.6**	**6 553.2**	**7 497.7**	**8 565.8**	**8 174.6**	..	..	..
45-82	**Business sector services**	**6 700.7**	**6 450.7**	**7 341.5**	**8 423.9**	**8 048.6**	..	..	..
45-47	**Wholesale and retail trade; motor vehicle and motorcycle repairs**	**361.9**	**276.7**	**247.3**	**355.5**	**311.3**	..	..	..
49-53	**Transportation and storage**	**28.0**	**31.8**	**51.6**	**55.5**	**70.9**	..	..	..
55-56	**Accommodation and food service activities**	..	..	..	..	..	..	..	..
58-63	**Information and communication**	**4 439.8**	**4 293.8**	**4 326.3**	**4 896.8**	**4 723.4**	..	..	..
58-60	Publishing, audiovisual and broadcasting activities	40.8	44.9	94.7	..	..	..	..	..
58	Publishing activities	..	..	..	..	..	..	..	..
59-60	Motion picture, video and TV programme production; broadcasting activities	..	..	..	..	..	..	..	..
59	Motion picture, video and TV programme production; sound and music	..	..	..	..	..	..	..	..
60	Programming and broadcasting activities	..	..	..	..	..	..	..	..
61	Telecommunications	1 611.1	1 340.6	1 243.3	1 390.7	..	..	..	..
62-63	IT and other information services	2 787.9	2 908.3	2 988.4	..	..	..	..	..
62	Computer programming, consultancy and related activities	..	..	..	..	..	..	..	..
63	Information service activities	..	..	..	..	..	..	..	..
64-66	**Financial and insurance activities**	**206.9**	**63.2**	**187.0**	**252.8**	**246.3**	..	..	..
68-82	**Real estate; professional, scientific and technical; administrative and support**	**1 664.1**	**1 785.2**	**2 529.2**	**2 863.3**	**2 696.8**	..	..	..
68	Real estate activities	15.2	0.0	0.0	31.5	29.2	..	..	..
69-75x72	Professional, scientific and technical activities, except scientific R&D	..	..	..	..	..	..	..	..
72	Scientific research and development	1 044.9	922.3	1 373.8	1 196.0	1 440.9	..	..	..
77-82	Administrative and support service activities	..	..	..	..	..	..	..	..
84-99	Community, social and personal services	101.9	102.5	156.2	141.9	125.9	..	..	..
84-85	Public administration and defence; compulsory social security and education	..	..	..	..	..	..	..	..
86-88	Human health and social work activities	..	..	..	..	..	..	..	..
90-93	Arts, entertainment and recreation	..	..	..	..	..	..	..	..
94-99	Other services; household-employers; extraterritorial bodies	..	..	..	..	..	..	..	..

.. Not available; e Estimated value

Note: Detailed metadata at: http://metalinks.oecd.org/anberd/20200813/2abe.

UNITED STATES

R&D expenditure in industry by main activity of the enterprise, current prices
ISIC Rev. 4

Million USD PPP

		2011	2012	2013	2014	2015	2016	2017	2018
	TOTAL BUSINESS ENTERPRISE	**294 093.0**	**302 250.0**	**322 528.0**	**340 728.0**	**355 821.0**	**374 685.0**	**400 100.0**	..
01-03	**AGRICULTURE, FORESTRY AND FISHING**	..	..	..	..	..	..	..	..
05-09	**MINING AND QUARRYING**	**2 733.0**	**2 815.0**	**3 997.0**	**4 703.0**	**4 012.0**	**3 296.0**	**3 150.0**	..
10-33	**MANUFACTURING**	**201 361.0**	**208 415.0**	**221 476.0**	**232 815.0**	**236 132.0**	**250 553.0**	**257 227.0**	..
10-12	Food products, beverages and tobacco	5 085.9 e	4 860.0 e	5 855.0	6 212.0	5 840.0	5 857.0 e	5 773.0	..
13-15	Textiles, wearing apparel, leather and related products	634.0	560.0	662.0	631.0	748.0	1 166.0	920.0	..
13	Textiles	..	..	..	..	..	..	..	..
14	Wearing apparel	..	..	..	..	..	..	..	..
15	Leather and related products, footwear	..	..	..	..	..	..	..	..
16-18	Wood and paper products and printing	1 732.0	1 469.0	1 392.0	1 319.0	1 157.0	1 259.0	1 726.0	..
16	Wood and wood products, except furniture	211.0	461.0	220.0	362.0	195.0	188.0	175.0	..
17	Paper and paper products	1 346.0	752.0	920.0	723.0	766.0	851.0	1 322.0	..
18	Printing and reproduction of recorded media	175.0	256.0	252.0	234.0	196.0	219.0	229.0	..
19-23	Chemical, rubber, plastic, non-metallic mineral products	60 267.2 e	62 956.0	66 885.0	71 553.0	72 210.0	78 997.0	80 381.0	..
19	Coke and refined petroleum products	1 484.2 e	894.0	242.0	234.0	214.0	381.0	316.0	..
20-21	Chemical and pharmaceutical products	55 324.0	57 226.0	61 664.0	66 300.0	68 196.0	73 575.0	74 977.0	..
20	Chemicals and chemical products	9 375.0	9 080.0	9 238.0	9 688.0	9 521.0	8 947.0	8 775.0	..
21	Pharmaceuticals, medicinal, chemical and botanical products	45 949.0	48 146.0	52 426.0	56 612.0	58 675.0	64 628.0	66 202.0	..
22	Rubber and plastic products	2 280.0	3 509.0	3 650.0	3 574.0	2 541.0	3 752.0	3 754.0	..
23	Other non-metallic mineral products	1 179.0	1 327.0	1 329.0	1 445.0	1 259.0	1 289.0	1 334.0	..
24-25	Basic metals, metal products, except machinery and equipment	2 508.0	2 574.0	2 836.0	2 808.0	2 889.0	2 831.0	2 955.0	..
24	Basic metals	655.0	741.0	624.0	677.0	628.0	592.0	749.0	..
25	Fabricated metal products, except machinery and equipment	1 853.0	1 833.0	2 212.0	2 131.0	2 261.0	2 239.0	2 206.0	..
26-30	Computer, electronic, optical products; electrical machinery, transport equipment	121 888.0	124 715.0	129 963.0	137 129.0	139 145.0	146 016.0	149 354.0	..
26	Computer, electronic and optical products	62 704.0	65 068.0	67 205.0	73 891.0	72 110.0	77 385.0	78 575.0	..
27	Electrical equipment	3 595.0	3 087.0	4 136.0	4 365.0	4 335.0	4 771.0	4 291.0	..
28	Machinery and equipment n.e.c.	14 709.0	14 254.0	12 650.0	12 128.0	13 426.0	12 585.0	13 197.0	..
29	Motor vehicles, trailers and semi-trailers	11 694.8 e	14 587.6 e	16 729.0	18 404.0	19 078.0	22 042.0	23 881.0	..
30	Other transport equipment	29 185.2 e	27 717.4 e	29 244.0	28 342.0	30 196.0	29 233.0 e	29 410.0	..
31-33	Furniture; repair, installation of machinery and equipment	9 245.9 e	11 281.0 e	13 883.0	13 162.0	14 142.0	14 427.8 e	16 117.0	..
31	Furniture	319.0	348.0	374.0	373.0	452.0	366.0	422.0	..
32	Other manufacturing	8 926.9 e	10 933.0 e	13 509.0	12 789.0	13 690.0	14 061.8 e	15 695.0	..
33	Repair and installation of machinery and equipment	..	..	..	..	..	..	..	..
35-39	**ELECTRICITY, GAS, WATER AND WASTE MANAGEMENT**	**386.0**	**348.0**	**294.0**	**310.0**	**480.0**	**351.0**	**317.0**	..
35-36	Electricity, gas and water	..	..	..	..	..	..	..	..
37-39	Sewerage, waste management and remediation activities	..	..	..	..	..	..	..	..
41-43	**CONSTRUCTION**	**775.0 e**	**760.0 e**	**248.0 e**	**204.0 e**	**520.0 e**	**255.0 e**	**587.0 e**	..
45-99	**TOTAL SERVICES**	**88 838.0 e**	**89 912.0 e**	**96 513.0 e**	**102 696.0 e**	**114 677.0 e**	**120 230.0**	**138 819.0**	..
45-82	**Business sector services**	**86 633.0**	**88 352.0**	**94 979.0 e**	**101 538.0**	**113 510.0**	**118 658.0**	**136 507.0**	..
45-47	**Wholesale and retail trade; motor vehicle and motorcycle repairs**	**2 617.0**	**3 177.0**	**1 886.0**	**1 727.0**	**3 301.0**	**2 021.0**	**9 851.0**	..
49-53	**Transportation and storage**	**81.0**	**178.0**	**411.0 e**	**679.0**	**403.0**	**488.0**	**1 147.0**	..
55-56	**Accommodation and food service activities**	..	..	..	..	..	..	..	..
58-63	**Information and communication**	**55 124.0**	**58 056.0**	**66 475.0**	**74 792.0**	**79 846.0**	**86 495.0**	**93 578.0**	..
58-60	Publishing, audiovisual and broadcasting activities	..	..	..	..	..	..	..	..
58	Publishing activities	28 435.0	28 987.0	35 675.0	36 140.0	33 346.0	33 574.0	34 338.0	..
59-60	Motion picture, video and TV programme production; broadcasting activities	..	..	..	..	..	..	..	..
59	Motion picture, video and TV programme production; sound and music	..	..	..	..	..	..	..	..
60	Programming and broadcasting activities	..	..	..	..	..	..	..	..
61	Telecommunications	2 157.0	2 824.0	3 041.0	3 755.0	3 607.0	4 004.8 e	3 744.0 e	..
62-63	IT and other information services	17 544.0	16 164.0	15 714.0	20 048.0	23 749.0	27 661.0	29 482.0	..
62	Computer programming, consultancy and related activities	13 259.0	11 251.0	9 268.0	11 019.0	14 333.0	15 747.0	13 327.0	..
63	Information service activities	4 285.0	4 913.0	6 446.0	9 029.0	9 416.0	11 914.0	16 155.0	..
64-66	**Financial and insurance activities**	**3 457.0**	**3 519.0**	**4 308.0**	**4 122.0**	**5 366.0**	**7 331.0**	**7 616.0**	..
68-82	**Real estate; professional, scientific and technical; administrative and support**	**25 355.0**	**23 421.0**	**21 899.0**	**20 218.0**	**24 594.0**	**22 324.0**	**24 313.0**	..
68	Real estate activities	71.0	21.0	92.0	207.0	233.0	449.0	579.0	..
69-75x72	Professional, scientific and technical activities, except scientific R&D	9 659.0	6 514.0	7 548.0	7 149.0	7 964.0	7 006.0	6 275.0	..
72	Scientific research and development	15 301.0	16 544.0	14 201.0	12 807.0	16 329.0	14 842.0	17 321.0	..
77-82	Administrative and support service activities	324.0	342.0	58.0	55.0	68.0	27.0	138.0	..
84-99	Community, social and personal services	..	..	..	..	..	..	..	..
84-85	Public administration and defence; compulsory social security and education	..	..	..	..	..	..	..	..
86-88	Human health and social work activities	741.0	675.0	526.0	501.0	758.0	848.0	1 101.0	..
90-93	Arts, entertainment and recreation	..	..	..	..	..	..	..	..
94-99	Other services; household-employers; extraterritorial bodies	..	..	..	..	..	..	..	..

.. Not available; e Estimated value

Note: Detailed metadata at: *http://metalinks.oecd.org/anberd/20200813/2abe.*

R&D expenditure in industry by main activity of the enterprise, constant prices
ISIC Rev. 4

2010 USD PPP

		2011	2012	2013	2014	2015	2016	2017	2018
	TOTAL BUSINESS ENTERPRISE	313 871.6	316 507.1	331 916.7	344 276.1	355 821.0	370 845.7	388 679.1	..
01-03	AGRICULTURE, FORESTRY AND FISHING		..						..
05-09	MINING AND QUARRYING	2 916.8	2 947.8	4 113.4	4 752.0	4 012.0	3 262.2	3 060.1	..
10-33	MANUFACTURING	214 903.1	218 245.9	227 923.1	235 239.4	236 132.0	247 985.7	249 884.4	..
10-12	Food products, beverages and tobacco	5 427.9 e	5 089.2 e	6 025.4	6 276.7	5 840.0	5 797.0 e	5 608.2	..
13-15	Textiles, wearing apparel, leather and related products	676.6	586.4	681.3	637.6	748.0	1 154.1	893.7	..
13	Textiles	..	..	..	..	..	..	..	..
14	Wearing apparel								
15	Leather and related products, footwear	..	..	..	..	..	..	..	..
16-18	Wood and paper products and printing	1 848.5	1 538.3	1 432.5	1 332.7	1 157.0	1 246.1	1 676.7	..
16	Wood and wood products, except furniture	225.2	482.7	226.4	365.8	195.0	186.1	170.0	..
17	Paper and paper products	1 436.5	787.5	946.8	730.5	766.0	842.3	1 284.3	..
18	Printing and reproduction of recorded media	186.8	268.1	259.3	236.4	196.0	216.8	222.5	..
19-23	Chemical, rubber, plastic, non-metallic mineral products	64 320.4 e	65 925.6	68 832.0	72 298.1	72 210.0	78 187.5	78 086.5	..
19	Coke and refined petroleum products	1 584.0 e	936.2	249.0	236.4	214.0	377.1	307.0	..
20-21	Chemical and pharmaceutical products	59 044.7	59 925.3	63 459.0	66 990.4	68 196.0	72 821.1	72 836.8	..
20	Chemicals and chemical products	10 005.5	9 508.3	9 506.9	9 788.9	9 521.0	8 855.3	8 524.5	..
21	Pharmaceuticals, medicinal, chemical and botanical products	49 039.2	50 417.0	53 952.1	57 201.5	58 675.0	63 965.8	64 312.2	..
22	Rubber and plastic products	2 433.3	3 674.5	3 756.3	3 611.2	2 541.0	3 713.6	3 646.8	..
23	Other non-metallic mineral products	1 258.3	1 389.6	1 367.7	1 460.0	1 259.0	1 275.8	1 295.9	..
24-25	Basic metals, metal products, except machinery and equipment	2 676.7	2 695.4	2 918.6	2 837.2	2 889.0	2 802.0	2 870.6	..
24	Basic metals	699.1	776.0	642.2	684.0	628.0	585.9	727.6	..
25	Fabricated metal products, except machinery and equipment	1 977.6	1 919.5	2 276.4	2 153.2	2 261.0	2 216.1	2 143.0	..
26-30	Computer, electronic, optical products; electrical machinery, transport equipment	130 085.3	130 597.8	133 746.2	138 557.0	139 145.0	144 519.8	145 090.7	..
26	Computer, electronic and optical products	66 921.0	68 137.2	69 161.3	74 660.5	72 110.0	76 592.1	76 332.1	..
27	Electrical equipment	3 836.8	3 232.6	4 256.4	4 410.5	4 335.0	4 722.1	4 168.5	..
28	Machinery and equipment n.e.c.	15 698.2	14 926.4	13 018.2	12 254.3	13 426.0	12 456.0	12 820.3	..
29	Motor vehicles, trailers and semi-trailers	12 481.3 e	15 275.7 e	17 216.0	18 595.6	19 078.0	21 816.1	23 199.3	..
30	Other transport equipment	31 148.0 e	29 024.8 e	30 095.3	28 637.1	30 196.0	28 933.5 e	28 570.5	..
31-33	Furniture; repair, installation of machinery and equipment	9 867.7 e	11 813.1 e	14 287.1	13 299.1	14 142.0	14 280.0 e	15 656.9	..
31	Furniture	340.5	364.4	384.9	376.9	452.0	362.2	410.0	..
32	Other manufacturing	9 527.3 e	11 448.7 e	13 902.2	12 922.2	13 690.0	13 917.7 e	15 247.0	..
33	Repair and installation of machinery and equipment	..	..	..	..	..	..	..	..
35-39	ELECTRICITY, GAS, WATER AND WASTE MANAGEMENT	412.0	364.4	302.6	313.2	480.0	347.4	308.0	..
35-36	Electricity, gas and water	..	..	..	..	..	..	..	..
37-39	Sewerage, waste management and remediation activities	..	..	..	..	..	..	..	..
41-43	CONSTRUCTION	827.1 e	795.8 e	255.2 e	206.1 e	520.0 e	252.4 e	570.2 e	..
45-99	TOTAL SERVICES	94 812.6 e	94 153.1 e	99 322.5 e	103 765.4 e	114 677.0 e	118 998.0	134 856.4	..
45-82	Business sector services	92 459.3	92 519.6	97 743.8 e	102 595.4	113 510.0	117 442.1	132 610.4	..
45-47	Wholesale and retail trade; motor vehicle and motorcycle repairs	2 793.0	3 326.9	1 940.9	1 745.0	3 301.0	2 000.3	9 569.8	..
49-53	Transportation and storage	86.4	186.4	423.0 e	686.1	403.0	483.0	1 114.3	..
55-56	Accommodation and food service activities	..	..	..	..	..	..	..	..
58-63	Information and communication	58 831.3	60 794.5	68 410.1	75 570.8	79 846.0	85 608.7	90 906.8	..
58-60	Publishing, audiovisual and broadcasting activities	..	..	..	..	..	..	..	..
58	Publishing activities	30 347.3	30 354.3	36 713.5	36 516.3	33 346.0	33 230.0	33 357.8	..
59-60	Motion picture, video and TV programme production; broadcasting activities	..	..	..	..	..	..	..	..
59	Motion picture, video and TV programme production; sound and music	..	..	..	..	..	..	..	..
60	Programming and broadcasting activities	..	..	..	..	..	..	..	..
61	Telecommunications	2 302.1	2 957.2	3 129.5	3 794.1	3 607.0	3 963.7 e	3 637.1 e	..
62-63	IT and other information services	18 723.9	16 926.5	16 171.4	20 256.8	23 749.0	27 377.6	28 640.4	..
62	Computer programming, consultancy and related activities	14 150.7	11 781.7	9 537.8	11 133.7	14 333.0	15 585.6	12 946.6	..
63	Information service activities	4 573.2	5 144.7	6 633.6	9 123.0	9 416.0	11 791.9	15 693.9	..
64-66	Financial and insurance activities	3 689.5	3 685.0	4 433.4	4 164.9	5 366.0	7 255.9	7 398.6	..
68-82	Real estate; professional, scientific and technical; administrative and support	27 060.2	24 525.8	22 536.5	20 428.5	24 594.0	22 095.3	23 619.0	..
68	Real estate activities	75.8	22.0	94.7	209.2	233.0	444.4	562.5	..
69-75x72	Professional, scientific and technical activities, except scientific R&D	10 308.6	6 821.3	7 767.7	7 223.4	7 964.0	6 934.2	6 095.9	..
72	Scientific research and development	16 330.0	17 324.4	14 614.4	12 940.4	16 329.0	14 689.9	16 826.6	..
77-82	Administrative and support service activities	345.8	358.1	59.7	55.6	68.0	26.7	134.1	..
84-99	Community, social and personal services	..	..	..	..	..	..	..	..
84-85	Public administration and defence; compulsory social security and education	..	..	..	..	..	..	..	..
86-88	Human health and social work activities	790.8	706.8	541.3	506.2	758.0	839.3	1 069.6	..
90-93	Arts, entertainment and recreation	..	..	..	..	..	..	..	..
94-99	Other services; household-employers; extraterritorial bodies	..	..	..	..	..	..	..	..

.. Not available; e Estimated value

Note: Detailed metadata at: *http://metalinks.oecd.org/anberd/20200813/2abe.*

R&D expenditure in industry by main activity of the enterprise, current prices
ISIC Rev. 4

Million USD PPP

		2011	2012	2013	2014	2015	2016	2017	2018
	TOTAL BUSINESS ENTERPRISE	..	..	..	..	1 164.9	1 111.8	1 241.3	..
01-03	**AGRICULTURE, FORESTRY AND FISHING**	..	..	..	..	149.2	151.5	161.8	..
05-09	**MINING AND QUARRYING**	..	..	..	..	7.6	8.9	30.3	..
10-33	**MANUFACTURING**	..	..	..	..	647.3	596.8	618.2	..
10-12	Food products, beverages and tobacco	..	..	..	..	..	..	..	..
13-15	Textiles, wearing apparel, leather and related products	..	..	..	..	..	..	..	..
13	Textiles	..	..	..	..	..	..	..	..
14	Wearing apparel	..	..	..	..	..	..	..	..
15	Leather and related products, footwear	..	..	..	..	..	..	..	..
16-18	Wood and paper products and printing	..	..	..	..	..	..	..	..
16	Wood and wood products, except furniture	..	..	..	..	..	..	..	..
17	Paper and paper products	..	..	..	..	..	..	..	..
18	Printing and reproduction of recorded media	..	..	..	..	..	..	..	..
19-23	Chemical, rubber, plastic, non-metallic mineral products	..	..	..	..	..	..	..	..
19	Coke and refined petroleum products	..	..	..	..	..	..	..	..
20-21	Chemical and pharmaceutical products	..	..	..	..	..	..	..	..
20	Chemicals and chemical products	..	..	..	..	..	..	..	..
21	Pharmaceuticals, medicinal, chemical and botanical products	..	..	..	..	..	..	..	..
22	Rubber and plastic products	..	..	..	..	..	..	..	..
23	Other non-metallic mineral products	..	..	..	..	..	..	..	..
24-25	Basic metals, metal products, except machinery and equipment	..	..	..	..	..	..	..	..
24	Basic metals	..	..	..	..	..	..	..	..
25	Fabricated metal products, except machinery and equipment	..	..	..	..	..	..	..	..
26-30	Computer, electronic, optical products; electrical machinery, transport equipment	..	..	..	..	..	..	..	..
26	Computer, electronic and optical products	..	..	..	..	..	..	..	..
27	Electrical equipment	..	..	..	..	..	..	..	..
28	Machinery and equipment n.e.c.	..	..	..	..	..	..	..	..
29	Motor vehicles, trailers and semi-trailers	..	..	..	..	..	..	..	..
30	Other transport equipment	..	..	..	..	..	..	..	..
31-33	Furniture; repair, installation of machinery and equipment	..	..	..	..	..	..	..	..
31	Furniture	..	..	..	..	..	..	..	..
32	Other manufacturing	..	..	..	..	..	..	..	..
33	Repair and installation of machinery and equipment	..	..	..	..	..	..	..	..
35-39	**ELECTRICITY, GAS, WATER AND WASTE MANAGEMENT**	..	..	..	..	37.2	32.5	53.0	..
35-36	Electricity, gas and water	..	..	..	..	..	..	..	..
37-39	Sewerage, waste management and remediation activities	..	..	..	..	..	..	..	..
41-43	**CONSTRUCTION**	..	..	..	..	1.2	1.2	0.0	..
45-99	**TOTAL SERVICES**	..	..	..	..	322.4	320.8	377.9	..
45-82	**Business sector services**	..	..	..	..	..	..	..	..
45-47	**Wholesale and retail trade; motor vehicle and motorcycle repairs**	..	..	..	..	..	..	..	..
49-53	**Transportation and storage**	..	..	..	..	..	..	..	..
55-56	**Accommodation and food service activities**	..	..	..	..	..	..	..	..
58-63	**Information and communication**	..	..	..	..	..	..	..	..
58-60	Publishing, audiovisual and broadcasting activities	..	..	..	..	..	..	..	..
58	Publishing activities	..	..	..	..	..	..	..	..
59-60	Motion picture, video and TV programme production; broadcasting activities	..	..	..	..	..	..	..	..
59	Motion picture, video and TV programme production; sound and music	..	..	..	..	..	..	..	..
60	Programming and broadcasting activities	..	..	..	..	..	..	..	..
61	Telecommunications	..	..	..	..	..	..	..	..
62-63	IT and other information services	..	..	..	..	..	..	..	..
62	Computer programming, consultancy and related activities	..	..	..	..	..	..	..	..
63	Information service activities	..	..	..	..	..	..	..	..
64-66	**Financial and insurance activities**	..	..	..	..	..	..	..	..
68-82	**Real estate; professional, scientific and technical; administrative and support**	..	..	..	..	..	..	..	..
68	Real estate activities	..	..	..	..	..	..	..	..
69-75x72	Professional, scientific and technical activities, except scientific R&D	..	..	..	..	..	..	..	..
72	Scientific research and development	..	..	..	..	..	..	..	..
77-82	Administrative and support service activities	..	..	..	..	..	..	..	..
84-99	Community, social and personal services	..	..	..	..	..	..	..	..
84-85	Public administration and defence; compulsory social security and education	..	..	..	..	..	..	..	..
86-88	Human health and social work activities	..	..	..	..	..	..	..	..
90-93	Arts, entertainment and recreation	..	..	..	..	..	..	..	..
94-99	Other services; household-employers; extraterritorial bodies	..	..	..	..	..	..	..	..

.. Not available

Note: Detailed metadata at: *http://metalinks.oecd.org/anberd/20200813/2abe.*

R&D expenditure in industry by main activity of the enterprise, constant prices
ISIC Rev. 4

2010 USD PPP

		2011	2012	2013	2014	2015	2016	2017	2018
	TOTAL BUSINESS ENTERPRISE	..	..	..	..	1 164.9	1 099.7	1 205.0	..
01-03	**AGRICULTURE, FORESTRY AND FISHING**	..	..	..	..	149.2	149.9	157.1	..
05-09	**MINING AND QUARRYING**	..	..	..	..	7.6	8.8	29.5	..
10-33	**MANUFACTURING**	..	..	..	..	647.3	590.4	600.1	..
10-12	Food products, beverages and tobacco	..	..	..	..	..	..	..	..
13-15	Textiles, wearing apparel, leather and related products	..	..	..	..	..	..	..	..
13	Textiles	..	..	..	..	..	..	..	..
14	Wearing apparel	..	..	..	..	..	..	..	..
15	Leather and related products, footwear	..	..	..	..	..	..	..	..
16-18	Wood and paper products and printing	..	..	..	..	..	..	..	..
16	Wood and wood products, except furniture	..	..	..	..	..	..	..	..
17	Paper and paper products	..	..	..	..	..	..	..	..
18	Printing and reproduction of recorded media	..	..	..	..	..	..	..	..
19-23	Chemical, rubber, plastic, non-metallic mineral products	..	..	..	..	..	..	..	..
19	Coke and refined petroleum products	..	..	..	..	..	..	..	..
20-21	Chemical and pharmaceutical products	..	..	..	..	..	..	..	..
20	Chemicals and chemical products	..	..	..	..	..	..	..	..
21	Pharmaceuticals, medicinal, chemical and botanical products	..	..	..	..	..	..	..	..
22	Rubber and plastic products	..	..	..	..	..	..	..	..
23	Other non-metallic mineral products	..	..	..	..	..	..	..	..
24-25	Basic metals, metal products, except machinery and equipment	..	..	..	..	..	..	..	..
24	Basic metals	..	..	..	..	..	..	..	..
25	Fabricated metal products, except machinery and equipment	..	..	..	..	..	..	..	..
26-30	Computer, electronic, optical products; electrical machinery, transport equipment	..	..	..	..	..	..	..	..
26	Computer, electronic and optical products	..	..	..	..	..	..	..	..
27	Electrical equipment	..	..	..	..	..	..	..	..
28	Machinery and equipment n.e.c.	..	..	..	..	..	..	..	..
29	Motor vehicles, trailers and semi-trailers	..	..	..	..	..	..	..	..
30	Other transport equipment	..	..	..	..	..	..	..	..
31-33	Furniture; repair, installation of machinery and equipment	..	..	..	..	..	..	..	..
31	Furniture	..	..	..	..	..	..	..	..
32	Other manufacturing	..	..	..	..	..	..	..	..
33	Repair and installation of machinery and equipment	..	..	..	..	..	..	..	..
35-39	**ELECTRICITY, GAS, WATER AND WASTE MANAGEMENT**	..	..	..	..	37.2	32.2	51.4	..
35-36	Electricity, gas and water	..	..	..	..	..	..	..	..
37-39	Sewerage, waste management and remediation activities	..	..	..	..	..	..	..	..
41-43	**CONSTRUCTION**	..	..	..	..	1.2	1.1	0.0	..
45-99	**TOTAL SERVICES**	..	..	..	..	322.4	317.3	366.9	..
45-82	**Business sector services**	..	..	..	..	..	..	..	..
45-47	**Wholesale and retail trade; motor vehicle and motorcycle repairs**	..	..	..	..	..	..	..	..
49-53	**Transportation and storage**	..	..	..	..	..	..	..	..
55-56	**Accommodation and food service activities**	..	..	..	..	..	..	..	..
58-63	**Information and communication**	..	..	..	..	..	..	..	..
58-60	Publishing, audiovisual and broadcasting activities	..	..	..	..	..	..	..	..
58	Publishing activities	..	..	..	..	..	..	..	..
59-60	Motion picture, video and TV programme production; broadcasting activities	..	..	..	..	..	..	..	..
59	Motion picture, video and TV programme production; sound and music	..	..	..	..	..	..	..	..
60	Programming and broadcasting activities	..	..	..	..	..	..	..	..
61	Telecommunications	..	..	..	..	..	..	..	..
62-63	IT and other information services	..	..	..	..	..	..	..	..
62	Computer programming, consultancy and related activities	..	..	..	..	..	..	..	..
63	Information service activities	..	..	..	..	..	..	..	..
64-66	**Financial and insurance activities**	..	..	..	..	..	..	..	..
68-82	**Real estate; professional, scientific and technical; administrative and support**	..	..	..	..	..	..	..	..
68	Real estate activities	..	..	..	..	..	..	..	..
69-75x72	Professional, scientific and technical activities, except scientific R&D	..	..	..	..	..	..	..	..
72	Scientific research and development	..	..	..	..	..	..	..	..
77-82	Administrative and support service activities	..	..	..	..	..	..	..	..
84-99	Community, social and personal services	..	..	..	..	..	..	..	..
84-85	Public administration and defence; compulsory social security and education	..	..	..	..	..	..	..	..
86-88	Human health and social work activities	..	..	..	..	..	..	..	..
90-93	Arts, entertainment and recreation	..	..	..	..	..	..	..	..
94-99	Other services; household-employers; extraterritorial bodies	..	..	..	..	..	..	..	..

.. Not available

Note: Detailed metadata at: http://metalinks.oecd.org/anberd/20200813/2abe.

CHINA

R&D expenditure in industry by main activity of the enterprise, current prices
ISIC Rev. 4

Million USD PPP

		2011	2012	2013	2014	2015	2016	2017	2018
	TOTAL BUSINESS ENTERPRISE	**187 684.1**	**222 798.0**	**256 819.7**	**287 795.3**	**314 404.2**	**350 958.0**	**387 240.6**	..
01-03	**AGRICULTURE, FORESTRY AND FISHING**	483.3	461.8	..	..	..	..	..	..
05-09	**MINING AND QUARRYING**	**7 206.5**	**7 956.4**	**7 750.2**	**7 867.6**	**7 148.1**	**7 068.0**	**7 270.7**	..
10-33	**MANUFACTURING**	**162 466.1**	**194 486.2**	**224 968.1**	**254 042.9**	**278 542.4**	**305 449.5**	**329 074.1**	..
10-12	Food products, beverages and tobacco	6 846.1	9 160.3	10 649.9	12 252.3	13 355.4	15 161.1	15 370.6	..
13-15	Textiles, wearing apparel, leather and related products	5 146.7	6 280.3	7 404.4	8 351.6	10 078.1	11 153.2	11 587.7	..
13	Textiles	3 880.2	3 921.4	4 484.7	5 083.2	6 000.2	6 356.1	6 610.2	..
14	Wearing apparel	..	1 579.3	1 960.6	2 121.4	2 602.8	3 091.5	3 132.0	..
15	Leather and related products, footwear	..	779.6	959.1	1 146.9	1 475.0	1 705.5	1 845.5	..
16-18	Wood and paper products and printing	2 549.4	3 383.9	4 112.7	4 673.6	5 412.4	6 426.8	7 336.7	..
16	Wood and wood products, except furniture	412.8	532.0	768.5	935.9	1 237.1	1 528.0	1 708.7	..
17	Paper and paper products	1 594.3	2 153.6	2 484.2	2 758.3	3 109.1	3 547.7	4 099.0	..
18	Printing and reproduction of recorded media	542.4	698.4	859.9	979.4	1 066.1	1 351.1	1 529.1	..
19-23	Chemical, rubber, plastic, non-metallic mineral products	30 750.1	37 456.2	44 670.5	51 284.9	55 923.3	61 687.4	67 165.5	..
19	Coke and refined petroleum products	1 784.2	2 319.3	2 527.5	3 048.7	2 913.7	3 457.2	4 155.7	..
20-21	Chemical and pharmaceutical products	21 107.3	25 578.7	30 414.2	34 666.5	37 978.4	40 836.7	44 016.6	..
20	Chemicals and chemical products	15 081.2	17 530.0	20 576.6	23 501.1	25 222.9	26 720.0	28 873.7	..
21	Pharmaceuticals, medicinal, chemical and botanical products	6 026.1	8 048.7	9 837.6	11 165.4	12 755.4	14 116.7	15 142.9	..
22	Rubber and plastic products	3 872.9	4 911.1	5 644.1	6 519.4	7 009.7	8 056.5	8 708.2	..
23	Other non-metallic mineral products	3 985.7	4 647.0	6 084.8	7 050.3	8 021.5	9 337.1	10 285.1	..
24-25	Basic metals, metal products, except machinery and equipment	23 224.2	30 865.8	32 942.4	35 009.0	35 118.6	36 728.2	40 921.3	..
24	Basic metals	20 049.5	25 540.6	26 433.6	27 822.2	26 951.5	27 296.9	31 193.2	..
25	Fabricated metal products, except machinery and equipment	3 174.7	5 325.2	6 508.8	7 186.9	8 167.1	9 431.3	9 728.1	..
26-30	Computer, electronic, optical products; electrical machinery, transport equipment	92 525.3	105 272.7	122 517.9	139 002.4	154 442.6	169 072.1	180 932.1	..
26	Computer, electronic and optical products	30 292.6	33 763.0	39 666.5	44 669.8	51 795.2	57 703.6	62 734.1	..
27	Electrical equipment	17 800.7	20 005.1	23 073.1	26 399.2	29 261.7	31 858.6	35 219.0	..
28	Machinery and equipment n.e.c.	22 031.7	25 556.0	30 000.8	33 225.2	34 666.3	35 918.2	37 809.6	..
29	Motor vehicles, trailers and semi-trailers	..	16 211.1	19 248.3	22 517.9	26 124.6	30 308.3	33 012.9	..
30	Other transport equipment	..	9 737.6	10 529.1	12 190.4	12 594.8	13 283.3	12 156.5	..
31-33	Furniture; repair, installation of machinery and equipment	1 424.2	2 067.0	2 670.3	3 469.0	4 212.0	5 220.8	5 760.1	..
31	Furniture	257.7	412.8	635.7	774.4	953.9	1 238.8	1 571.3	..
32	Other manufacturing	1 083.0	1 516.2	1 814.2	2 407.5	2 918.7	3 466.4	3 773.4	..
33	Repair and installation of machinery and equipment	83.5	138.1	220.3	287.2	339.5	515.6	415.5	..
35-39	**ELECTRICITY, GAS, WATER AND WASTE MANAGEMENT**	**1 333.9**	**1 481.0**	..	..	..	..	..	..
35-36	Electricity, gas and water	..	..	..	..	..	..	..	..
37-39	Sewerage, waste management and remediation activities	..	..	..	..	..	..	..	..
41-43	**CONSTRUCTION**	**4 144.7**	**4 279.7**	..	..	..	..	..	..
45-99	**TOTAL SERVICES**	**12 049.6**	**14 132.9**	..	..	..	..	..	..
45-82	**Business sector services**	..	..	..	..	..	..	..	..
45-47	**Wholesale and retail trade; motor vehicle and motorcycle repairs**	..	..	..	..	..	..	..	..
49-53	**Transportation and storage**	..	..	..	..	..	..	..	..
55-56	**Accommodation and food service activities**	..	..	..	..	..	..	..	..
58-63	**Information and communication**	..	..	..	..	..	..	..	..
58-60	Publishing, audiovisual and broadcasting activities	..	..	..	..	..	..	..	..
58	Publishing activities	..	..	..	..	..	..	..	..
59-60	Motion picture, video and TV programme production; broadcasting activities	..	..	..	..	..	..	..	..
59	Motion picture, video and TV programme production; sound and music	..	..	..	..	..	..	..	..
60	Programming and broadcasting activities	..	..	..	..	..	..	..	..
61	Telecommunications	..	..	..	..	..	..	..	..
62-63	IT and other information services	..	..	..	..	..	..	..	..
62	Computer programming, consultancy and related activities	..	..	..	..	..	..	..	..
63	Information service activities	..	..	..	..	..	..	..	..
64-66	**Financial and insurance activities**	..	..	..	..	..	..	..	..
68-82	**Real estate; professional, scientific and technical; administrative and support**	..	..	..	..	..	..	..	..
68	Real estate activities	..	..	..	..	..	..	..	..
69-75x72	Professional, scientific and technical activities, except scientific R&D	..	..	..	..	..	..	..	..
72	Scientific research and development	..	..	..	..	..	..	..	..
77-82	Administrative and support service activities	..	..	..	..	..	..	..	..
84-99	Community, social and personal services	..	..	..	..	..	..	..	..
84-85	Public administration and defence; compulsory social security and education	..	..	..	..	..	..	..	..
86-88	Human health and social work activities	..	..	..	..	..	..	..	..
90-93	Arts, entertainment and recreation	..	..	..	..	..	..	..	..
94-99	Other services; household-employers; extraterritorial bodies	..	..	..	..	..	..	..	..

.. Not available

Note: Detailed metadata at: *http://metalinks.oecd.org/anberd/20200813/2abe.*

R&D expenditure in industry by main activity of the enterprise, constant prices
ISIC Rev. 4

2010 USD PPP

		2011	2012	2013	2014	2015	2016	2017	2018
	TOTAL BUSINESS ENTERPRISE	200 437.3	233 468.7	264 472.4	290 872.0	314 404.2	347 154.2	375 898.2	..
01-03	**AGRICULTURE, FORESTRY AND FISHING**	516.2	484.0	..	..	..	..	..	..
05-09	**MINING AND QUARRYING**	7 696.1	8 337.4	7 981.1	7 951.7	7 148.1	6 991.4	7 057.7	..
10-33	**MANUFACTURING**	173 505.7	203 800.9	231 671.6	256 758.8	278 542.4	302 139.0	319 435.5	..
10-12	Food products, beverages and tobacco	7 311.3	9 599.0	10 967.3	12 383.3	13 355.4	14 996.7	14 920.4	..
13-15	Textiles, wearing apparel, leather and related products	5 496.4	6 581.1	7 625.0	8 440.9	10 078.1	11 032.3	11 248.3	..
13	Textiles	4 143.9	4 109.2	4 618.4	5 137.6	6 000.2	6 287.2	6 416.6	..
14	Wearing apparel	..	1 655.0	2 019.0	2 144.1	2 602.8	3 058.0	3 040.3	..
15	Leather and related products, footwear	..	816.9	987.6	1 159.2	1 475.0	1 687.0	1 791.4	..
16-18	Wood and paper products and printing	2 722.6	3 546.0	4 235.2	4 723.5	5 412.4	6 357.2	7 121.8	..
16	Wood and wood products, except furniture	440.8	557.4	791.4	945.9	1 237.1	1 511.5	1 658.6	..
17	Paper and paper products	1 702.6	2 256.8	2 558.3	2 787.8	3 109.1	3 509.2	3 978.9	..
18	Printing and reproduction of recorded media	579.2	731.8	885.5	989.9	1 066.1	1 336.5	1 484.3	..
19-23	Chemical, rubber, plastic, non-metallic mineral products	32 839.5	39 250.2	46 001.6	51 833.2	55 923.3	61 018.8	65 198.3	..
19	Coke and refined petroleum products	1 905.4	2 430.4	2 602.8	3 081.3	2 913.7	3 419.7	4 034.0	..
20-21	Chemical and pharmaceutical products	22 541.5	26 803.8	31 320.5	35 037.1	37 978.4	40 394.1	42 727.3	..
20	Chemicals and chemical products	16 106.0	18 369.6	21 189.7	23 752.4	25 222.9	26 430.4	28 028.0	..
21	Pharmaceuticals, medicinal, chemical and botanical products	6 435.5	8 434.2	10 130.8	11 284.8	12 755.4	13 963.7	14 699.3	..
22	Rubber and plastic products	4 136.1	5 146.4	5 812.2	6 589.1	7 009.7	7 969.1	8 453.1	..
23	Other non-metallic mineral products	4 256.5	4 869.6	6 266.1	7 125.7	8 021.5	9 235.9	9 983.8	..
24-25	Basic metals, metal products, except machinery and equipment	24 802.3	32 344.1	33 924.0	35 383.3	35 118.6	36 330.1	39 722.7	..
24	Basic metals	21 411.9	26 763.8	27 221.2	28 119.6	26 951.5	27 001.0	30 279.6	..
25	Fabricated metal products, except machinery and equipment	3 390.5	5 580.3	6 702.7	7 263.7	8 167.1	9 329.1	9 443.2	..
26-30	Computer, electronic, optical products; electrical machinery, transport equipment	98 812.5	110 314.6	126 168.7	140 488.4	154 442.6	167 239.6	175 632.6	..
26	Computer, electronic and optical products	32 351.0	35 380.0	40 848.5	45 147.3	51 795.2	57 078.2	60 896.6	..
27	Electrical equipment	19 010.2	20 963.2	23 760.7	26 681.4	29 261.7	31 513.3	34 187.5	..
28	Machinery and equipment n.e.c.	23 528.7	26 779.9	30 894.8	33 580.4	34 666.3	35 528.9	36 702.1	..
29	Motor vehicles, trailers and semi-trailers	..	16 987.5	19 821.9	22 758.6	26 124.6	29 979.8	32 046.0	..
30	Other transport equipment	..	10 203.9	10 842.9	12 320.7	12 594.8	13 139.3	11 800.4	..
31-33	Furniture; repair, installation of machinery and equipment	1 521.0	2 166.0	2 749.8	3 506.1	4 212.0	5 164.2	5 591.4	..
31	Furniture	275.2	432.5	654.6	782.7	953.9	1 225.4	1 525.2	..
32	Other manufacturing	1 156.6	1 588.8	1 868.3	2 433.2	2 918.7	3 428.8	3 662.9	..
33	Repair and installation of machinery and equipment	89.2	144.7	226.9	290.2	339.5	510.0	403.3	..
35-39	**ELECTRICITY, GAS, WATER AND WASTE MANAGEMENT**	1 424.6	1 551.9	..	..	..	..	..	..
35-36	Electricity, gas and water	..	..	..	..	..	..	..	..
37-39	Sewerage, waste management and remediation activities	..	..	..	..	..	..	..	..
41-43	**CONSTRUCTION**	4 426.4	4 484.6	..	..	..	..	..	..
45-99	**TOTAL SERVICES**	12 868.4	14 809.8	..	..	..	..	..	..
45-82	**Business sector services**	..	..	..	..	..	..	..	..
45-47	**Wholesale and retail trade; motor vehicle and motorcycle repairs**	..	..	..	..	..	..	..	..
49-53	**Transportation and storage**	..	..	..	..	..	..	..	..
55-56	**Accommodation and food service activities**	..	..	..	..	..	..	..	..
58-63	**Information and communication**	..	..	..	..	..	..	..	..
58-60	Publishing, audiovisual and broadcasting activities	..	..	..	..	..	..	..	..
58	Publishing activities	..	..	..	..	..	..	..	..
59-60	Motion picture, video and TV programme production; broadcasting activities	..	..	..	..	..	..	..	..
59	Motion picture, video and TV programme production; sound and music	..	..	..	..	..	..	..	..
60	Programming and broadcasting activities	..	..	..	..	..	..	..	..
61	Telecommunications	..	..	..	..	..	..	..	..
62-63	IT and other information services	..	..	..	..	..	..	..	..
62	Computer programming, consultancy and related activities	..	..	..	..	..	..	..	..
63	Information service activities	..	..	..	..	..	..	..	..
64-66	**Financial and insurance activities**	..	..	..	..	..	..	..	..
68-82	**Real estate; professional, scientific and technical; administrative and support**	..	..	..	..	..	..	..	..
68	Real estate activities	..	..	..	..	..	..	..	..
69-75x72	Professional, scientific and technical activities, except scientific R&D	..	..	..	..	..	..	..	..
72	Scientific research and development	..	..	..	..	..	..	..	..
77-82	Administrative and support service activities	..	..	..	..	..	..	..	..
84-99	Community, social and personal services	..	..	..	..	..	..	..	..
84-85	Public administration and defence; compulsory social security and education	..	..	..	..	..	..	..	..
86-88	Human health and social work activities	..	..	..	..	..	..	..	..
90-93	Arts, entertainment and recreation	..	..	..	..	..	..	..	..
94-99	Other services; household-employers; extraterritorial bodies	..	..	..	..	..	..	..	..

.. Not available

Note: Detailed metadata at: *http://metalinks.oecd.org/anberd/20200813/2abe.*

R&D expenditure in industry by main activity of the enterprise, current prices
ISIC Rev. 4

Million USD PPP

		2011	2012	2013	2014	2015	2016	2017	2018
	TOTAL BUSINESS ENTERPRISE	**648.1**	**715.9**	**470.5**	**650.6**	**920.3**	**1 270.0**	**1 526.1**	..
01-03	**AGRICULTURE, FORESTRY AND FISHING**	3.4	6.0	6.8	8.0	10.8	15.1	11.6	..
05-09	**MINING AND QUARRYING**	0.0 e	0.1	0.5 e	17.9	20.8	13.6	14.4	..
10-33	**MANUFACTURING**	336.5	299.9	247.5	336.2	379.3	464.4	484.3	..
10-12	Food products, beverages and tobacco	4.2	10.8	11.4	31.7	4.7	5.4	15.4	..
13-15	Textiles, wearing apparel, leather and related products	0.9 e	5.7	2.6	2.6	2.0	1.4	3.1	..
13	Textiles	0.1 e	0.7 e	0.1	0.3	0.1	0.2	2.3 e	..
14	Wearing apparel	0.2 e	0.7 e	0.4	1.3	1.6	0.7	0.7 e	..
15	Leather and related products, footwear	0.6 e	4.3	2.2	0.4	0.2	0.5	0.1 e	..
16-18	Wood and paper products and printing	0.0 e	0.0 e	0.1 e	0.8	0.2	0.0	0.8	..
16	Wood and wood products, except furniture	..	..	..	..	..	..	..	..
17	Paper and paper products	..	..	..	..	..	..	..	..
18	Printing and reproduction of recorded media	..	..	..	..	..	..	..	..
19-23	Chemical, rubber, plastic, non-metallic mineral products	98.5 e	35.3 e	32.9 e	45.9	35.2	47.5	29.0	..
19	Coke and refined petroleum products	0.0	0.0 e	0.0 e	0.0	0.0	0.0	0.0	..
20-21	Chemical and pharmaceutical products	86.2	30.3	28.4	45.1	34.4	46.0	27.9	..
20	Chemicals and chemical products	61.3	3.5	3.3	6.3	6.5	9.1	6.8	..
21	Pharmaceuticals, medicinal, chemical and botanical products	24.9	26.8	25.1	38.8	27.9	37.0	21.1	..
22	Rubber and plastic products	12.2	3.2	4.1	0.2	0.1	0.9	0.4	..
23	Other non-metallic mineral products	0.2 e	1.8	0.3	0.6	0.7	0.6	0.8	..
24-25	Basic metals, metal products, except machinery and equipment	16.0	8.5	9.6	10.7	8.2	9.5	7.2	..
24	Basic metals	11.4	4.0	4.9	4.9	2.2	1.8	1.7	..
25	Fabricated metal products, except machinery and equipment	4.6	4.5	4.7	5.7	6.0	7.6	5.5	..
26-30	Computer, electronic, optical products; electrical machinery, transport equipment	215.5	232.1	188.5	238.9	324.7	395.8	424.8	..
26	Computer, electronic and optical products	13.8	60.8	40.2	16.2	37.8	44.9	15.1	..
27	Electrical equipment	46.1	18.7	14.6	13.6	23.0	29.1	25.9	..
28	Machinery and equipment n.e.c.	6.8	20.6	13.1	13.2	9.0	7.7	5.4	..
29	Motor vehicles, trailers and semi-trailers	141.9	124.3	114.7	187.1	253.8	311.2	367.2	..
30	Other transport equipment	6.9	7.8	5.9	8.8	1.1	2.9	11.2	..
31-33	Furniture; repair, installation of machinery and equipment	1.4	7.5 e	2.3 e	6.3	4.3	4.9	3.9	..
31	Furniture	0.1 e	0.1 e	0.1 e	0.5	0.2	0.7	0.9	..
32	Other manufacturing	0.0 e	2.3	0.8	1.3	1.3	2.4	0.8	..
33	Repair and installation of machinery and equipment	1.2 e	5.1	1.4	4.4	2.8	1.7	2.2	..
35-39	**ELECTRICITY, GAS, WATER AND WASTE MANAGEMENT**	0.6 e	3.4	1.6	1.4	1.4	0.9	1.1	..
35-36	Electricity, gas and water	0.2 e	2.7	1.3 e	1.2 e	1.2	0.7	0.8	..
37-39	Sewerage, waste management and remediation activities	0.4 e	0.6	0.3 e	0.2 e	0.2	0.3	0.3	..
41-43	**CONSTRUCTION**	6.6	0.5	0.5 e	1.2	1.2	1.3	54.6	..
45-99	**TOTAL SERVICES**	300.9	406.0	213.7	286.0	506.8	774.6	960.1	..
45-82	**Business sector services**	300.8	403.1	213.7	283.1	504.7	771.9	931.3	..
45-47	**Wholesale and retail trade; motor vehicle and motorcycle repairs**	14.7	29.6	17.8	33.2	13.5	29.5	16.1	..
49-53	**Transportation and storage**	4.1	..	..	12.2	0.3	0.9	0.2 e	..
55-56	**Accommodation and food service activities**	..	1.8	1.3	0.7	0.0	0.0	0.0 e	..
58-63	**Information and communication**	114.3	127.4	46.0	69.6	121.9	275.8	187.0	..
58-60	Publishing, audiovisual and broadcasting activities	55.8	2.2	0.0	9.7	30.8	122.1	134.0	..
58	Publishing activities	..	2.1						
59-60	Motion picture, video and TV programme production; broadcasting activities	..	0.1	..	..	..	..	..	
59	Motion picture, video and TV programme production; sound and music	..	..	..	..	..	..	..	
60	Programming and broadcasting activities	..	..	..	..	..	..	..	
61	Telecommunications	..	13.1	1.2	2.4	1.3	28.7	7.9	..
62-63	IT and other information services	..	112.1	44.8	57.5	89.8	125.1	45.1	..
62	Computer programming, consultancy and related activities	56.8	76.6	32.0	57.4	89.7	124.6	44.7	..
63	Information service activities	..	35.6	12.7	0.1	0.2	0.6	0.4	..
64-66	**Financial and insurance activities**	..	..	..	..	0.0	0.0	0.0	..
68-82	**Real estate; professional, scientific and technical; administrative and support**	166.3	244.3	..	..	369.0	465.6	728.0	..
68	Real estate activities	0.0 e	2.7	..	..	0.0	0.0	0.0	
69-75x72	Professional, scientific and technical activities, except scientific R&D	29.6	47.2	15.8	15.0	164.3	289.9	569.7	
72	Scientific research and development	136.3	191.8	131.6	150.4	204.6	175.5	157.9	
77-82	Administrative and support service activities	0.3 e	2.7	..	1.9	0.1	0.2	0.5	
84-99	Community, social and personal services	0.1	2.9	0.0	2.8	2.1	2.7	28.8	
84-85	Public administration and defence; compulsory social security and education	..	..	..	..	0.0	0.0	0.0	
86-88	Human health and social work activities	..	..	..	..	2.1	2.2	28.1	
90-93	Arts, entertainment and recreation	..	..	..	..	0.0	0.5	0.7	
94-99	Other services; household-employers; extraterritorial bodies	..	..	..	..	0.0	0.0	0.0	..

.. Not available; e Estimated value

Note: Detailed metadata at: *http://metalinks.oecd.org/anberd/20200813/2abe.*

ROMANIA

R&D expenditure in industry by main activity of the enterprise, constant prices
ISIC Rev. 4

2010 USD PPP

		2011	2012	2013	2014	2015	2016	2017	2018
	TOTAL BUSINESS ENTERPRISE	**678.4**	**726.8**	**474.6**	**653.9**	**920.3**	**1 190.8**	**1 373.3**	..
01-03	**AGRICULTURE, FORESTRY AND FISHING**	**3.6**	**6.1**	**6.9**	**8.0**	**10.8**	**14.2**	**10.4**	..
05-09	**MINING AND QUARRYING**	**0.0 e**	**0.1**	**0.5 e**	**18.0**	**20.8**	**12.8**	**13.0**	..
10-33	**MANUFACTURING**	**352.2**	**304.5**	**249.6**	**337.9**	**379.3**	**435.5**	**435.8**	..
10-12	Food products, beverages and tobacco	4.4	10.9	11.5	31.9	4.7	5.0	13.9	..
13-15	Textiles, wearing apparel, leather and related products	1.0 e	5.7	2.7	2.6	2.0	1.4	2.8	..
13	Textiles	0.1 e	0.7 e	0.1	0.3	0.1	0.2	2.0 e	..
14	Wearing apparel	0.2 e	0.7 e	0.4	1.3	1.6	0.7	0.7 e	..
15	Leather and related products, footwear	0.6 e	4.4	2.2	0.4	0.2	0.4	0.1 e	..
16-18	Wood and paper products and printing	0.0 e	0.0 e	0.1 e	0.8	0.2	0.0	0.7	..
16	Wood and wood products, except furniture	..	..	..	..	..	..	..	..
17	Paper and paper products	..	..	..	..	..	..	..	..
18	Printing and reproduction of recorded media	..	..	..	..	..	..	..	..
19-23	Chemical, rubber, plastic, non-metallic mineral products	103.1 e	35.9 e	33.1 e	46.2	35.2	44.5	26.1	..
19	Coke and refined petroleum products	0.0	0.0 e	0.0 e	0.0	0.0	0.0	0.0	..
20-21	Chemical and pharmaceutical products	90.2	30.8	28.7	45.3	34.4	43.2	25.1	..
20	Chemicals and chemical products	64.2	3.5	3.3	6.3	6.5	8.5	6.1	..
21	Pharmaceuticals, medicinal, chemical and botanical products	26.1	27.2	25.4	39.0	27.9	34.7	19.0	..
22	Rubber and plastic products	12.7	3.2	4.1	0.2	0.1	0.8	0.4	..
23	Other non-metallic mineral products	0.2 e	1.8	0.3	0.6	0.7	0.5	0.7	..
24-25	Basic metals, metal products, except machinery and equipment	16.8	8.7	9.7	10.7	8.2	8.9	6.5	..
24	Basic metals	12.0	4.1	4.9	5.0	2.2	1.7	1.6	..
25	Fabricated metal products, except machinery and equipment	4.8	4.6	4.8	5.8	6.0	7.1	5.0	..
26-30	Computer, electronic, optical products; electrical machinery, transport equipment	225.6	235.6	190.1	240.1	324.7	371.2	382.3	..
26	Computer, electronic and optical products	14.4	61.7	40.5	16.3	37.8	42.1	13.6	..
27	Electrical equipment	48.2	19.0	14.7	13.6	23.0	27.3	23.3	..
28	Machinery and equipment n.e.c.	7.1	20.9	13.2	13.3	9.0	7.2	4.8	..
29	Motor vehicles, trailers and semi-trailers	148.5	126.2	115.7	188.0	253.8	291.8	330.4	..
30	Other transport equipment	7.3	7.9	6.0	8.9	1.1	2.7	10.1	..
31-33	Furniture; repair, installation of machinery and equipment	1.4	7.7 e	2.3 e	6.3	4.3	4.6	3.5	..
31	Furniture	0.1 e	0.1 e	0.1 e	0.5	0.2	0.7	0.8	..
32	Other manufacturing	0.0 e	2.4	0.8	1.3	1.3	2.3	0.7	..
33	Repair and installation of machinery and equipment	1.3 e	5.2	1.4	4.5	2.8	1.6	2.0	..
35-39	**ELECTRICITY, GAS, WATER AND WASTE MANAGEMENT**	**0.7 e**	**3.4**	**1.6**	**1.4**	**1.4**	**0.8**	**1.0**	..
35-36	Electricity, gas and water	0.2 e	2.8	1.3 e	1.2 e	1.2	0.6	0.7	..
37-39	Sewerage, waste management and remediation activities	0.5 e	0.6	0.3 e	0.2 e	0.2	0.2	0.3	..
41-43	**CONSTRUCTION**	**6.9**	**0.5**	**0.5 e**	**1.2**	**1.2**	**1.2**	**49.1**	..
45-99	**TOTAL SERVICES**	**315.0**	**412.2**	**215.5**	**287.4**	**506.8**	**726.3**	**864.0**	..
45-82	**Business sector services**	**314.9**	**409.2**	**215.5**	**284.5**	**504.7**	**723.8**	**838.0**	..
45-47	**Wholesale and retail trade; motor vehicle and motorcycle repairs**	**15.4**	**30.1**	**18.0**	**33.4**	**13.5**	**27.7**	**14.5**	..
49-53	**Transportation and storage**	**4.3**	..	..	**12.3**	**0.3**	**0.9**	**0.1 e**	..
55-56	**Accommodation and food service activities**	..	**1.8**	**1.3**	**0.7**	**0.0**	**0.0**	**0.0 e**	..
58-63	**Information and communication**	**119.6**	**129.3**	**46.4**	**70.0**	**121.9**	**258.7**	**168.3**	..
58-60	Publishing, audiovisual and broadcasting activities	58.4	2.2	0.0	9.8	30.8	114.4	120.6	..
58	Publishing activities	..	2.1	..	..	..	..	..	..
59-60	Motion picture, video and TV programme production; broadcasting activities	..	0.1	..	..	..	..	..	..
59	Motion picture, video and TV programme production; sound and music	..	..	..	..	..	..	..	..
60	Programming and broadcasting activities	..	..	..	..	..	..	..	..
61	Telecommunications	..	13.3	1.2	2.5	1.3	26.9	7.2	..
62-63	IT and other information services	..	113.8	45.1	57.8	89.8	117.3	40.6	..
62	Computer programming, consultancy and related activities	59.5	77.7	32.3	57.7	89.7	116.8	40.2	..
63	Information service activities	..	36.1	12.8	0.1	0.2	0.5	0.4	..
64-66	**Financial and insurance activities**	..	..	..	..	**0.0**	**0.0**	**0.0**	..
68-82	**Real estate; professional, scientific and technical; administrative and support**	**174.0**	**248.0**	..	..	**369.0**	**436.5**	**655.1**	..
68	Real estate activities	0.0 e	2.7	..	..	0.0	0.0	0.0	..
69-75x72	Professional, scientific and technical activities, except scientific R&D	31.0	47.9	16.0	15.1	164.3	271.8	512.7	..
72	Scientific research and development	142.7	194.7	132.7	151.1	204.6	164.6	142.1	..
77-82	Administrative and support service activities	0.3 e	2.7	..	1.9	0.1	0.1	0.4	..
84-99	Community, social and personal services	0.1	2.9	0.0	2.9	2.1	2.5	25.9	..
84-85	Public administration and defence; compulsory social security and education	..	..	..	..	0.0	0.0	0.0	..
86-88	Human health and social work activities	..	..	..	..	2.1	2.0	25.3	..
90-93	Arts, entertainment and recreation	..	..	..	..	0.0	0.5	0.6	..
94-99	Other services; household-employers; extraterritorial bodies	..	..	..	..	0.0	0.0	0.0	..

.. Not available; e Estimated value

Note: Detailed metadata at: http://metalinks.oecd.org/anberd/20200813/2abe.

SINGAPORE

R&D expenditure in industry by main activity of the enterprise, current prices
ISIC Rev. 4

Million USD PPP

		2011	2012	2013	2014	2015	2016	2017	2018
	TOTAL BUSINESS ENTERPRISE	**5 194.4**	**5 023.0**	**5 228.0**	..	..	..	..	..
01-03	**AGRICULTURE, FORESTRY AND FISHING**	**0.0**	**0.0**	**0.0**	..	..	..	..	..
05-09	**MINING AND QUARRYING**	**0.0**	**0.0**	**0.0**	..	..	..	..	..
10-33	**MANUFACTURING**	**2 467.5**	**3 024.7**	**3 010.1**	..	..	..	..	..
10-12	Food products, beverages and tobacco	19.5	25.0	24.2	..	..	..	..	..
13-15	Textiles, wearing apparel, leather and related products	1.0	0.9	0.6 e	..	..	..	..	..
13	Textiles	0.0	..	..	..	..	..	..	..
14	Wearing apparel	0.7	..	..	..	..	..	..	..
15	Leather and related products, footwear	0.3	..	..	..	..	..	..	..
16-18	Wood and paper products and printing	3.5	3.6 e	3.2	..	..	..	..	..
16	Wood and wood products, except furniture	0.0	0.0 e	0.0	..	..	..	..	..
17	Paper and paper products	2.7	3.0 e	2.8	..	..	..	..	..
18	Printing and reproduction of recorded media	0.8	0.6 e	0.4	..	..	..	..	..
19-23	Chemical, rubber, plastic, non-metallic mineral products	248.7	273.4	351.8 e	..	..	..	..	..
19	Coke and refined petroleum products	1.2	1.4	1.0 e	..	..	..	..	..
20-21	Chemical and pharmaceutical products	229.4	265.6	345.1	..	..	..	..	..
20	Chemicals and chemical products	97.6	112.3	202.3	..	..	..	..	..
21	Pharmaceuticals, medicinal, chemical and botanical products	131.8	153.4	142.8	..	..	..	..	..
22	Rubber and plastic products	14.3	2.7	3.0	..	..	..	..	..
23	Other non-metallic mineral products	3.8	3.6	2.7	..	..	..	..	..
24-25	Basic metals, metal products, except machinery and equipment	23.1	30.1 e	43.8	..	..	..	..	..
24	Basic metals	1.6	1.6 e	3.1	..	..	..	..	..
25	Fabricated metal products, except machinery and equipment	21.5	28.5	40.7	..	..	..	..	..
26-30	Computer, electronic, optical products; electrical machinery, transport equipment	2 094.1	2 556.3	2 452.3	..	..	..	..	..
26	Computer, electronic and optical products	1 644.2	2 059.1	1 805.6	..	..	..	..	..
27	Electrical equipment	24.7	15.7	31.9	..	..	..	..	..
28	Machinery and equipment n.e.c.	209.4	220.6	308.8	..	..	..	..	..
29	Motor vehicles, trailers and semi-trailers	49.6	55.0	61.7	..	..	..	..	..
30	Other transport equipment	166.1	205.9	244.4	..	..	..	..	..
31-33	Furniture; repair, installation of machinery and equipment	77.5	135.4	134.2	..	..	..	..	..
31	Furniture	17.1	16.9	16.3	..	..	..	..	..
32	Other manufacturing	60.5	118.5	117.9	..	..	..	..	..
33	Repair and installation of machinery and equipment	0.0	0.0	0.0	..	..	..	..	..
35-39	**ELECTRICITY, GAS, WATER AND WASTE MANAGEMENT**	**13.9**	**10.9**	**15.2**	..	..	..	..	..
35-36	Electricity, gas and water	0.1	0.0	0.0	..	..	..	..	..
37-39	Sewerage, waste management and remediation activities	13.8	10.9	15.2	..	..	..	..	..
41-43	**CONSTRUCTION**	**2.5**	**1.5**	**1.8**	..	..	..	..	..
45-99	**TOTAL SERVICES**	**2 710.4**	**1 986.0**	**2 200.9**	..	..	..	..	..
45-82	**Business sector services**	**2 700.6**	**1 976.4**	**2 165.0**	..	..	..	..	..
45-47	**Wholesale and retail trade; motor vehicle and motorcycle repairs**	**575.1**	**613.3**	**824.2**	..	..	..	..	..
49-53	**Transportation and storage**	**46.6**	**31.1**	**46.3**	..	..	..	..	..
55-56	**Accommodation and food service activities**	**0.0**	**0.0**	**0.0**	..	..	..	..	..
58-63	**Information and communication**	**160.7**	**169.8**	**174.1**	..	..	..	..	..
58-60	Publishing, audiovisual and broadcasting activities	39.4	54.5	45.4	..	..	..	..	..
58	Publishing activities	37.6	54.2	45.3	..	..	..	..	..
59-60	Motion picture, video and TV programme production; broadcasting activities	1.8	0.3	0.2	..	..	..	..	..
59	Motion picture, video and TV programme production; sound and music	1.8	0.3	0.2	..	..	..	..	..
60	Programming and broadcasting activities	0.0	0.0	0.0	..	..	..	..	..
61	Telecommunications	5.7	3.5	6.7	..	..	..	..	..
62-63	IT and other information services	115.6	111.8	122.0	..	..	..	..	..
62	Computer programming, consultancy and related activities	112.9	108.9	116.1	..	..	..	..	..
63	Information service activities	2.7	2.9	5.9	..	..	..	..	..
64-66	**Financial and insurance activities**	**105.3**	**102.6**	**107.6**	..	..	..	..	..
68-82	**Real estate; professional, scientific and technical; administrative and support**	**1 812.9**	**1 059.6**	**1 012.7**	..	..	..	..	..
68	Real estate activities	0.0	0.0	0.0	..	..	..	..	..
69-75x72	Professional, scientific and technical activities, except scientific R&D	319.6	266.7	191.6	..	..	..	..	..
72	Scientific research and development	810.2	787.7	814.6	..	..	..	..	..
77-82	Administrative and support service activities	683.1	5.2	6.6	..	..	..	..	..
84-99	Community, social and personal services	9.9	9.6	35.9	..	..	..	..	..
84-85	Public administration and defence; compulsory social security and education	4.3	3.2	2.3 e	..	..	..	..	..
86-88	Human health and social work activities	4.5	6.1	33.3	..	..	..	..	..
90-93	Arts, entertainment and recreation	0.0	0.0	0.0	..	..	..	..	..
94-99	Other services; household-employers; extraterritorial bodies	1.1	0.3	0.2 e	..	..	..	..	..

.. Not available; e Estimated value

Note: Detailed metadata at: *http://metalinks.oecd.org/anberd/20200813/2abe.*

R&D expenditure in industry by main activity of the enterprise, constant prices
ISIC Rev. 4

2010 USD PPP

		2011	2012	2013	2014	2015	2016	2017	2018
	TOTAL BUSINESS ENTERPRISE	**5 541.4**	**5 261.0**	**5 380.4**	..	..	..	..	..
01-03	**AGRICULTURE, FORESTRY AND FISHING**	**0.0**	**0.0**	**0.0**	..	..	..	..	..
05-09	**MINING AND QUARRYING**	**0.0**	**0.0**	**0.0**	..	..	..	..	..
10-33	**MANUFACTURING**	**2 632.3**	**3 168.0**	**3 097.9**	..	..	..	..	..
10-12	Food products, beverages and tobacco	20.8	26.2	24.9	..	..	..	..	..
13-15	Textiles, wearing apparel, leather and related products	1.1	0.9	0.6 e	..	..	..	..	..
13	Textiles	0.0	..	..	..	..	..	..	..
14	Wearing apparel	0.7	..	..	..	..	..	..	..
15	Leather and related products, footwear	0.4	..	..	..	..	..	..	..
16-18	Wood and paper products and printing	3.7	3.7 e	3.3	..	..	..	..	..
16	Wood and wood products, except furniture	0.0	0.0 e	0.0	..	..	..	..	..
17	Paper and paper products	2.9	3.1 e	2.9	..	..	..	..	..
18	Printing and reproduction of recorded media	0.8	0.7 e	0.4	..	..	..	..	..
19-23	Chemical, rubber, plastic, non-metallic mineral products	265.3	286.3	362.1 e	..	..	..	..	..
19	Coke and refined petroleum products	1.3	1.5	1.0 e	..	..	..	..	..
20-21	Chemical and pharmaceutical products	244.7	278.2	355.2	..	..	..	..	..
20	Chemicals and chemical products	104.2	117.6	208.2	..	..	..	..	..
21	Pharmaceuticals, medicinal, chemical and botanical products	140.6	160.6	147.0	..	..	..	..	..
22	Rubber and plastic products	15.2	2.9	3.1	..	..	..	..	..
23	Other non-metallic mineral products	4.1	3.8	2.7	..	..	..	..	..
24-25	Basic metals, metal products, except machinery and equipment	24.7	31.6 e	45.1	..	..	..	..	..
24	Basic metals	1.7	1.7 e	3.2	..	..	..	..	..
25	Fabricated metal products, except machinery and equipment	23.0	29.9	41.9	..	..	..	..	..
26-30	Computer, electronic, optical products; electrical machinery, transport equipment	2 233.9	2 677.4	2 523.8	..	..	..	..	..
26	Computer, electronic and optical products	1 754.1	2 156.7	1 858.2	..	..	..	..	..
27	Electrical equipment	26.3	16.4	32.8	..	..	..	..	..
28	Machinery and equipment n.e.c.	223.4	231.0	317.8	..	..	..	..	..
29	Motor vehicles, trailers and semi-trailers	52.9	57.6	63.5	..	..	..	..	..
30	Other transport equipment	177.2	215.7	251.5	..	..	..	..	..
31-33	Furniture; repair, installation of machinery and equipment	82.7	141.8	138.1	..	..	..	..	..
31	Furniture	18.2	17.7	16.8	..	..	..	..	..
32	Other manufacturing	64.5	124.1	121.3	..	..	..	..	..
33	Repair and installation of machinery and equipment	0.0	0.0	0.0	..	..	..	..	..
35-39	**ELECTRICITY, GAS, WATER AND WASTE MANAGEMENT**	**14.8**	**11.4**	**15.6**	..	..	..	..	..
35-36	Electricity, gas and water	0.1	0.0	0.0	..	..	..	..	..
37-39	Sewerage, waste management and remediation activities	14.7	11.4	15.6	..	..	..	..	..
41-43	**CONSTRUCTION**	**2.6**	**1.5**	**1.9**	..	..	..	..	..
45-99	**TOTAL SERVICES**	**2 891.5**	**2 080.1**	**2 265.1**	..	..	..	..	..
45-82	**Business sector services**	**2 881.0**	**2 070.0**	**2 228.1**	..	..	..	..	..
45-47	**Wholesale and retail trade; motor vehicle and motorcycle repairs**	**613.5**	**642.4**	**848.3**	..	..	..	..	..
49-53	**Transportation and storage**	**49.7**	**32.5**	**47.6**	..	..	..	..	..
55-56	**Accommodation and food service activities**	**0.0**	**0.0**	**0.0**	..	..	..	..	..
58-63	**Information and communication**	**171.5**	**177.9**	**179.2**	..	..	..	..	..
58-60	Publishing, audiovisual and broadcasting activities	42.0	57.1	46.8	..	..	..	..	..
58	Publishing activities	40.1	56.8	46.6	..	..	..	..	..
59-60	Motion picture, video and TV programme production; broadcasting activities	1.9	0.4	0.2	..	..	..	..	..
59	Motion picture, video and TV programme production; sound and music	1.9	0.4	0.2	..	..	..	..	..
60	Programming and broadcasting activities	0.0	0.0	0.0	..	..	..	..	..
61	Telecommunications	6.1	3.6	6.9	..	..	..	..	..
62-63	IT and other information services	123.3	117.1	125.6	..	..	..	..	..
62	Computer programming, consultancy and related activities	120.4	114.1	119.5	..	..	..	..	..
63	Information service activities	2.9	3.0	6.1	..	..	..	..	..
64-66	**Financial and insurance activities**	**112.3**	**107.5**	**110.7**	..	..	..	..	..
68-82	**Real estate; professional, scientific and technical; administrative and support**	**1 934.0**	**1 109.8**	**1 042.3**	..	..	..	..	..
68	Real estate activities	0.0	0.0	0.0	..	..	..	..	..
69-75x72	Professional, scientific and technical activities, except scientific R&D	341.0	279.4	197.1	..	..	..	..	..
72	Scientific research and development	864.3	825.0	838.3	..	..	..	..	..
77-82	Administrative and support service activities	728.7	5.4	6.8	..	..	..	..	..
84-99	Community, social and personal services	10.5	10.0	36.9	..	..	..	..	..
84-85	Public administration and defence; compulsory social security and education	4.5	3.3	2.4 e	..	..	..	..	..
86-88	Human health and social work activities	4.8	6.4	34.3	..	..	..	..	..
90-93	Arts, entertainment and recreation	0.0	0.0	0.0	..	..	..	..	..
94-99	Other services; household-employers; extraterritorial bodies	1.2	0.3	0.2 e	..	..	..	..	..

.. Not available; e Estimated value

Note: Detailed metadata at: *http://metalinks.oecd.org/anberd/20200813/2abe*.

R&D expenditure in industry by main activity of the enterprise, current prices
ISIC Rev. 4

Million USD PPP

		2011	2012	2013	2014	2015	2016	2017	2018
	TOTAL BUSINESS ENTERPRISE	**19 949.5**	**21 606.6**	**23 286.9**	**25 129.3**	**26 182.6**	**27 725.7**	**30 898.6**	**34 809.1**
01-03	**AGRICULTURE, FORESTRY AND FISHING**	..	..	..	..	..	..	..	..
05-09	**MINING AND QUARRYING**	..	..	..	..	..	..	..	..
10-33	**MANUFACTURING**	**18 440.2**	**19 776.2**	**21 272.5**	**22 992.8**	**23 986.3**	**25 396.2**	**28 254.2**	**31 863.9**
10-12	Food products, beverages and tobacco	141.5	166.6	146.0	154.4	151.9	174.8	192.1	204.5
13-15	Textiles, wearing apparel, leather and related products	246.6	265.5	261.4	292.0	311.6	397.2	406.5	536.3
13	Textiles	126.6	125.8	117.4	127.3	134.8	183.3	175.8	204.8
14	Wearing apparel	12.6	11.4	13.1	13.1	11.5	11.4	14.4	14.8
15	Leather and related products, footwear	107.4	128.4	130.9	151.5	165.3	202.5	216.4	316.7
16-18	Wood and paper products and printing	38.9	42.0	55.4	42.4	50.8	40.8	35.2	44.0
16	Wood and wood products, except furniture	1.0	0.9	1.4	4.0	6.2	8.0	3.1	3.4
17	Paper and paper products	16.7	17.8	12.3	10.5	11.4	8.3	10.5	15.9
18	Printing and reproduction of recorded media	21.2	23.3	41.7	27.9	33.2	24.5	21.6	24.7
19-23	Chemical, rubber, plastic, non-metallic mineral products	1 293.6	1 406.5	1 485.8	1 604.9	1 595.9	1 723.2	1 866.8	2 087.4
19	Coke and refined petroleum products	80.4	97.8	138.2	148.8	140.5	130.4	119.9	150.3
20-21	Chemical and pharmaceutical products	970.5	1 040.3	1 099.0	1 175.3	1 183.8	1 300.6	1 365.4	1 485.3
20	Chemicals and chemical products	643.2	690.2	703.9	685.8	727.0	743.0	797.8	943.0
21	Pharmaceuticals, medicinal, chemical and botanical products	327.3	350.2	395.1	489.5	456.8	557.5	567.6	542.3
22	Rubber and plastic products	198.9	225.7	209.3	227.0	221.2	246.0	287.4	351.5
23	Other non-metallic mineral products	43.7	42.7	39.3	53.8	50.4	46.2	94.0	100.3
24-25	Basic metals, metal products, except machinery and equipment	324.3	325.4	350.2	355.3	357.4	398.3	353.0	398.3
24	Basic metals	169.9	168.3	177.6	174.4	172.4	177.9	167.9	187.5
25	Fabricated metal products, except machinery and equipment	154.5	157.1	172.6	181.0	185.0	220.5	185.0	210.8
26-30	Computer, electronic, optical products; electrical machinery, transport equipment	16 229.2	17 381.1	18 764.2	20 330.3	21 288.5	22 399.9	25 101.1	28 249.7
26	Computer, electronic and optical products	14 473.2	15 607.0	16 855.8	18 264.8	19 240.9	20 243.3	22 778.2	25 632.5
27	Electrical equipment	610.7	632.4	639.8	637.2	640.8	633.2	677.1	718.4
28	Machinery and equipment n.e.c.	573.9	521.0	589.4	678.7	696.4	752.2	901.4	1 042.4
29	Motor vehicles, trailers and semi-trailers	307.1	343.2	375.3	439.7	408.7	433.2	441.3	526.9
30	Other transport equipment	264.4	277.4	303.8	309.9	301.7	338.0	303.1	329.5
31-33	Furniture; repair, installation of machinery and equipment	166.1	189.1	209.5	213.5	230.1	261.8	299.5	343.7
31	Furniture	8.4	10.7	7.2	9.2	10.6	12.2	3.7	10.2
32	Other manufacturing	157.7	178.4	202.3	204.3	219.5	249.6	295.8	333.5
33	Repair and installation of machinery and equipment	0.0	0.0	0.0	0.0	0.0	0.0	0.0	0.0
35-39	**ELECTRICITY, GAS, WATER AND WASTE MANAGEMENT**	**44.2**	**48.7**	**38.8**	**37.7**	**51.1**	**53.2**	**62.7**	**74.3**
35-36	Electricity, gas and water	42.6	47.5	37.6	36.5	49.0	52.3	60.3	71.5
37-39	Sewerage, waste management and remediation activities	1.6	1.2	1.2	1.3	2.2	0.9	2.4	2.9
41-43	**CONSTRUCTION**	**10.0**	**12.2**	**14.1**	**17.9**	**14.6**	**15.3**	**15.5**	**19.2**
45-99	**TOTAL SERVICES**	**1 455.0**	**1 769.5**	**1 961.5**	**2 080.8**	**2 130.5**	**2 261.0**	**2 566.2**	**2 851.7**
45-82	**Business sector services**	**1 276.0**	**1 568.0**	**1 757.2**	**1 846.6**	**1 896.5**	**2 025.0**	**2 274.7**	**2 537.2**
45-47	**Wholesale and retail trade; motor vehicle and motorcycle repairs**	**51.3**	**99.1**	**103.9**	**119.3**	**112.1**	**136.5**	**279.4**	**319.7**
49-53	**Transportation and storage**	**12.1**	**12.6**	**16.0**	**17.6**	**17.8**	**25.5**	**35.6**	**31.9**
55-56	**Accommodation and food service activities**	**0.7**	**0.3**	**0.5**	**0.1**	**0.1**	**1.2**	**3.5**	**4.3**
58-63	**Information and communication**	**871.8**	**875.5**	**995.3**	**1 029.8**	**1 051.4**	**1 124.5**	**998.1**	**1 131.3**
58-60	Publishing, audiovisual and broadcasting activities	13.3	18.5	28.6	30.8	27.4	29.7	98.4	111.8
58	Publishing activities	11.3	15.5	23.1	22.4	20.1	22.9	92.2	102.4
59-60	Motion picture, video and TV programme production; broadcasting activities	2.0	3.0	5.5	8.4	7.3	6.8	6.3	9.4
59	Motion picture, video and TV programme production; sound and music	0.2	0.4	4.2	3.0	3.6	2.0	3.3	2.6
60	Programming and broadcasting activities	1.8	2.6	1.4	5.4	3.8	4.7	2.9	6.8
61	Telecommunications	257.6	262.5	260.6	253.8	246.9	264.0	281.3	276.9
62-63	IT and other information services	600.8	594.5	706.0	745.2	777.1	830.7	618.4	742.6
62	Computer programming, consultancy and related activities	536.5	557.5	665.3	696.3	713.8	763.8	570.7	664.7
63	Information service activities	64.3	37.0	40.7	49.0	63.3	67.0	47.7	77.9
64-66	**Financial and insurance activities**	**124.2**	**150.6**	**159.8**	**183.2**	**206.4**	**231.3**	**288.6**	**324.1**
68-82	**Real estate; professional, scientific and technical; administrative and support**	**216.0**	**429.9**	**481.7**	**496.6**	**508.6**	**506.1**	**669.5**	**725.9**
68	Real estate activities	0.8	1.2	1.7	2.5	1.9	2.1	5.7	6.0
69-75x72	Professional, scientific and technical activities, except scientific R&D	128.4	338.2	389.7	400.5	413.5	408.9	547.6	583.9
72	Scientific research and development	80.4	82.9	80.8	83.9	84.6	86.3	105.2	123.7
77-82	Administrative and support service activities	6.4	7.6	9.5	9.8	8.6	8.7	11.0	12.3
84-99	Community, social and personal services	179.0	201.5	204.3	234.2	234.0	236.0	291.5	314.4
84-85	Public administration and defence; compulsory social security and education	0.0	0.1	0.1	0.2	0.2	0.3	2.0	2.5
86-88	Human health and social work activities	176.4	199.5	202.3	232.1	232.2	234.0	285.1	304.2
90-93	Arts, entertainment and recreation	0.0	0.0	0.0	0.0	0.0	0.0	2.1	1.8
94-99	Other services; household-employers; extraterritorial bodies	2.6	1.9	1.9	1.9	1.7	1.7	2.4	6.0

.. Not available

Note: Detailed metadata at: *http://metalinks.oecd.org/anberd/20200813/2abe.*

R&D expenditure in industry by main activity of the enterprise, constant prices
ISIC Rev. 4

2010 USD PPP

		2011	2012	2013	2014	2015	2016	2017	2018
	TOTAL BUSINESS ENTERPRISE	**21 291.2**	**22 625.6**	**23 966.2**	**25 391.8**	**26 182.6**	**27 442.2**	**30 017.8**	**33 011.7**
01-03	**AGRICULTURE, FORESTRY AND FISHING**	..	..	..	..	..	..	..	..
05-09	**MINING AND QUARRYING**	..	..	..	..	..	..	..	..
10-33	**MANUFACTURING**	**19 680.4**	**20 708.9**	**21 893.1**	**23 233.0**	**23 986.3**	**25 136.5**	**27 448.9**	**30 218.6**
10-12	Food products, beverages and tobacco	151.0	174.5	150.2	156.0	151.9	173.0	186.6	194.0
13-15	Textiles, wearing apparel, leather and related products	263.2	278.0	269.1	295.0	311.6	393.2	394.9	508.6
13	Textiles	135.2	131.7	120.9	128.7	134.8	181.4	170.8	194.2
14	Wearing apparel	13.5	11.9	13.5	13.2	11.5	11.3	13.9	14.0
15	Leather and related products, footwear	114.6	134.4	134.7	153.1	165.3	200.4	210.2	300.3
16-18	Wood and paper products and printing	41.5	43.9	57.0	42.9	50.8	40.4	34.2	41.7
16	Wood and wood products, except furniture	1.1	0.9	1.4	4.1	6.2	7.9	3.0	3.2
17	Paper and paper products	17.8	18.7	12.7	10.6	11.4	8.3	10.2	15.0
18	Printing and reproduction of recorded media	22.6	24.4	42.9	28.2	33.2	24.3	21.0	23.5
19-23	Chemical, rubber, plastic, non-metallic mineral products	1 380.6	1 472.9	1 529.2	1 621.7	1 595.9	1 705.5	1 813.6	1 979.6
19	Coke and refined petroleum products	85.9	102.4	142.2	150.3	140.5	129.1	116.5	142.6
20-21	Chemical and pharmaceutical products	1 035.8	1 089.4	1 131.1	1 187.6	1 183.8	1 287.3	1 326.5	1 408.6
20	Chemicals and chemical products	686.5	722.7	724.4	692.9	727.0	735.4	775.0	894.3
21	Pharmaceuticals, medicinal, chemical and botanical products	349.3	366.7	406.7	494.7	456.8	551.8	551.4	514.3
22	Rubber and plastic products	212.2	236.3	215.5	229.3	221.2	243.5	279.2	333.3
23	Other non-metallic mineral products	46.7	44.7	40.4	54.4	50.4	45.7	91.3	95.1
24-25	Basic metals, metal products, except machinery and equipment	346.2	340.7	360.4	359.0	357.4	394.3	342.9	377.7
24	Basic metals	181.3	176.2	182.8	176.2	172.4	176.0	163.2	177.8
25	Fabricated metal products, except machinery and equipment	164.9	164.5	177.6	182.9	185.0	218.2	179.8	199.9
26-30	Computer, electronic, optical products; electrical machinery, transport equipment	17 320.7	18 200.8	19 311.6	20 542.7	21 288.5	22 170.9	24 385.6	26 791.0
26	Computer, electronic and optical products	15 446.6	16 343.0	17 347.6	18 455.6	19 240.9	20 036.3	22 128.9	24 309.0
27	Electrical equipment	651.8	662.3	658.4	643.8	640.8	626.7	657.8	681.3
28	Machinery and equipment n.e.c.	612.5	545.6	606.6	685.8	696.4	744.5	875.7	988.6
29	Motor vehicles, trailers and semi-trailers	327.7	359.4	386.3	444.3	408.7	428.8	428.7	499.7
30	Other transport equipment	282.2	290.4	312.6	313.1	301.7	334.5	294.5	312.5
31-33	Furniture; repair, installation of machinery and equipment	177.3	198.1	215.6	215.7	230.1	259.2	290.9	326.0
31	Furniture	9.0	11.2	7.4	9.2	10.6	12.1	3.6	9.7
32	Other manufacturing	168.3	186.9	208.2	206.4	219.5	247.1	287.4	316.3
33	Repair and installation of machinery and equipment	0.0	0.0	0.0	0.0	0.0	0.0	0.0	0.0
35-39	**ELECTRICITY, GAS, WATER AND WASTE MANAGEMENT**	**47.2**	**51.0**	**40.0**	**38.1**	**51.1**	**52.7**	**60.9**	**70.5**
35-36	Electricity, gas and water	45.5	49.7	38.7	36.8	49.0	51.8	58.6	67.8
37-39	Sewerage, waste management and remediation activities	1.7	1.3	1.3	1.3	2.2	0.9	2.3	2.7
41-43	**CONSTRUCTION**	**10.7**	**12.7**	**14.5**	**18.1**	**14.6**	**15.1**	**15.0**	**18.2**
45-99	**TOTAL SERVICES**	**1 552.9**	**1 853.0**	**2 018.7**	**2 102.6**	**2 130.5**	**2 237.9**	**2 493.1**	**2 704.4**
45-82	**Business sector services**	**1 361.8**	**1 642.0**	**1 808.5**	**1 865.9**	**1 896.5**	**2 004.3**	**2 209.8**	**2 406.2**
45-47	**Wholesale and retail trade; motor vehicle and motorcycle repairs**	**54.7**	**103.8**	**107.0**	**120.6**	**112.1**	**135.1**	**271.4**	**303.1**
49-53	**Transportation and storage**	**12.9**	**13.2**	**16.5**	**17.8**	**17.8**	**25.2**	**34.6**	**30.3**
55-56	**Accommodation and food service activities**	**0.7**	**0.3**	**0.6**	**0.1**	**0.1**	**1.2**	**3.4**	**4.1**
58-63	**Information and communication**	**930.4**	**916.7**	**1 024.3**	**1 040.6**	**1 051.4**	**1 113.0**	**969.7**	**1 072.9**
58-60	Publishing, audiovisual and broadcasting activities	14.2	19.4	29.5	31.1	27.4	29.4	95.6	106.0
58	Publishing activities	12.1	16.2	23.8	22.6	20.1	22.7	89.6	97.1
59-60	Motion picture, video and TV programme production; broadcasting activities	2.1	3.2	5.7	8.5	7.3	6.7	6.1	8.9
59	Motion picture, video and TV programme production; sound and music	0.2	0.5	4.3	3.0	3.6	2.0	3.3	2.5
60	Programming and broadcasting activities	2.0	2.7	1.4	5.5	3.8	4.7	2.8	6.4
61	Telecommunications	274.9	274.8	268.2	256.4	246.9	261.3	273.2	262.6
62-63	IT and other information services	641.2	622.5	726.6	753.0	777.1	822.2	600.8	704.2
62	Computer programming, consultancy and related activities	572.6	583.8	684.7	703.5	713.8	755.9	554.4	630.4
63	Information service activities	68.7	38.8	41.9	49.5	63.3	66.3	46.4	73.9
64-66	**Financial and insurance activities**	**132.5**	**157.7**	**164.5**	**185.1**	**206.4**	**228.9**	**280.3**	**307.4**
68-82	**Real estate; professional, scientific and technical; administrative and support**	**230.6**	**450.2**	**495.7**	**501.8**	**508.6**	**500.9**	**650.4**	**688.4**
68	Real estate activities	0.9	1.3	1.7	2.5	1.9	2.1	5.5	5.7
69-75x72	Professional, scientific and technical activities, except scientific R&D	137.0	354.2	401.1	404.6	413.5	404.7	532.0	553.7
72	Scientific research and development	85.8	86.8	83.2	84.8	84.6	85.4	102.2	117.3
77-82	Administrative and support service activities	6.8	8.0	9.8	9.9	8.6	8.6	10.7	11.6
84-99	Community, social and personal services	191.1	211.0	210.2	236.6	234.0	233.6	283.2	298.2
84-85	Public administration and defence; compulsory social security and education	0.0	0.1	0.1	0.2	0.2	0.3	1.9	2.3
86-88	Human health and social work activities	188.2	208.9	208.2	234.6	232.2	231.6	277.0	288.5
90-93	Arts, entertainment and recreation	0.0	0.0	0.0	0.0	0.0	0.0	2.0	1.7
94-99	Other services; household-employers; extraterritorial bodies	2.8	2.0	1.9	1.9	1.7	1.7	2.3	5.7

.. Not available

Note: Detailed metadata at: *http://metalinks.oecd.org/anberd/20200813/2abe.*